Machiavelli,
Leonardo,
and the Science of Power

The Frank M. Covey, Jr.
Loyola Lectures in Political Analysis

Thomas S. Engeman
GENERAL EDITOR

Our late colleague Richard S. Hartigan founded the Frank M.
Covey, Jr., Lectures in Political Analysis to provide a continuing forum for the reanimation of political philosophy. The
lectures are not narrowly constrained by a single topic nor do
they favor a particular perspective. Their sole aim is to foster
serious theoretical inquiry, with the expectation that this effort
will contribute in essential ways to both human knowledge
and political justice.

Frontispiece. Peter Paul Rubens' copy of Struggle around the Standard from Leonardo's *Battle of Anghiari* (c. 1604), black chalk, pen and ink heightened with gray and white, 17 1/4 x 25 inches (45.2 X 63.4 cm). Courtesy of Cabinet des Dessins, Musée du Louvre, Paris.

Machiavelli, Leonardo,

and the

Science of Power

Roger D. Masters

UNIVERSITY OF NOTRE DAME PRESS
NOTRE DAME AND LONDON

Copyright © 1996 by
University of Notre Dame Press
Notre Dame, Indiana 46556
All Rights Reserved

Manufactured in the United States of America

Library of Congress Cataloging-in-Publication Data

Masters, Roger D.
    Machiavelli, Leonardo, and the science of power / Roger D.
Masters.
        p.   cm. — (Frank M. Covey Jr. Loyola lectures in political
analysis)
    Includes index.
    ISBN 0-268-01416-7 (alk. paper)
        1. Machiavelli, Niccolò, 1469–1527—Contributions in
political science.   2. Leonardo da Vinci, 1452–1519—
Contributions in political science.   3. Power (Social sciences)
I. Title.   II. Series.
JC143.M4M387   1995
320.1'092—dc20   94-40484
                                                            CIP

Book design by Wendy Torrey and Jeannette Morgenroth
Set in 10–13 Galliard by Books International
Printed and bound by Edwards Brothers, Inc.

∞ *The paper used in this publication meets the minimum
requirements of the American National Standard for Information
Sciences—Permanence of Paper for Printed Library Materials,
ANSI Z 39.48-1984.*.

In Memoriam

Henry W. Ehrmann
(1908–1994)

"I have observed in him those qualities strongly desired
in a good friend by his friend and in a citizen
by his native city."

Contents

$\mathcal{L}$ist of Illustrations

Introduction

Indeed, it is evident that the philosophy of nature is indispensable.

Leo Strauss[1]

What is the difference between right and wrong? Can we know anything about justice and morality in the sense that we know truths in physics or chemistry? Because modern science seems to create a gulf between facts and values, these perennial questions have become particularly acute.

We live in a time marked by a lack of consensus on moral or legal principles. "Cultural diversity" has come to symbolize not merely respect for others, but an inability to explain why some forms of behavior are superior to others. "Just Do It"—a popular motto on T-shirts in some places—has become the tacit standard of many in business, politics, law, and everyday life. For the terrorist as for the literary deconstructionist, commitment is the measure of right and wrong.

Most of us, of course, continue to respect moral standards and legal obligations. But the reasons for what we do seem unclear. For every practical issue, politicians and preachers proclaim diametrically opposed views with equal fervor. Is it a question of abortion? For some, the answer is a fetus's "right to life"; for others, it is a woman's "right to choose." Should we pay taxes? For some, governmental activity is always inherently suspect and "no new taxes" an almost sacred refrain; for others, social obligation extends to a guarantee of equal opportunity if not equal success to all.

Since antiquity, such issues have been the focus of serious thought about human nature and society. In private life, the ordinary person confronts similar issues, often wondering why social norms and laws exist. Little wonder that theologians and political philosophers have offered diverse answers to the questions asked by every growing child, not to mention every intelligent citizen.

In the Western tradition, the concept of human nature has generally been central to the religious doctrines and secular theories that explain society, law, and morality. The origins and character of our species have also been a matter of scientific study since the ancient Greeks. As a result, issues of moral and political thought touch on the findings of natural science as well as on philosophic theories and religious doctrines.

Since Darwin published *The Origin of Species* in 1858, the need to relate questions of human nature and society to the natural sciences has become even more obvious. This century has seen unparalleled advances in the scientific understanding of evolution and human biology: we know more today about our species' nature than ever before. Paradoxically, however, this century has also seen an unparalleled division between the study of nature and the study of morality, law, and politics.

My book is part of a growing concern to respond to this situation. Over the last twenty years, along with other scholars, I have suggested a return to the naturalistic tradition of Western thought, in which a scientific study of human life is directly relevant to questions of morality and law.

In my own teaching, research, and publication I have tried to integrate evolutionary biology, political psychology, political philosophy, law, and human ethology. The organization of the present book, while unorthodox, thus reflects an effort to bring together two traditions that have drifted apart over the last century.

To explore the issues of political philosophy as they have been articulated in the past, I set out to focus on a single thinker—Niccolò Machiavelli. This great and subtle Florentine is often said to have founded a modern "scientific" study of human affairs. To assess the *truth* of Machiavelli's theories, however, we must consider what is known, today, about hominid evolution and the natural factors influencing social behavior. This procedure is particularly necessary now that Darwinian evolutionary theory is generally accepted within the scientific community as the explanation of human origins.

To compare Machiavelli's theories with scientific findings, it is first necessary to state his theories accurately. This turns out to be more difficult than might first appear. Scholars have proposed very different interpretations of *The Prince, Discourses on Titus Livy,* and other works by Machiavelli. It is, therefore, necessary to read the texts carefully in order to define Machiavelli's theory of human nature before we can test it against the latest scientific research. In so doing, I realized that scholars have ignored some critical evidence.

At the outset of *The Prince,* Machiavelli tells us that his knowledge is based on his "long experience of modern things" as well as "continuous reading of ancient ones." When reading and interpreting his work, particular attention therefore needs to be given to Machiavelli's political career. Machiavelli held high office in the Florentine Republic from 1498 until the overthrow of Piero Soderini's regime in 1512. I now believe that his thought was particularly shaped by an event in this career: Machiavelli's meeting, during his mission to the court of Cesare Borgia in 1502, with Leonardo da Vinci (who at that time was serving as Borgia's architect and military engineer).

After giving the Covey Lectures on which this book is based, I discovered, almost by accident, that the lives of Machiavelli and Leonardo intersected. Although Leonardo's biographers and many art historians believe they became close friends in 1502, the extent of their contacts has been questioned by intellectual historians. Most political theorists have been unaware that Machiavelli's thought might have been influenced by the most extraordinary artist, engineer, and scientific innovator of the Renaissance. When I came across the statement that they were friends (while looking at a book on Leonardo at the Chicago Art Institute bookshop), I did not expect how difficult it would be to establish the truth of the story.

Neither Machiavelli nor Leonardo mentions the other by name in writings or letters that have survived; this is not conclusive, however, since both were legendary for their elusiveness or deviousness. Leonardo's *Notebooks* contain amazing things—including passages that seemingly relate to Machiavelli's works—but no conclusive evidence. Machiavelli's secondary works, including poems written before *The Prince* as well as *The Art of War,* provide little more than tantalizing hints. Only after completing an account pieced together from secondary sources did I discover that many relevant documents, although published in Italian, have never been translated into English or analyzed with adequate care by Machiavelli's biographers.

As Second Chancellor of the Florentine Signoria and Secretary to the Committee known as the Ten of War, Machiavelli wrote extensive letters and memoranda that are still in the Florentine archives. His dispatches from the court of Cesare Borgia in 1502–1503, the so-called *Legations to Valentino,* refer to conversations with an unnamed "friend" or "first secretary" of Cesare.

This purely circumstantial evidence was immeasurably strengthened by the discovery of additional documents reproduced below. Letters and archival materials prove that between 1503 and 1506, Machiavelli's responsibilities included four projects on which Leonardo da Vinci was involved. One of these, an attempt to divert the Arno River during the siege of Pisa, is especially important: a letter from the field proves that Leonardo visited the site on 23 July 1503 and played a role in the adoption of the project (Appendix I.2). Machiavelli's dispatches from Florence demonstrate that he took an active role in supervising the attempted diversion (Appendix I.4). As I will show, this experience had a lasting impact on Machiavelli, whose writings echo views of science, warfare, and technology found only in Leonardo's *Notebooks*. This influence is of the greatest importance because Leonardo himself had worked out visionary plans for a political system that foreshadowed modern industrial societies.

Chapter one introduces the argument by setting forth the historical evidence concerning the relationship between Leonardo da Vinci and Machiavelli. I trace the careers of Leonardo and Machiavelli, with particular emphasis on the period between 1502 and 1508 when they were most likely to have met and talked with each other. While many points remain uncertain and we cannot be sure that their acquaintance ever constituted close friendship, the documents establish that Machiavelli knew Leonardo to some degree.[2] As a result, no comprehensive account of Machiavelli's political thought can ignore his political experiences between 1500 and 1512.

Based on this historical account, the next two chapters set forth an interpretation of Machiavelli's political teaching that is not shared by all commentators and scholars. When the Florentine Republic fell in 1512, Machiavelli was arrested and tortured on charges of conspiring against the new Medici rulers. These circumstances, too often neglected when reading and interpreting *The Prince*, confirm the old view that Machiavelli was an exceptionally deceptive writer who often "hid" his republican principles.

Chapter two is devoted to the problem of how to read Machiavelli's *Prince*. In it, I briefly describe Machiavelli's political career and the context in which he wrote, contrast *The Prince* with the *Discourses on Titus Livy*, and examine his own statements of his "intention." Both correspondence and published works confirm the view that he wrote in what he himself called a "covert" manner. To avoid the criticism that such an interpretation is impossible to prove, I will suggest specific criteria for discovering implicit meanings in a theoretical text, and show that Machiavelli's writings meet these standards of evidence.

The substance of Machiavelli's political philosophy is summarized in chapter three. Focusing on a careful reading of *The Prince*, I explain why he repeatedly suggested that he had found a "new way" of thinking about human life, abandoning otherworldly piety and transforming ancient political philosophy in the light of the needs of political practice. But while challenging both pagan Greek rationalism and Christian faith, Machiavelli somehow preserves and builds on both traditions.

Machiavelli's "new way" can properly claim to open the possibility of what came to be called modern thought and politics. He bases political and moral principles on a secular or pagan view of human nature, substituting observation of the world for biblical revelation as the means to knowledge. But he does not simply go back to the conception of human virtue and morality that Western tradition had derived from philosophers like Plato and Aristotle. Instead, Machiavelli's understanding is also shaped by a reflection on the primacy of political practice and an awareness of the new scientific perspective explored by Leonardo da Vinci.

The result is a this-worldly view of history, opening the hope that events can be partly controlled or shaped by human intelligence, art, and choice. Our world of science and technology seems but a development of this perspective, according to which humans can create new things just as, in *Genesis,* Yahweh created the heavens, the earth, and all living things.

In the Bible, Moses and the Israelites are saved by God's parting of the Red Sea. As a Florentine political official, in 1503–1504 Machiavelli consulted Leonardo on the engineering plans for diverting the Arno River to defeat Pisa; this experience, and Leonardo's writings, suggest that Machiavelli had both theoretical and practical reasons to think that human science and technology could be used to achieve ends once sought only by prayer. Although Machiavelli's experience of working with Leonardo could have indicated such a transformation of values would be possible, it also revealed its dangers if science and technology were not controlled by political prudence.

A superficial reading of *The Prince* not only obscures these deeper insights, but even confuses Machiavelli's judgments in political matters. By considering the text carefully and relating it to the *Discourses on Titus Livy,* it will become evident that Machiavelli's principles lead to an emphasis on a government of "law" primarily dependent on the "people" and backed by "force." In a profound sense, he laid the foundation of modern "constitutional" or "democratic" political regimes. If so, we are entitled to ask whether Machiavelli's science of power is valid in the light of contemporary natural science.

Because Machiavelli professed to base his political understanding on the "effectual truth of the thing" and claimed that successful leaders must "use" both the "beast" and the "man," it is especially appropriate to confront his remarks about human nature with the scientific understanding of our species' evolution and biology. The nature of animal social behavior is now a subject of extensive study, both in field and laboratory research. A reconsideration of Machiavelli's theories in the light of these studies is especially appropriate because biologists now describe the capacity for deception and social manipulation in monkeys and apes as "Machiavellian intelligence." The next three chapters therefore survey the findings of the life sciences as they relate to the emergence of social cooperation, law, and political leadership in human affairs.

Chapter four, "Using the Beast: Animal Dominance and Human Leadership," begins from a famous passage in chapter eighteen of *The Prince*. There, Machiavelli distinguishes between the "nature" of "man" and "beast," and counsels the leader—the individual Machiavelli calls "the prince" (*il principe*)—to "pick" the "lion" and the "fox" to control the "wolves." What does Machiavelli mean when using the "lion," the "fox," and the "wolves" as symbols of the basic social and political problems facing humans?[3] What do we know about animal social behavior, and how does it relate to problems of leadership and social cooperation in our own species? Clearly we cannot know the natural foundations of society without understanding the origins of the social behavior exhibited by lions, foxes, and wolves—not to mention birds, bees, and whales.[4]

Chapter five turns to the specifically human institution of governments and the centralized state. Machiavelli is famed not only for his concept of the prince, but for an emphasis on "the state" (*lo stato*). Knowing the roots of dominance and status among animals does not resolve the question of how centralized governments arise in human affairs.[5] To assess Machiavelli's theory of the state, it is necessary to reconsider the assumption of human selfishness in the philosophic tradition from the Greek Sophists to modern social contract theories, relating the origin of government to contemporary models in rational choice or game theory as well as evolutionary biology.[6]

Chapter six considers Machiavelli's view of the relations between leaders and led in the light of observational studies of animal social behavior, with emphasis on the role of television in contemporary Western societies. The Machiavellian "economy of power," resting on the triad of love, hate, and fear, corresponds to the essential components in the behavioral repertoire of primates; facial displays of the emotions and social signals corresponding to these three motives play a central role in human leadership.

An examination of the average citizen's emotions and judgments when watching leaders reveals the central role of the *mode of communication* between the leaders and led, and leads to a surprising reconsideration of Machiavelli as political thinker.

In effect, over the last two centuries Machiavelli has had a popular reputation as a teacher of evil.[7] At a time when political life was conceptualized in terms of individual "rights," Machiavelli seemed somewhat anachronistic. Even for those who view him as a republican, Machiavelli's concerns are often reduced to the narrow question of how far effective leaders need to violate the social norms of an established, stable society.

By focusing on the mode of communication between leaders and citizens, we gain a better idea of the reasons for these interpretations of Machiavelli. The constitutional regimes characteristic of modernity, particularly after the revolutions of the late eighteenth century in the United States and France, relied on the newspapers as the essential mode of political communication; the result was the emergence of the political party, an institution not predicted by Machiavelli. In a political universe dominated by political discourse based on printing Machiavelli's teaching seemed to many obsolete.

Television, by profoundly changing the mode of communication, has recreated—on the larger scale of the nation-state—many of the issues characteristic of the Renaissance cities of Italy. In returning to what appears to be a more direct or unmediated interaction between leaders and led, television seems to have returned us to the era of Machiavellian politics.

In chapter seven, I reconsider the extent to which Machiavelli's thought can clarify contemporary life. To understand modernity and its crisis, or even to ascertain the extent to which Machiavelli can be called a modern, it is necessary to define the central attribute of our epoch. This characteristic can be found, I argue, in the integration of scientific theory, technological innovation, commerce, industry, and politics. Whereas theory and practice were divorced, albeit for different reasons, in antiquity and the Middle Ages, after the Renaissance there came to be a close reciprocal relationship between scientific theories and technological or social practice.

Chapter seven then summarizes the way Leonardo da Vinci and Machiavelli contributed to this specifically modern view of science, technology, and politics. I show that Leonardo's life and work were focused on radical innovations, everywhere challenging the distinction between theory and practice inherited from the past. In domains as diverse as painting, mathematics, physics, hydraulics, military engineering, architecture, and comparative anatomy, Leonardo introduced concepts and practices often centuries before they were fully realized in the modern West. More to the point, Leonardo extended these concepts to the study of human nature, society, and law, foreseeing a modern community based on private property and scientific technology.

These developments help explain why Machiavelli would have been influenced by his encounter with Leonardo. Whether the two men were once close friends or merely contemporaries whose direct contact was limited to consultation on official projects, their work can be said to symbolize the origins of modernity. To cite but one example, both Leonardo and Machiavelli saw how artillery had changed the nature of warfare by giving a strategic advantage to the offense, ending the defensive invulnerability of the feudal castle, and requiring substantial changes in military architecture and planning. From this, as can be seen in *The Prince* and *Discourses* as well as *The Art of War*, Machiavelli saw the necessity for a new political form, which he called "the state" (*lo stato*), based on a citizen army, prudent leadership, and effective laws.

Although Leonardo and Machiavelli both innovated in important ways, neither developed fully the political implications of the modern view of theory and practice. As an illustration of the further transformations that occurred to make possible our highly technological civilization, with its conquest of the globe and its never-ending revolutions of scientific theory, technology, and socio-economic change, I will show how Hobbes radicalized Machiavelli's view of human potentiality. Machiavelli's famous image of fortune as a river, which at one level might refer to the ill-fated project to redirect the Arno, illustrates the possibility of a partial control of human history; for Machiavelli himself, theory can never be a complete guide to practice.

Hobbes moves far beyond this by seeking a geometrical certainty in the scientific theory that is to guide practice. The consequences were not only the origins of liberalism in the concept that all men have an equal "natural right" to life and liberty, but a thoroughgoing integration of theory and practice. In place of the need for prudent legislators and leaders, Hobbes and those who follow in this tradition seek universal enlightenment. The consequences are a society of never-ending change, devoted to the myth of progress and subject to the dangers of ideological tyranny and technological disaster.

My conclusion assesses the continued value of Machiavelli's perspective. The contemporary predicament could be described as an impossibility either to continue the modern quest for a limitless conquest of nature or to return to the earlier perspectives of classical antiquity and medieval Christianity. The civilization of the West has, since the sixteenth century, been based on a creative tension between a modern science of technological power, ancient traditions of reasoned justice, and religious beliefs in the limitations of human activity. Since Bacon spoke of the "conquest of nature," we have been dedicated to using the power of science to resolve social conflict. In assessing the depth of the contemporary crisis, I suggest it may be beneficial to reconsider Machiavelli's science of power as a means of integrating the wisdom of the ancients with the effectual realities of the present.

In reassessing the contemporary condition in the light of Machiavelli's contribution to modernity, I would be failing in my duties should I neglect to thank Loyola University of Chicago for providing the occasion for the lectures that gave rise to this book. Since human institutions cannot be divorced from the individuals who animate them, I have a particular debt to the late Professor Richard Hartigan, whose invitation to present the Covey Lectures in Political Analysis was the stimulus for relating Machiavelli's thought to recent scientific studies of human nature. As one who taught and wrote wisely on the necessity for a return to the naturalistic tradition in political philosophy, Dick provided both friendship and support for those like myself who shared in the quest for rational standards of justice and law. His loss has been widely felt; it is a great sadness that he did not live to see the final fruit of the lectures he encouraged me to give.

After beginning to write this book, as I have noted, I discovered the evidence that Machiavelli worked with Leonardo da Vinci and was probably influenced by this experience. In exploring this relationship, and in countless other ways, special thanks are due my former student John T. Scott, now a scholar who often teaches his former professor. In addition to commenting critically on the drafts of this essay, John has been indefatigable in locating valuable references on the relations between Machiavelli and Leonardo, and in focusing my attention on the fundamental issues.

When the first draft of this book was almost completed, William Connell provided a model of vigorous but informed scholarly criticism of an earlier draft chapter, presenting firmly the case against the supposed friendship of Machiavelli and Leonardo. In a subsequent letter, he most generously alerted me to Denis Fachard's study of Machiavelli's assistant and friend, Biagio Buonaccorsi, published in France almost twenty years ago, as well as to John M. Najemy's recent analysis of the Machiavelli-

Vettori correspondence. These works, which do much to bring Machiavelli's political career to life, were invaluable and, combined with more thorough research of my own, led me to the documents reproduced in Appendix I. At a time when anonymous reviewers all too frequently indulge in hasty reading and prejudiced evaluation, Professor Connell demonstrated that the best traditions of fair-minded intellectual inquiry are very much alive.

As these remarks indicate, no scholar works alone. Today more than ever, thought and reflection entail obligations to others. Among those to whom I am particularly indebted, but who should not be held responsible for my errors, are (in addition to those just mentioned): Richard Alexander, Larry Arnhart, E. Donald Elliott, Wolfgang Fikentscher, Robert Frank, Siegfried Frey, Margaret Gruter, Michael T. McGuire, Heinrich Meier, Thomas Pangle, Michael Platt, William Rodgers, Jr., Glendon Schubert, Denis G. Sullivan, Lionel Tiger, Robert Trivers, and Edward O. Wilson. Two dear friends, Allan Bloom and Henry Ehrmann, contributed greatly to my understanding but did not live to correct my most recent errors.

Last but far from least, scholars have obligations to individuals and institutions who play a critical role in the support of the endeavor of writing. This work was completed while enjoying the leisure of a Senior Faculty Fellowship from Dartmouth College. The time and resources thereby made available would, however, not have been of use without the love and support of my wife Sandy. To all these, my thanks and appreciation.

Chapter One

Leonardo and Machiavelli

. . . come haveno più mesi fa Lionardo di ser Piero da Vinci, cittadino fiorentino, tolto a dipignere uno quadro della Sala del Consiglio grande. . . . Actum in palatio dictorum Dominorum presentibus Nicolao Domini Bernardi de Machiavellis. . . . [1]

. . . havendo in questo caso ad dire l'opinione nostra, ci piaceva più quel primo disegno che questo ultimo, perché entrando Arno per due vie, et l'una et l'altra non molto largha. . . . [2]

It is unconventional to begin a book on one thinker by describing the life of another. There is little choice, however. I will argue that Machiavelli sought to introduce a novel view of human politics, based in part on Leonardo da Vinci's innovations in science and technology. This argument forces me to establish that Leonardo's work and thought were known to Machiavelli. Such a task is all the more imperative because, while art historians have often spoken of their friendship, students of political theory and intellectual history have rarely even mentioned they were contemporaries. As a result, most scholars are surprised to discover that a relationship between Machiavelli and Leonardo was even possible.

Did Machiavelli know Leonardo? Although it may at first seem a trivial historical detail, an answer to this question can illuminate our understanding of Western civilization. The modern epoch has been dominated by commerce and industry, the centralized nation-state, truly global economic and socio-political interactions, and—above all—a close integration of scientific theory and technical or social practice.[3] Historians of science, of art, and of technology have often discussed Leonardo da Vinci's place in the transition to this epoch.[4] Likewise, in the history of political and social thought, scholars have frequently debated the extent to which Niccolò Machiavelli was "modern."[5]

Most intellectual historians have doubted that these two Florentine contemporaries were friends or ignored the possibility entirely. There is good reason for this. There does not seem to be a single explicit reference to Machiavelli in the voluminous *Notebooks* of Leonardo.[6] Conversely, Machiavelli never discusses Leonardo in his writings—even though there would have been ample reason to do so when describing the behavior of Cesare Borgia in 1502/3, since at that time Leonardo was Cesare's chief military engineer and Machiavelli himself was Florentine emissary at Cesare's court.[7] Despite this silence, there is strong evidence that they knew each other and some reason to believe that the two may have been, at least at one time, friends. Indeed, the absence of explicit mention of Leonardo in anything written by Machiavelli (apart from the public document cited as first epigraph to this chapter) may actually reinforce the substantive importance of the contacts between them.

Students of political theory who seem unaware that Machiavelli might have known Leonardo sometimes speak at length of the similarities between them.[8] Although there are hints, parallels, and circumstantial evidence of meetings between them, critics charge that there is no solid proof of direct contact.[9] On the other hand, many distinguished scholars— including Kenneth Clark, Giorgio Santillana, and Carlo Pedretti—have spoken of the "friendship" between Leonardo and Machiavelli.[10] Even those who question whether the two were personally acquainted need to admit that the parallels noted below justify a comparison between Leonardo and Machiavelli.[11]

As I shall argue, the absence of evidence does not constitute evidence of absence: although Machiavelli does not discuss Leonardo da Vinci by name, there are plausible reasons for this fact.[12] Moreover, part of the obscurity may be due to our own prejudices: the influence of Leonardo is particularly evident in Machiavelli's discussion of military strategy and the technological transformation of warfare by artillery, a topic rarely examined in detail by commentators on Machiavelli's political thought.[13] Posed in the historical context, it will be clear not only that Leonardo marked a major step in the emergence of the modern view of science and technology, but that Machiavelli shared—whether through personal interaction or mere propinquity—a similar approach to human knowledge and action.

To determine whether Leonardo directly influenced Machiavelli or they are merely parallel but independent innovators, it is necessary to summarize what we know about the career of Leonardo and its intersection with that of Machiavelli. The ambiguities just noted make it prudent to formulate a "maximal" and a "minimal" interpretation of their relationship. I will therefore distinguish between the minimum agreed evidence (based on undisputed facts), and the hypothesis that Machiavelli and Leonardo became close friends during the years 1502 to 1507 (possibly followed by a break after Leonardo went to Milan and entered the service of King Louis XII of France). The truth must be somewhere between the undisputed factual evidence of contacts between them and the extrapolation of intimate friendship made by some scholars. In assessing the question, the secretive practices of both Leonardo and Machiavelli will force us to consider apparently extraneous historical events and textual passages much as a detective would sift the clues in an unsolved case.

I. *The Life and Work of Leonardo*

Leonardo da Vinci was born in 1452 in the village of Anchiano, near Vinci—some twenty miles from the center of Florence.[14] Because he was illegitimate—his father, Ser Piero da Vinci (a notary from a family of local gentry) having refused to marry his mother (who was of a lower class)— the young Leonardo was forced to make his own way. In 1469, while his father was living in the Palazzo del Podestà in Florence, Leonardo began an apprenticeship with the painter Verrocchio, whose prestigious workshop during this period included Botticelli, Perugino, Ghirlandaio, and Lorenzo di Credi. By 1472, Leonardo's name was listed on the register of Florentine painters. Four years later, along with three other young men, Leonardo was anonymously accused of sodomy, though the charge was never proven and he was ultimately acquitted.[15] From 1477 to 1482, Leonardo worked as an independent artist in Florence, receiving several major commissions (some of which, including an altarpiece for Chapel San Bernardo in the Palazzo Vecchio, were never completed); from this time are dated the portrait of *Ginevra de Benci* (1474–80; see Figure 1.1),[16] preparatory work for the *Adoration of the Magi* (1481), *St. Jerome* (c. 1481), and the first drawings of mechanical devices.

In 1482, Leonardo offered his services to Ludovico Sforza (il Moro) of Milan, having written that in addition to his abilities as sculptor and painter, he had plans for such technological innovations as bridges, devices to control water, and a variety of military innovations.[17] Leaving Florence without completing another important commission (the *Adoration of the Magi* for the Monastery of Saint Donato at Scopeto), Leonardo was to work in Milan until 1499. During these years, in addition to his paintings—of which the most notable was *The Last Supper* at Santa Marie della Grazie (1495–98)[18]—Leonardo explored radical new techniques in sculpture and other arts, wrote his treatise on painting, studied natural science, designed a variety of new weapons (Figure 1.2) as well as industrial machines (Figure 1.3), and engaged in extensive contacts with the mathematician Pacioli and other scientists and theologians at the court of Milan. While making a name for his outstanding musical ability (much of his time at court being occupied with planning and executing pageants, games, and entertainments for Sforza), Leonardo also sketched architectural plans, including a radical urban planning scheme for the city; from this period comes the remarkable map of Milan, with its combination of aerial perspectives (Figure 1.4).[19] After the fall of Ludovico and his capture by the French army, Leonardo traveled to Mantua and Venice before returning to Florence in the spring of 1500.[20]

In 1498, two years before Leonardo's return to Florence, Savonarola had been declared a heretic and burned, leading to the establishment of the Florentine Republic in which Machiavelli was named Second Chancellor and Secretary of the Committee of Ten (responsible for foreign policy and war).[21] In 1500, as is clear in *The Prince*, Machiavelli was on diplomatic mission to Nantes, where he met with Georges d'Amboise, minister of Louis XII and Cardinal of Rouen.[22]

In August 1502, Leonardo accepted Cesare Borgia's invitation to serve as "our most excellent and dearly beloved architect and general engineer . . . charged with inspecting the places and fortifications of our states."[23] This decision has been called "a surprising step" and a "strange decision," especially since before leaving Milan two years earlier, Leonardo had been offered such a position by Cesare and had turned it down.[24] While we do not know why Leonardo took this position, there is no question that he served in Cesare Borgia's court throughout the autumn and winter of 1502/3.

In early September 1502, Machiavelli joined Francesco Soderini, the Bishop of Volterra, on a mission to Cesare Borgia. Later that month, Francesco's brother Piero Soderini was elected Gonfalonier (head of state) of Florence for life. Machiavelli then returned to Cesare's court, where he was in attendance from October through the end of the year. As private correspondence shows, Machiavelli was close to both Soderini brothers and highly valued by others in the Signoria for the accurate "description" and "judgment" in his reports from "Duke Valentino's" court.[25]

Figure 1.1. Leonardo da Vinci, *Ginevra de Benci* (c. 1476), oil on wood panel, 15 1/4 x 14 1/2 inches (38.8 x 36.7 cm). Courtesy of the National Gallery of Art, Washington, D.C. (Ailsa Mellon Bruce Fund).

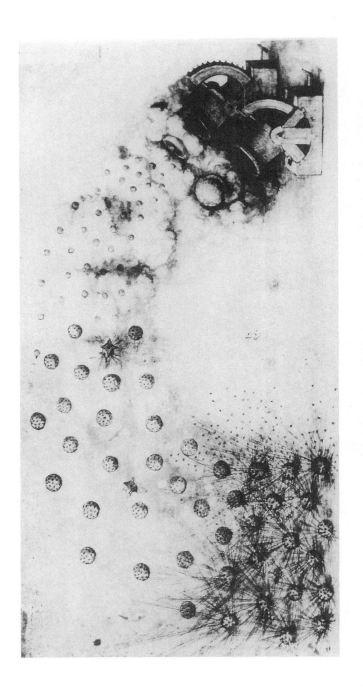

Figure 1.2. Leonardo da Vinci, Design for a Shrapnel-firing Cannon. Codex Atlanticus, folio 9, verso a. Courtesy of Veneranda Biblioteca Ambrosiana. "This huge mortar looks much like the powerful new cannon used in the American Civil War . . . The shrapnel are filled with powder and pocked with holes so that upon impact they will explode and scatter deadly fragments. Leonardo describes the shrapnel shell, in his Manuscript B, as 'the most deadly machine that exists . . . the ball in the center bursts and scatters the others which fire in such time as is needed to say an Ave Maria.' Leonardo hated war, calling it 'beastly madness.' Even in this, he seems to anticipate many scientists of the 20th century—abhorring war and yet putting his great genius into its employ" (Birn Dibner, "Machines and Weaponry," in Reti, *Unknown Leonardo*, 188–189).

Figure 1.3. Leonardo da Vinci, Design for a Digging Machine. Codex Atlanticus, folio 1, verso b. Courtesy of Veneranda Biblioteca Ambrosiana. "He was also aware of the inefficiency of men equipped only with hand shovels, and he designed the big treadmill-powered digging machine shown here. . . . For the Arno plan Leonardo's Florentine superiors had calculated it would take 2,000 workers about six months to dig the necessary canals. They miscalculated by a multiple of 5" (Ludwig H. Heydenreich, "The Military Architect," in *The Unknown Leonardo*, ed. Ladislao Reti [New York: McGraw Hill, 1974], 143). For evidence that this design was intended specifically for the Arno diversion, see Carlo Pedretti, *Literary Works of Leonardo da Vinci* (Berkeley: University of California Press, 1977), 2.179–180.

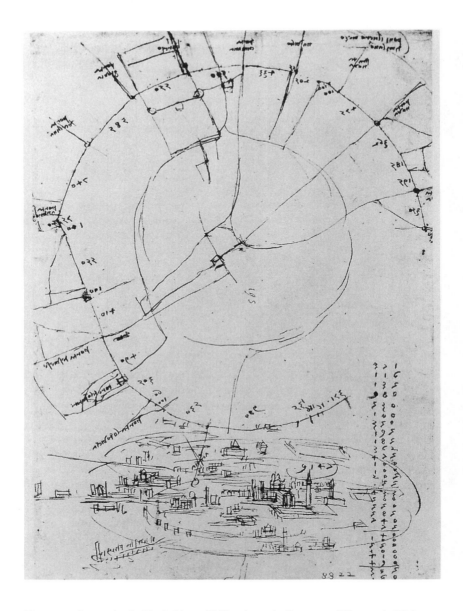

Figure 1.4. Leonardo da Vinci, Map of Milan (1490s). Courtesy of Veneranda Biblioteca Ambrosiana. "Below the circular plan of the city is a view in perspective. The cathedral is near the center and to the left is the Castello Sforzesco" (Maria Costantino, *Leonardo: Artist, Inventor, Scientist* [New York: Crescent Books, 1993], 27).

II. *Machiavelli's Relations with Leonardo*

According to a widely accepted account, it was during the autumn of 1502 that Machiavelli first met Leonardo da Vinci in person.[26]

> While he was accompanying Cesare, Leonardo made the acquaintance of a little man with malicious eyes, thin lips, and short hair. Niccolò Machiavelli, the secretary of the Florentine Republic, had been sent to Romagna as an observer.[27]

Machiavelli refers explicitly in *The Prince* to his discussions with Cesare that took place the following year,[28] but he nowhere writes about this meeting, about Leonardo's service as Cesare's military engineer, or about Leonardo's return to Florence in 1503. Why, then, should anyone believe the story that Machiavelli met Leonardo in 1502?

To consider the possibility that Machiavelli and Leonardo met in Cesare Borgia's court, first we must turn to Machiavelli's official reports to the Florentine government during his mission of 1502/3—the so-called *Legations to Valentino*.[29] In assessing these documents, however, it is important to recall that, in Renaissance letter-writing, "obscurity" was often considered "permissible" by no less an authority than Erasmus. Machiavelli, as a diplomat in delicate and sometimes dangerous situations, often remained silent or used indirect phrasing (and even ciphers) in his writing—a practice that would have been especially prudent when reporting from the court of a ruler as brutal and as unpredictable as Cesare Borgia.[30]

When he first arrived at Cesare's court, Machiavelli wrote in a dispatch that "it's part of my assignment to write you [the Signoria] how many visitors are at this nobleman's court, where they are staying, and many other local particulars."[31] Given that assignment, is it likely that a man as inquisitive as Machiavelli would have failed to meet someone as well-known as Leonardo, a Florentine serving as Cesare's military engineer and advisor? Though a reported meeting between Machiavelli and Leonardo in Nuvarola on 2 November 1502 is in doubt, Machiavelli wrote his superiors on 1 November that he had verified a conversation with Cesare's aide, Messer Agobito, by talking "to another who is also acquainted with this Lord's secrets"; then on 3 November, Machiavelli writes of a "long" conversation with an unnamed high official serving Cesare: "one of the first Secretaries, who confirmed everything I wrote in my other letters."[32] Since these dispatches list others by name and describe Machiavelli's meeting with the French commander and his officers, listing "Monsignore di Montison . . .

Baron di Bierra, Monsignore Lo Grafis et Monsignore di Borsu, luoghite-nenti di Fois, Miolans et Dunais," it is obvious that Machiavelli chose *not* to name the "first secretary" of Cesare whom he met in early November.

Several days later, on 8 November 1502, Machiavelli again wrote of a nameless "friend" whose analysis he thought important to communicate to the Signoria.[33] In his letter of 26 December Machiavelli wrote that Borgia's "chief secretaries have many times asserted to me that he does not tell them anything except when he orders it."[34] Was one of these un-named people Leonardo da Vinci? We cannot say with certainty.[35]

Machiavelli's reticence to name his contacts is easily explained by the danger that his reports might be intercepted by Cesare, but it leaves us with probabilities rather than absolute proof. Although Machiavelli's *Legations to Valentino* do not definitively establish that he talked with Leonardo frequently, these letters make a meeting in Imola during November seem highly likely. From Leonardo's diary (Manuscript L in Paris), we know he traveled extensively with Cesare to Imola, Cesena, Rimini, Urbino, Pesaro, and Piombino; Leonardo's magnificent map of Imola (Figure 1.5), a forti-fied town which Cesare took from Jacopo Appiani two years earlier, ap-parently dates from autumn 1502.[36] Since Machiavelli was in Imola from October to early December 1502, it is hard to believe that the Florentine emissary did not meet Cesare's "general engineer and architect" at official functions; Machiavelli's dispatches suggest he met virtually everyone of importance present in Cesare's court, making it reasonable to suppose that the two Florentines met there if not elsewhere.[37]

Although some scholars still doubt that they met, there is no question that Machiavelli knew of Leonardo by reputation. This is proven by a letter sent to Machiavelli in 1503, announcing the birth of his first son and reas-suring Machiavelli that he could not be cuckold because the boy looked just like his father: "Congratulations! Truly your Madonna Marietta did not deceive you, for he is your spitting image. Leonardo da Vinci would not have done a better portrait."[38] While this phrase—apparently the only explicit mention of Leonardo in Machiavelli's extant private papers—has been used to claim the two were not friends, it surely demonstrates ac-quaintanceship.[39]

In March 1503, Leonardo returned to Florence as suddenly as he had departed. He soon was engaged in the first of four projects in which he served the Republic. On three matters, Leonardo served as a technical ad-visor or consulting architect for projects associated with military and foreign affairs: the fortification of La Verucca, a fort deemed essential to

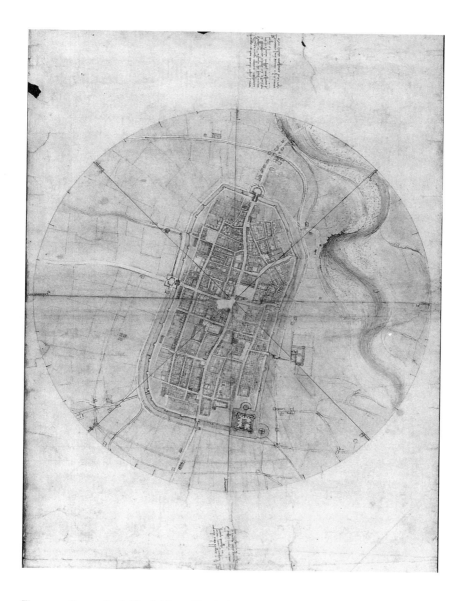

Figure 1.5. Leonardo da Vinci, Map of Imola (c. 1503), pen, ink and watercolor, 17 1/3 x 22 2/3 inches (44 x 60.2 cm). Windsor Castle, Royal Library 12284. Courtesy of The Royal Collection © Her Majesty Queen Elizabeth II. "The castle of Imola appears at the lower left of the plan, surrounded by a moat. At either side of the drawing are notes in Leonardo's mirror writing which refer to the geography, distance, and bearings of towns and cities of military interest to Cesare Borgia, Leonardo's patron" (Costantino, *Leonardo*, 93).

Figure 1.6. Leonardo da Vinci, Scheme for Canalizing the River Arno. Courtesy of Biblioteca Nacional, Madrid.

the siege of Pisa; the decision to divert the Arno River in order to deprive the Pisans of water and force their capitulation; and a technical mission to improve the port and fortress of Piombino in order to maintain the favor of its ruler, Jacopo IV Appiani. The remaining commission was more visible to the public: the painting of a large mural in the Grand Council Hall of the Palazzo della Signoria. To understand the likelihood that Machiavelli knew and worked with Leonardo, it is necessary to describe these events chronologically in the context of Florentine politics.

When Machiavelli came to office, one of the essential issues facing the Republican government was the rebellion of Pisa, which was besieged without success by the Florentines. On 14 June 1503, Machiavelli formulated a plan to attack the fortress of La Verruca, a key strategic point in the Pisan campaign. The attack was successful, and on 21 June of that year Leonardo visited the site to plan modifications in order to make it "impregnable." In this context, Leonardo drew maps from an aerial perspective, using a new point of view outlined in both his *Treatise on Painting* and the dedication to Machiavelli's *Prince*.[40]

Shortly thereafter, Leonardo was again consulted by the government, this time with regard to a plan to divert the river Arno as a means of successfully concluding the siege of Pisa.[41] On 23 July 1503, Leonardo went to the Florentine camp to advise on the feasibility of the project; Francesco Guiducci's memorandum of 24 July 1503 to the Committee of Ten (the governmental body responsible for military affairs, which Machiavelli served as Secretary) records Leonardo's approval of the diversion project (see Appendix I.2 A). Leonardo, the only one of several *Maestri d'Acqui* (hydraulic engineers) named in this memorandum, was exceptionally well qualified, since he had studied the dynamics of water extensively and, a decade earlier, developed a detailed plan to divert the Arno for peaceful purposes.

Leonardo's *Notebooks* contain evidence of his involvement in the attempted diversion of the Arno. In designing his earlier scheme, Leonardo had drawn extensive and highly detailed maps of the Arno river valley; indeed, one component of the earlier plan had been a tunnel under Serravalle, the route ultimately followed by the autostrada from Florence to the sea.[42] When working as a military architect for Cesare Borgia, Leonardo drew new maps, some of which use the aerial perspective (Figure 3.2). With regard to the military project directed against Pisa, probably in conjunction with his visit to the field in July 1503, Leonardo drew yet another map which indicates the location of a single canal diverting the Arno to the Stagno (Figure 1.6).

Machiavelli had other responsibilities in addition to the military campaign against Pisa. On 18 August 1503, Pope Alexander VI died—apparently, it is now surmised, as a result of poison Borgia intended for one of the Orsini; Cesare, who probably consumed by accident some of the poison, survived its effects but soon lost power. The election of Pope Pius III on 22 September was almost immediately followed by the new pope's death on 16 October and the election of Julius II as his successor on 31 October. We know that Machiavelli was in Rome at this time, both from his official report to the Florentine Signoria announcing the election of Julius and from his description of the conversation with Cesare in *The Prince*.[43]

During the summer of 1503, Soderini had decided to have large frescos painted in the newly completed Grand Council Hall of the Palazzo della Signoria. Because of the importance of the work, it can be assumed that the choice of artists was a significant political matter. Since Michelangelo also had supporters (his statue of David had been commissioned by the city in 1501 and ultimately he was asked to paint a mural on another wall of the Council Hall), some art historians believe Machiavelli's views may well have been crucial, either when Leonardo received the commission in October 1503 or later when Soderini complained about paying Leonardo because he seemed too slow in completing the painting.[44] Despite Machiavelli's diplomatic activities at this time, as one of Soderini's closest collaborators he could hardly have been unaware of Leonardo's commission and the controversies it entailed.[45]

From 1503 to 1506 Leonardo worked on the cartoon of his painting for the Council Hall, the famous *Battle of Anghiari* (Frontispiece, Figures 1.7 and 4.5). To acquaint Leonardo with the event, a description of the battle was written in his notebooks by another hand; although a few scholars once thought this might be written by Machiavelli himself, the description is now thought to be in the handwriting of Agostino Vespucci, one of Machiavelli's assistants at the Signoria. The same handwriting is found on an important letter from Leonardo to Cardinal Ippolito d'Este written in 1507.[46] It should go without saying that handwriting on both of these documents by Agostino Vespucci provides especially strong evidence of a close working relationship with Machiavelli.

Meanwhile, with the strong support of Machiavelli himself, Soderini and the Signoria embarked on the work required for the diversion of the Arno. Scholars have disagreed on the precise roles of Leonardo and Machiavelli in this project. Because Leonardo was primarily occupied with *The Battle of Anghiari*, his contribution to the diversion seems to have been

Figure 1.7. Leonardo da Vinci., Study for Central and Left Groups for *Battle of Anghiari* (c. 1503–04), pen and ink, 5 3/4 x 6 inches (14.5 x 15.2 cm). Courtesy of Galleria dell' Accademia, Venice.

limited to consultation on viability and design; there is no evidence that Leonardo himself worked in the field. The evidence marshaled by Fachard shows that an architect named Colombino was the principal specialist in charge and that Machiavelli, while delegating routine organization to Buonaccorsi and relying on Giuliano Lapi and others for direction in the field, followed the project closely. In particular, on several occasions, Machiavelli warns those in the field of the danger of relying too much on Colombino's engineering skill (see Appendix I.4).

Leonardo's drawings for *The Battle of Anghiari* advanced only slowly, in part because he sought to depict the movement of battle with hitherto unknown perfection. The only formal document I have found linking the names of Leonardo and Machiavelli dates from this period. On 4 May 1504, to ensure completion of the mural which Leonardo had begun the preceding October, the Signoria agreed to give Leonardo "an advance of thirty-five florins and . . . a monthly salary of fifteen florins" on condition that he "finish the composition [i.e., the cartoon] of the *Battle* by the following February" and providing that a separate contract would be drawn up for painting the mural itself; the text indicates that Machiavelli witnessed the action.[47]

Meanwhile, work on the Arno project was hampered by limited funds. The estimated number of laborers needed to dig the canal proved five times too low. It has been argued that this mistake could not have been due to Leonardo, whose notebooks from the 1490s reveal careful calculations of the manpower necessary to build such channels as well as designs for machines to do the work more efficiently. As difficulties mounted, Machiavelli seems to have become greatly concerned about the outcome.

Of the ninety-five memoranda that Machiavelli himself wrote on the project, the critical text is dated 20 September 1504 (Appendix I.4). Writing to Giuliano Lapi, Machiavelli says that "we prefer" the "first plan" of the diversion to the "second plan." The first plan seems to correspond to the map of the diversion drawn by Leonardo that was discovered in Madrid in 1970 (Figure 1.6); the second seems the same as the final project attributed to Colombino in Buonaccorsi's *Sunmario* and illustrated by the map in his *Diary* (Figure 1.11). Although Machiavelli makes his preference clear, he concludes his letter by authorizing Lapi to use his judgment in the light of necessities in the field.[48]

The next day, Machiavelli again wrote Lapi—this time with urgency— warning that the plan being followed had a potentially disastrous defect. With the canals proposed in the "second plan," Machiavelli notes, the water will not flow as anticipated and the entire project could be destroyed (Machiavelli to Lapi, 21 September 1504; Appendix I.4). According to Buonaccorsi's description of the events, this is precisely what happened: due to the depth of the diversionary canals, the Arno only flowed into them when the river was in flood; as the river fell, water flowed backwards from the weir into the river, destroying the works and forcing abandonment of the project (Appendix I.5).[49]

While the texts cited by Fachard and reproduced in Appendix I contradict Pedretti's hypothesis that Machiavelli and Leonardo worked extensively together in implementing the planned diversion, these texts do prove that Machiavelli was precisely informed on the technical aspects of the diversionary canals—and that he criticized the work in the field on the basis of an earlier design by an unnamed specialist. There is no evidence that Machiavelli, apparently trained as a humanist and poet, either studied hydraulic engineering or had the practical experience with the flow of rivers of the typical *Maestri d'Acqui*. While Leonardo is the most plausible source for Machiavelli's criticism of Colombino, Berardi, and other engineers, even skeptics need to admit that Machiavelli's administrative oversight of the diversion of the Arno reveals extensive knowledge of the technical problems of channeling rivers through "dikes and banks."[50]

Whether caused by political shortcomings in financing or technical errors in execution, a partially completed section of the new channel collapsed after about a year's work. Despite Machiavelli's entreaties, the Signoria abandoned the attempt to redirect the river in October 1504, and pursued the war by more conventional means.[51] Blame for the failure was directed at Colombino, who had been criticized in Tomassino's letter to the Committee of Ten on 28 September 1504 (Appendix I.4F). Buonaccorsi's personal draft describing the disaster names Colombino as the engineer responsible for the revised plan, although the manuscript revised for circulation deletes this identification (see Appendix I.5). When Piero Soderini's brother Francesco learned of the failure, his letter to Machiavelli likewise attributes it to the "fault of those engineers, who went so far wrong."[52]

After the projected diversion of the Arno failed, Machiavelli himself refers to it in *The First Decennale*, a poem written in late 1504 that recounts the political events in Italy from 1494 to 1504: in the war against Pisa, "you [Florence] tried to turn the Arno aside through different courses."[53] Neither in this passage nor in general remarks about attempts to divert rivers while besieging cities, does Machiavelli refer to his own role in this attempt. Hence Machiavelli's silence about Leonardo's advice on the Arno project could well be interpreted as part of a broader reticence to speak about his own failures.

Other events indicate that Machiavelli continued his contacts with Leonardo after the plan to rechannel the Arno was abandoned. It became important for Florence to gain the goodwill of Jacopo Appiani, newly restored ruler of the strategic port city of Piombino, whose deposition by Cesare Borgia in 1499 had been tacitly supported by Florence. Earlier in 1504, Machiavelli went on a diplomatic mission to Piombino to secure Jacopo's benevolent neutrality toward Florence's rivalry with Pisa and Sienna. To implement the agreements reached at that meeting, in November 1504 Leonardo was sent to Piombino to provide technical assistance in redesigning the fortifications and port, which he knew well from previous work there under Cesare.[54]

In 1505, Leonardo requested—and received from the Signoria—additional funds to complete *The Battle of Anghiari*. On 6 June, he recorded in his *Notebooks* that "I began to paint in the palace." Although the results were astounding, the painting itself was a failure; because Leonardo chose to paint with experimental materials that proved defective, the painting was never finished and—after his death—had to be destroyed.[55]

During these years, Leonardo was engaged in other activities, some of which might also have led him to encounter Machiavelli. Although the *Mona Lisa* is usually dated from this period of Leonardo's work, for present purposes it is probably more important that he continued his studies of science and technology, including most notably the construction of a flying machine with which Leonardo himself attempted to fly.[56] As will be shown below, Leonardo's innovations in military technology seem to parallel Machiavelli's innovations in military strategy, suggesting a parallelism—and perhaps a direct influence—that has escaped prior commentators.

On 30 May 1506, Leonardo went to Milan, now under the control of the French king, Louis XII, promising to return after three months to complete *The Battle of Anghiari*. In August, Charles d'Amboise, the Governor of Milan, requested an extension of Leonardo's leave from Florence. While Leonardo was in Milan as the French king's "regular painter and engineer," his uncle died and Leonardo returned to Florence to defend his inheritance against a legal challenge. This event might be important because Leonardo's notebooks contain the draft of a letter to a "Messer Nicolò" seeking legal assistance. Although Beltrami and several other scholars believe it was addressed to Machiavelli in 1507,[57] other specialists like Pedretti date the letter in 1514 and suggest the addressee is Niccolò Michelozzi, a humanist who was Machiavelli's successor in the Chancery after the Florentine Republic fell in 1512.[58] While the letter does not prove the existence of a close and long-standing personal relationship between Machiavelli and Leonardo, it reminds us of the possibility if not the likelihood that they would have met again at the Rucellai gardens while Leonardo was in Florence in 1507 and 1508.[59]

After 1509, Leonardo worked in Milan until the expulsion of the French in 1512. In addition to painting *The Virgin and Child with St. Anne and a Lamb* (Figure 4.6) and *St. John the Baptist*, Leonardo's major activities during this time included extensive anatomical studies (Figure 1.8); among his major architectural projects was the design of a villa for Charles d'Amboise remarkable for its complex irrigation and artistic water distribution system.[60] In 1512, the French were driven from Milan by a coalition of the pope, the Venetians, and the Spaniards; in the same year, the Florentine Republic was overthrown and the Medici returned to power.

Leonardo left Milan on 24 September 1513, and after visiting Florence briefly, went to Rome on 1 December to enter the service of Giuliano de' Medici.[61] While in Rome, Leonardo did not receive the major artistic commissions given to other painters patronized by the Medici (including Donato Bramante, Raphael, and Michelangelo). Instead, Giuliano commissioned him to draft an ambitious plan for draining the Pontine Marshes and to work on a solar mirror for use in cloth-making, although he did complete several paintings for Baldassare Turini, a papal notary.[62]

Machiavelli, meanwhile, found himself out of power and without resources. After the Medici returned to power in Florence in 1512, Machiavelli was accused of participating in a plot against them, arrested, and tortured; on his release from jail, he returned to his home in San Casciano, outside of Florence, with the condition that he could neither leave the territory of Florence nor enter the Signoria for one year. It is at this time that he wrote *The Prince*, as recorded in his famous letter to Vettori of 13 December 1513, which states that the work is being dedicated to Giuliano de' Medici.[63]

In 1515, Lorenzo di Piero de' Medici, Giuliano's nephew, was named Governor of Florence; Leonardo seems to have returned to Florence to design stables and a new Medici palace for the younger Lorenzo.[64] After the death of Giuliano de' Medici in 1516, Leonardo found his way back to the service of the French, moving to Romorantin and then Amboise with King Francis I. During this period, however, Leonardo continued to work

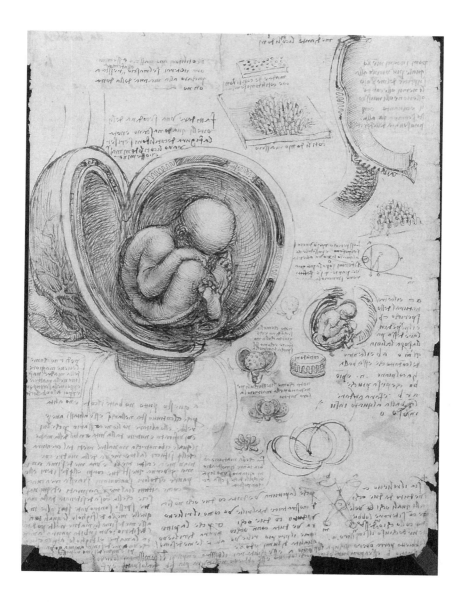

Figure 1.8. Leonardo da Vinci, Embryo in the Uterus (c. 1510), pen and ink, 11 7/8 x 8 1/2 inches (30.1 x 21.4 cm). Windsor Castle, Royal Library 19102r. Courtesy of The Royal Collection © Her Majesty Queen Elizabeth II.

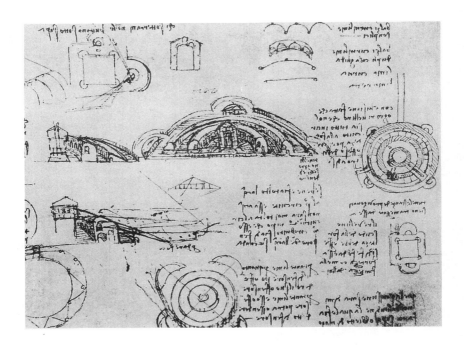

Figure 1.9. Leonardo da Vinci, Design for a Fortress. Codex Atlanticus, folio 48, recto b. Courtesy of Veneranda Biblioteca Ambrosiana. Upper left: Leonardo's note reads "Along as many lines as the defender can strike at the offender, the offender will be able to strike at the defender." Upper right: Leonardo notes "to open fire." "Out of his labors at Piombino, Leonardo evolved a design for a fortress so different its like would not be seen for centuries. . . . Outposts on the four corners furnish flanking fire. Concentric fortified rings provide firing positions for the defenders of the citadel. Between the rings are trench-like areas that could be flooded if the enemies breached the outer walls, enabling the defenders to retreat to strongpoints in the innermost rings" (Heydenreich, "The Military Architect," 162–163).

for Lorenzo de' Piero de Medici, who was aligned with the French court; hence, when Lorenzo married Madeleine de la Tour d'Auvergne in 1518, the festivities at the royal court in Amboise included a *Paradise* play that Leonardo originally designed for Sforza in Milan a generation earlier.[65]

After moving to France, although Leonardo's ability to paint seems to have been limited by a stroke, he designed a new palace at Romorantin for Francis I. Although the project was abandoned at Leonardo's death, it has been speculated that Leonardo's projects influenced the castle at Chambord, which is conventionally viewed as the first major building of the French Renaissance.[66] His activity reduced by ill health, Leonardo was on exceptionally close terms with the French king; he died on 2 May 1519 at the Chateau of Amboise—according to Vasari, in the arms of King Francis I— at the age of sixty-seven.[67]

In these years, Machiavelli continued to write, completing both *The Prince* (changing the dedication from Giuliano to Lorenzo di Piero de' Medici, according to most accounts after the former's death in 1516) and the *Discourses on Titus Livy*. Although neither was published in Machiavelli's lifetime, we now know that *The Prince* was not materially changed after 15 September 1520 (the latest date possible for one of the three extant manuscript copies made by Buonaccorsi).[68] Thereafter, Machiavelli wrote and published *The Art of War*, a dialogue on military strategy of greater importance than has usually been recognized, as well as plays and fables, of which the most famous is *Mandragola*.[69] In addition to reading these works in the gardens of the Rucellai family—the famous Orti Oricellari for which Leonardo designed a novel fountain[70]—Machiavelli finally secured a commission from the Medici in 1519 to write a history of Florence; dedicated to Pope Leo X, the *Florentine Histories* was published in 1525.

A number of passages in these works provide evidence of Leonardo's influence on Machiavelli. Apart from textual parallels between Machiavelli's *Prince* and Leonardo's *Notebooks* to be discussed at length below, there are important similarities between Leonardo's innovations and Machiavelli's views of military strategy as outlined in the *Discourses on Titus Livy* and *The Art of War*. For example, Leonardo seems to have been the first to understand how massed artillery changed the balance of forces between offense and defense by destroying the invulnerability of the traditional thick-walled medieval castle; Machiavelli emphatically endorses this view.[71] As a result, Leonardo envisaged a radically new way of building fortifications with lower curved walls and moats (Figure 1.9), an innovation adopted with some modifications in Machiavelli's *Art of War*.

Leonardo's *Notebooks* contain other indications of potential influence on Machiavelli's thought. When Machiavelli seeks an example to show that, apart from cannon and gunpowder, technical innovations usually have little effect on the outcome of battles, he speaks "of elephants, of scythed chariots and of other strong opponents that the Roman infantry opposed."[72] Every schoolboy knows of Hannibal's use of elephants when crossing the Alps, but the reference to scythed chariots is more obscure; although such a device is described in Xenophon's *Anabasis* as an invention used by the Persians against the Greeks, it was also used by Archelaus against Romans under the command of Sulla. Machiavelli's use of this illustration might reflect Leonardo's drawings of such a device (Figure 1.10), which accompany pictures of other machines of war.[73]

Another example of possible influence occurs in Book VI of the *Florentine Histories*, where Machiavelli describes a violent and highly destructive windstorm that devastated the Val d'Arno on 24 August 1456. Although there is no published record of this tornado, which occurred thirteen years before Machiavelli himself was born, his account is exceptionally vivid:

> a whirlwind of a cloud, huge and dense, which reached almost two miles wide throughout its course . . . driven by superior forces, whether they were natural or supernatural, broke on itself and fought within itself; and the shattered clouds, now rising toward the sky, now descending toward the earth, crashed together; and then they moved in circles with very great velocity and stirred up ahead of them a wind violent beyond all measure. . . . From these clouds, so broken and confused, from such furious winds and such frequent flashes, arose a noise never before heard from any earthquake or thunder of any kind or greatness; from it arose such fear that anyone who heard it judged that the end of the world had come and that earth, water, and the rest of the sky and the world would return mixed together to its ancient chaos.[74]

Leonardo was four years old at the time the storm passed through the valley, and his *Notebooks* contain striking drawings of such a storm as well as verbal descriptions of similar cataclysms. As a result, Pedretti claims that this passage must have been the result of Machiavelli's conversations with Leonardo.[75]

A final indication of the relationship between Machiavelli and Leonardo comes from the last years of Machiavelli's life, when he was engaged in missions in the Romagna as an advisor to his friend Francesco Guicciardini, then governor of Modena. In September 1526 Guicciardini wrote Robert

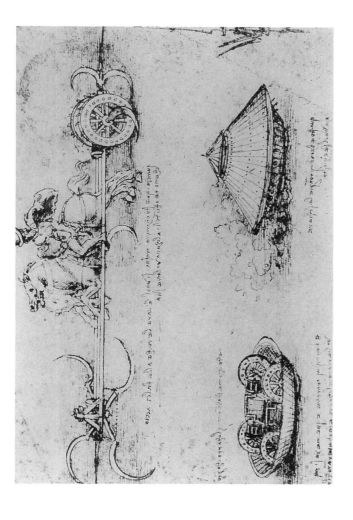

Figure 1.10. Leonardo da Vinci, A Scythed Chariot, an Armoured Vehicle, and a Partisan (c. 1485–88), pen, ink, and wash, 6 7/8 x 9 5/8 inches (17.3 x 24.6 cm). Courtesy of the British Museum.

Accioatoli that "I sent you, in a letter from Machiavelli from the camp of Cremona, a drawing of these trenches that is not in the hand of Leonardo da Vinci."[76] While this probably merely means that the drawing is of poor quality (and not that Machiavelli had in his possession other architectural sketches by Leonardo), Guiccardini's usage implies that without the specification, his correspondent might expect Machiavelli's description of a military site to be accompanied by a drawing as good as those of Leonardo.

In Machiavelli's last years, although his *Mandragola* was successfully performed, he never regained the status of his years as Secretary to the Signoria. Even his patronage from the Medici, secured after years of effort, worked against him. When the Medici were again overthrown in 1527, Machiavelli offered his services to the new republic but, ironically, was rebuffed shortly before his death on 22 June 1527. It was only posthumously that his most famous works were published: *The Discourses on Titus Livy* in 1531 and *The Prince* in 1532.

III. The Facts and Their Interpretation

To interpret such a tangled web of detail, it will be useful to begin from a summary of the agreed facts:

- Leonardo and Machiavelli were Florentine contemporaries who had ample opportunities to meet when the former was serving Cesare Borgia as military architect (1502/3). At least one letter to Machiavelli confirms that, by 1503, he must have known of Leonardo by reputation.
- Several ambiguous passages in Machiavelli's *Legations to Valentino* (especially in his letters of 3 November, 8 November, and 26 December 1502) might be interpreted as referring to Leonardo.
- After both returned to Florence, on at least four occasions Machiavelli was responsible for a project on which Leonardo worked or was consulted: the fortification of La Verruca in the Val d'Arno (1503); the attempt to redirect the Arno in the war between Florence and Pisa (1503/4); the painting of *The Battle of Anghiari* in the Palace of the Signoria (1503–1506); and the technical mission to Jacopo Appiani of Piombino (1504).
- On 23 July 1503, Leonardo went to the site to assess the feasibility of diverting the Arno; documents recording his approval of the

project and Machiavelli's later memoranda concerning its execution indicate that they must have known each other.

○ As preparation for painting *The Battle of Anghiari*, a description of the event in Leonardo's *Notebooks* is written by Machiavelli's secretary, Agostino Vespucci; the same handwriting appears in a letter that Leonardo sent to Cardinale Ippolito d'Este in 1507, when seeking support in the contest over the will of his uncle.

○ As Second Chancellor of the Signoria, Machiavelli had direct knowledge of the conflict between Leonardo and Soderini over payments to the artist and his failure to complete *The Battle of Anghiari*: the decision of 4 May 1504, setting the terms of Leonardo's future work, was witnessed by Machiavelli. Moreover, it would have been impossible for anyone working in the Signoria to be unaware of Leonardo's extraordinary and well-known painting.

○ Although Machiavelli delegated day-to-day direction of the abortive effort to redirect the Arno in the war against Pisa (1503/4), documentary evidence shows his awareness of technical details in the plans being followed. The famous comparison of fortune with a river (*Prince*, ch. 25) can be read, at one level, as referring to Leonardo's projects to control the flow of rivers, many of which were directed toward economic development (projects in the Arno and Adda river valleys and the Pontine Marshes) rather than to military purposes.

○ As will be shown in following chapters, there are other passages in *The Prince*—notably the description of those who "sketch landscapes" in the dedication—which are parallel to texts by Leonardo and seem inspired by him. Also of importance are the discussion of fortresses (*Prince*, ch. 20) and the prince's need to study "nature of sites" (*Prince*, ch. 14), both of which reveal views like those of Leonardo.

○ Machiavelli's military strategy, as developed in both the *Discourses on Titus Livy* and *The Art of War*, accepts innovations found only in the work of Leonardo and shows the influence of his views of warfare.

○ In *Florentine Histories* (Book VI, ch. 24), Machiavelli presents a vivid first-hand description of a violent tempest that devastated the Val d'Arno in 1456, when Leonardo was four years old and thirteen years before Machiavelli's birth; Leonardo himself described and drew such a storm, and there are no other contemporary records of the cataclysm of 1456.

Beneath these personal contacts and textual parallels is a deeper similarity in the conceptions of theory, practice, and human history set forth in Leonardo's *Notebooks* and Machiavelli's *Prince, Discourses,* and *Florentine Histories.*[77] The evidence that Leonardo and Machiavelli knew of each other, combined with the possibility they may have been friends between 1502 and 1507 (and perhaps as late as 1515), suggests that similarities in their views could be the result of shared interests and direct influence. Even should scholars reject this interpretation, the parallels suggest the need to consider Machiavelli's contribution to modernity in the light of the similarity between his views and Leonardo's innovative integration of theory and practice.

As if to confirm these parallels, Machiavelli's silence concerning Leonardo extends to silence concerning Machiavelli's own role in any of the four projects on which they seem to have collaborated. Two of these events are described in a general way by Machiavelli, albeit without mentioning his own involvement: the diversion of the Arno (*First Decennale*) and the fortification of La Verruca (*Discourses,* II, 24). The failure to discuss Leonardo thus appears to be part of a broader reticence of Machiavelli.

Leonardo is known for the immense range of his inventive projects, many of which anticipated Western technological developments by three or four centuries. Machiavelli shows great reticence about the strategic importance of innovations, arguing that most are essentially deceptions whose effect depends on the naïveté of the enemy.[78] Could there be something in Leonardo's view of science, technology, and human life which Machiavelli either rejects or prefers to hide from his readers? Perhaps the puzzle, which has led us on the chase for obscure clues, is itself the message Machiavelli wished to give his most acute readers.

The historical record alone is insufficient ground for a final conclusion on the nature and extent of the relationship between Machiavelli and Leonardo. As indicated by Machiavelli's failure to mention such collaborators as Biagio Buonaccorsi, many people and events were not recorded in Machiavelli's letters and writings. It is therefore necessary to focus on the only evidence that Machiavelli unambiguously bequeathed to us—the texts of his major writings. But if Machiavelli was as "Machiavellian" as he is reputed to have been, how can we understand what he wrote? To analyze Machiavelli's thought, we must first discover how to read his work.

Chapter Two

On Reading Machiavelli's "Prince"

Machiavelli's The Prince *is the book of republicans.*
Rousseau

*T*his essay considers Niccolò Machiavelli to be one of the greatest thinkers in Western civilization. To justify this conclusion, I will focus on *The Prince*. This book is well known, has been historically important, and, in Machiavelli's own words, can enable a reader "to understand in a very short time all that I have learned and understood."[1] But how should we read Machiavelli's *Prince?* Is it merely a book of circumstance, written to gain Machiavelli a job with the Medici? Is it an amoral—or immoral—justification of the use of power for its own sake? Does it contradict the longer and ostensibly more complete *Discourses on Titus Livy*, or does it present the same understanding that Machiavelli expressed in his other works?

These questions are important because Machiavelli is so often said to have inaugurated "modern" thought. Typically, *The Prince* is described as the first *scientific* study of politics and human affairs. In our curriculum, Machiavelli usually represents the end of the "classic" and "medieval" periods, which were based on theological and philosophical premises distant from contemporary life; his teaching is presented as the beginning of the intellectual horizon known as "modernity."[2] Before reflecting on Machiavelli's thought, it is therefore prudent to clarify how his work should be read.

Although it is commonplace to rank *The Prince* among the "great books," this conventional assessment raises two questions. First, was Machiavelli a writer of the depth and importance of Plato, Aristotle, Hobbes, Rousseau, or Hegel—that is, does his thought form a philosophical system that could be *true* and hence can be considered meaningful in the light of contemporary natural science? And second, was he somehow exceptionally devious—one might almost say "Machiavellian"—in presenting a serious political philosophy in the guise of a handbook for selfish leaders?

Unfortunately, much of what is said or written about Machiavelli and his works fails to consider these questions.[3] If the answer to either or both is negative, he was little more than the epitome of political thought in Renaissance Italy and an author of considerable historical importance. If both answers are positive, Machiavelli understood "the effectual truth of the matter" of human life and still has something to teach us. Such a claim implies that Machiavelli might even have transformed what we call epistemology, ontology, logic, or other abstract inquiries when writing what appears to be advice to political leaders. As a result, an attempt to assess Machiavelli as a major philosopher (the first of the questions posed above) entails a hard look at the deceptive nature of his writings (the second query).

There is good reason to examine both questions with an open mind. In the *Discourses on Titus Livy*—generally regarded as Machiavelli's most complete work—the author flatly asserts that he seeks to "enter upon *a new way, as yet untrodden by anyone else*" (*Discourses*, I, Pref.; p. 97). Machiavelli compares himself to Columbus, acknowledging that such innovation carries great risks: "it has *always been no less dangerous to discover new ways and methods than to set off in search of new seas and unknown lands*" (ibid.). Similarly, in *The Prince* Machiavelli asserts that he will "*depart from the orders of others*" (*Prince*, ch. 14; p. 61). Even Machiavelli's most celebrated literary work, the comedy *Mandragola*, begins with a Prologue in which the author introduces the play as a "*new case.*"[4]

Machiavelli's claim to radical novelty is not limited to political advice in the narrow sense: on the contrary, when he compares "all men that are praised," Machiavelli lists "founding a religion" as leading to the "most" praise, followed by founding "either republics or kingdoms," then deeds of "army commanders" and "men of letters," and finally those of "any man who excels in some art and in the practice of it" (*Discourses*, I, 10; pp. 134–135). Is Machiavelli's "new way" merely a work of the "art" of writing by a "man of letters" interested in "what the modes and government of a prince should be with subjects and with friends" (*Prince*, ch. 14; p. 61)? Or, in some sense, can his work claim to be as fundamental and praiseworthy as the founding of a new religion?

To address these questions, we must bear in mind two things. First, Machiavelli's own stated goal is "that which I believe to be for the *common benefit of all*" (*Discourses*, Pref.; p. 97): despite the apparent nationalism of the last chapter of *The Prince*, even of that book the author says "my intent is to write something useful to *whoever understands it*" (*Prince*, ch. 15; p. 61). Machiavelli's explicit intention in writing his most famous works is not limited to any one political community—or indeed to any one kind of human being.[5] Could Machiavelli, like Socrates, be a philosopher who turned to human life and morality as more important than studies of "nature" more generally? Like Plato or Aristotle, he seems to be concerned with the "good life" and the means to achieve it. If, like Demetrius of Phalerum of the Peripatetic School, Machiavelli seems to focus on political life as the highest practical human goal, this may reflect considerations of the "useful" as distinct from an abstract or disembodied "truth."[6]

Second, we need to remember Machiavelli's classification of the three kinds of human intelligence: "*there are three kinds of brains: one that understands by itself; another that discerns what others understand, the third that understands neither by itself nor through others*; the first is most excellent, the second excellent, and the third useless" (*Prince*, ch. 22; p. 92). If Machiavelli claimed to open "a new way," he must have placed himself in this highest category. And if he claimed to have one of the few human brains "that understands by itself," there may be profound reasons—beyond Machiavelli's political fortunes after the fall of the Florentine Republic—for his decision to present his reflections on human nature and nature in a somewhat devious manner.

Although these questions may seem far-fetched, recently published evidence of Machiavelli's early career gives us reason to challenge the traditional interpretations of *The Prince*. We now know that Machiavelli was trained as a humanist and, as a young man, personally copied Lucretius's *De rerum natura*.[7] While at the court of Cesare Borgia in October 1502, he asked his assistant, Biagio Buonaccorsi, to procure a copy of Plutarch's *Lives*—a request that was difficult for Buonaccorsi to satisfy.[8] While it cannot be said with certainty whether Machiavelli and Leonardo discussed questions concerning the relationship between natural science and philosophy,[9] a private letter from Bartolomeo Vespucci, Professor of Astronomy at Padua, indicates that in 1504 Machiavelli had written that he considered the science of astronomy essential for understanding human affairs.[10] By 1506, as Machiavelli's letter to Giovan Battista Soderini shows (see Appendix II.1), he had already outlined his mature understanding of the relationship between the diversity of human natures and fortune. All these details suggest that, before writing *The Prince*, Machiavelli was concerned with issues that go far beyond the practical politics of six-teenth-century Florence.

I propose, therefore, that we embark on a rereading of *The Prince* with an openness to three distinct possibilities. First, Machiavelli may write with hidden or esoteric meanings, so that what serious or philosophic readers discover in his works is not evident to the casual reader. Second, Machiavelli may be more interested in what was traditionally called philosophy or theoretical wisdom than has been imagined—an interest which, as I will show, could have been reinforced by the relationship with Leonardo da Vinci discussed in the last chapter.[11] Last but not least, Machiavelli's novelty may concern the relationship between theory and practice rather than details on the domain of either pragmatic political advice or philosophic speculation—and in this regard, we cannot ignore Machiavelli's own experiences as Second Secretary of the Florentine Republic, especially when they provide concrete information about the meaning of the texts of his work.

To explore these three possibilities with an open mind demands much of the reader. Lest we show ourselves to be "useless," we should try to show that we are at least of the second category "that discerns what others understand." To do so, we will need to read more closely than has been the habit of many modern commentators.

I. Is The Prince a Satire?

Conventional wisdom treats Machiavelli's *The Prince* as an astute, cynical, and amoral (if not immoral) guide to the use of power. Any reader can see that, on the surface, this is a reasonable impression. The first question we need to raise, therefore, is whether Machiavelli wrote in a devious or misleading way. Can *The Prince* be read as a satire on the ambition of rulers?

Serious thinkers have sometimes claimed precisely this. When Rousseau discusses monarchy in *The Social Contract*, for example, he asserts:

> The best kings want to be able to be wicked if it so pleases them, without ceasing to be the masters. . . . This is what Samuel so strongly pointed out to the Hebrews; and what Machiavelli showed with clarity. While pretending to give lessons to kings, he gave great ones to the people. *Machiavelli's* The Prince *is the book of republicans.*[12]

At this point, Rousseau adds a footnote on his claim that *The Prince* is a deceptive book:

Machiavelli was an honorable man and a good citizen; but being attached to the Medici household, he was forced, during the oppression of his homeland, to disguise his love of freedom. The choice of his execrable hero is in itself enough to make manifest his *hidden intention*; and the contrast between the maxims of his book *The Prince* and those of his *Discourses on Titus Livy* and his *History of Florence* shows that this profound political theorist has had only superficial or corrupt readers until now.[13]

Does the evidence support this interpretation?

Many critics have been hesitant to accept the view that an author has a "secret" (or "esoteric") meaning, pointing out that such interpretations can subject a text to the whims and biases of the interpreter.[14] Caution in this regard is prudent. In general, one should reserve the attribution of a "hidden intention" to works that satisfy three criteria:

- The historical and intellectual context should justify the practice of writing in a devious or insincere manner.
- There should be hints, in the public writings being considered, of contradictions or confusions that direct a careful reader to the possibility of a hidden meaning.
- Correspondence or other information about the author's private life should indicate an awareness of deceptive writing and, if possible, the intention to practice it.

Or, to put it more simply, we should follow Rousseau's suggestion that Machiavelli's own career and "the contrast" between his different works are relevant to an understanding of *The Prince*.

II. Machiavelli's Republican Career and the Medici

As chapter one has indicated, rather more is known about Machiavelli's life and career than about most of the great thinkers of antiquity.[15] Born in 1469, he was a young man when Lorenzo the Magnificent, ruler of Florence, died in the fateful year 1492. After the reestablishment of the Florentine Republic and the interlude of "fundamentalist" piety under Savonarola (1494–1498), leadership passed to Piero Soderini, who was elected Gonfalonier for life in 1502. In 1498, Machiavelli was named to the post of Secretary (or Chancellor) to the Second Chancery—and thereafter also was named to the post of Secretary to the Ten of Liberty and Peace (a committee with responsibility for military and foreign affairs). Perhaps more important, Soderini employed the young Niccolò Machiavelli personally on many delicate foreign negotiations, including the missions to France and to the court of Cesare Borgia cited in *The Prince*.[16]

In studying Machiavelli's writings, it is therefore essential to keep in mind that he spent the years from 1498 to 1512 as a public figure, actively engaged in the political life of his native Florence. As a specialist in foreign and military affairs, he was particularly committed to a policy of establishing a native militia, replacing the mercenary troops and condottieri who seemed both unreliable and dangerous to the young republic. And as a committed supporter of Piero Soderini, Machiavelli was perceived as a defender of the republican form of government that replaced the autocratic rule of the Medici family.[17]

In September 1512, after the citizen's militia organized by Machiavelli suffered a disastrous military defeat at Prato, Piero Soderini was overthrown and the Medici returned to power. Machiavelli was imprisoned and, suspected of complicity in a plot to restore the republic, tortured. He was then released to his country house (in Sant' Andrea in Percussina, near San Casciano), required to post a bond of a thousand florins, forbidden either to enter the Palazzo (or seat of government) or to leave the territory of Florence for one year.[18] By March 1513, therefore, Machiavelli found himself under something akin to house arrest, under suspicion by the restored Medici rulers of Florence who were dedicated to uprooting memories of the short-lived republic.

In the year 1513, we know from correspondence that Machiavelli continued to think and write about politics. In January 1513, he had written Soderini a long and guarded letter outlining the role of fortune (in terms similar to chapter twenty-five of *The Prince*), comparing the careers of Hannibal and Scipio (parallel to the comparison in *The Prince*, chapter seventeen).[19] After his imprisonment in February and March, Machiavelli's friend Vettori, who continued to hold the post of Florentine ambassador to Rome under the Medici, asked his opinion of a truce between Spain and France;[20] Machiavelli replied on 20 April, admitting that "although I have sworn neither to think of nor discuss politics," he would "break my vow" and answer Vettori's request.[21] This correspondence with Vettori continued throughout the year, culminating in a long letter dated 10 December 1513 which has been called "the most famous letter in Italian literature."[22]

Machiavelli's letter to Vettori provides critical evidence about Machiavelli's life at the time as well as his intentions in writing *The Prince*. In reading it, however, we must bear in mind that Machiavelli had to consider the possibility that his letter could be intercepted and read (or misread) as a subversive document; indeed, the letter begins with a reference to just such a possibility. Years later, writing the historian Guiccardini, Machiavelli remarked that *"for a long time I have not said what I believed, nor do I ever believe what I say, and if indeed sometimes I do happen to tell the truth, I hide it among so many lies that it is hard to find."*[23] Even in private correspondence, one cannot always be sure that Machiavelli is simply telling the truth, the whole truth, and nothing but the truth.[24]

Machiavelli begins his famous letter of 10 December 1513 by acknowledging his friend Vettori's letter of 23 November.[25] After indicating that he had been afraid of being blamed because Vettori's prior correspondence may have been improperly divulged, Machiavelli goes on to praise Vettori for continuing his ambassadorial functions "orderedly and quietly":

> And because *Fortune wants to do everything*, she wants us to allow her to do it, to remain quiet and not give trouble, and to *await the time when she allows men something to do*; and then it will be right for you to give more effort, to watch things more, and *for me to leave my villa* and say: 'Here I am.'

While this explicitly indicates that Machiavelli will continue to avoid political activity (which, had the letter been intercepted by the Medici, could hardly have been unwelcome), what is the "something to do" that Fortune will allow? Is it any role in political life, or action associated with republican government?

Machiavelli proceeds to describe his current mode of life and activity for his friend in Rome: "I stay in my villa, and since these last chance events occurred,[26] I have not spent, to add them all up, twenty days in Florence." There follows a long description of "catching thrushes with my own hands" and an account of going "to a wood of mine that I am having cut down," giving rise to controversies and Machiavelli's decision not to deliver promised wood to several "citizens."[27] The letter goes on:

> When I leave the wood, I go to a spring, and from there to an aviary of mine. I have a book under my arm, Dante or Petrarch, or one of the minor poets like Tibullus, Ovid, and such. I read of their amorous passions and their loves; I remember my own and enjoy myself for a while in this thinking. Then I move on along the road to the inn; I speak with those passing by; I ask them news of their places; I learn various things;

and I note the various tastes and different fancies of men. In the meantime comes the hour to dine, when I eat with my company what food
this poor villa and tiny patrimony allow. Having eaten, I return to the
inn; there is the host, ordinarily a butcher, a miller, two bakers. With
them I become a rascal for the whole day, playing at *cricca* and *tric-trac*,
from which arise a thousand quarrels and countless abuses with insulting
words, and most times we are fighting over a penny and yet we can be
heard shouting from San Casciano. Thus involved with these vermin I
scrape the mold off my brain and I satisfy the malignity of this fate of
mine, as I am content to be trampled on this path so as to see if she will
be ashamed of it.

After this day of trivial events, Machiavelli turns to serious thought:

When evening has come, I return to my house and go into my study. At
the door I take off my clothes of the day, covered with mud and mire,
and I put on my regal and courtly garments; and decently reclothed, I
enter the ancient courts of ancient men, where, received by them lovingly, I feed on the food that alone is mine and that I was born for. There
I am not ashamed to speak with them and to ask them the reason for
their actions; and they in their humanity reply to me. *And for the space of
four hours I feel no boredom, I forget every pain, I do not fear poverty,
death does not frighten me. I deliver myself entirely to them.*[28]

As Machiavelli goes on to explain, his nocturnal dialogue with the past
bore lasting fruit.

And because Dante says that to have understood without retaining does
not make knowledge,[29] I have noted what capital I have made from
their conversation and have *composed a little work* De Principatibus (On
Principalities) *where I delve as deeply as I can into reflections on this subject, debating what a principality is, of what kinds they are, how they are
acquired, how they are maintained, why they are lost.* And if you have ever
been pleased by any of my whimsies,[30] this one should not displease you;
and to a prince, and especially to a new prince, it should be welcome. So
I am addressing it to his Magnificence, Giuliano.[31] Filippo Cassavecchia
has seen it; he can give you an account in part both of the thing in itself
and of the discussions I had with him, although I am all the time fattening and polishing it.

In addition to a vivid image of Machiavelli's daily life, here we have a
specific discussion of his most famous work, albeit with a different title

(*De Principatibus,* or *On Principalities,* rather than *Il Principe* as the work is known to us) and a different addressee.[32] After describing the work we know as *The Prince,* Machiavelli turns to Vettori's invitation to join him in Rome:

> You wish, magnificent ambassador, that I leave this life and come to enjoy your life with you. I will do it in any case, but what tempts me now is certain dealings of mine that I will have done in six weeks.[33] What makes me be doubtful is that the Soderini are there, whom I would be forced, if I came, to visit and speak with. *I should fear that at my return I would not expect to get off at my house, but I would get off at the Bargello,*[34] for although this state has very great foundations and great security, yet it is new, and because of this suspicious; nor does it lack wiseacres who, to appear like Pagolo Bertini, would let others run up a bill and leave me to think of paying. I beg of you to relieve me of this fear, and then I will come in the time stated to meet you anyway.

> *I have discussed with Filippo this little work of mine, whether to give it to him or not; and if it is good to give it, whether it would be good for me to take it or send it to you.* Not giving it would make me fear that at the least it would not be read by Giuliano and that this Ardinghelli would take for himself the honor of this latest effort of mine.[35] The necessity that chases me makes me give it, because I am becoming worn out, and I cannot remain as I am for a long time without becoming despised because of poverty, besides the desire I have that these Medici lords begin to make use of me even if they should begin by making me roll a stone. For if I should not then win them over to me, I should complain of myself; and through this thing, if it were read, one would see that I have neither slept through nor played away the fifteen years I have been at the study of the art of the state. And anyone should be glad to have the service of one who is full of experience at the expense of another. And one should not doubt my faith, because having always observed faith, I ought not now be learning to break it. Whoever has been faithful and good for forty-three years, as I have, ought not to be able to change his nature, and of my faith and goodness my poverty is witness.

This discussion of Machiavelli's intention in writing *The Prince* obviously requires some consideration in deciding how to read the book.

The famous letter to Vettori reminds us of a number of things, each of which is germane to the questions with which we began:

- In December 1513, Machiavelli still feared a repetition of his impris-onment and torture earlier in the year and, for this reason, did not wish to initiate any political action in his own name. Because Soderini was alive and in Rome, moreover, Machiavelli did not feel he could accept Vettori's invitation to go there lest he be immedi-ately arrested on his return to Florence. At the time of writing *The Prince*, Machiavelli had very good reasons to be exceedingly cir-cumspect.
- Although Machiavelli disliked his absence from power, and feared the loss of reputation due to poverty, during his evening studies of the ancients, Machiavelli says: "I feel no boredom, I forget every pain, I do not fear poverty, death does not frighten me. I deliver myself entirely to them." Despite his emphatic preference for the active life of politics, Machiavelli was no stranger to scholarship and knew its unique pleasures.[36]
- Machiavelli sought—and openly said he sought—employment from the Medici. But the letter to Vettori hardly proves that his decision to seek a position was an attempt to exercise power at all costs rather than a device to guarantee his immunity from the "chance events" of torture, imprisonment, and possible death.[37] Indeed, Machi-avelli's willingness to accept any position ("even if they should begin by making me roll a stone") could be interpreted as a tactic of self-defense, designed more to gain "favor" and avoid being "despised" than to exercise power and influence.
- Although Machiavelli describes the manuscript as addressed to Giuliano de' Medici, he explicitly treats the question of whether or not to send it to him as a matter of discussion and prudence. Not only did he discuss the idea with Filippo Cassavecchia and ask Vet-tori's advice, but his own justification is external "necessity" (not the logic of his argument).
- Machiavelli's book about "what a principality is, of what kinds they are, how they are acquired, how they are maintained, why they are lost" was originally entitled *De Principatibus* (*On Principalities*), a title retained at the head of chapter one of our editions. As we know, the manuscript that was published after Machiavelli's death[38] is called *Il Principe* or *The Prince* (with the title in Italian rather than Latin), and is dedicated to Lorenzo de' Medici[39] (rather than to Giuliano). Since Machiavelli seems to have left this work to be pub-lished, with some important changes introduced after December

1513,[40] his intention in writing cannot be limited to the circumstance of his desire for and need of political employment.

While Machiavelli's correspondence at the time of writing *The Prince* and beginning the *Discourses* does not settle the question of how to interpret his major works, it provides valuable evidence on several critical points. Machiavelli had a self-interest in writing in a devious or deceptive manner.[41] And if we can believe his subsequent assertion to Guiccardini, Machiavelli actually admitted to this practice: "if indeed sometimes I do happen to tell the truth, I hide it among so many lies that it is hard to find." Of the three requisites for discovering a meaning "between the lines" of a serious book, historical evidence provides indications of the first (the possibility was known and there was reason to use it) and the third (the author left some indication in private correspondence that is consistent with the existence of a "hidden intention"). It remains to turn to the final criterion, emphasized by Rousseau: are there contradictions or confusions in Machiavelli's texts that can only be understood on the assumption that the author was intentionally devious? Do these contradictions justify an interpretation of *The Prince* that departs sharply from the conventional understanding of Machiavelli as an amoral exponent of power politics and an apologist of the prince's use of force and deceit?

III. The Discourses on Titus Livy *and* The Prince

That *The Prince* is somehow a deceptive book can be inferred from a number of puzzles. I have noted that, in 1513, Machiavelli himself gave it a different title (*On Principalities*) which has survived as the inner title, just before chapter one. Other puzzles abound. Why, in a book written in Italian, did the author use Latin chapter headings? Who is meant by the direct addressee ("you"), sometimes given in the singular ("Tu") and sometimes in the plural ("Voi")? More broadly, for whom was the book written?

The question of the addressee of *The Prince* is made explicit by its Dedicatory Letter to Lorenzo de' Medici, headed in Latin (*Nicolaus Maclavellus ad Magnificum Lavrentium Medicem*). Since the younger Lorenzo, nephew of Pope Leo X, had died in 1519, why did Machiavelli leave this dedication in the manuscript, and why did his literary heirs publish it when the book finally appeared in 1532? To be sure, Lorenzo's uncle Giuliano, to whom Machiavelli thought of addressing the manuscript in 1513, died in

1516. This would imply that Machiavelli revised his manuscript between 1516 and 1519, and then left it unchanged during the last nine years of his life.[42] Machiavelli does not seem to have changed *The Prince* after 1520, the date of manuscript copies written by his friend Biagio Buonaccorsi.[43] Whatever the reason for changing the addressee from Giuliano to Lorenzo, the meaning of the published work seems somehow related to this dedication.

To resolve the puzzle, it is well to focus on the text with some care. Machiavelli begins the Dedicatory Letter to *The Prince* by citing conventional proprieties:

> It is *customary most of the time* for those who desire to acquire favor with a Prince to come to meet him with things that they care most for among their own or with things that they see please him most. Thus one sees them many times being presented with horses, arms, cloth of gold, precious stones and similar ornaments worthy of their greatness. Thus, since I desire to offer myself to your Magnificence with some testimony of my homage to you, *I have found nothing in my belongings that I care so much for and esteem so greatly as the knowledge of the actions of great men, learned by me from long experience with modern things and a continuous reading of ancient ones.* (*Prince*, Dedicatory Letter; p. 3)

Machiavelli seeks favor with Lorenzo de' Medici. He follows the custom of offering a prince valued things. But between the two types of gift—those valued by the prince himself (things that "please him") or those valued by the givers (things the givers "care most for among their own")—Machiavelli chooses a gift based on his own standards of value ("I have found nothing in my belongings that I care so much for and esteem so greatly").

Are we to interpret this offer at face value? Rousseau suggests that *The Prince* be contrasted to the *Discourses on Titus Livy*, a work which also begins with a dedicatory letter. Because the *Discourses* seem to be mentioned at the beginning of chapter two of *The Prince,* and both works were published posthumously, it is not far-fetched to assume that Machiavelli himself wanted us to compare them. That suspicion is underlined by the sharp contrast between the Dedicatory Letters to the two works.

The *Discourses* are dedicated not to one man, but to two: "Niccolò Machiavelli to Zanobi Buondelmonti and Cosimo Rucellai, Greeting." In this Dedicatory Letter, Machiavelli quite directly criticizes the practice of dedicating books to a ruler:

> when I reflect on the many mistakes I may have made in other circumstances, I know that I have made no mistake at any rate in this, that I

have chosen to dedicate these my discourses to you in preference to all others; both because, in doing so, I seem to be showing some gratitude for benefits received, and also because I seem in this to be *departing from the usual practice of authors, which has always been to dedicate their works to some prince, and, blinded by ambition and avarice, to praise him for all his virtuous qualities when they ought to have blamed him for all manner of shameful deeds.* (*Discourses,* Dedicatory Letter; pp. 94–95)[44]

Was the dedication to *The Prince* merely a "mistake," due to a moment in which Machiavelli was "blinded by ambition and avarice"? Or are we intended to contrast the two Dedicatory Letters and, thereby, gain a perspective on the devious nature of Machiavelli's intention?

It might seem that we are intended to treat the *Discourses on Titus Livy* as Machiavelli's definitive work: "For in it I have set down *all that I know and have learnt from a long experience of, and from constantly reading about, political affairs*" (ibid.). In contrast, *The Prince* is as it were the short course in Machiavelli's political thought:

I have found nothing in my belongings that I care so much for and esteem so greatly as the knowledge of the actions of great men, learned by me from long experience with modern things and a continuous reading of ancient ones. Having thought out and examined these things with diligence for a long time, and *now reduced them to one small volume,* I send it to your Magnificence. (*Prince,* Dedicatory Letter; p. 3)

There is no indication that *The Prince* is less reliable than the *Discourses*—merely that it would give Lorenzo "the capacity to be able *to understand in a very short time all that I have learned and understood* in so many years and with so many hardships and dangers for myself" (ibid.).

In dedicating *The Prince* to Lorenzo, Machiavelli then refers explicitly to his intention—but does so in a deliberately ambiguous way:

Therefore, your Magnificence, take this small gift in the spirit (*animo*) with which I send it. If your Magnificence considers and reads it diligently, you will learn from it my extreme desire that *you arrive at the greatness that fortune and your other qualities promise you.* (*Prince,* Dedicatory Letter; p. 4)[45]

But what is "the greatness that fortune" and Lorenzo's "other qualities promise" at the time Machiavelli is presumed to have written these lines, between 1516 and 1519?[46]

IV. *Machiavelli's Intention in* The Prince

Few interpreters of *The Prince* go beyond the surface meaning of Machiavelli's offer to work for the Medici. But there seems to be some kind of puzzle in the dedication. This puzzle is by no means limited to the contradictory implications of the dedication to the *Discourses*. On the contrary, one finds even greater difficulties within the text of *The Prince* itself.

If Machiavelli intended Lorenzo to understand "in a very short time all that I have learned and understood," then presumably he meant for Lorenzo to understand the dangers of flattery from those who follow the customary behavior of "*those who desire to acquire favor with a Prince.*" It therefore seems reasonable to consider Machiavelli's dedication in the light of the discussion of flattery in *The Prince* (ch. 23).[47] In that discussion, Machiavelli points out that every ruler confronts a basic problem because advisors need to know "that they do not offend you in telling you the truth; but when everyone can tell you the truth, they lack reverence for you."[48]

The ubiquitous problem of getting good advice can be solved, Machiavelli suggests, by adopting the following strategy:

> Therefore, *a prudent prince* must hold to a third mode, *choosing wise men in his state*; and only to these should he give freedom to speak the truth to him, and *of those things only that he asks about and nothing else*. . . . A prince, therefore, should always take counsel, but *when he wants*, and not when others want it; on the contrary, he should discourage everyone from counseling him about anything *unless he asks it of them*. (*Prince*, ch. 23; pp. 94–95)

In two different places in this chapter, Machiavelli emphatically notes that princes should reject unsolicited advice. Yet the Dedicatory Letter—and the book as a whole—offers unsolicited advice. And, as chapter twenty-three of *The Prince* points out, a prince who would accept such advice "either *falls headlong because of flatterers* or changes often because of the variability of views, from which *a low estimation of him arises*" (ibid.).

The teaching of *The Prince* itself suggests that its Dedicatory Letter is some kind of trap. Were the Medici to give Machiavelli a position of influence, this act itself would contradict the "mode that never fails" in determining "how a prince can know his minister":

> When you see a minister thinking more of himself than of you, and in all actions looking for something useful to himself, one so made will

never be a good minister; never will you be able to trust him. (*Prince,* ch. 22; p. 93)

Machiavelli apparently offers his services because he needs a job; his choice of a gift to please Lorenzo is explicitly based on the standards of the donor, not those of the recipient. If Lorenzo, to whom *The Prince* is dedicated, had indeed given its author a position as advisor, he would demonstrate that he lacks prudence.

Such a conclusion is important because, as Machiavelli goes on to point out, the relationship between a ruler and his advisors is crucial;

> For this is a *general rule that never fails*: that a prince who is not wise by himself cannot be counseled well, unless indeed by chance he should submit himself to one person alone to govern him in everything, who is a very prudent man. In this case he could well be, but it would not last long because that *governor would in a short time take away his state.* (*Prince*, ch. 23; p. 95)[49]

If the addressee of *The Prince* accepts Machiavelli's advice and gives him employment, he will either be badly advised or—having turned all power over to his advisor—lose power to him.

For today's reader, these contradictions suggest a need to reconsider Machiavelli's intention. Machiavelli allowed the text of *The Prince* to circulate among friends and left it to be published posthumously. For us, if not for Lorenzo, the Dedicatory Letter needs to be read as some kind of instruction, rather than as a request for a job that is to be taken literally. What, then, was Machiavelli's purpose?

V. Machiavelli's Intention: Writing at Multiple Levels

The puzzle of Machiavelli's intentions is clarified by his own statement in the matter. In chapter fifteen of *The Prince*, he tells us flatly about "my intent." Although the passage is well known, it bears careful rereading in the light of what has just been noted.

> It remains now to see what the modes and government of a prince should be with subjects and with friends. And because I know that many have written of this, I fear that in writing of it again, I may be held presumptuous, especially since *in disputing this matter I depart from the orders of others.* But since *my intent is to write something useful to whoever*

understands it, it has appeared to me more fitting to go directly to the
effectual truth of the thing than to the imagination of it. (p. 61)

Machiavelli's addressee is "whoever understands" his work. His intention
is to be "useful" to such a person. And this utility is directly associated
with Machiavelli's novelty.[50]

It would seem that Machiavelli did indeed write deviously, and that his
deception was somehow related to his innovation. In the *Discourses*, he
claims that "impelled by the natural desire I have *always* had to labour, re-
gardless of anything, on that which I believe to be *for the common benefit
of all*, I have decided to enter upon a new way, as yet untrodden by
anyone else" (*Discourses*, I, Pref.; p. 97).[51] If we credit this bold assertion, Machiavelli's labors in writing *The Prince* were also "for the common
benefit of all."

Somehow that common good requires acts of deception (cf. *Discourses*,
II, 13). But was Machiavelli aware of the tradition of writing to deceive?
Can we credit him with such "Machiavellian" deviousness? Consider Machiavelli's famous remark on the distinction between laws ("proper to
man") and force (the characteristic of "beasts"):

> it is necessary for a prince to know well how to use the beast and the
> man. This role was *taught covertly to princes by ancient writers*, who
> wrote that Achilles, and many other princes, were given to Chiron the
> centaur to be raised. To have as teacher a half-beast, half-man means
> nothing other than that a prince needs to know how to use both na-
> tures. (*Prince*, ch. 18; p. 69)

Machiavelli not only knows about devious or "esoteric" writing; he asserts
that "ancient writers" used this technique to teach princes.[52] Insofar as his
own work is directed to potential or actual rulers, is it impossible that he
would teach "covertly"?

Earlier, I suggested three criteria that need to be met before we can say
with some plausibility that a writer used the device of indirect or deceptive
communication.

- First, the historical and social context needs to create a reason for
  using this method—and, as a former official of the Florentine
  Republic suspected of seeking the overthrow of the Medici, Machiavelli's context provided ample enough reason.
- Second, the published texts should contain contradictions or puzzles that seem impossible to resolve without concluding that, unless

the author was a fool, these passages point to partially hidden meanings—and such puzzles are evident if we contrast the dedication of
The Prince with that of the *Discourses* or with the text of *The Prince*
itself.

   ○ And finally, the author should indicate that he is aware of this
technique—and, even without knowing his emphatic statement to
this effect in his correspondence, Machiavelli's knowledge of this
method is demonstrated by the explicit reference to "covert" writing in ancient thought (*Prince*, ch. 18).

In reading *The Prince*, we should indeed take seriously Rousseau's assertion that Machiavelli has a "hidden intention."

    It follows that Machiavelli's claim for novelty must also be taken very
seriously. But if Machiavelli actually did articulate "a new way, as yet untrodden by anyone" (*Discourses*, I, Pref.; p. 93), he discovered something
in his experience and his studies that was entirely new.[53] Machiavelli thus
must claim to have a "brain" that "understands by itself"—the highest
kind of intelligence, which is "very excellent" (*Prince*, ch. 22; p. 92). In
short, Machiavelli quietly implies that his theory is a rival to anything
humans have ever thought, be it in the realm of philosophy as exemplified
by Socrates and the traditions elaborated by Plato, Xenophon, and Lucretius, or of religion as exemplified by Jesus and the tradition elaborated
by St. Paul, St. Augustine, or St. Thomas Aquinas.

    At first, of course, it appears that Machiavelli is only concerned with pol-
itics in the narrow sense. But on important occasions, he will explicitly refer
to other "philosophers" and "answer" their arguments (e.g., *Discourses*,
II, 5; p. 288). Machiavelli's hesitancy in talking about the philosophic con-
templation he describes so movingly in the letter to Vettori may itself
be based on principle, for in the *Florentine Histories* he speaks of a political
and moral cycle of history in which philosophy and letters play a corrupt-
ing role:

it has been observed by the prudent that letters come after arms and
that, in provinces and cities, captains arise before philosophers. For, as
good and ordered armies give birth to victories and victories to quiet,
*the strength of well-armed spirits cannot be corrupted by a more honorable
leisure than that of letters*, nor can leisure enter into well-instituted cities
with *a greater and more dangerous deceit than this one*. This was best understood by Cato when the philosophers Diogenes and Carneades, sent
by Athens as spokesmen to the Senate, came to Rome. When he saw

how the Roman youth was beginning to follow them about with admiration, and *since he recognized the evil that could result to his fatherland
from this honorable leisure, he saw to it that no philosopher could be accepted in Rome.* (*Florentine Histories*, V, 1; p. 185)

Philosophy—which in Machiavelli's time included "natural philosophy"
or science—is "honorable" but "dangerous," and should be prohibited in
"well-instituted cities." That Machiavelli is generally silent on his own
philosophical or scientific pretensions could, then, be part of a carefully
worked out transformation of all prior thought.[54]

Deceptive or so-called "esoteric" writing might be not only necessary
as a means to prevent difficulty with the Medici, but prudent for deeper
reasons. Many other philosophers, not to mention some religious traditions, have practiced "covert" instruction when it is assumed that public
or open teaching would have negative effects.[55] But how is one to know
the meaning of a text written in this manner? Isn't it an invitation to the
commentator's whimsy and self-interest to move away from the plain
meaning of the text?

The answer can best be stated by listing some of the means for drafting a
written text that is likely to be read by the censors or rulers of a hostile
regime (Machiavelli's situation in Florence when he wrote *The Prince*).
One or more of the following devices are available to get around cen-
sorship:

- Include many details, especially at the outset of the argument. Censors are easily bored.
- Make an orthodox or inoffensive general statement, which you do
  not believe, then later qualify it with an exception that makes your
  point. Censors are usually lazy and will not go beyond first impressions; if they do, you always have the excuse of the general
  statement.
- Use words with an unexpected or inverted meaning, much as
  teenagers call desirable things "terrible" or "awful." Censors will
  be confused and not bother to figure out the reason.
- Introduce a problem with an ambiguous discussion which is only
  clarified later; your intended reader will go through the text more
  than once to be sure your meaning is grasped, whereas the censor
  is only likely to read through once.
- Present allegories or comparisons that have an obvious point and a
  less visible implication. Better yet, make two different comparisons

to the same thing, and leave it to your reader to work out the implications. The censor will never bother.
- Contradict yourself from time to time and leave it to the intended reader—who goes through the text more than once—to figure out why you have done so. The censor will conclude you are confused.

To be sure, great care is needed when reading in this manner. For that reason, I will focus specifically on *The Prince*, in order to show how reading it as a "covert" teaching of "princes" leads to an understanding of Machiavelli's thought. Other works can then be used to contradict my interpretation. In this way, the proposed reading of *The Prince* will function as an hypothesis, with the evidence to confirm or disconfirm it being Machiavelli's other writings and his political experience.

What, then, is the "new way" that led Machiavelli to "depart from the orders of others"? How does Machiavelli's understanding of human nature, based on "long experience with modern things and a continuous reading of ancient ones" (*Prince*, Dedicatory Letter; p. 3), differ from the perspective of both Christianity and pagan antiquity? Before we can use Machiavelli as a touchstone for understanding the findings of contemporary science, we need to restate his theories clearly and succinctly. It is to that task that the next chapter is devoted.

Chapter Three

Machiavelli's Science of Human Nature

I am Machevill . . . And hold there is no sin but ignorance.
Christopher Marlowe[1]

*I*n order to reconsider Machiavelli's thought in the light of contemporary science, it is first necessary to understand what he meant to teach us. In the last chapter, I sought to establish that Machiavelli is a serious political thinker who had reason to write with what Rousseau called a "hidden intention." Although many scholars in recent times have criticized the method of reading associated with deceptive or so-called "esoteric" writing, historical evidence indicates that after his imprisonment and torture, Machiavelli had good reasons to hide his opinions. I have argued that when Machiavelli himself points out how "ancient writers" taught princes "covertly," he is suggesting *The Prince* should be studied as a book with a covert meaning. In fact, I have tried to show that any other approach to the text leads either to hopeless confusion or to the conclusion that Machiavelli is not a major thinker whose theories could claim to be true.

The evidence that Machiavelli wrote in a devious manner does not, however, itself demonstrate that he had a coherent or systematic theory of human nature and politics. Because Machiavelli so openly endorses republican regimes in the *Discourses,* if he is consistent, *The Prince* must also contain a republican political teaching despite its superficial endorsement of autocratic princely rule. To discover Machiavelli's meaning, therefore, it will be necessary to show that a consistent philosophical teaching underlies the apparently diverse perspectives set forth in his works.

Because *The Prince* seems to be addressed to a particular individual under specific circumstances, is it appropriate to focus the restatement of Machiavelli's general understanding of human nature and politics on this

49

work? There are at least three main reasons for doing so: First, any interpretation of Machiavelli that is not based on *The Prince* could be challenged on the grounds, so often used by commentators, that he changed his mind from one work to another. If Machiavelli wrote in a devious or "covert" manner, hiding a consistent philosophical position in diverse messages, we should be able to understand his theory by focusing on a single text, rereading passages with more care than a supporter of the Medici might have done in 1513. Second, in the intellectual and political history of the West, *The Prince* has been Machiavelli's most influential work. Since many commentators focus on the question of whether Machiavelli sought to restore ancient pagan traditions, reflected his times, or was the first "modern," it seems reasonable to focus on the work that is most likely to have played a role in the emergence of modernity.[2] Finally, because *The Prince* has become Machiavelli's best-known work, most of those familiar with the Western intellectual tradition will have read the book; hence a careful reading of *The Prince* provides the most convenient way to reconsider Machiavelli's theory in the light of contemporary knowledge of human behavior.

These arguments also imply that if Machiavelli did have a coherent theory, it is presented in different ways in his various writings. In effect, Machiavelli introduces each of the major works as giving a specific perspective on human affairs. If we are to understand *The Prince* and its relation to his thought as a whole, it will be necessary to bear in mind Machiavelli's explicit description of the intended audience or point of view that is elaborated in some other writings:

- The *Discourses on Titus Livy* is the most extensive presentation of Machiavelli's teaching, directed to "those who know how to govern a kingdom" and who, "on account of their innumerable good qualities, deserve to be" princes or rulers.[3] Because it is to explore all human political life, both ancient (pagan) and modern (Christian), the *Discourses* focus on the greatest regime known to have existed: republican Rome.
- The *Florentine Histories* focus on the relationship between domestic and foreign policy in a single human community, a perspective that is "useful to the citizens who govern republics." Because Machiavelli is himself a citizen of Florence, the *Histories* focus on his native city, but it is intended to be "understood in all times."[4]
- *The Prince* emphasizes the founder or legislator who, like Moses, Cyrus, Theseus, or Romulus, established "altogether new princi-

palities" or regimes (*Prince*, ch. 6; pp. 21–25). Although each of these leaders was "a man rising newly" whose honor came from "the new laws and the new orders found by him,"[5] *The Prince* also explores—and is dedicated to—the ruler who, like Cesare Borgia, seeks to achieve his ends through "fortune and the arms of others" rather than "virtue and his own arms" (*Prince*, ch. 7; pp. 25–33).

- *The Art of War* presents in dialogue form the teaching of *The Prince* (chs. 12–14) and *Discourses* (Book II, esp. chs. 16–18) concerning the "good arms" required in any lasting state as "defenses" of "all the arts that are provided for in a state for the sake of the common good of man."[6] Since Machiavelli's own experience in Florentine politics was centered on military and diplomatic matters—and since he saw to it that this work was published in his own lifetime—the tendency to ignore *The Art of War* may be a reflection of scholarly bias. Attention to this work is especially important if one is to understand Machiavelli's novel analysis of the emerging political transformations due to artillery and other new military technology.[7]

- As I will suggest at the end of this chapter, even the *Mandragola*, Machiavelli's famous comedy, fits this pattern—presenting his teaching in a form that would lead the general "audience" or common people to "understand a new case born in this city" and to be "tricked" as Lucrezia is in the play.[8]

While my restatement of Machiavelli's principles is based on *The Prince*, it will therefore take into consideration these other works.

I. Human Nature and Power

From the outset of *The Prince*, we are told that human things look different depending on one's point of view:

> For just as those who sketch landscapes place themselves down in the plain to consider the nature of mountains and high places and to consider the nature of low places place themselves high atop mountains, similarly, *to know well the nature of peoples one needs to be prince, and to know well the nature of princes one needs to be of the people.* (*The Prince*, Dedicatory Letter; p. 4)

The diversity of perspectives in Machiavelli's works, which I have claimed is crucial to understanding his thought, therefore reflects a basic problem in human affairs—namely the tendency for one's judgment to be influenced by one's point of view or situation.

In comparing himself to "those who sketch landscapes," Machiavelli may have had a specific artist in mind. In the first chapter, it was shown that Leonardo da Vinci was serving as military architect for Cesare Borgia when the Florentine Republic sent Machiavelli to Cesare's court in 1502, and that after Leonardo's return to Florence in 1503, Machiavelli sent Leonardo on several technical missions of great importance. In addition, Machiavelli played a role in negotiating the terms for Leonardo's painting of a large fresco in the Palazzo della Signoria of Florence, the famous *Battle of Anghiari*.[9]

The possibility that Machiavelli as author of *The Prince* is comparing himself to the artist Leonardo da Vinci is suggested by a passage in the latter's *Treatise on Painting*: "The painter is lord of all types of peoples and of all things. If he wants valleys, if he wants from high mountain tops to unfold a great plain extending down to the sea's horizon, he is lord to do so; and likewise if from low plains he wishes to see high mountains."[10] While this parallel between the description of "those who sketch landscapes" by Leonardo and Machiavelli might be accidental, further evidence that Leonardo's thought and writings influenced Machiavelli will be noted below. As a result, it is worth reflecting for a moment on the implications of Leonardo's view of the landscape painter.

In the passage of the *Treatise on Painting* just cited, Leonardo goes on to add that the multiplicity of perspectives makes possible "a proportioned and harmonious view of the whole, that can be seen simultaneously, at one glance, just as things in nature."[11] By his ability to imagine a scene from more than one angle, moreover, Leonardo created an "aerial perspective" which transcends the distinction between mountain top and plains;[12] among examples of this new technique are the background of the *Mona Lisa* (Fig. 3.1) and maps that "seem to have been drawn from the air, as if Leonardo had been able to construct and pilot aloft his flying machine."[13] It is likely that Machiavelli knew of this perspective from the maps portraying the site of the Florentines' attempt to rechannel the Arno, since he seems to have used Leonardo's map to critique the plan adopted by Colombino (cf. Figures 1.6, 1.11, and 3.2).[14] Does Machiavelli's comparison of his writing with the work of "those who sketch landscapes" imply the claim to understand human life from an olympian or god-like detachment?

As a former statesman reduced to private life due to "a great and continuous malignity of fortune," Machiavelli has experienced both the

Figure 3.1. Leonardo da Vinci, *Mona Lisa* (c. 1505–1513), oil on wood panel, 30 x 20 7/8 inches (77 x 53 cm). Courtesy of Musée du Louvre, Paris. Note the aerial perspective used for the background, creating the illusion that the figure of Mona Lisa is floating in the air.

Figure 3.2. Leonardo da Vinci, Bird's Eye View of Part of Tuscany (c. 1502–1503), pen, ink, and watercolor, 10 7/8 x 15 7/8 inches (27.5 x 40.1 cm). Windsor Castle, Royal Library 12683. Courtesy of The Royal Collection © Her Majesty Queen Elizabeth II.

perspective of power and that of the common "people." Like Leonardo's painter, who can present "a proportioned and harmonious view of the whole," Machiavelli's unusual capacity to see things from different points of view gives him a deeper knowledge of human nature than others, and especially than a hereditary ruler.[15] Machiavelli can therefore claim he understands the nature of both common men and rulers—and thus has a more inclusive perspective than either taken alone.[16]

As if to underscore the importance of multiple perspectives for gaining general knowledge of political life, Machiavelli uses the grammatical device of direct address ("you"), sometimes shifting from singular to plural without apparent reason in a way that many commentators have found puzzling.[17] Consider how Machiavelli presents one of his broadest descriptions of human nature:

> For one can say this generally of men: that they are ungrateful, fickle, pretenders and dissemblers, evaders of danger, eager for gain. While *you do them good, they are yours, offering you their blood, property, lives, and children, as I said above,* when the need for them is far away; but *when it is close to you, they revolt.* (*Prince*, ch. 17; p. 66)

As a general rule, humans are unreliable or selfish. From the perspective of the prince or ruler, this disembodied perspective means that offers of support only last as long as *"you* do them good" and do not prevent *"them"* from rebelling in the time of need.

In this passage, "you" is the singular and familiar *Tu.*[18] Since elsewhere Machiavelli often uses the impersonal point of view when speaking about the prince,[19] such direct address, as if Machiavelli were talking personally to a ruler like Lorenzo de' Medici or Cesare Borgia, connotes a *perspective,* not a *subject matter.* Thus the earlier passage to which Machiavelli refers in chapter seventeen ("as I said before") seems to be in chapter nine, which makes the same substantive point with different pronouns:

> For such a prince [a prince "about to ascend from a civil order to an absolute one" who governs "by means of magistrates"] cannot found himself on what he sees in quiet times, *when citizens have need of the state, because then everyone runs, everyone promises, and each wants to die for him when death is at a distance; but in adverse times, when the state has need of citizens, then few of them are to be found.* (p. 42)

This passage corresponds to the formula in chapter seventeen, but uses "him" rather than "you" to describe the situation of the Medici in Florence, in which princes seek to transform a republic ("civic order") to absolute rule but rule with the aid of magistrates.[20]

The ability to see things from the perspective of either the common people or the prince thus permits Machiavelli to understand human nature in a more general way than either. This means, however, that any specific statement needs to be qualified by its context. Earlier in chapter nine, for example, Machiavelli seems to contradict the general rule about the fickle nature of the people which occurs later in that chapter and is restated in chapter seventeen.

> He who comes to the principality with the aid of the great maintains himself with more difficulty than one who becomes prince with the aid of the people . . . And let no one resist my opinion on this with that trite proverb, that whoever founds on the people founds on mud. For that is true when a private citizen lays his foundation on them, and allows himself to think that the people will liberate him if he is oppressed by enemies or by the magistrates . . . But *when a prince who founds on the people knows how to command and is a man full of heart*, does not get frightened in adversity, does not fail to make other preparations, and with his spirit and his orders keeps the generality of people inspired, *he will never find himself deceived by them and he will see he has laid his foundations well*. (*Prince*, ch. 9; pp. 39, 41)

The "general" rule of human unreliability applies to private citizens, and to princes who seek to establish absolute rule or to rule with the aid of the aristocrats or nobles (the "great"); it does not apply to a prince who "knows how to command and is a man full of heart." If such a ruler bases his power on the people, "he will *never* find himself deceived by them."

On the surface, Machiavelli teaches that humans are generally unreliable and selfish—and so they are. But he also gives us examples of princes whose survival depended on extraordinary faithfulness and courage on the part of the people. In chapter nine, he cites "Nabis, prince of the Spartans" as one who "withstood a siege by all Greece and by one of Rome's most victorious armies, and defended his fatherland and his state against them" (p. 41).[21] Agathocles the Sicilian was able to "live for a long time secure in his fatherland, defend himself against external enemies, and never be conspired against by his citizens" (*Prince*, ch. 7; p. 37).[22] Since both of these rulers are elsewhere described as "tyrants," the point is not that human nature is inherently or usually good or virtuous in the traditional sense.

Rather, Machiavelli seems to be emphasizing a diversity or malleability that depends on individuals and circumstances.

Because humans are generally selfish, it is a mistake to *rely* on goodness: "a man who wants to make a profession of good in all regards must come to ruin *among so many who are not good*" (*Prince*, ch. 15; p. 61). But human nature itself is variable in at least two important ways. Some individuals are good, brave, or faithful by "nature." And in some situations, most or all people can be led to behave in ways that are good—though to do so requires a political art, the creation of "good laws and good arms" by effective political leaders. As Machiavelli puts it explicitly, "the nature of peoples is variable" (*Prince*, ch. 6; p. 24).

That individuals differ by "nature" as well as by "nurture" is implied by the twin requirements of the successful ruler who bases his power on the people because he "*knows how to command and is a man full of heart*" (cited above). While the knowledge may depend on instruction, it would seem that bravery or "spirit" is a personal characteristic of a different order. People "proceed variously: one with caution, the other with impetuosity; one with violence, the other with art; one with patience, the other with its contrary" (*Prince*, ch. 25; p. 99). Elsewhere, with regard to himself Machiavelli speaks of "the *natural desire* I have *always* had to labour . . . on that which I believe to be for the common benefit of all" (*Discourses*, I, Pref.; p. 97), and comments that "whoever has been faithful and good for forty-three years, as I have, ought *not to be able to change his nature*" (letter to Vettori, Appendix II). As observation confirms, it is often the case that a man "cannot deviate from what *nature inclines him to*" (*Prince*, ch. 25; p. 100).[23]

In an important chapter of the *Discourses*, Machiavelli explains the political importance of these differences, which we would describe as matters of "personality" or "temperament."

> For one sees that in what they do some men are impetuous, others look about them and are cautious; and that, since in both cases they go to extremes and are unable to go about things in the right way, in both cases they make mistakes. On the other hand, he is likely to make fewer mistakes and to prosper in his fortune when circumstances accord with his conduct, as I have said, and *one always proceeds as the force of nature compels one.* (*Discourses*, III, 9; p. 430)

Good fortune or success is often a matter of the accidental "conformity" between a person's "behavior" and "the times"; indeed, this is one of the major advantages of leadership in "a republic" in which there are "*diverse citizens with diverse dispositions*" (ibid., pp. 430–431).[24]

In addition to individual differences among humans, social circumstances change. What Machiavelli calls the "variability of the good" arises because the "quality of the times" changes (ibid., pp. 99–100). Human nature is thus malleable to the degree that the natural selfishness and shortsightedness of most people can be overcome. Such successful manipulation of human nature is particular illustrated by "*the highly virtuous actions performed in ancient kingdoms and republics,* by their kings, their generals, their citizens, their legislators, and by others who have gone to the trouble of serving their country" (*Discourses,* I, Pref.; p. 98).[25] But what Machiavelli calls "human conditions" do not permit rulers either to rely on the goodness of their subjects, or to be good themselves in every respect (*Prince,* ch. 15; p. 61). The result is that "great variability of things which have been seen and are seen every day, beyond human conjecture" which most people describe as "fortune" or chance (*Prince,* ch. 25; p. 98).

Human nature is thus characterized by selfishness and shortsightedness, by ambition and conflict, but also sometimes by knowledge and bravery, by virtue and devotion to the common good. The consequence is a world of change and unpredictability. In many matters, it is not possible to have fixed rules of conduct because of the diversity and complexity of situations. As a result, for example, a "prince can gain the people to himself in many modes, for which one cannot give certain rules because the modes vary according to circumstances" (*Prince,* ch. 9; pp. 40–41).

II. Fortune, History, and the State

Because of the "variability of things" produced by the differences in human character and the frequent propensity to selfishness, it is difficult to predict the outcome of events. As a consequence,

> many have held and hold *the opinion that worldly things are so governed by fortune and by God,* that men cannot correct them with their prudence, indeed that they have no remedy at all; and on account of this they might judge that one need not sweat much over things but let oneself be governed by chance. (*Prince,* ch. 25; p. 98)

While this unpredictability of history can be attributed to "fortune" or to "God," in the famous chapter that follows this statement Machiavelli speaks only of "fortune": provisionally, we might say that "God" is merely one of the popular names for "fortune" or "chance."

Machiavelli's comparison between fortune and a "river" is well known, but it needs careful reconsideration. Because human events so often seem unpredictable,

> I liken her [fortune] to one of those *violent rivers which, when they become enraged flood the plains, ruin the trees and the buildings, lift earth from this part, drop in another*; each person flees before them, everyone yields to their impetus without being able to hinder them in any regard. (*Prince*, ch. 25; p. 98)

History is thus like the River Arno, which occasionally floods the city of Florence: most of the time tranquil; on rare but overpowering occasions, utterly destructive of human life and well-being.

Sometimes, however, the "river" of fortune can be controlled. Machiavelli goes on:

> And although they [rivers] are like this, *it is not as if men, when times are quiet, could not provide for them with dikes and dams so that when they rise later, either they go by a canal or their impetus is not so wanton nor so damaging.* It happens similarly with fortune, which shows her power where virtue has not been put in order to resist her and therefore turns her impetus where she knows that dams and dikes have not been made to contain her. (*Prince*, ch. 25; pp. 98–99)[26]

If the effects of floods can be controlled by understanding the nature of rivers, then the effects of historical unpredictability or fortune should likewise be limited by understanding human nature.

Although most commentators and readers have stopped their consideration of the analogy at this point, there are good reasons to analyze it more closely. The comparison between fortune and a river brings to mind the plan to channel the river Arno with "dikes and dams" to defeat Pisa that was executed by Florence under Machiavelli's direction in 1503/4. Not only was this ill-fated attempt to control a river part of the "effectual reality" of Machiavelli's experience as Second Secretary to the Florentine Republic, but it specifically concerns the extent to which human knowledge (in this case, Leonardo's scientific knowledge as a military architect and expert in hydraulics) can control the historical events (a long and inconclusive war between Florence and Pisa which ultimately did not end until 1509).

A good summary of the events discussed in chapter one is contained in Heydenreich's account of Leonardo's career as a "military architect":

> In the spring of 1503 Leonardo was again in Florence, having given up his post with Cesare Borgia probably during the course of the winter. His native town took him forthwith into its service as military engineer. Florence was then engaged in a troublesome and protracted war with Pisa. . . . In 1503 the Florentine Republic opened a new campaign against Pisa, and here emerged the daring plan to divert the course of the Arno River in order to cut off the Pisans from access to the sea, since from this the besieged town was constantly able to obtain supplies. Historical sources and documents reveal that the forceful project was especially promoted by Machiavelli, the secretary of state for war in the Florentine governing council, and that it won the support of Piero Soderini, the chief official of the Republic of Florence.[27]

While some sources suggest that Leonardo originated or directed the plan, the evidence published by Fachard (reproduced in part in Appendix I) shows that work in the field was directed by an architect named Colombino. Although Leonardo visited the site in July 1503 to assess the feasibility of the plan, it was Machiavelli who was responsible for overseeing its execution.[28] After the canal filled with water and collapsed in October 1504, Machiavelli sought unsuccessfully to persuade the Signoria to continue.[29]

Leonardo's technical expertise on the diversion of the Arno was extensive because years before he had developed in detail another, essentially peaceful plan of a similar kind (see Figure 1.6):

> Leonardo had an abiding interest in changing the course of the Arno— but not to cut Pisa off from the sea. He wanted to create a great waterway to open Florence to the sea and bring agricultural and economic benefits to all Tuscany. The Arno was nonnavigable from Florence to Pisa because of its tortuous bends and sudden variations in level. The idea of diverting a long section of it into a man-made canal dated back more than a century before Leonardo's birth. From about 1490 on, Leonardo made it his own, and drew a number of maps, and studies.[30]

Whatever the extent of communication between Machiavelli and Leonardo during the unsuccessful military project of 1503/4, there can be no question that both men devoted extensive energy to conceptualizing human efforts to channel the Arno for political purposes.[31]

In November 1504, immediately after the abandonment of the scheme to divert the Arno, Leonardo was dispatched—again apparently by Machiavelli—on a mission to Piombino, where he spent six or seven weeks consulting on the military fortifications and port facilities; some of this work also required expertise in the control of water, as is evident from Leonardo's notes taken at the time.[32] Whatever the extent of the friendship between Machiavelli and Leonardo, therefore, the technology of redirecting rivers seems to be a practical interest they shared.

These facts in Machiavelli's political career reinforce the need to look more closely at the comparison between fortune and a river—and the notion of controlling chance with "dikes and dams"—in chapter twenty-five of *The Prince*. Detailed analysis of this famous allegory is rendered all the more necessary because Machiavelli also uses it in a poem "On Fortune":

As a rapid torrent, swollen to the utmost, destroys whatever its current anywhere reaches,
and adds to one place and lowers another, shifts its banks, shifts its bed and its bottom, and makes the earth tremble where it passes,
so Fortune in her furious onrush many times, now here now there, shifts and reshifts the world's affairs.[33]

In another poem, which Allan Gilbert suggests may have been written around 1509, Machiavelli speaks of "all Italy" as "shattered by a strong sea of troubles."[34] Machiavelli clearly thought of human history and fortune as resembling the flow of water—often calm but occasionally erupting into overpowering violence and chaos.

Because chapter twenty-five of *The Prince* seeks to show that prudent leaders can control history, the ultimate failure of the diversion of the Arno might explain why Machiavelli does not mention either the project or Leonardo in *The Prince*.[35] For that very reason, however, Leonardo's theories of nature and technology—and particularly his analysis of the role of floods in human history—may have been profoundly important for Machiavelli. Like Plato's allegory of the Cave, therefore, careful analysis of Machiavelli's comparison between fortune and a river is needed to reveal its meaning.

If the chance events in history can be compared to the natural forces of a flood, can we decode the equivalence of the other terms? Most specifically, what is the human equivalent of the "dikes and dams" that can control flooding rivers? And, if this passage provides one of Machiavelli's central statements of the relationship between human endeavor and inanimate nature, why does he end the same chapter of *The Prince* by comparing fortune with a woman, using a metaphor of rape that seemingly contradicts the analogy between fortune and a river?

Since the "violent river" obviously corresponds to the unforeseen events of human history, the moment at which it is "enraged" would correspond to warfare. Moments of either foreign invasion or civil unrest destroy the plans and tranquillity of individuals. Such eruptions "flood the plains"—that is, they inundate the community with soldiers. Wars "ruin the trees and the buildings"—that is, they destroy both the natural resources and the human constructions on which civilization rests. Invasions "lift earth from this part, drop in another"—that is, some individuals, groups, or states benefit and rise in status and power while others fall. And "each person flees before them, everyone yields to their impetus"—that is, both as individuals and as a community, humans cannot control the effects of violence and war.

In the analogy between fortune and a river, then, the "earth" seems to represent human beings, the "trees" the natural resources, and the "buildings" the arts, sciences, and civilizations made by humans. "Water" stands for events, which at flood tide exceed human control; hence, in the last chapter of *The Prince*, foreign invasions of Italy are described as "these *floods* from outside" (ch. 26; p. 105). But "virtue can be put in order to resist" fortune and "turn her impetus": precisely because human nature is malleable, there are excellent or praiseworthy human possibilities that can limit the effects of war and violence. The essential question, then, is how should we interpret the "dikes and dams" that prudent men can use so that the river's waters, "when they rise later, either they go by a canal or their impetus is not so wanton nor so damaging"?

The immediate sequel in the analogy provides the clue.

> And if you consider *Italy*, which is the seat of these variations and that which has given them motion, you will see *a country without dams and without any dike*. If it had been *diked by suitable virtue, like Germany, Spain, and France*, either this flood would not have caused the great variations that it has, or it would not have come here. (*Prince*, ch. 25; p. 99)[36]

Italy has *neither* "dams" nor "dikes"; Germany, Spain, and France have "dikes"—but Machiavelli is silent here on whether they also have fully developed "dams."

The difference between Italy on the one hand and Germany, Spain, and France on the other is thus a key to the provisions that can be made against fortune. Italy, which has repeatedly been invaded and devastated by foreign troops, symbolizes the vulnerability of human societies. Since Germany, Spain, and France have diverse political systems—the Germans are "free," whereas the Spanish and French have monarchies—what they share cannot be a form of government. In chapter three of *The Prince* (p. 8), Machiavelli discusses the French king Louis XII's short-lived conquest of Italy, indicating that he apparently had "the strongest of armies" but could not maintain control because he lost the "support of the inhabitants." Apparently, the "dikes" in the famous analogy of a river are the military forces which permit rulers to conquer and societies to defend themselves from foreign invasion. If so, then the "dams" would be the means by which "the inhabitants" are "channeled": if "dikes" are armies, "dams" seem to be laws.[37]

As is demonstrated by Machiavelli's other works, the image of the "flood" to describe "fortune" is part of a broader theory of human history. In one of the most important general discussions of history in the *Discourses*, Machiavelli argues that there are recurrent cycles in which "records of times gone by are obliterated by diverse causes, of which some are due to men and some to heaven" (II, 5; p. 288). Whereas the human causes arise "when a new religious institution comes into being" and its "founders" seek to "wipe out" traces of older beliefs and institutions (ibid., pp. 288–289),

> The causes due to heaven are those which wipe out a whole generation and reduce the inhabitants in certain parts of world to but a few. This is brought about *by pestilence or by famine or by a flood and of these the most important is the last*. (Ibid., pp. 289–290)

Like the biblical story of Noah and the flood, Machiavelli's analogy between fortune and a river is a way of reflecting on what actually happened.
The pattern of these cycles is described in the *Florentine Histories*:

> Usually provinces go most of the time, in the changes they make, from *order to disorder and then pass again from disorder to order, for worldly things are not allowed by nature to stand still*. As soon as they reach their ultimate perfection, having no further to rise, they must descend; and similarly, once they have descended and through their disorders arrived at the ultimate depth, since they cannot descend further, of necessity

they must rise. Thus *they are always descending from good to bad and rising from bad to good.* (V, 1; p. 185)

Or, as Machiavelli put it in the *Discourses*, even the natural "floods, pestilences and famines" have a political function,

> when the craftiness and malignity of man has gone as far as it can go, the world must needs be purged in one of these three ways, so that mankind, being reduced to comparatively few and humbled by adversity, may adopt a more appropriate form of life and grow better. (*Discourses*, II, 5; p. 290)

Knowledge of these changes makes it possible to form "composite bodies" like "states and religious institutions" that are "better constituted and have a longer life" (*Discourses*, III, 1; p. 385). The analogy between fortune and a river in *The Prince* stands for a deeper theory of history that Machiavelli elaborated more fully in the *Discourses* and the *Florentine Histories*.

Machiavelli's view of the effects of natural catastrophe on history could well have been influenced by discussions with Leonardo, who wrote that floods are—*in actual fact*—the main agency of historical disaster and political change:

> *Amid all the causes of the destruction of human property, it seems to me that rivers hold the foremost place on account of their excessive and violent inundations* . . . against the irreparable inundation caused by swollen and proud rivers no resource of human foresight can avail; for in a succession of raging and seething waves gnawing and tearing away high banks, growing turbid with the earth from ploughed fields, destroying the houses therein and uprooting the tall trees, it carries these as its prey down to the sea which is its lair, *bearing along with it men, trees, animals, houses, and lands, sweeping away every dike and every kind of barrier,* bearing along the light things, and devastating and destroying those of weight, creating big landslips out of small fissures, filling up with floods the low valleys, and rushing headlong with destructive and inexorable mass of waters. (*Notebooks,* ed. I. Richter, 26–27)

Leonardo's view, first drafted in the 1490s, resembles Machiavelli's image of fortune as a river and may also help to explain why, at the end of chapter twenty-five, Machiavelli provides an apparently contradictory analogy by saying that "fortune is a woman" (p. 101).

After Machiavelli's description of the need to build "dikes and dams" to channel the river of fortune "when times are quiet," it should strike the reader as puzzling that Machiavelli should use the image of a rape to symbolize the control of fortune.

> I judge this indeed, that it is better to be impetuous than cautious, *because fortune is a woman*; and it is necessary, *if one wants to hold her down, to beat her and strike her down*. (*Prince*, ch. 25; p. 101)

It should be obvious that, if fortune is like a river, it cannot be treated like a woman: beating and striking the flooding waters won't keep the rising river within its banks. As Leonardo puts it in his *Notebooks*,

> That a river which is to be turned from one place to another *must be coaxed and not treated roughly or with violence*; and to do this a sort of dam should be built into the river, and then lower down another one projecting farther and in like manner a third, fourth, and fifth so that the river may discharge itself into the channel allotted to it, or by this means it may be diverted from the place it has damaged as was done in Flanders according to what I was told by Niccolò di Forzore. (*Notebooks*, ed. I. Richter, 351–352)

The two metaphors for history—a river and a woman—seem flatly in contradiction.[38]

The paradox can be resolved if the image of raping "fortune" is considered as a description of the violent actions by the individual leader which are needed at the foundation of "new laws and new arms."[39] As Machiavelli emphasizes when discussing the great founders in chapter six of *The Prince*:

> *the nature of peoples is variable*, and it is *easy to persuade them* of something, but *difficult to keep them in that persuasion*. And thus things must be ordered in such a mode that when they no longer believe, one can make them believe by force. Moses, Cyrus, Theseus, and Romulus would not have been able to make their peoples observe their constitutions for long if they had been unarmed, as happened in our times to Brother Girolamo Savonarola. (p. 24)

Machiavelli might have added that the same thing had happened to him personally, when the proposed canal to divert the Arno was abandoned as soon as the Florentine Signoria could no longer be persuaded that the plan would ultimately work.[40] Science or technology without political prudence is useless, and without the political will to use force on occasion, cautious attempts to rechannel events will ultimately fail.

For Machiavelli, what is often called the relationship between "man and nature" is ultimately political. Without control over human nature, all control over inanimate nature can be lost.[41] The "state" (*lo stato*) is the arena of stability which humans, with art, can construct as a defense against the natural changeability of circumstances.[42] In another of the best-known lines of *The Prince* (ch. 7, p. 48), Machiavelli asserts that "the principal foundations all states have, new ones as well as old or mixed, are *good laws and good arms.*" It is from the combination of control over foreign invasion and domestic unrest that stability arises. "Dikes" (good armies) protect a society against the flood of foreign invaders; "dams" (good laws) channel the passions of the society's own citizens.

Most readers of *The Prince* have, of course, stressed the sentence of chapter twelve immediately following the statement that "good laws and good arms" are the "principal foundations" of all states:

> And because there cannot be good laws where there are not good arms, and where there are good arms there must be good laws, I shall leave out the reasoning on laws and shall speak of arms. (p. 48)

The logic of this disingenuous phrase needs attention. There "cannot be good laws where there are not good arms": military force is a necessary condition of civil peace. "All the armed prophets conquered and the unarmed ones were ruined" (*Prince*, ch. 6; p. 24). But this necessary condition is not necessary *and sufficient* : it is "armed *prophets*" who conquer, not all those—including King Louis XII of France—who merely have "the strongest of armies."[43]

If good armies are necessary but not sufficient conditions of a stable state, what is the role of the laws, symbolized by the "dams" of the allegory of the river? Machiavelli's phrase is tantalizing: "*where there are good arms there must be good laws.*" The Italian has the sense of "there ought to be" or "there should be": one expects good laws to exist in a community with good armies—but this expectation may not always be fulfilled. Good laws are sufficient for good armies, but they are not necessary for them. In other words, communities with good laws all have good armies, but some good armies exist in societies without good laws. France and Spain have "dikes"—the "strongest of armies"—yet they do not have "dams."

This interpretation of the phrase "where there are good arms there must be good laws" is confirmed at the outset of the book Machiavelli devotes to "good arms." In the Preface to *The Art of War*, Machiavelli stresses the need for a citizen army in which the "civilian life and the military life" are "closely united," as they were under the "ancient ways" of pagan political virtue. Hence, the principal reason why the ancient military virtues have not been recovered in the centuries following the corruption and fall of Rome is "that our way of living today, as a result of the Christian religion, does not impose the same necessity for defending ourselves as antiquity did."[44]

Machiavelli elsewhere confirms the need to go beyond the purely military preconditions of political stability. In *Florentine Histories,* he emphasizes that consideration of military conflict and war without an understanding of domestic politics makes it impossible to understand human events. The histories of Florence written by d'Arezzo and Poggio explained "everything in detail" about the "wars waged by the Florentines with foreign princes and peoples," but "as regards civil discords and internal enmities, and the effects arising from them, they were altogether silent about the one and so brief about the other as to be of no use to readers or pleasure to anyone" (*Florentine Histories,* Pref.; p. 6). This matters because:

> *if no other lesson is useful to the citizens who govern republics,* it is that which shows *the causes of the hatreds and divisions in the city,* so that when they become wise through the dangers of others, they may be able to maintain themselves united. (Ibid.)

Domestic affairs ("civil discords and internal enmities") are sources of violence and unpredictability—indeed, they can lead to foreign invasion, as in the discontents that led Italians to invite Louis XII to invade them the first time (*Prince,* ch. 3; p. 8).

The control over unforeseen events thus requires both good laws and good arms. Indeed, while Machiavelli does not discuss good laws in chapter twelve of *The Prince* ("I shall leave out the reasoning on laws and shall speak of arms"), he includes both when he directly addresses potential rulers in chapter eighteen:

> Thus you must know that there are *two kinds of combat: one with laws, the other with force.* The first is proper to man, the second to beasts . . . a prince needs to know how to use both natures; and *the one without the other is not lasting.* (p. 69)[45]

The specifically human constraint on selfishness is the law. While law is not sufficient by itself, for the reason that "all unarmed prophets fail," force also has only limited efficacy (though to be sure the limitations of brute force differ from those concerning laws).[46]

The "state," then, is that domain of stability in the sea of chaos produced by the variations in human passion and natural events. The land, however, only remains dry insofar as human action has produced the "dikes and dams"—the armies and the laws—which constrain ambition and selfishness both within and outside the community. Human societies are what Machiavelli calls "compound" or unnatural bodies, created by human art or convention. But this creation cannot be the product of collective deliberation, since collective deliberation presupposes the existence of accepted rules. Hence, as Machiavelli puts it in the *Discourses*:

> One should take it as a general rule that rarely, if ever, does it happen that a state, whether it be a republic or a kingdom, is either well-ordered at the outset or radically transformed *vis-à-vis* its old institutions *unless this be done by one person*. (*Discourses*, I, 9; p. 132)

Because it is possible to be "a prince in a republic" (e.g., *Discourses*, I, 10; p. 136), the same prudential rules are appropriate for "rulers of a republic or of a kingdom" (ibid., I, 12; p. 143; I, 16; p. 155; I, 25; p. 176, *et passim*). An individual with such "sole authority" (ibid., p. 134) or "founder" (ibid., I, 10; pp. 134–135) is, in *The Prince*, discussed in the context of "altogether new principalities, where there is a new prince" (ch. 6; p. 32).

The highest examples of leadership discussed in *The Prince* thus concern the individual leader whose actions form a community, providing a domain of respite against the chaos and uncertainty of the "human condition." Since new principalities "are acquired either with the arms of others or with one's own, either by fortune or by virtue" (ch. 1; p. 6), there are two principal situations in which it is possible for an individual to create an "entirely new" state:

> And because the result of becoming prince from private individual presupposes either virtue [*virtù*] or fortune, it appears that one or the other of these two things relieves in part many difficulties; nonetheless, he who has relied less on fortune has maintained himself more. (*Prince*, ch. 6; p. 22)

Dependence on "fortune" or chance apparently means that a leader has benefited from the good luck that his natural inclination or choice of action has coincided with the external circumstances. What, then, does Machiavelli mean by *virtù*, that most difficult of terms in his lexicon?

For ancient Greek philosophers in the Socratic tradition, one form of virtue (*arete*) was human excellence in a moral and political sense. Many modern translators, accustomed to the Christian understanding of "virtue," have difficulty applying the same connotations to Machiavelli's use of the word: hence some render his use of *virtù* by "ingenuity" or "cleverness" as well as "virtue." While I will return to this issue below, it should be evident that Machiavelli views human virtue as associated with the ability to control fortune. For example, if fortune "had been diked by suitable virtue," war would not have had as serious effect in Italy—or, indeed, might not have occurred there at all (*Prince*, ch. 25; p. 99). The two principal types of "new princes" are those who rise to power through "virtue and their own arms" (*Prince*, ch. 6) or through "fortune and the arms of others" (*Prince*, ch. 7). Virtue, then, concerns the ability of human prudence, will, and action to control the effects of human nature and history.

Machiavelli writes as if "virtue" and "fortune" were two distinct attributes, parallel to having "one's own arms" or "the arms of others." But Machiavelli's *virtù* is not a trait an individual can possess, like courage, intelligence, or moderation. Because virtue represents the control over fortune, not only is the definition of the former merely the absence of the latter, but the circumstance supposedly defining the *means* of gaining power is only known by the historical *results*: "in the actions of all men, and especially of princes, where there is no court to appeal to, *one looks to the end*" (*Prince*, ch. 18; p. 71). The temptation to read "end" (*fine*) here as goal or intention should be resisted in the light of the next sentence: "So let a prince win and maintain his state: the means will always be judged honorable, and will be praised by everyone" (ibid.). "It is a sound maxim that reprehensible actions may be justified by their effects, and that *when the effect is good*, as it was in the case of Romulus [who killed his brother], *it always justifies the action*" (*Discourses*, I, 9; p. 132). Not only do the "ends justify the means"; the end or results virtually *define* the means.

III. The "Example" of Cesare Borgia

To understand this point, it is well to follow Rousseau's advice and consider more precisely the possibility that Machiavelli's "choice of his execrable hero"—Cesare Borgia—"is in itself enough to make manifest his hidden intention."[47] In chapter seven of *The Prince* (pp. 25ff), Machiavelli discusses "New Principalities That Are Acquired by Others' Arms and Fortune." He uses as his principal example "Cesare Borgia, called Duke Valentino by the vulgar," adding "I do not know what better teaching I could give to a new prince than the example of his actions" (*Prince*, ch. 7; pp. 26–27).

Chapter six makes clear that the highest and most praiseworthy princes gain power through virtue and their own arms, as did Moses, Cyrus, Theseus, and Romulus. As a result, Cesare would seem to be the highest exemplar of the wrong kind of prince. From the structure of the argument, therefore, one might presume that his "example" will indicate something to avoid, not something to be imitated. At first, however, this seems not to be the case:

> Cesare Borgia, called Duke Valentino by the vulgar, acquired his state through the fortune of his father [Pope Alexander VI] and lost it through the same, notwithstanding the fact that he made use of every deed and did all those things that should be done by a prudent and virtuous man to put his roots in the states that the arms and fortune of others had given him. (Ibid., pp. 26–27)

After cataloguing Cesare's deeds, Machiavelli adds that "the duke had laid very good foundations for his power" (ibid., p. 29) and "he would soon have succeeded, if Alexander had lived" (ibid., p. 30).

As we first read chapter seven, it appears that Cesare failed because of events he could not have foreseen or prevented.

> But if at the death of Alexander the duke had been healthy, everything would have been easy for him. And he told me, on the day that Julius II was created, that *he had thought about what might happen when his father was dying, and had found a remedy for everything, except that he never thought that at his death he himself would also be on the point of dying.* (Ibid., p. 32)

Bad luck—fortune, in Machiavelli's terms—cannot always be controlled. Cesare's failure "was not his fault" (ibid., p. 27), or so it would seem.

In the next and last paragraph of the chapter, Machiavelli seemingly reinforces the view that Cesare could not have done otherwise and is thus a model to follow:

> Thus, if I summed up all the actions of the duke, *I would not know how to reproach him*; on the contrary, it seems to me he should be put forward, as I have done, to be imitated by all those who have *risen to empire through fortune and by the arms of others.* (Ibid.)

The astute reader needs to remember, here, that Cesare is called "the duke" (the term of address used "by the vulgar"—ibid., p. 27); that he rose "to empire" (that is to power not based on popular support or republican ideals); and above all that he is an example of coming to power "through fortune and by the arms of others" (modes that contrast, unfavorably, with those of the founders described in chapter six).

Only with these things in mind is one prepared for the end of the chapter, for having just said "*I would not know* how to reproach" Cesare, Machiavelli concludes:

> *One* could only indict him *in the creation* of Julius as pontiff, in which *he made a bad choice*; for, as was said, though he could not make a pope to suit himself, he could have kept anyone from being pope. (Ibid., p. 33)

And, after explaining in detail why Cesare should have blocked the election of Julius II,[48] Machiavelli concludes:

> *So the duke erred in this choice and it was the cause of his ultimate ruin.*

The assertion is flat and uncompromising: Cesare made a mistake in "this choice," and that mistake—not fortune beyond human control—"was the cause of his ultimate ruin."[49] After all, Machiavelli does "know" something about the reasons for Cesare's failure.[50]

One is thus encouraged to go back to the earlier statement that led the reader to believe that Cesare had no way of avoiding the election of Julius II. Machiavelli tells us that "he told me"—the evidence is first hand[51]—that he "had found a remedy for everything" that might happen when his father was dying, "except that he never thought that at his death he himself would also be on the point of dying." In other words, Cesare was either relying on his own last-minute intervention during the conclave to elect a successor to Alexander VI or had concluded that Giuliano delle Rovere, the future Julius II, need not be blocked. Either way, Cesare is twice described by Machiavelli has having made a "choice" and, by not preventing the election of an Italian "whom he had offended," Cesare caused his own defeat.[52]

This interpretation is confirmed by Machiavelli's diplomatic dispatches at the time of these events. If the comparison of fortune and a river in chapter twenty-five of *The Prince* is illuminated by Machiavelli's experience of attempting to divert the Arno in 1504, the analysis of Cesare in chapter seven is also a reflection of events Machiavelli witnessed first hand. For example, on 23 October 1503 (before the election of Julius II), Machiavelli wrote his superiors in Florence that "the government of this Lord [Cesare] since I have been here has rested only on his good fortune."[53] On 30 October, just before the conclave to elect a new pope, "the belief that it must be San Piero in Vincola [the future Julius II] has so much increased that there are those who give odds of sixty to a hundred on him."[54] Finally, on 4 November 1503, after the election of Julius II, Machiavelli reports the judgment of some "prudent" observers that:

> this Pontiff, having for his election had need of the Duke, to whom he made big promises, can do nothing else than keep him expectant in this way; yet they fear, if the Duke does not adopt some other plan than remaining in Rome, that he will be deceived, because they know the natural hatred which His Holiness has always had for him; the Pope cannot so soon have forgotten the exile in which he spent ten years. Yet *the Duke lets himself be carried away by that rash confidence of his.*[55]

In fact, Cesare did stay in Rome—and Julius did trick him, effectively putting him under arrest and taking control of his cities and troops. Cesare's failure was his own fault.[56]

To appreciate fully the importance of this evidence, we need to consider several additional points:

- The "fortune" that brought Cesare to power was the ambition of his father, Pope Alexander VI. Later Machiavelli describes Cesare as merely the "instrument" of his father; indeed, it was Alexander who "did all the things I discussed above in the actions of the duke" (*Prince*, ch. 11; p. 46).
- In this circumstance, the question of who controlled the papacy should have been the primary concern for Cesare; as Machiavelli puts it, "the duke, *before everything else*" should have secured a Spanish or French pope. If the goal was the creation of a large central Italian state based on the papacy, rivalry with other Italians and considerations of the balance of power should have made this choice perfectly obvious.
- Even if ill, Cesare could have vetoed Julius II had this been a clearly determined policy: "though he was half-alive, he remained secure . . . if he could not make pope whomever he wanted, at least it would not be someone he did not want" (*Prince*, ch. 7; p. 32). Having always been dependent on his father—the "fortune" that brought him to power—Cesare did not know enough to have made the correct choice.
- Cesare Borgia was in the same situation as Lorenzo de' Medici: *The Prince* is dedicated to a close relative of the pope (nephew rather

than son, to be sure), and it was the pope (Leo X, Giovanni de' Medici) who had designs to use Lorenzo (and before him, Giuliano de' Medici) to establish a large central Italian state. Machiavelli underscores this parallel by explicitly connecting Leo X to the tradition of Alexander VI (*Prince*, ch. 11; pp. 46–47).

Insofar as there is an irony in the dedication to Lorenzo (as has been argued above), the apparent praise of Cesare takes on a new tone. If we read *The Prince* as "a book of republicans" (to use Rousseau's phrase), the Medici leaders in Florence are "new princes" like Cesare Borgia, not founders in the true sense who can claim to establish a lasting regime.[57] And if this is possible, Machiavelli could be highly ironic when he says "*I do not know what better teaching I could give to a new prince than the example of his actions*" (ch. 7, p. 27). Cesare is indeed an outstanding example of something the new prince should *avoid*.

This interpretation of the text is confirmed by another historical detail that seems to have escaped most modern commentators. Machiavelli quotes Cesare as saying that "he never thought that at his [father's] death *he himself would also be on the point of dying*" (*Prince*, ch. 7; p. 32). It was reasonable that Cesare did not expect to be "dying" when his father died in August 1503, since he was only twenty-six at the time. But Cesare actually did not die until 1507. Cesare seems to have exaggerated the cause of his own failure—as ambitious men often do—when he told Machiavelli he was so sick that he was "*on the point of dying*."[58]

Cesare's singular "bad luck"—the cause of Alexander's death—was widely rumored in Rome in 1503: after describing the poison used by the Borgias to kill many rivals ("a white powder of an agreeable taste . . . which did not work on the spot, but slowly and gradually"), Burckhardt adds that "at the end of their career father and son poisoned themselves with the same powder by accidentally tasting a sweetmeat intended for a wealthy cardinal."[59] Whether true or not, such a rumor would have been known not only to Machiavelli, but to the Medici and other informed contemporaries. In this light, Cesare's remark that "*he never thought that at his* [Alexander's] *death he himself would also be on the point of dying*" takes on particular irony.

Why then the praise of Cesare's "virtue"? The "example" of Cesare Borgia in chapter seven is complex. The specific deeds of Duke Valentino, which had generated his reputation as a totally unscrupulous and violent man, are not at issue for Machiavelli. The "spirit" and boldness to use force as a means to create a new regime are identical to the actions of the praiseworthy founders described in chapter six; without such actions, it is impossible to conquer fortune. While in this sense Borgia's actions illustrate political virtue, it is the *absence* of the correlative goal of establishing "good laws" which seems to be associated with the defect of Borgia's procedure. Borgia illustrates the problem of treating fortune as a woman without also building "dikes and dams" against the flood.

To be an "entirely new prince," Cesare Borgia would have had to come to power with his "own arms" and with "virtue." Why does Machiavelli characterize Cesare, who might be considered a leader seeking to create his own armies, among those who relied on "the arms of others"? Like Romulus, who killed his own brother in order to found Rome, did Cesare need to plan his father's murder in order to ensure that the papacy was entirely under his control? Only in this case could Cesare have controlled the timing of Pope Alexander's death and avoided the unexpected coincidence of his father's death and his own illness, of which Machiavelli says Cesare complained.[60]

According to this interpretation, the defect of Borgia might be attributed to a lack of understanding of politics and his failure to establish an "entirely new principality." These faults reflect, in turn, Cesare's dependence on his father and his failure to combine "good laws" (the form of "combat" that is "proper to man") with the use of force (which is natural to "beasts"). As Burckhardt describes the events in 1503, "Cesare isolated his father, murdering brother, brother-in-law, and other relations and courtiers whenever their favour with the Pope or their position in any other respect became inconvenient to him"; as a result, Alexander VI is said to have "lived in hourly dread of Cesare."[61] Moreover, a contemporary reported that Alexander VI told the Venetian ambassador that he planned to have Cesare succeed him as pope: "I will see to it," Alexander is reputed to have said, "that one day the Papacy shall belong either to him or to you [the Venetian ambassador]." Is Machiavelli's praise of Cesare due to Duke Valentino's secret goal of killing his father and becoming pope himself, with the aim of secularizing the states controlled by the Church and annihilating the papacy? If so, Machiavelli's subtle criticism of Cesare might concern the way the plan was bungled.[62]

The true founders, deserving of the highest praise, combine both force and law. Moses, Romulus, Cyrus, and Theseus were all willing to kill or deceive if need be, but the result was a lasting regime. Only such leaders are "great men" who provide the "*greatest examples*" (*Prince*, ch. 6;

p. 22). Such founders, like "armed prophets," not only "remain powerful, secure, honored, and prosperous," but they are "*held in veneration*" (ibid., pp. 24–25). The discussion of Cesare Borgia in chapter seven can only be understood in the context of the praise of Moses, Romulus, Cyrus, and Theseus in the preceding chapter—and Cesare's failure to succeed in creating a new order equivalent to the Mosaic Law or the Roman republic.

There is a crucial difference between those who combine force and law (and hence whose success can be attributed to "virtue") and those who, like Cesare, use only force (and, when they fail, blame "fortune"). To underline this contrast, Machiavelli's next chapter is "Of Those Who Have Attained a Principality Through Crimes" (*Prince*, ch. 8; pp. 34–38). Here, he focuses on the career of Agathocles the Sicilian, who "became king of Syracuse not only from private fortune but from a mean and abject one" by means of "a life of crime at every rank of his career" (p. 34).

After cataloguing the crimes of Agathocles, which included having "all the senators and the richest of the people killed by his soldiers," Machiavelli notes that he "held the principate of that city without any civil controversy" (pp. 34–35). Since Moses, Romulus, Cyrus, and Theseus were classified as having come to power by "virtue," whereas Cesare is described as depending on "fortune," we might wonder whether Agathocles will be classified along with those described in chapter six or in chapter seven. Instead, Machiavelli claims that "one cannot attribute to fortune or to virtue what he [Agathocles] achieved without either" (p. 35).

The apparent puzzlement arises because different criteria are involved in using the terms "fortune" and "virtue." On the one hand, "whoever might consider the actions and virtue of this man will see nothing or little that can be attributed to fortune": Agathocles was not like Cesare Borgia because, "after infinite betrayals and cruelties" he still "could live for a long time secure in his fatherland, defend himself against external enemies, and never be conspired against by his citizens" (p. 37). But Agathocles cannot be classified along with Moses, Romulus, Cyrus, and Theseus either: "one cannot call it virtue to kill one's citizens, betray one's friends, to be without faith, without mercy, without religion; these modes can enable one to acquire empire, but not glory" (p. 35).

If Machiavelli were as "Machiavellian" as is often proclaimed, why should this be? Later, we are told that Agathocles was successful because his cruelties were "*well used*"; such praiseworthy acts of violence are "done at a stroke, out of the necessity to secure oneself, and then are not persisted in" (pp. 37–38). One is reminded of the description of Moses when, coming down Mount Sinai with the Tables of the Law for the first time, he confronted the Israelites worshipping the Golden Calf. Hence, as Machiavelli says, "if one considers *the virtue of Agathocles* . . . and the greatness of his spirit . . . one does not see why he has to be judged inferior to any *most excellent captain*" (p. 35).[63]

The key seems to be how we describe the actions of a leader after the fact and in light of the consequences: "one cannot *call it virtue* to kill one's citizens, betray one's friends, to be without faith, without mercy, without religion." These deeds may be—and typically are—necessary at the founding of "new modes and orders." But such *deeds themselves* cannot be *called* virtue. Indeed, when Machiavelli refers to them in discussing "the greatest examples" (like Moses), he uses indirect language: "And thus things must be ordered in such a mode that *when they no longer believe one can make them believe by force*" (*Prince*, ch. 6; p. 24).

Agathocles' cruelty is called both "well committed" (because it was done effectively) and "savage" (because it was not done toward the end of producing good and lasting laws). As a "most excellent captain," Agathocles—like Hiero of Syracuse (*Prince*, ch. 6; p. 25) or Francesco Sforza of Milan (ch. 7; pp. 26–27) and unlike Cesare or Liveretto da Fermo (ch. 8; pp. 35–36)—was successful, finding "some remedy for their state with God and with men" (p. 38). But his deeds "do not *allow him to be celebrated among the most excellent men*"—like Moses, Romulus, Cyrus, or Theseus—because, unlike them and like Cesare or Liveretto, he did not found a lasting regime.[64]

That this is the essential criterion for judging founders is made explicit in the *Discourses*:

> the security of a republic or of a kingdom, therefore, does not depend upon its ruler governing it prudently during his lifetime, but upon *his so ordering it that, after his death, it may maintain itself in being*. (*Discourses*, I, 11; p. 142)

Indeed, the explicit criticism of Christianity lies in just such a failure:

> If such a religious spirit [as that of the pagan Romans] had been kept up by the ruler of the Christian commonwealth as was ordained for us by its founder, Christian states and republics would have been much more united and much more happy than they are. (*Discourses*, I, 12; p. 144)[65]

The outcomes or results of a leader's actions—not his goals or aims—are the only reasonable criterion for judging him.

IV. Standards of Praise and Blame

The comparison between the leaders or princes described in chapters six through eight of *The Prince* will confound the reader who seeks to use language in a conventional manner. Machiavelli describes as "virtue" the "means" used by Moses or Romulus because the *consequences* of their actions were "excellent," not because the *acts* themselves were praiseworthy. The ends—i.e., the results, rather than the intentions—*define* the means even more than they justify them: after the success of Moses, we tend to forget the scene described in Exodus 32.[66] How many Americans are aware of the nature of the first printed reference to George Washington?[67]

The standards of praise and blame in human affairs are thus relative, not absolute and fixed:

> *in the actions of all men,* and especially of princes, where there is no court to appeal to, *one looks to the end.* So *let a prince* win and *maintain his state: the means* will always be judged honorable, and *will be praised by everyone.* (*Prince*, ch. 18; p. 71)

Success retroactively determines how we think of historical events—and presumably the same thing occurs in private life.[68] Standards of "praise and blame"—in other words, standards of morality—are relative in time and place.

This general understanding of praise and blame should be kept in mind when reading "Of Those Things for Which Men and Especially Princes Are Praised and Blamed" in chapter fifteen. After emphasizing for the second time in this famous chapter that he is "leaving out what is imagined about a prince and discussing what is true" (p. 61), Machiavelli goes on:

> I say that all men, whenever one speaks of them, and especially princes, since they are placed higher, are noted for *some of the qualities that bring them either blame or praise.* And this is why someone is considered liberal, someone mean (using a Tuscan term because *avaro* [greedy] in our language is still one who desires to have something by violence, *misero* [mean] we call one who refrains too much from using what is his); someone is considered a giver, someone rapacious; someone cruel, someone merciful; the one a breaker of faith, the other faithful; the one effeminate and pusillanimous, the other fierce and spirited; the one humane, the other proud; the one lascivious, the other chaste; the one honest, the other clever; the one hard, the other agreeable; the one grave, the other

light; the other religious, the other unbelieving, and the like. And I know that everyone will confess that it would be a very laudable thing to find in a prince *all of the above-mentioned qualities that are held good.* (pp. 61–62)

Why does Machiavelli give us such a long list of "qualities"? And which ones of them "are held good"?[69]

The terms usually reserved for praise sometimes come first ("liberal," "giver," "humane," "honest," "grave," "religious"), sometimes second ("merciful," "faithful," "chaste," "agreeable"), and—in at least one pair ("effeminate and pusillanimous" versus "fierce and spirited")—it might be wondered which ones "are held good" by most people or by "the vulgar." That this long list is meant to emphasize the mutability of standards of praise and blame is underscored by the first pair, contrasting "liberal" with "mean": Machiavelli tells us he is "using a Tuscan term because *avaro* [greedy] *in our language* is still one who desires to have something by violence, *misero* [mean] *we call* one who refrains too much from using what is his." For Christians, "charity" is one of the cardinal virtues; it is "better to give than to receive." But what is the opposite of "liberality" or being a "giver"? Either one can be "mean" or miserly, or one can be "rapacious" or "greedy": in the first case, not giving because one keeps what one has; in the second taking from others "by violence" rather than giving to them.

Elsewhere, Machiavelli is quite explicit in advising princes to the "mean" rather than "rapacious": (e.g., *Prince,* ch. 21; p. 91). Christian teachings treat both traits as equally bad or blameworthy. The Roman soldiers "loved a prince with a military spirit who was insolent, cruel, and rapacious" as a means to "give vent to their avarice and cruelty" (*Prince,* ch. 19; p. 76). In contrast, the Roman "people loved quiet, and therefore loved modest princes" (ibid.). In short, if one considers the triad of qualities ("liberal" or giving, "mean" or modest, "rapacious" or violent), each has been considered "good" or praiseworthy by some humans and bad by others.

Machiavelli's use of a "Tuscan" term to underscore the variability of standards of praise and blame points to the difference between the traditions of Tuscany (the region of Florence) and those of the remainder of Italy. This difference reflects the changes in language brought by history, the subject of a chapter of the *Discourses* entitled "Changes of Religion and of Language, Together with Such Misfortunes as Floods or Pestilences, Obliterate the Records of the Past." At the end of this most important chapter, Machiavelli notes that prior to the rise of the Roman republic, Tuscany had an independent civilization:

There was, then, as we have said before, *a time when Tuscany was a powerful country*, full of religion and of virtue, *with its own customs and its own language*, all of which we know was *wiped out* by the power of Rome, so that of it, as has been said, there remains nought but the remembrance of its *name*. (*Discourses*, II, 5; p. 290)

Earlier in this chapter, Machiavelli notes that "language" can sometimes survive to transmit remembrance of the past after "religion" has been obliterated, as "the retention of the Latin language" permitted knowledge of pagan antiquity after Christianity "abolished all pagan institutions, all pagan rites, and destroyed the records of the theology of the ancients" (ibid., p. 289).

In this contrast, "language" seems to refer to the "names" or words, whereas "religion" stands for the beliefs of a society, or the way these words are used. Among the "modes and orders" of human life, religion plays a central role by determining standards of praise and blame, and all good regimes depend decisively on the religious beliefs of the many or "vulgar." Religions are human institutions or creations, and indeed the highest praise of any human action is reserved for the individual who founds a religion.[70]

Many ancient thinkers had, of course, emphasized the relativity of human affairs. Protagoras, for example, insisted that even the sensations and feelings most people consider to be natural are ultimately dependent on human habit and custom: "sweet and sour are by convention." Unlike the pre-Socratics and sophists, for whom the relativity of all standards of praise and blame led to a denial of natural criteria of judgment, Machiavelli insists that there is a human nature, that it is knowable, and that knowledge of the human condition is essential to prudent and successful action.

The very first sentence of *The Prince* should be enough to show that some human things are unchanging and independent of convention: "*All* states, *all* dominions that *have held and do hold* empire over men *have been and are* either republics or principalities" (ch. 1; p. 5). The double repetition of a past tense and a present tense, so apparently redundant, can only reinforce the impression that on some matters, times do not change the human condition. When Machiavelli remarks in the dedication that his knowledge is based on "long experience with modern things and a continuous reading of ancient ones," he implies that knowledge of the "ancient" (pagan) times is relevant to "modern" (Christian) life.

The point is made explicit in the *Discourses*: "men are born and live and die in an order which remains ever the same" (I, 11; p. 142).[71] This constancy of the human condition is, indeed, a corollary of the constancy of nature more broadly: hence, in the Preface, Machiavelli explains his focus on ancient things as an attempt to show that his contemporaries are foolish to believe the deeds of pagan Romans are impossible to imi-tate, "as if the heaven, the sun, the elements and man had in their motion, their order, and their potency, become different from what they used to be" (*Discourses*, I, Pref.; pp. 98–99). Nature—and human nature—have a con-stant "order" despite the varying conventions of praise and blame. Indeed, without this conception of the "nature" (and "natures") of men, embed-ded in a broader view of the "nature" of "things," Machiavelli could not elaborate a definition of human "excellence" as a guide to political action.

V. The Economy of Power

Standards of praise and blame provide us with the view of human action from the perspective of society at large or of the "vulgar." Reflection on the variability of these standards and of their origins shows that humans create religious and political institutions, which have the effect of forming standards of praise and blame. And since the creation of religious and po-litical institutions is in almost all cases the work of individuals, the study of human nature leads to distinction between the perspective of the ruler or prince and that of the people. *The Prince* is particularly important because it examines human "things" from the perspective of the prince, and espe-cially the "entirely new" prince who is shaping or reshaping the "modes and orders" of a human community.

From the perspective of the "people" or the "vulgar," judgments depend on varying standards of praise and blame; from the perspective of the ruler (or those capable of being or judging rulers), judgments depend on the unchanging maxims or rules concerning human nature and politics. These rules, which form the substance of Machiavelli's prudential teaching about politics, comprise a science that could be called the "economy of power."

The name is easily justified. Immediately after Machiavelli's well-known statement that "generally" men are ungrateful, fickle, pretenders and dissemblers, evaders of danger, eager for gain" (*Prince*, ch. 7; p. 66) he adds:

And that prince who has founded himself entirely on their words, stripped of other preparation, is ruined; for *friendships that are acquired at a price* and not with greatness and nobility of spirit *are bought*, but they *are not owned* and when the time comes they *cannot be spent*.

There are two modes of acquiring "friendship": another person can be "acquired at a price" or "with greatness and nobility of spirit." The former would seem to be actions of cost and benefit as measured by pleasure and pain (or what Plato calls "desire"); the latter concern those relations based on honor and glory (in Platonic psychology, *thymos* or spirit). While Machiavelli seems to share the psychological categories developed in Plato's *Republic*,[72] it seems that desire or appetite needs to be at the center of the leader's concern.

The calculus of appetite is of primary concern for the prince because "utility" is more fundamental than "obligation." Machiavelli goes on:

And men have less hesitation to offend one who makes himself loved than one who makes himself feared; for *love is held by a chain of obligation*, which, because men are wicked, is *broken at every opportunity for their own utility*,[73] but *fear is held by a dread of punishment that never forsakes you*. (Ibid., pp. 66–67)

Since most men are primarily concerned "with their own utility," Machiavelli directly addresses the prince or leader and reminds him that "you" should rely on the "dread of punishment." Fear is more reliable than love because it can be controlled by the ruler: "a wise prince should found himself *on what is his, not on what is someone else's*" (*Prince*, ch. 17; p. 68).

Human emotions have a constant nature, in contrast to the terms of praise and blame which vary from one time or place to another. In assessing the feelings or principles of behavior on which princes should rely, Machiavelli can thus claim to answer universal or general questions. These answers are formulated as his famous teaching about love, fear, and hate:

[A] dispute arises whether it is better to be loved than feared, or the reverse. The answer is that one would want to be both the one and the other; but because it is difficult to put them together, *it is much safer to be feared than loved*, if one has to lack one of the two. The prince should nonetheless make himself *feared in such a mode* that if he does not acquire love, he *escapes hatred*, because being feared and not being hated can go together very well. (Ibid., pp. 66–67)

In the exercise of power, fear is preferable to love, and love is preferable to hate. For princes or rulers, Machiavelli replaces the Christian "law of love" with a new calculus in which being feared is to be preferred.

This economy of power settles, at least from the ruler's perspective, the issue of praise and blame which Machiavelli had described in relativist terms in chapter fifteen. Hence, in chapter seventeen, Machiavelli adds that the prince can combine "being feared and not being hated"

> if he *abstains from the property of his citizens and his subjects,* and from their women; and if he also needs to proceed against someone's life, he must do it when there is suitable justification and manifest cause for it. But above all, *he must abstain from the property of others,* because men forget the death of a father more quickly than the loss of a patrimony; Furthermore, causes for taking away property are never lacking, and *he who begins to live by rapine always finds cause to seize others' property,* and, on the contrary, causes for taking life are rare and disappear more quickly. (p. 67)

Of the triad of terms which introduces the list of "qualities" of praise and blame (*Prince,* ch. 15; p. 61), being "greedy" (*avaro*) or desiring to "have something by violence" is worse for a ruler than being "mean" (*misero*) or refraining "too much from using what is his").

The economy of power arises from predictable or natural tendencies: "men forget the death of a father more quickly than the loss of a patrimony." Honor or "spirit," which would lead men to avenge the rape of their wives or the murder of their kinsmen, is of course a danger in politics; elsewhere, Machiavelli gives many examples of the way such passionate behavior has destroyed lives and careers.[74] But material "utility" is an even stronger incentive for most humans. By assuring the "citizens" of a republic or the "subjects" of a monarchy their "patrimony," rulers of any regime can avoid "being hated" and hence prevent the spread of spirited opposition to a substantial portion of the society.

The same criterion explains why "liberality" or "giving" is dangerous for a ruler.

> [I[f one wants to maintain a name for liberality among men, it is necessary not to leave out any kind of lavish display, so that a prince who has done this will always consume all his resources in such deeds. In the end it will be necessary, *if he wants to maintain a name for liberality,* to burden the people extraordinarily, to be *rigorous with taxes,* and to *do*

all those things that can be done to get money. This will begin to make him hated by his subjects. (*Prince,* ch. 16; p. 63)

Giving (unless based on conquest of foreigners) and taking are equally dangerous, for both will give rise to hatred and contempt. Neither Christian "love" and charity, nor selfish "greed" are prudent for the political leader. "In our time, we have not seen great things done *except by those who have been considered mean*" (*Prince,* ch. 16; p. 63).

In much the same way, Machiavelli resolves the question of praise and blame with regard to being "cruel" or "merciful," contradicting the Christian doctrine according to which mercy is good and cruelty bad. With citizens, cruelties that are "well used" or "done at a stroke, out of the necessity to secure oneself" are praiseworthy (*Prince,* ch. 8; pp. 37–38); with soldiers, "it is above all necessary not to care about a name for cruelty" (ch. 17; p. 67). Similarly, praise and blame with regard to the fourth pair of qualities introduced in chapter fifteen—"the one a breaker of faith, the other faithful" (p. 62)—is decided against Christian doctrine: "one sees by experience *in our times* that the princes *who have done great things are those who have taken little account of faith*" (ch. 18; p. 69).

Machiavelli seeks a fundamental transformation in the standards of praise and blame that dominate "modern" times or "our times," which is to say the Christian era. Having shown how "breaking faith" is superior to "faithfulness," "meanness" is superior to either "liberality" or "greed," and "cruelty" superior to "mercy," Machiavelli adds that he has "spoken of the most important of the qualities mentioned above" (*Prince,* ch. 19; p. 71). Of the cardinal Christian virtues—"faith, hope, and charity"—two are qualities of *blame* in the actions of princes and the third is focused on human affairs. Although some commentators argue that Machiavelli was a believing Christian opposed to the corruption of the Catholic Church, his target was the entire "education" associated with the decline in the love of "liberty" and declining esteem for "worldly honour" created by "our religion"—i.e., by the basic principles of Christianity.[75] At the risk of anachronism, one can almost speak of what Nietzsche called "the transvaluation of values."

That Machiavelli sought such a radical transformation of the moral standards of European society can be shown in many other ways. Perhaps the most interesting concerns the first of his major writings to be published in his own lifetime. Unlike *The Prince* or the *Discourses,* we are less in doubt about Machiavelli's responsibility for our texts of *The Art of War* (published in Florence in 1521), and *Mandragola* (his play, first produced in 1517 and published in 1518). Although *The Art of War* has already been mentioned at several points, his famous comedy—ignored by many conventional political theorists—can be read as a symbolic epitome of Machiavelli's teaching. Such an interpretation of *Mandragola* is particularly justified by the Prologue, in which the author himself comes on stage and informs the audience that he hopes they "might be tricked" as the character Lucrezia is in the play.[76]

To understand *Mandragola* and its relationship to Machiavelli's political writings, it will be necessary to summarize the plot. The hero is a man named Callimaco Guadagni, who was sent to Paris at the age of ten and, after the French invasion of Italy in 1494 resolved to remain there to study; in 1504, now thirty, he has returned to Florence because he has been told that a woman named Lucrezia, the wife of Nicia Calfucci, is so beautiful that he is "burning with such a desire to be with her, that I don't know where I am."[77] "Messer Nicia" is an old, impotent man, but "Madonna Lucrezia" is an extraordinary virtuous wife as well as a great beauty. The action of the play concerns the way Callimaco, through a character named Ligurio, solicits the assistance of the priest Timoteo, who convinces the elderly Nicia that his wife must sleep with a man in order to have an heir. Lucrezia is resistant,[78] but with the help of the priest, who promises absolution in return for alms, Nicia agrees to convince his wife and supervise the act.[79] Callimaco seduces the lovely Lucrezia, who falls in love with him without Nicia realizing that he has been the agent of his own cuckoldry. As the play ends with everyone content, Timoteo leads them all "into the Church" where they are to "say the regular prayers" and then "go dine."[80]

The comedy of the play is of course that an old husband (Nicia) uses every stratagem to overcome the virtue of his beautiful wife (Lucrezia) so that she will be unfaithful to him. The priest (Timoteo) is the knowing accomplice in the seduction. And because the act is perfectly planned and executed, everyone is happy by the end of the play: Nicia (who now thinks he will have a son), Lucrezia (who has discovered the joys of sexuality), Callimaco (whose desires have been satisfied), and Timoteo (who has received a generous payoff for the Church).

Symbolically, I would interpret the play as follows: the audience of the play represents the city of Florence; Nicia the old, established standards of praise and blame; Lucrezia the possibility of human desire; and Friar Timoteo the Catholic Church. Callimaco—his name is that of the first head of Ptolemy's great library of Alexandria, the man reputed to have put in order all the works of Greek poetry and philosophy—represents learning; Ligurio, the "link" or connection between the characters who makes it possible for each to achieve his or her goals, is Machiavelli himself.

What does it mean for the audience to be "tricked" as was Lucrezia, which the Prologue makes the explicit intention of the author? The "people" are to adopt new standards of morality, abandoning the otherworldliness of Christ's teaching in favor of tasting the pleasures of the body. Machiavelli achieves this by releasing the desires that had been hidden in the traditional secular knowledge of the West, epitomized by Callimaco (whose attentions are redirected from his studies in Paris to the conquest of Lucrezia in Florence). And this is to be done within the context of the traditional religion: Machiavelli does not pretend to overthrow the Church, but rather promises it material benefits (Lucrezia's gift of ten *grossi* to Timoteo in the final scene).

That something of this sort is the meaning of the play is confirmed by a song for the outset of the play which Machiavelli wrote in 1526:

> Because life is brief
> and many are the pains
> which, living and struggling, everyone sustains,
>
> *let us follow our desires,*
> passing and consuming the years,
> *because whoever deprives himself of pleasure*
> to live with anguish and with worries
> *doesn't know* the tricks
> of the world, or by what ills
> and *by what strange happenings*
> *all mortals are almost overwhelmed.*[81]

Machiavelli's goal is to allow humans to "follow our desires" in this world because "life is brief" and the afterlife apparently irrelevant.

By channeling desire, an effective political order can make it possible to achieve happiness. The song added by Machiavelli in 1526 concludes:

> Besides, we have been brought here
> by the name of him[82] who governs you,
> in whom can be seen all
> the goods gathered in the eternal countenance.
> For such heavenly grace,
> for so happy a state,

you can be glad,
rejoice, and give thanks—to the one who gave him to you.[83]

A secularized church and a government dedicated to the "new case" described in Machiavelli's play can give humans "heavenly grace" on earth and make humans "glad, rejoice, and give thanks."

Machiavelli's innovation is thus an astute combination of ancient knowledge and desire (symbolized by Callimaco), cleverness (Ligurio), and Christianity (Friar Timoteo), by which material pleasure (Lucrezia)—repressed by the established, barren traditions (Nicia)—becomes accessible to "you" (the audience). The Roman republic had been founded after the rape of Lucrezia (cf. *Discourses*, III, 2, 5, and 26). The new republic will be based on a seduction of Lucrezia that is aided and abetted by a Machiavellian alliance between the Christian Church and pagan knowledge.

Machiavelli remarks in *The Prince* that perfection or an "imagined principality"—one thinks of Paul's "kingdom of heaven" or Augustine's *City of God* as well as of Plato's *Republic*—is impossible. He frequently counsels accepting necessity: "a prince who wants to maintain his state is often forced not to be good" (*Prince*, ch. 19; p. 77). It is necessary to learn to choose "the less bad as good" (*Prince*, ch. 21, p. 91). But these counsels are not merely the political prudence of the ancient pagans. They are also a new kind of religion, which turns Christian values upside down rather than obliterating them openly. In a letter to his friend Guiccardini dated 17 May 1521, Machiavelli writes:

> I was on the privy seat when your messenger came, and just then I was thinking of the absurdities of this world, and I was giving all my attention to imagining for myself a preacher after my mind for the place at Florence, and he would be just what would please me, because in this I intend to be as obstinate as in my other opinions. And *because I never failed that city by not benefiting her when I could—if not with deeds, with words, if not with words, with gestures—I do not intend to fail her this time either.* It is true that I know I am opposed, as in many other things, to the opinion of the citizens there: they would like a preacher who would show them the road to Paradise, and I should like to find one who would teach them the way to go to the house of the Devil because *I believe the true way of going to Paradise would be to learn the road to Hell in order to avoid it.*[84]

Chapter Four

$\mathcal{U}$sing the $\mathcal{B}$east: $\mathcal{A}$nimal $\mathcal{D}$ominance and $\mathcal{H}$uman $\mathcal{L}$eadership

The task of philosophy is to resolve the fundamental question regarding human nature.

Alexandre Kojève[1]

Machiavelli asserts he can teach "the effectual truth" of human life in place of the "imagined" things believed by most people, princes and common citizens alike. As one perceptive scholar puts it, "it was a huge and audacious claim," for Machiavelli apparently has "the ability to leap over the pitfalls and ambiguities of everyday speech into a realm of understanding based on direct contact with things"—a realm which reveals "possibilities for action in which the notorious gap—properly understood and manipulated—between conventional speech and things becomes a source of power."[2] Machiavelli can be called one of the originators of modernity because his practical political teaching is based on a scientific theory of human nature. If so, the serious reader needs to inquire whether Machiavelli's understanding of "things" is actually true. To do so, we must turn from historical analysis and textual commentary to questions of a different kind.

Are Machiavelli's theories confirmed by recent scientific research on human nature and animal social behavior? It is appropriate to compare Machiavelli's *Prince* with the findings of contemporary biology for several reasons. Machiavelli explicitly says the leader needs to "use the man and the beast." Human politics cannot be understood without an inquiry into the "necessities" of social behavior, and many of these "facts" are described by Machiavelli in terms that compare humans with nonhuman animals. It follows that the truth of his theory will depend to some extent on how human nature relates to the nature of nonhuman species (like lions, foxes, and wolves).

Whereas Machiavelli based his theory of human nature and politics on practical experience and the study of both ancient and modern events (*Prince*, Dedicatory Letter; p. 3), we have access to further evidence of the "effectual truth of the thing." The broad outlines of hominid evolution have been confirmed by fossils of ancestors who lived in Africa as much as 2.5 million years ago. Animal social behavior and its relationship to the physical and social environment have been explained by observation and experiment in ethology, behavioral ecology, and comparative zoology. The structure and functions of the central nervous system are being revealed by neuroanatomy, neurochemistry, and cognitive neuroscience. Do these fields confirm or contradict the teachings of *The Prince*?

Such an effort may seem anachronistic. Darwin's *Origin of Species* was published over three centuries after Machiavelli's *Prince*. Although we cannot read back into Machiavelli the perspective of neo-Darwinian biology, it should not be presumed that he was unaware of such an approach to human nature. He knew Lucretius's *De rerum natura*—one of the principal ancient texts to explain human origins through a process of evolution—having copied a humanist manuscript edition of the work as a young man;[3] when describing human beginnings in the *Discourses*, Machiavelli asserts that humans "lived for a time scattered like the beasts" (I, 2; p. 106). And, if he talked extensively with Leonardo da Vinci, Machiavelli would have encountered a contemporary for whom "the description of man . . . includes that of such creatures as are almost the same species, as Apes, Monkeys, and the like."[4] Whatever these historical details, Machiavelli's claim concerns a truth about the unchanging "nature"—or rather, "natures"—of human beings. Is his theory true?

I. Machiavelli on "Man" and "Beast"

In the last chapter, I argued that Machiavelli understood human nature as unreliable and shortsighted rather than simply wicked. In this view, history has generally been a flow of uncontrolled events—the "fortune" which most individuals blame for undesirable outcomes. Wars, conflicts, riots, famines, and other unpredictable events cannot be prevented by exhorting people to exercise the Christian virtues of faith, hope, and charity: the necessities of human nature are such that, at the critical moment, promises of good behavior evaporate in the face of natural desires. It is prudent to assume that others will be selfish because, at the urgent moment when altruism is needed, selfishness is so likely.

For Machiavelli, this situation can be overcome only through a science of both "the nature of the people" and "the nature of the prince" (*Prince,* Dedicatory Letter; p. 4). From the popular perspective, human rulers are likely to be selfish, cowardly, venal, or simply incompetent. Most of those who come to power do so through luck rather than ability ("fortune and the arms of others") and easily lose control because they do not know what to do. Cesare Borgia, the model of such leaders, blamed "fortune" when he lost power; although Cesare was bold enough to succeed, "the cause of his ruin" was that "the duke erred" in the "choice" of his father's successor as pope (*Prince*, ch. 6; p. 33).

The people are equally unpredictable and shortsighted. "A prince cannot found himself on what he sees in quiet times, when citizens have need of the state, because then everyone runs, everyone promises, and each wants to die for him when death is at a distance"; despite such promises, "in adverse times, when the state has need of citizens, then few of them are to be found" (*Prince*, ch. 9; p. 42). Indeed, the tendency of popular behavior to differ "according to circumstances" is so great that "one cannot give certain rules" for the way a prince should get popular support (*Prince,* ch. 9; pp. 39–40).

This unpredictability of human nature can only be controlled by founders of "new modes and orders" who establish lasting regimes. Such leaders are unusual "princes," like Moses, Cyrus, Theseus, and Romulus, whose success can be attributed to reliance on "virtue" and their "own arms" (*Prince*, ch. 6; pp. 21–24). History or fortune does little more than "give opportunity to someone prudent and virtuous to introduce a form that would bring honor to him and good to the community of men" (*Prince*, ch. 16; p. 102).

The goal or end for Machiavelli is thus not merely "honor" for the ambitious prince, but the "good to the community of men" that comes from the establishment of "good arms and good laws" (*Prince*, ch. 12; p. 48). The obstacle to this goal, however, is human nature itself. Princes must fight for control—and the considerations entailed in this "combat" give rise to Machiavelli's central statement concerning the relationship between humans and other animals.

> Thus, you must know that there are two kinds of combat: one with *laws*, the other with *force*. The first is proper to *man*, the second to

beasts; but because the first is often not enough, one must have recourse to the second. Therefore *it is necessary for a prince to know well how to use the beast and the man.* This role was taught covertly to princes by ancient writers, who wrote that Achilles, and many other ancient princes, were given to Chiron the centaur to be raised, so that he would look after them with his discipline. To have as teacher a half-beast, half-man means nothing other than that a prince needs to know how to use both natures; and the one without the other is not lasting.

Thus, since a prince is compelled of necessity to know well how *to use the beast*, he should *pick the fox and the lion*, because the lion does not defend itself from snares and the fox does not defend itself from wolves. So *one needs to be a fox to recognize snares and a lion to frighten the wolves.* Those who stay simply with the lion do not understand this. (*Prince*, ch. 18; p. 69)

A careful reading of this famous passage contradicts the superficial interpretations of Machiavelli. The successful leader must *combine* the reliance on the "human" element—rivalry or "combat" with "laws"—with the use of "force" associated with different "beasts"; these animal attributes are, however, multiple, symbolized by three different species: lion, fox, and wolves.

The lion represents power—the ability to "defend" against an attacker (an ability lacking in the fox, which "does not defend itself from wolves"). This power seems to be effective insofar as it does *not* need to be used: the lion apparently can defend itself against wolves in part because a wolf is usually not tempted to attack such a large and powerful mammal.

The fox represents cleverness—the ability to "defend" against hidden dangers (which is lacking in the lion, which "does not defend itself from snares"). This ability presumes an intelligence that enables an animal to avoid conflict: the fox apparently can avoid snares by "recognizing" and avoiding dangers where other animals, like the lion, cannot.

In this comparison, what are the "wolves"? While the lion is called "fierce" and the fox "astute" (*Prince*, ch. 19; p. 79), Machiavelli does not give a similar adjective to this species—nor does he use the singular: the third of the animal natures is the plurality of individual wolves who need to be "frightened" so that they will not attack. By implication, wolves—predators outside the camp, perpetually a danger in the night—stand for the desires, ambitions, or threats of the many.

While at first a modern reader is tempted to read Machiavelli's references to the "beast" as something akin to a Hobbesian state of nature, such a conclusion is not justified. Hobbes is well known for comparing humans with wolves (*homo homini lupus est*): that is, unlike Machiavelli, Hobbes reduces the political problem to a single species and a single principle (the desire for self-preservation). In contrast, Machiavelli tells us in chapter eighteen that the prince should "pick the fox and the lion" as the "natures" that he will "use"; Severus, an example of a successful leader, "knew how to use *the persons of the fox and the lion*, whose natures I say above are necessary for a prince to imitate" (*Prince*, ch. 19; p. 78).

The fox, lion, and wolves are symbols or totems of natural attributes shared by many "beasts." Machiavelli is silent about other elements of what we would call the mammalian behavioral repertoire, though he implies that the horse—the half of the centaur symbolizing the beast for the ancients—should not be imitated by leaders. The animal natures that need to guide human leaders are found among wild or *undomesticated* species: power, cleverness, and the predatory threats of outsiders.

In suggesting that the prince "pick" the first two of these "natures" for imitation, however, Machiavelli tacitly recognizes that humans are social animals. The "wolves" which must be "frightened" by the prince are, of course, other humans—like the centurion who killed Antoninus (*Prince*, ch. 19; p. 79); wolves are sociable mammals who hunt in packs. Desire and pleasure—which become the individual's right to self-preservation for Hobbes and Locke—are as social as power or dominance (symbolized by the lion) and cleverness or manipulation (symbolized by the fox). And, of course, the horse that was "picked" as a symbol by the ancient teachers is a domesticated animal who depends on a master or owner for food.

Machiavelli does not recommend that a prince study the social behavior of lions, foxes, or wolves in the wild, and then base his actions on what he has seen.[5] But ethological research like that of George Schaller, Konrad Lorenz, and Benson Ginsburg has taught us much about the "effectual truth" of the social life within groups of these "beasts": all three are highly gregarious animals in which cooperation and altruism are more pronounced than the competition and conflict which, for Hobbes, represent "the natural condition of mankind." Does this mean that Machiavelli's teaching is false or irrelevant?

To assess Machiavelli's theory of human nature in the light of contemporary biology, we need to consider the status of the behavioral attributes or traits which Machiavelli personified in the image of the lion, the fox, and the wolves (as well as of the centaur). What is the role of "combat"—intraspecific competition—within mammals and especially nonhuman primates? How are power (being sufficiently "fierce" to deter threat or attack) and cleverness (being sufficiently "astute" to "recognize" and avoid trouble) related to the omnipresent danger from attack by other individuals ("wolves" who desire to take what one has) or environmental risks ("snares" that are hidden in the places where one lives)?

Today, political theorists need no longer personify these attributes of animal nature in the manner of Beatrix Potter stories. We can turn to the research of ethologists and behavioral ecologists for an understanding of when and why animals exhibit the behavior we observe. And, in so doing, we find that humans are naturally sociable beings who, as Machiavelli suggests, share elements of the behavioral repertoire of other species.

Machiavelli was thus correct to insist that the leader must combine that which is "proper to man" (based on the use of verbal language and the "law" it makes possible) with the behaviors associated with the "beast." But is the "way" of the "beast" really to be associated with "force," as Machiavelli suggests at the outset of the famous passage in chapter eighteen? Exactly what does animal leadership teach us about human nature?

II. The Nature of Social Behavior

Evolution can no longer be viewed as an unproved hypothesis or "theory" (in that sense used by creationists). We must take it as demonstrated that processes of nondirected mutation and natural selection, as well as genetic drift and other secondary factors, account for the diversification and perpetuation of living things. But what is this theory and how does it relate to questions of social behavior?[6]

EVOLUTION, BEHAVIOR, AND THE ENVIRONMENT

Sometimes it is still said that there is no "evidence" proving Darwinian theory. Assuming that biological theories do not have the certainty of a geometric proof—for in this sense it has been clear since Hume that no scientific theory can ever be definitively proven—skeptics are simply wrong. A single case should suffice: the well-known example of the peppered moth (*Biston botularia*), whose colors changed to provide protection as the bark of trees was darkened by the soot of industrialization. And since a picture is worth a thousand words, look at the evidence (Figure 4.1).[7]

In pre-industrial climates or places without polluted air, tree trunks are light. Moths, to avoid predators (Machiavelli's "wolves"), evolved the

Figure 4.1. "Adaptation is exemplified by 'industrial melanism' in the peppered moth (*Biston betularia*). Air pollution kills the lichens that would normally colonize the bark of tree trunks. On the dark, lichenless bark of an oak tree near Liverpool in England the melanic (*black*) form is better adapted: it is better camouflaged against predation by birds than the light, peppered wild type [*top*], which it largely replaced through natural selection in industrial areas of England in the late 19th century. Now air quality is improving. On a nearby beech tree colonized by algae and the lichen *Lecanora conizaeoides*, which is itself particularly well adapted to low levels of pollution, the two forms of the moth are equally conspicuous (*middle*). On the lichened bark of an oak tree in rural Wales, the wild type is almost invisible (*bottom*), and in such areas it predominates" (Richard C. Lewontin, "Adaptation," *Scientific American* 239 [September 1978]: 212–213). Photographs courtesy of J. A. Bishop, University of Liverpool.

adaptation of colors blending perfectly into the tree trunks. With industrialization, however, the tree trunks were blackened. Those moths that had dark coloration by "accident"—i.e., through a process of genetic mutation which is not directed by conscious will or divine plan—were now protected from predators.

In this case, natural selection is said to "favor" the dark or melanistic mutant because it has greater average "reproductive success" than the ancestral, light form (or "morph"). To understand the process, however, we should not allow words to trap us. From the perspective of nature as a whole, what counts is the *relationship* between the environment, other species, and the color—or shape, social behavior, and foraging habits—of an animal. Of particular importance, as recent research shows, is the distinction between the physical environment (usually stable over the lifetime of an individual organism) and selective pressures that can evolve more rapidly in response to an animal's physical development or behavior (as in host-parasite and predator-prey interactions).[8]

Machiavelli's images in the famous passage on "man and beast" in chapter nineteen are remarkable, for they reflect in a poetic way precisely this complexity. The dangers confronting any animal include "snares" (risks in the environment) and "wolves" (predators, which is to say other living things). And in response to these dangers, there is a multiplicity of responses (the "natures" of the fox, the lion—or the horse and man symbolized by the centaur) which form a palette of possibly "adaptive" responses.

Adaptations, like the coloration of the peppered moth, represent ways by which animals continue to survive in a changing world. Those changes themselves are not directed or planned, do not represent "progress," and thus resemble what Machiavelli calls "fortune" in chapter twenty-four of *The Prince*. Moreover the ecosystem is a compound of the physical environment and the behavior of other living species, as Machiavelli suggests. Finally, for mammals and especially primates—and hence most particularly for humans—behavior is a critical mode of adaptation to the surrounding world.

This last point is of particular importance. Most of us have little difficulty appreciating the concept of natural selection when it is applied to bodily structures and colors. We can see the function served by hawks' wings or wolves' teeth, just as we can see why the moth's color is adaptive. It is harder to see how social behavior evolves, and especially how such behavior patterns are adaptations to the environment rather than "things" or fixed attributes to be studied in isolation from the surrounding world.

Here, Machiavelli's metaphoric use of lion, fox, and wolves to symbolize behaviors should not be taken too literally. In fact, the behaviors of animals are usually responses to the social as well as physical environment. Just as Machiavelli teaches that the prince should "pick" the "natures" that are "necessary" under the circumstances, so evolutionary biology shows that the behaviors of other animals are adapted to the social context—and often represent what scientists call a "strategy" (as if the results of evolutionary processes amount to a choice among possibilities).[9]

Instinctive responses are, obviously, not consciously chosen by the individual animal: a hawk didn't "pick" the behavior of predation any more than a moth could have chosen its color. But at the level of entire species, since the typical behavioral responses result from the impersonal process we call natural selection, Machiavelli's image can best be seen as a metaphor for the range of possibilities from which evolution has favored some behaviors rather than others.

When we consider adaptation as the consequence of an impersonal or non-directed process, there is no reason to exclude social behavior from evolutionary analysis—and, in fact, it is impossible to do so. Observe and try to identify birds. A standard handbook will tell you the colors of feathers, head, or legs that characterize a red-tailed hawk or turkey vulture. In the field, alas, the sun often makes it impossible to see these features. But you can still tell the dihedral wing position and wobbling flight patterns of the turkey vulture from the red-tailed hawk's very different mode of flying.

Behavior is as much a defining characteristic of species as body shape and color. Any good field guide describes many things about a bird's behavior—typical habitat, range, flight patterns, and the like—as well as the coloration of the still (or stuffed) bird. Indeed, the recent publication of *The Birder's Handbook* provides a magnificent tool for the amateur bird-watcher precisely because it focuses on behavior, assuming that one also has access to the conventional guide with its pictures of plumage, size, and shape.[10]

If evolution entails a selection of behavior, for which Machiavelli's image of "picking" among alternative "natures" is a suitable metaphor, this selection must be understood as a response to the environment—and *not* some arbitrary or disembodied choice of an ideal form or shape in the abstract. Once again, Machiavelli's teaching is congruent with what we now know of evolutionary theory.

Consider the case of fortresses discussed in chapter twenty of *The Prince*. In nonhuman species, the analog can be defined as any bodily structure or behavior that provides passive defense against potential predators; in this sense, the moth's color is its "fortress" against birds that feed on insects. Whether any such defensive trait is consistent with survival cannot be demonstrated in the abstract, however: everything depends on the social as well as the physical environment. As Machiavelli puts it, "Fortresses are thus useful or not according to the times, and if they do well for you in one regard, they harm you in another" (*Prince,* ch. 20; p. 86).

SOCIAL BEHAVIOR, DOMINANCE, AND NATURAL SELECTION

The social behavior of any "beast" thus reflects a relationship between that animal, the physical environment, and other species with which it is in contact. Consider the social organization of hamadryas baboons. If we look at a typical scene of these animals (Figure 4.2), we can see a pattern of behavior: the troop is composed of smaller groups, each consisting of dominant males (physically larger than the females) surrounded by several females and their young.[11]

This pattern of spacing reflects a variety of social behaviors. The adult males seem to "herd" several females and seek to monopolize the opportunity for copulation with them. When another male approaches one of these females, the dominant male threatens him and drives him off. Should a female be tempted to move away from proximity to the dominant male, he will threaten her—and, if the threat does not suffice, bite her painfully on the neck.

Surrounding the male and these females are their young offspring. This structure, too, is the residue of species-typical behaviors. As males mature, for example, they are threatened and eventually driven away by the dominant male. As females mature, they are subsequently attracted and herded by a male as part of a one-male group. The troop as a whole is a local population of these groups, in which there are further complexities such as status differences as well as cooperative relationships between different adults.

In the literature of primatology, the one-male groups of hamadryas baboons are often called "harems"—one of the many cases of reading human social behavior back into the analysis of animals (as Thelma Rowell has pointed out so effectively).[12] The reason for avoiding such anthropomorphism is not that it implies the baboons consciously choose to form this kind of group: can we be sure, after all, that the Turkish sultan really *chose* to form a harem?

Many cultural practices can hardly be said to have been picked by the individuals who observe them. Whether or not humans really choose to form the different kinship systems described by anthropologists is as much of a question as whether some animals show intention and choice in their behavior: to know the answer, in both cases one needs careful observation and study, not arbitrary definitions and armchair dicta.[13] Conversely, it is often impossible to deny that nonhuman animals have intentions, shaping their behavior by what seems indistinguishable from human intentionality.[14]

The primary reason not to call the hamadryas one-male group a "harem" is that it implies the existence of a type or kind of social structure in the abstract. When looking at Figure 4.2, it is easy to forget that the pattern of spacing among the hamadryas reflects the savanna (the physical environment in the background of the picture) and the leopards and other predators (present but not visible) as well as the previous behaviors of individual baboons. These circumstances are as much a part of baboon social structure as the behaviors of adult male and females or infants contributing to the spatial distribution we see.

Social behavior among nonhuman animals is thus nature's solution to the problem of surviving and reproducing *in a specific albeit changing social as well as physical environment* (which is what is meant by "natural selection"). If we are trapped by Machiavelli's poetic metaphor—thinking that the lion *is* the power or the "fierce" behavior, and the fox *is* the cleverness or the "astute" behavior—we surrender the effectual truth of evolutionary biology for imagined realities. Faced with human hunters, the lion is weak and the subject of predation; faced by determined farmers defending their chickens, the fox is often trapped by snares designed for the purpose.

When social behavior is considered in this way, the issues of traditional political philosophy take on new light. Following the work of David Barash, in *The Nature of Politics* I illustrated the problem with the example of marmots.[15] The woodchuck, all too familiar as the animal who enjoys our garden peas before we pick them, does not form social groups. A related species, the Olympic Marmot, forms tightly cooperative social groups in alpine meadows high on the Olympic mountains. Why?

Living in wooded or forest environments, with dispersed food supplies and predators, woodchucks are asocial because the costs of cooperation are greater than the benefits. Food supplies are widely spread and cannot be defended or harvested more effectively by groups than by individuals. Giving a warning cry at the approach of a hawk may benefit other woodchucks, but it obviously makes it easier for the predator to locate the altruistic caller and prey on it.

Figure 4.2. Baboons on the savannah. The spatial distribution of predators, food, and other resources influences the structure of social groups within as well as between species. Hence the physical environment can be as much a factor in group formation as the species being observed. Photograph courtesy of Jeanne and Stuart Altmann and University of Chicago Alumni Magazine.

Society always has some costs—even if only the cost that one needs to attend to others. These costs are greater than the benefits for the woodchuck, but not for the Olympic marmot. High on alpine meadows, the growing season is short. The environment is, so to speak, less friendly: cooperation pays. Under these circumstances, we observe social groups.

The considerations underlying these advantages and disadvantages of social behavior are studied in the biological discipline known as "behavioral ecology."[16] When specialists speak of animals as having "strategies of survival," they do not mean that each individual woodchuck or marmot makes conscious choices; they mean that the costs and benefits of alternative social behavior can be defined and predicted by the scientific observer. And once formalized as a scientific theory, one can predict which types of behavior are more likely to arise in any particular environment.

It is no longer appropriate to ask whether human nature is *either* "selfish" *or* "altruistic." The very formulation of this question implies that social behavior is a fixed trait. Not only is this false when we consider differences between species; it is often false for a single species. Barash cites the example of the yellow-bellied marmot, intermediate between the woodchuck and Olympic marmot: for this animal, the extent of social cooperation varies depending on the altitude and microenvironment within which they are living.[17]

Behavioral ecology is thus capable of converting the philosophical question of social cooperation and competition into scientific matters of fact. Depending on food sources, predators, nesting sites, climate, and previously evolved social and bodily structures, animals will be as asocial as the woodchuck or as cooperative within the group as the Olympic marmot.

Where cooperation is beneficial, ecological factors of food supply and predation determine whether animals are likely to form one-male groups like the hamadryas, multi-male groups like those of chimpanzees, large herds like the African wildebeest, or other social patterns. It is not necessary to go to Africa to see what is involved. Among bird species that we recognize daily, as *The Birder's Handbook* shows in detail, there are wide variations in social behavior that can be explained by behavioral ecology and the theory of natural selection.

Although research in this discipline has advanced rapidly over the last twenty-five years, nonspecialists have often been confused by the claims and criticisms directed at "sociobiology." Most specifically, much attention has been directed to "reproductive success" and "inclusive fitness" in the selection of social behavior among animals. It is, we are told, impossible that such factors play the same role among humans as in other species because human behavior is freely "chosen" or determined by culture, whereas animal social life is the product of "instinct" and necessity.[18]

Reflection on Machiavelli's account of human leadership leads one to wonder. He speaks of the need to "pick" modes of behavior, but this advice to actual or potential leaders is needed because, most of the time, humans do *not* effectively choose what they do. If Machiavelli's theory has had a persistent fascination, it is because the erroneous choices of leaders, symbolized by Cesare Borgia's mistake (*Prince*, ch. 7; p. 33), remind us of this fact. If you doubt it, read the newspaper.

For Machiavelli, the human condition can only be understood if the intelligent—we would say, the scientific—observers stand back and analyze the different effects of behaviors in various circumstances. And this is exactly what the behavioral ecologist or field ethologist does in the study of animals. It would seem that consideration of the "effectual truth of the thing" requires that we keep an open mind about whether animals ever show intentionality and choice (I will show below that, by any reasonable standard, they do). Equally important, at the level of the behavior of species like the lion, the fox, or the wolf, the environmental considerations producing selfishness and social cooperation need to be studied objectively and applied to human life: even the most rational human cannot escape what Machiavelli everywhere calls "necessity."

Careful observation of the nonhuman primates, our closest animal relatives, show the importance of this point. Among chimpanzees and great apes, and even to a lesser degree among monkeys, there can no longer be a question of intentionality, choice, and some forms of consciousness.[19] It is, indeed, only fitting that biologists who study "strategic" manipulation of social behavior among primates have called these traits "Machiavellian intelligence."[20]

III. Dominance and Subordination

When we consider social life as a natural phenomenon, one of the first things that comes to light—especially among mammals—is differences in status or dominance. For Machiavelli, the lion represents "power"—the potential of using force that others find "fierce" enough to deter attack or uninvited approach. For the behavioral ecologist or ethologist, dominant status in a social group is precisely such an ability to dissuade rivals from competing for advantageous resources of food, access to females, nesting sites, and the like.

From an anthropomorphic perspective, power seems attractive. When a man looks at the scene of the hamadryas baboon (Figure 4.2) or thinks of the harem of a sultan, he often imagines the pleasures of controlling many females. From the perspective of nature, such high status is a trade-off between costs and benefits: there are always costs of dominance or power, and they must be outweighed by benefits in a specific environment. Otherwise, animals will be as asocial as the marmot or orangutan. Rousseau's critique of Hobbes in the *Second Discourse* was not without reason.

Dominance does, of course, have its benefits. Insofar as natural selection favors traits or behaviors most likely to enhance reproductive success, it is valuable to have differential access to food, copulation with fertile mates, or better nesting sites. It is not hard to see, for instance, that the dominant male in the hamadryas one-male group or the chimpanzee troop has a reproductive advantage associated with the "power" to intimidate others.

At what price? Dominance also has costs. If it is beneficial for males to gain dominant status, as among hamadryas or chimpanzees, males will compete for dominance. To become dominant, conflict—at least to the extent of threat and intimidation displays if not a battle to the death—is necessary. And the control over females by the dominant male is never perfect, since females often copulate with other, lower status males. Whenever the benefits of competition for dominance are exceeded by the costs of the entire social process, animals tend to form egalitarian flocks or loose networks, or—in environments with abundant, widely distributed food and few predators—to remain asocial.[21]

Even where animals form dominance relationships, high status has costs that are not always exceeded by the leader's benefits. The dominant individual often engages in defense of other members of the group against predators. Dominant hamadryas males have been observed to risk (and suffer) death in order to defend females and young against a leopard. And since the subordinate males also benefit from the dominant male's defense against predators, there are benefits to being of low status.

Dominant primates also engage in other social behaviors that are costly, providing benefits to the group that can be compared to collective goods. Often, the dominant male or female will engage in dispute settlement: when lower status individuals threaten each other, the conflict may be highly arousing to bystanders (as among chimpanzees). Social dominance is often associated with intervention in such squabbles, limiting the danger of aggressiveness to the benefit of those with lower status.

Because many of the benefits of dominance are shared by all members of the group and many of the costs are borne primarily by the dominant individual, status hierarchies of various types emerge as a trade-off of responses to diverse environmental circumstances. When asocial behavior or anonymous herding is not adaptive, we often see some form of social hierarchy or dominance. But even so, there can be advantages of subordinate status as well as of dominance. And in any case, the costs and benefits depend on the environment as well as on the behavior of others.

Take the apparent benefits of dominance in access to estrous females among either the one-male groups of hamadryas baboons or the multi-male groups of chimpanzees (or other species with similar social structures). The dominant male's benefit of enhanced access to estrous females is counterbalanced if subordinate males have opportunities to copulate.

As long as the dominant male is vigilant, threats directed at potential male rivals and the female target of their interest may well exclude subordinates. But the dominant male is sometimes inattentive or distracted. Subordinates can take advantage of such lapses, with the added advantage that a successful copulation transfers the cost of defending the pregnant female to what one might anthropomorphically call the "cuckold."[22]

The benefits of dominance are also related to the environment. Vigilance depends on the possibility of seeing others: one-male groups that are possible in the savanna environment of the hamadryas are not likely for chimpanzees living in forest settings. If an estrous female can momentarily escape behind the nearest bush, it will be more difficult for a dominant male to attend to a number of females. Among chimpanzees, dominant males form temporary consortships with estrous females rather than lasting one-male groups in which an individual male herds or controls the behavior of several females.

Not only the fact of rivalry, but its consequences thus depend on the environment and the "strategies" or behaviors that have evolved within it. When Machiavelli speaks of "combat" using either the "nature" of "the beasts" or that of "men," he reminds us that law is simply another mode of regulating the competition for status that we also find among nonhuman animals. And when he speaks of the leader's need to "pick" the beast to "imitate," Machiavelli points to the changing behavioral needs depending on time, place, and circumstance. Thus far, contemporary behavioral ecology seems to be a gloss on *The Prince*, telling us with more precision exactly the kind of factual information that Machiavelli himself sought to glean from his "long experience with modern things and a continuous reading of ancient ones" (*Prince*, Dedicatory Letter; p. 3).

IV. Chimpanzees, Baboons, and Orangutans

It might be objected that evolutionary theory shows that the lion or the fox have followed distinct lines of descent, far removed from hominid evolution. Many critics of popularizations of ethology by Konrad Lorenz and Robert Ardrey objected strenuously to comparisons between humans and other species as varied as birds or insects.[23] Since each animal species may develop a distinct behavioral repertoire, it is not self-evident that observations of lions can be applied to humans without deforming the evidence.

Machiavelli explicitly treats his references to nonhuman animals as a metaphor, speaking of the lion or the fox as a "person" to be imitated. Is the study of ethology and behavioral ecology merely a metaphoric or poetic way of describing human behavior, subject to all the dangers of impressionistic assessments parading in the cloak of rigorous science?

To avoid this charge, it is well to focus more precisely on the nonhuman primates. Since Darwin—and indeed, since Rousseau's *Second Discourse*—it has been evident that humans evolved from primate ancestors and thus are phylogenetically related to the other great apes. Leonardo da Vinci was already clearly aware of the kinship between humans, apes, and monkeys.[24] Because Machiavelli adopts something like an evolutionary perspective on human origins, presumably derived from such ancient texts as Lucretius or Polybius (e.g., *Discourses,* I, 2; p. 106), it is reasonable to consider the social behavior of other primates when assessing the truth of Machiavelli's theory of human nature.

If humans evolved from the anthropoid apes, our repertoire of behavior should be influenced—or in some way limited—by those traits shared by most or all surviving species of nonhuman primates. Not only are the bodily shapes, neuroanatomy, and biochemistry of monkeys and apes similar to those of humans, many behaviors among primates have been conserved across species and are found in humans as well. Those tempted to deny this fact would do well to study Eibl-Eibesfeldt's magisterial text and other research in the field called "human ethology."[25]

Facial displays, to be discussed at length in chapter five, provide an important example. Often described as "expressions" of emotions, facial gestures also serve as social signals: sometimes we smile because we are happy, but sometimes we smile merely to be polite. As Paul Ekman and his colleagues have shown, facial displays of anger, fear, sadness, surprise, and the like are accurately decoded in every known human culture.[26]

Facial expressions are thus cross-cultural universals which play a central role in defining human nature. But similar expressions are observed in monkeys and apes. Go to the zoo and watch the chimpanzees or the macaques: it is surprisingly easy to tell when individuals are threatening or curious, reassuring others or fearful of them.

Studies of nonhuman primates can thus provide useful information about animal social behavior that presumably corresponds to Machiavelli's concept of the "beast" in human behavior. Such research has the added advantage that it cannot be viewed as merely metaphor or poetic comparison. There is a difference between traits inherited from a common ancestor and similarities in different lines of descent that have evolved independently.

As specialists put it, there is a distinction between "homology" due to common ancestry and "analogy" or "parallelism." Birds and moths have wings to solve a common need to fly, but these structures evolved quite separately. In contrast, the legs of chimpanzees and humans have a similar structure reflecting descent from common primate ancestors.[27]

Since over ninety percent of the genes of chimpanzees and humans are "homologous" in this sense, the observed similarities in body shape and behavior can be supported at the genetic level. This is why many new medications are given to monkeys or apes to test whether there will be adverse side effects in humans. It is curious that critics of the comparisons between the social behavior of humans and other animals rarely challenge drug testing as a way of predicting pharmacological and even behavioral effects on humans.

There is a final advantage in turning to the social behavior of primates as a basis for exploring the natural component of human politics. Machiavelli speaks of diverse animal "natures" among which the leader ("prince") should "pick" the most appropriate and effective. But how do the traits of power or dominance, personified by the lion, relate to the defensive cleverness symbolized by the fox or the desires represented by the wolves?

The study of ethology is thus essential if we are to assess the truth of Machiavelli's theories in the light of contemporary science. Is there any pattern in the behavior of primates, or are these different traits like dishes in a cafeteria, to be chosen according to the individual's taste? Equally important, how do these elements of animal behavior relate to the way of "man," based on the "use" of "law" as an element of "combat" or social competition?

Because detailed surveys of the parallels and differences between human politics and the social behaviors of nonhuman primates are available,[28] this discussion will focus on two elements of behavior: the cues providing information in social interaction and the resulting patterns of social organization. Each level of analysis reveals traits common to virtually all nonhuman primates and likely to underlie human social behavior.

HEDONIC AND AGONIC MODES OF BEHAVIOR

In *The Expression of the Emotions in Man and Animals* (1872),[29] Darwin stressed what he called the "principle of antithesis." Display behaviors that are associated with opposed functions or consequences will tend to have diametrically opposite features. If the dog wags his tail when happy or content, this display is likely to be absent in a canine threat display; if the ears are forward and erect in threat, they are likely to be relaxed in expressions of happiness (Figure 4.3).

As Darwin went on to show, there is no one display which communicates reassurance, threat, or fear across all species. Cats tend to wag their tails immediately before pouncing on prey or when otherwise aroused and threatening. Indeed, for a series of bodily displays, dogs and cats have diametrically opposed cues when threatening others or when showing happiness and reassurance in relation to their masters.

The nonverbal behavior of animals therefore forms a *system* of cues. In studying primates, Michael Chance focused on two sets of oppositions in order to analyze more completely the structure of these behaviors. One, which he called "agonic," is associated with competition, threat, and fear; the other, "hedonic," concerns reassurance, pleasure, and bonding.[30]

In most mammals, and especially primates, natural selection has, quite predictably, made it relatively easy for one animal to tell the difference between threat and fear or submission. Cues of threat or aggressiveness are typically opposite to those of fearfulness and submission, as is clear when a dog or cat threatens another (Figure 4.3). In this case, for example, the tail and hair are erect in the threat display, and down as cues of fear and submission.

What Machiavelli calls "combat" or rivalry for power obviously corresponds to what ethologists call the "agonic" mode of behavior. The "fierce" traits that Machiavelli associates with the lion are thus associated with "agonic" social displays, such as the response to threat with counter-threat. As we will see below, the advice that leaders imitate the lion cannot be dissociated from the prediction that the prince is most secure when subjects "fear" him without "hatred" (*Prince*, ch. 17; pp. 66–67).

Among nonhuman primates, however, most social behavior is not competitive at all. For example, in over twenty years of observing chimpanzees, Jane Goodall reports that males initiated aggressive interactions in only 1.6 percent of the observation hours—and that such behaviors were seen in females during only 0.6 percent of the observed time. Social bonding, grooming, reassurance, play, and other positive or intrinsically pleasurable behaviors are essential components of the primate behavioral repertoire and actually make up the largest proportion of the behavior of chimpanzees.[31]

Ethologists like Chance describe these behaviors as "hedonic." Such hedonic or pleasurable behavior typically entails lower levels of arousal than competition and rivalry. Hedonic displays are, moreover, characterized by cues that are dramatically different from the entire dimension of threat and fear associated with agonistic behavior.

In social psychology, a parallel distinction is made between "positive" and "negative" emotions, which can be related to positive and negative reinforcement—or, more broadly, to pleasure and pain.[32] But unlike the older formulation of the utilitarians, the ethologists' distinction between "hedonic" or socially pleasurable and "agonic" or competitive behavior can be defined objectively, observed, and measured.

Nonverbal displays are not, however, simple all-or-none signals like a dot or a dash in Morse Code. Rather, they are expressions that admit of more or less intensity (technically called analog as distinct from digital signals). As a result, hedonic (or social pleasurable) and agonic (or competitive) behaviors need to be understood as independent dimensions that can be blended in a variety of subtle combinations.[33]

Hedonic behaviors are typically associated with the formation of bonds between individuals. They also characterize reassurance or calming behavior, most especially after competitive interactions. As Figure 4.4 indicates, we have no difficulty perceiving this type of social behavior among chimpanzees and other primates.

For example, agonic cues—whether of threat and aggression or of fear and submission—tend to involve rigid body postures and abrupt movements. Head positions tend to be vertical and characterized by fixed eye contact or total aversion of face and eyes. In contrast, hedonic behavior

Figure 4-3: Darwin's Illustration of Threat and Appeasement Displays of Dogs and Cats, reproduced from Charles Darwin, *The Expression of the Emotions in Man and Animals* (Chicago: University of Chicago Press, 1965), Figures 7–10, pp. 54–55, 58–59. In each pair, the top illustration is threat, the bottom is appeasement.

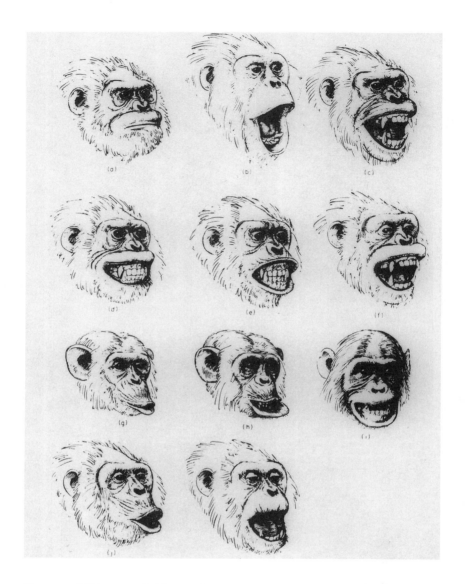

Figure 4.4. "Chimpanzee facial expressions: (a) 'Glare'; anger, type 1; (b) 'waa bark': anger, type 2; (c) 'scream calls': fear-anger; (d) 'silent bared teeth': 'type 1, horizontal bared-teeth' submission; (e) 'silent bared teeth': 'type 2, vertical bared-teeth': fear-affection (?); (f) 'silent bared teeth': 'type 3, open-mouthed bared teeth': affection; (g) 'pout face': desiring-frustration (?); (h) 'whimper face': frustration-sadness (?), type 1 or type 1–2 transition (infant); (i) 'cry face': frustration-sadness, type 2 (infant); (j) 'hoot face': excitement-affection (?); (k) 'play face': playfulness." From I. Eibl-Eibesfeldt, *Human Ethology* (New York: Aldine de Gruyter, 1989), 470; figure originally from *Darwin and Facial Expressions*, ed. P. Ekman (Orlando, Fla.: Academic Press, 1973), used with permission.

entails smoother or more fluid motions, brief eye contact broken by looking away and then resumed, and the head is tilted from side to side. As Jan van Hooff showed in a survey of the facial displays of monkeys and apes, a number of such cues are common throughout the primate family and can be observed in humans as well.[34]

For Machiavelli, "those who stay simply with the lion" do not "understand" the need for the cleverness personified by the fox (*Prince*, ch. 18; p. 69). That cleverness is apparently manifested most particularly in the extent to which a "prudent lord" should "observe faith." Interestingly enough, however, Machiavelli does not suggest an animal personification of keeping faith; keeping faith is by implication the "nature" associated with the "kind of combat" that is "with laws" and "proper to man" (ibid.).

What Machiavelli describes as the difference between "man" and "beast" thus seems to parallel Michael Chance's distinction between "hedonic" and "agonic" behavior in the social interactions of nonhuman primates. The different "natures" that Machiavelli associates with different species (lion, fox, wolves, man) are thus elements of a behavioral repertoire organized around the distinction between hedonic or positive and agonic or competitive behavior, with the latter in turn divided into threat or dominance and fear or submissiveness.

That Machiavelli himself saw the human condition in these terms is clear from his discussion of the "friendships" of the prince in chapter eighteen. In contemporary terms, friendship reflects the social bonds associated with hedonic behavior among nonhuman primates. For Machiavelli, such relationships are characterized by "love" and contrasted to "fear" and "hatred" of the prince by his subjects.

> And men have less hesitation to offend one who makes himself loved than one who makes himself feared; for *love* is held by a chain of obligation, which, because men are wicked, is broken at every opportunity for their own utility, but *fear* is held by a dread of punishment that never forsakes you.
>
> The prince should nonetheless make himself *feared* in such a mode that if he does not acquire *love*, he escapes *hatred*, because *being feared and not being hated can go together very well*. (*Prince*, ch. 17; pp. 66–67)

The triad of love, hatred, and fear—corresponding to social relationships of obligation or friendship, power, and subordination—characterizes Machiavelli's theory of leadership and human nature. It also corresponds to basic elements in the behavioral repertoire of our nearest evolutionary relatives, the monkeys and apes.

Different species, however, show diverse ways of organizing reassurance, threat, and fear. Baboon social interactions are characterized by a higher proportion of agonic interactions, whereas chimpanzees more frequently engage in hedonic behaviors. Patterns of organizing social life can thus be described, in part, by the frequency with which a group of animals exhibits hedonic or agonic displays and emotions.[35]

These differences in modes of behavior are also associated with problem solving. When animals are highly aroused, whether in competitive or hedonic interactions, learning is less likely to occur. This is most particularly the case when an individual is highly fearful or terrorized. In contrast, mild fear or anxiety, capable of inciting the comparison of alternatives (and thereby inhibiting enthusiastic pleasure without generating terror) facilitates learning.[36]

Teachers often have had similar experiences. Students who are relaxed and self-confident but concerned about how well they will do on the examination are, all things considered, much more likely to be successful than those who are either terrorized and fearful or enthusiastically engaged in social (or sexual) behavior.

These considerations suggest that Machiavelli's mode of presentation may have misled readers in one important respect. The categories of behavior set forth in *The Prince* seem to correspond quite exactly to those defined by contemporary ethologists and psychologists. But when Machiavelli personifies these categories as different "natures," symbolized or personified by different animals, he generally associates bonding or hedonic behavior, love, and obligation with "man" as contrasted with the competitive elements of "force" and "astuteness" attributed to animals like the lion and the fox.

It would be incorrect to conclude that the difference between competition (Figure 4.5) and bonding (Figure 4.6) corresponds with the conventional nature-nurture dichotomy—or, more broadly, with actual differences between humans and nonhuman animals. Although Machiavelli describes competition as the way of the "beast," he uses the fox to personify learning, intelligence, or astuteness (today often attributed to humans as distinct from animals). Machiavelli associates the fox's "cleverness" with the animal component of human nature, whereas contemporary critics of comparisons between humans and animals treat such traits as uniquely human.

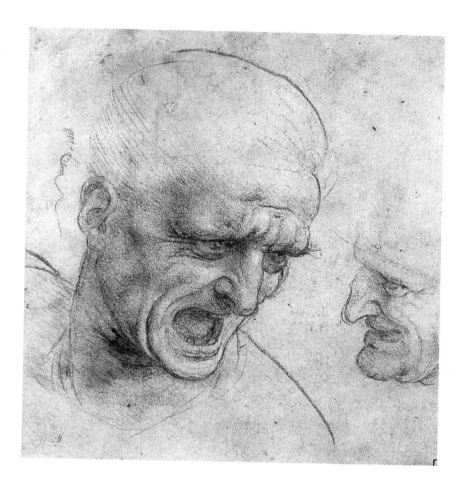

Figure 4.5. Leonardo da Vinci, Head of Man Shouting, sketch for *Battle of Anghiari* (c. 1505) black and red chalk, 7 1/2 x 7 1/8 inches (19.2 x 18.8 cm). Courtesy of Szépmüvészeti Muzeum, Museum of Fine Arts, Budapest. Threat display of brows accentuates the aggressive effects of shouting.

Figure 4.6. Leonardo da Vinci, *Virgin and Child with St. Anne and a Lamb* (c. 1508), oil on wood panel , 66 1/8 x 44 inches (168 x 112 cm). Courtesy of Musée du Louvre, Paris. Notice affiliative displays on all three faces as well as St. Anne's touching gesture.

In other words, Machiavelli makes it seem that the specifically human element in human nature is social bonding or obligation. But this is his poetic or symbolic presentation of the behavioral repertoire, and not a descriptive analysis of the difference between human and nonhuman species.[37] If Machiavelli expects anything of his most intelligent human students, it is their ability to learn the astuteness of the fox on the basis of reading and thinking about *The Prince.*

Machiavelli's distinction between man and beast is, thus, very different from that in Hobbes and later thinkers. It is as if Hobbes took the Machiavellian distinction, intended as a Beatrix Potter–like personification of traits, to be a literal description of the fact that animals are not sociable beings who form bonds or obligations with others. And since, for Hobbes, it is impossible to make contracts with "beasts," the man-animal contrast takes on a different tone in Hobbesian thought—a tone that has tended to characterize political philosophy ever since.[38]

V. *Political Leadership from Machiavelli to Konrad Lorenz*

It was remarked above that ethologists view primate social behavior in terms of underlying dimensions or theoretically derived categories. Whereas Machiavelli seems to list distinct "natures" and passions in a descriptive manner, contemporary scientists define agonic and hedonic modes of interaction and seek to trace this distinction in the display behavior (or the neurochemistry, neurophysiology, genetics, or individual experience) of animals.

In addition to the distinction between hedonic and agonic modes of behavior, ethologists have another dimension of social interaction that differs from one species or group to another. In some primate species, a single individual serves as the center of the attentional focus of other members of a group. In others, attentional patterns take a different form.

The ethologist Michael Chance describes this dimension as the difference between "acentric" and "centric" attention structures. By this he merely means that one can observe the extent to which group members focus their attention on a single individual, particularly at moments of indecision or arousal. More recently sociologists have spoken of the difference between loose social "networks" and more rigid dominance structures.[39]

The more that the focus of attention is limited to a single individual at such times, the more that individual seems likely to play a dominant role in the group. Such a definition of dominance diverges from the character-istic concept of power as differential control over resources. Or rather, as the center of the group's attentional structure, the leader controls the at-tention of others—a social resource that is sometimes more important than food or shelter.

Some primate species are more tightly organized around a focus on a common individual; others are less so. Where animals are described as asocial, as in the orangutan—those great apes in Borneo whose social be-havior is as diffuse as the woodchuck—one can say that attention structures are acentric. That is, animals tend to avoid each other rather than to gaze at or attend to their fellows.

In contrast, baboons form attention structures that tend to be focused primarily on the one-male groups that are tightly bonded by agonic dis-plays. Rhesus macaques form hierarchical multi-male groups, in which flows or patterns of attention generally parallel the structure of status.

Chimpanzees seem intermediate. The dominant male is periodically a center of attention, but hedonic behavior comes to play a more central role in behavior, particularly as the adult matures. Such a social system makes possible more fluid group patterns and more complex associative learning among chimpanzees than for baboons or rhesus monkeys. Marked in the common chimpanzee (*Pongo pongo*), this pattern of a changing network of bonds is even more pronounced in the bonobos or pygmy chimpanzees, a species which has only recently been studied with care.[40]

Machiavelli's concept of leadership among humans can thus be related to the tendency of nonhuman primates to form dominance hierarchies as-sociated with patterns of attention. In the nonhuman primates, leadership arises when environmental circumstances make group coordination or de-fense beneficial. For the orangutan as for the woodchuck, the ecological setting makes asocial behavior more adaptive than bonded groups; in other primates, there are varied degrees of social integration depending on both the species' traits and the population's physical environment.

Where the environment favors group formation among primates, leadership can be described as natural. And, at least among chimpanzees, as Frans de Waal has shown in detail, the greater intelligence of the species makes possible not only the formation of coalitions, but deception, planning, and even something akin to political murder and warfare.

The group sizes of nonhuman primates are, however, generally limited to less than one hundred. Small face-to-face bands, like those of human hunter-gatherers, do not have formal governments or political officers. In such simple human societies, there is an informal leader who can be abandoned or challenged at any time. Insofar as the way of the man is associated with "law," the "natures" described by ethologists are clearly insufficient to explain the origin of the state based on a centralized government.

In humans, according to Machiavelli, leadership requires a mixture of intelligence and power. It is based on desires, and particularly the desire for glory, which Machiavelli seeks to channel into the quest for immortal fame for the exceptional prince or founder—and into rivalry for power under the law for most men. But these attributes are necessary because, for Machiavelli, the state is unstable and must be founded by an extraordinary act.

In order to move beyond Machiavelli's treatment of the "beast" to a fuller consideration of the human condition, it is therefore necessary to study the state. Machiavelli apparently views the institution of a centralized government and written legal system, while symbolized by the "natures" unique to humans, to be somehow "unnatural." Is this so? It is to the status of government and law—that which Machiavelli considers the specifically human things—that we now turn.

Subsequent modern thinkers from Hobbes and Locke to Rousseau focused on this problem by conceiving of a "state of nature" in which no government or state exists. For Hobbes, this condition was a "war of all against all" because humans seek only power; for Locke it is epitomized by the peaceful interaction of small groups in the woods of America (where mutually beneficial exchanges are subject to the "inconvenience" of degenerating into a Hobbesian state of war); for Rousseau, in contrast, the state of nature is a condition of isolated, asocial individuals "without war and without liaison," unable to speak, unlikely to cooperate, and even less likely to compete.

Are these formulations superior to Machiavelli's more elusive and more symbolic analysis of human politics as a combination of the "natures" of both the "beast" and "man," with the beast-like principles in turn personified by the fox, the lion, and wolves?[41] In assessing this question, we will have particular reason to focus on the role of individual leadership, so central to Machiavelli but muted in Rousseau and largely absent in the theories of Hobbes and Locke.

Chapter Five

Using the Man: The Biological Nature of the State

To preserve Nature's chiefest boon, that is freedom, I can find means of offence and defence, when it [the state] is assailed by ambitious tyrants, and first I will speak of the situation of the walls, and also I shall show how communities can maintain their good and just Lords.
Leonardo da Vinci[1]

Machiavelli's thought rests on a subtle notion of human nature. He sees traits and passions like those of other animals combined with the uniquely human attributes of language, self-consciousness, and foresight. Recent studies confirm his view that human leadership exhibits many characteristics that we share with nonhuman primates as well as some not found in other animals. Without an understanding of our animal heritage, political or social projects are likely to fail—or at best to have quite unintended consequences.[2]

Evolutionary biology supports Machiavelli's argument that political science needs to consider *both* what he called the "beast" and the "man." Although contemporary ethology modifies Machiavelli's views of our mammalian heritage in some details, it confirms his position on a central point. Governments and laws—for Machiavelli, "the state" (*lo stato*)—are not found among animals. Without language and the capacities related to it, political institutions do not exist.[3]

An obvious illustration is the size of social groups in humans as contrasted with other animals. Human societies with centralized governments, while varied in other respects, are enormous compared to the bands of 50 to 100 individuals which are the largest groups usually found among nonhuman primates. The existence of governments ruling populations of thousands, not to mention millions, is a phenomenon that needs to be explained.[4]

To be sure, very large aggregations of animals sometimes come together for mutual benefit. "Flocks of a million or more starlings and blackbirds" are not uncommon, and roosts of the "Red-billed Quelea," an African bird, "may number tens of millions of individuals." Older and younger individuals of the same species, and even different kinds of birds, may "join communal roosts for different reasons," including defense from predation, "information" about food sources or the environment, and perhaps warmth.[5]

These flocks or "colonies" do not explain institutions like the centralized government or state for a number of reasons:

- Although very large roosting colonies are found in a few species of birds, they do not tend to occur among mammals and are never observed in primates.
- Nothing in the evidence of hominid evolution stretching back several million years to our australopithecine ancestors indicates groups larger than a band of 50–100 members prior to the emergence of domestication within the last 20,000 years.
- Among pre-literate bands and villages of human hunter-gatherers—or, to use the term preferred by some to reflect the food supplies provided by women, "gatherer-hunters"—groups rarely exceed 100 or 200 members.
- The emergence of large human populations in the early civilizations occurred in river valleys, such as the Tigris and Euphrates (Mesopotamia) and Nile (Egypt), when agriculture, domesticated animals, social stratification, centralized governments, and writing transformed the human condition; similar phenomena were observed in China and India.[6]
- Even in the New World, the independent development of states seems to coincide with radical transformations of both the natural environment and human social structure, contrasting sharply with the mode of livelihood and social patterns of human hunter-gatherers and nonhuman primates.
- For the longest period of human history, population increases led to the splitting up of groups; in classical antiquity, even after the formation of governments, city-states responded to growing num-

bers by sending out "colonies" to occupy new territory.[7] Humans seem to have had a deeply rooted propensity to avoid the formation of large groups.

○ The animal societies most comparable to the human state occur among social insects, like those bees and ants living in complex communities with social stratification, coordinated activity, and a division of labor; these social systems depend on a biology of mating among insects, technically known as "haplo-diploid," that is totally different from that found in mammals.[8]

○ The centralized state differs from animal societies in the extent to which individuals can be coerced to obey lasting rules established by a small group of individuals, whose members usually gain some material advantages from their specialized positions of power or authority.

Whatever the case for birds and insects, humans (like other large mammals) evolved as a species that "naturally" live in small and dispersed groups whose members only cooperate with others in the band. From an evolutionary perspective, therefore, the existence of centralized states with large populations is a *biological* puzzle.

Machiavelli was acutely aware of this problem. Although he wrote over three centuries before Darwin, his understanding of the origin of the state is not inconsistent with evolutionary theory: "These variations of government among men are due to chance. For *in the beginning of the world, when its inhabitants were few, they lived for a time scattered like the beasts*" (*Discourses*, I, 2; p. 106).

Machiavelli's use of the phrase "the beginning of the world" need not imply the biblical view that humans were present from the seventh day of creation. In *Discourses*, II, 5 (pp. 289–290), he endorses the view that the world is very old if not eternal, asserting that there have been periodic natural disasters in the form of floods, pestilence, and famine that destroy most of the living populations (see above, chapter three). Machiavelli explains these events with what seems like a crude version of what Stephen Jay Gould and others have called the evolutionary model of "punctuated equilibria": "when nature has accumulated too much superfluous material, it frequently acts . . . by means of a purge [that] restores health to the body" (*Discourses*, II, 5; p. 290).[9]

What we call the state transforms our earlier social life, creating a "mixed" or compound body different from the "simple bodies" of individuals (ibid.).

According to Machiavelli, this transition is associated with population increases, the need for defense from other groups, and leadership based on individual boldness or physical prowess: "with the *multiplication of their offspring, they drew together* and, in order the better to be able *to defend themselves*, began to look about for a man stronger and more courageous than the rest, *made him their head, and obeyed him*" (*Discourses*, I, 2; p. 107). Later, after "men learned how to distinguish what is honest and good from what is pernicious and wicked, . . . they took to *making laws and to assigning punishments* to those who contravened them. The notion of justice thus came into being" (ibid.).

For Machiavelli, then, there was historical evolution from dispersed animal life to groups with leaders, the development of language and self-awareness, and ultimately governments based on laws and punishments. What is the difference between these premises and those of others who share Machiavelli's view of human nature? And how does a contemporary scientific understanding of the origins and nature of political institutions compare to this account?

I. Human Nature and Selfishness: The Sophists, Machiavelli, and Hobbes

In the *Discourses*, Machiavelli makes an apparently astounding remark:

> *All writers on politics* have pointed out, and throughout history there are plenty of examples which indicate, that in constituting and legislating for a commonwealth *it must needs be taken for granted* that *all men are wicked* and that they will *always* give vent to the malignity that is in their minds *when opportunity offers.* (*Discourses*, I, 3; pp. 111–112)

This does not mean that all men *are* wicked, particularly in sense of Judeo-Christian "original sin"; rather, as noted in chapter three, political leaders should take it "for granted" that human promises are *unreliable* and will be violated "when opportunity offers." Because there are "so many who are not good" (*Prince*, ch. 15; p. 61), Machiavelli claims that "*all* writers on politics" have begun from this assumption.

Machiavelli does not claim any novelty for his view of human selfishness and shortsightedness. If his thought opened a "new way," it was surely not for the view that humans are primarily animals concerned with their own self-interest. Among his contemporaries, for example, Leonardo was particularly scathing in his assessment of human behavior.[10]

Much the same view of human selfishness can be found at the origins of Western political thought in the teaching of the pre-Socratics. Of particular relevance is the elaboration of a theory of individual hedonism by the Greek Sophists. While perhaps best known in the speeches of Thrasymachus in Plato's *Republic*, this position had been spelled out by a number of thinkers; Plato's Socrates is thus responding to what had become a widely held view of human nature in early Greek political thought.[11] To understand Machiavelli's theory of human nature and politics, it is useful to reconsider its origins in ancient Greece.

The extant fragments of Antiphon the Sophist's treatise *On Truth* provide a good example of the antecedents of Machiavelli's position. According to Antiphon, justice is a human "convention" that violates individual self-interest:

> A man, therefore, would practise justice in the way most advantageous to himself if, in the presence of witnesses, he held the laws in high esteem, but, in the absence of witnesses, and when he was by himself, he held in high esteem the rules of nature. The reason is that the *rules of the laws are adventitious, while the rules of nature are inevitable*; and again that the *rules of the laws are created by covenant and not produced by nature*, while the rules of the nature are exactly the reverse.[12]

By "nature," individuals seek individual pleasure and the avoidance of pain. Actions are "inimical to nature," according to Antiphon, if "they involve more suffering when less is possible, less pleasure when more is possible, and injury when freedom from injury is possible."[13]

In this view, justice and law are "restraints on nature" which have been accepted as a necessary evil. Humans have agreed to "laws" only because their absence led to conflict; if one can violate legal rules with impunity, it is natural to do so. Antiphon's proof is that a man "who transgresses legal rules, is free from shame and punishment whenever he is unobserved by those who made the covenant"; in contrast, when someone violates "natural" principles, "the evil consequences are none the less, if he is entirely unobserved, and none the greater, if he is seen of all men."[14]

Machiavelli's surprising claim that "all writers" have begun from this assumption of human selfishness might be justified by the importance given to the Sophist view by Socrates and those influenced by his teaching. In Plato's *Republic*, for example, Glaucon summarizes the Sophist challenge to Socrates very accurately:

> they say that doing *injustice is naturally good*, and *suffering injustice bad*, but that the bad in suffering injustice far exceeds the good in doing

it; so that, when they do injustice to one another and suffer it and taste
of both, it seems *profitable*—to those who are not able to escape the one
and choose the other—to *set down a compact* among themselves neither
to do injustice nor to suffer it.[15]

Glaucon's statement agrees with the texts of Antiphon and other
Sophists: if a "just man" is given "license to do whatever he wants," he
will commit "injustice" just as the ancestor of Gyges did after discovering
a ring that made him invisible.[16]

While Plato, Aristotle, and the schools that followed them claim there
is a justice "according to nature," these ancient critics of the Sophists
typically argued that education and training are needed to practice virtue.[17]
Pagan philosophers were thus aware of the problem of selfishness and the
obstacles it poses in the formation of cities. And, of course, the Christian
doctrine of original sin provides a different explanation for the expectation
that humans will violate the laws whenever it is in their self-interest to
do so.[18]

After Machiavelli, the emphasis on human selfishness came to be the
foundation of a major tradition in Western political thought. For Hobbes,
as for the Sophists, human societies are the result of a "contract" or agreement among selfish individuals whose obedience depends on perceived
self-interest. As transformed by Locke, these premises underlie the theory
of a social contract among individuals endowed with a "natural right"
to "life, liberty, and property"—or, in the terms used by Jefferson in the
Declaration of Independence, "inalienable" rights to "life, liberty, and
the pursuit of happiness."

Machiavelli's theory of the state thus begins from assumptions that can
be traced to the origins of Western political thought, and which have persisted to our own times. Moreover, the view that governments rest on a
calculus of costs and benefits (or utility) by naturally self-interested individuals has persisted as one of the major approaches in the social sciences.
It is therefore particularly important to consider how contemporary scientists reassess the origin of the centralized state in relation to this view of
human nature.

II. The "Prisoner's Dilemma" and the Limits of Cooperation

In contemporary biology, the problem of selfishness necessarily arises when
evolutionary theorists try to explain helping or cooperation among ani-

mals. If behavior has been shaped by natural selection, neo-Darwinian theory predicts that individuals should compete for scarce resources rather than share. Of two animals, the one who sacrificed in order to help others would be the less likely to survive and thus pass on genes to future generations. Helping or giving something useful to another at a cost to oneself—often called "altruism" by biologists[19]—would therefore seem to be eliminated by natural selection.

Although the element of competition in nature was stressed by Darwin himself, it is only recently that the principle of natural selection has been used to analyze social behavior more rigorously. Formalized by William D. Hamilton,[20] this approach is often called "sociobiology"—a term popularized by Edward O. Wilson.[21] While many critics have been particularly vocal in asserting that this theory necessarily implies genetic determinism and is vitiated by ideological bias,[22] in fact the approach merely applies a cost-benefit approach, like that of the Sophists or of Machiavelli, to the analysis of animal behavior.[23] For this reason, a number of economists have pointed out that the theories of their discipline are formally identical to the neo-Darwinian theory of natural selection.[24]

This approach to the problem of social cooperation is widely known from a model in game theory known as the "Prisoner's Dilemma." The model assumes two individuals who calculate rationally to maximize their benefits, whether by increasing gains or reducing losses. This formalization has also been used by biologists, however, since it applies to any two organisms that act *as if* they maximize individual benefits—and natural selection is presumed to favor individuals whose behavior does precisely this.[25]

The general situation is described by Diagram 5.1. Two individuals (*A* and *B*) can either cooperate with each other or behave selfishly. But if their behavior is determined separately, as would be the case if each "chooses" a "strategy" independently, there can be four possible outcomes: *A* and *B* both cooperate (mutual benefit), *A* cooperates but *B* does not (from *A*'s perspective, the path of "virtue," revealingly called the "sucker's" strategy by many game theorists); *A* doesn't cooperate but *B* does (selfishness from *A*'s point of view, often called the strategy of "defecting" or "cheating"), or neither cooperates (mutual harm or conflict).

Probably the best-known model of this sort is the Prisoner's Dilemma, in which two individuals who cannot communicate with each other must choose between different strategies. The outcome of each combination of strategies is measured by a presumed "pay-off." The particularity of the

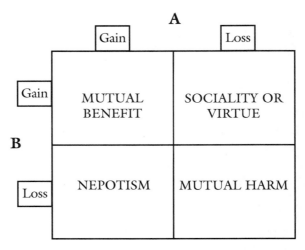

Diagram 5.1: Four Types of Social Behavior, based on classifications of W. D. Hamilton, E. O. Wilson, D. Barash, and others. (From Roger D. Masters, *Nature of Politics* [New Haven, Conn.: Yale University Press, 1989], 156. © Yale University Press. Used with permission.)

Prisoner's Dilemma arises from the relative values of these outcomes: for each individual, the benefits of cheating are highest, followed by cooperating, and then by mutual harm, with virtue (or the "sucker" pay-off) having the worst outcome.

In the Prisoner's Dilemma, although cooperation has greater joint benefits than any other outcome, because each individual calculates independently, both are led to behave selfishly. The result, paradoxically, is the worst of all outcomes for the two jointly. A typical matrix for this game theoretical model is presented in Diagram 5.2.[26]

Biologists, game theorists, economists, and political scientists have noted many situations that resemble the Prisoner's Dilemma.[27] As in Hobbes's "war of all against all," it is often not cost-effective to cooperate because others are so likely to exploit the outcome. If one is not sure of reciprocity or sharing, the path of "virtue" seems indeed to be that of the "sucker." And, needless to add, this is precisely the class of situations that Machiavelli claims the statesman ought "always" to expect.

Those who have studied the logic of the Prisoner's Dilemma have shown a number of ways out of the "trap." Robert Axelrod has long emphasized the role of repeated "plays" of the game under circumstances in which the roles of cooperation ("virtue") and cheating ("selfishness")

A's Strategy

	Silent	Talk
Silent	A = +9 B = +9 MUTUAL BENEFIT	A = +10 B = −10 NEPOTISM*
Talk	A = −10 B = +10 SOCIALITY OR VIRTUE	A = −9 B = −9 MUTUAL HARM

B's Strategy

Diagram 5.2: Prisoner's Dilemma: Nonkin. "Game matrix for a typical Prisoner's Dilemma. Assumptions. Two person game in which communication or behavioral coercion between A and B is impossible and payoffs are transitive and commensurable (cheating > cooperating > joint punishment > virtue or being a 'sucker'—or, to use conventionally adopted symbols, T > R > P > S). It is also necessary that 'the positive effect of cooperation on the fitness of the recipient must exceed its negative effects on the fitness of the donor. This condition implies that R > (T+S)/2 > P (Boyd 1988, 214). In this example, T (cheating) = +10; R (cooperating) = +9; P (punishment) = −9; S (virtue) = −10. Nepotism (private self-interest—here 'cheating' by talking when other is silent) and sociality (virtue—here being silent while the other talks) are defined in terms of A's payoffs." (From Roger D. Masters, *Nature of Politics* [New Haven, Conn.: Yale University Press, 1989], 152. © Yale University Press. Used with permission.)

might be reversed in the future.[28] In such instances, individuals seem to learn modes of reciprocity. Called "reciprocal altruism" by Robert Trivers, and either "direct" or "indirect reciprocity" by Richard D. Alexander, all that seems needed is a repeated series of Prisoner's Dilemma situations in which individuals can remember the outcome of preceding games.[29]

In Axelrod's computer simulations of repeated games of Prisoner's Dilemma, the best strategy usually is tit-for-tat. A rational player does best over the long run by cooperating in the first game and then choosing, in each following game, a strategy based on what the rival did in the prior game: cooperate if that player cooperated; be selfish if that player was selfish. Such phenomena can be observed in the behavior of nonhuman animals, indicating that the logic of the situation is not dependent on conscious calculation.[30]

Other devices can also lead to cooperation. Whereas Axelrod focuses on repetitions of the same game, Trivers pointed to a single situation when future role reversal is possible. It costs more than it benefits me to rescue a drowning man, but if the circumstances are likely to be reversed in the future, it becomes beneficial to reciprocate. Alexander and others broadened the point by showing how cooperation may arise not only from direct reciprocity, but from the "indirect" reciprocity due to reputation. If a bystander is watching, my failure to save the drowning man, once known to a broader community, may have substantial costs.

These considerations explain many paradoxes in human behavior. With insight and elegance, Robert Frank has shown how the capacity to communicate emotion through facial expressions and other nonverbal behavior can be a mechanism for enhancing the probability of social cooperation. If it is difficult to control these emotional expressions, a signal of each individual's disposition is akin to communication between the jail cells of a Prisoner's Dilemma. Emotions can make it "rational" to keep one's commitments to help others—or to resist passing temptations against one's long-term self-interest.[31]

Finally, but from the perspective of evolutionary theorists most important of all, kinship provides another reason why competing individuals might cooperate without violating the principles of natural selection.[32] Natural selection concerns the transmission of genes to future generations, not "survival of the fittest" in the sense of the strongest, toughest, or nastiest (as Social Darwinists believed in the last century). What is called "fitness" is merely "reproductive success" compared to others. And because kin share genes, one way of contributing to "reproductive success" is to help close relatives.[33]

Elsewhere, I have symbolized this by recomputing the outcomes in a Prisoner's Dilemma between full siblings (Diagram 5.3). Since kin share genes, each gains a proportion of the other's benefit represented by the "coefficient of relatedness" (that is, the proportion of genes that are identical by descent). Since full brothers, for example, share fifty percent of their genes, one-half of an individual's benefit accrues to a brother helping him; hence the evolutionary process known as kin selection can lead to cooperation in many (but not all) potentially competitive situations.[34]

A's Strategy

	Silent	Talk
Silent	A = +13.5 B = +13.5 MUTUAL BENEFIT	A = +5 B = −5 NEPOTISM*
Talk	A = −5 B = +5 SOCIALITY OR VIRTUE	A = −13.5 B = −13.5 MUTUAL HARM

B's Strategy

Diagram 5.3: Prisoner's Dilemma: Kin "Game martix for Prisoner's Dilemma with same assumptions as in Figure 5.2, except that participants are kin (either full siblings or parent-offspring) with a coefficient of relatedness of r =.5. Hence in each cell, A adds .5 of B's payoff in Figure 5.2 to his own payoff, and B does the same for A's payoffs. *As in Figure 5.2, nepotism (private self-interest) and sociality (virtue) are defined in terms of A's payoff." (From Roger D. Masters, Nature of Politics [New Haven, Conn.: Yale University Press, 1989], 166. © Yale University Press. Used with permission.)

It is little wonder, then, that family groups are likely to cooperate—especially when threatened by nonkin. Nor should it be surprising that the terms of kinship are applied to political communities (citizens as "children" of the "fatherland," and hence as "brothers"). During millions of years of hominid evolution, considerations of self-interest limited human groups to bands of approximately 50 to 100; for most of human experience, socially cooperative populations rarely exceeded the size of groups among social mammals.

Evolutionary theory thus confirms Machiavelli's perspective. It seems reasonable to say of early humans, as he does, that "in the beginning of the world, when its inhabitants were few, they lived for a time scattered like the beasts." If so, how did human politics emerge in groups of hunter-gatherers like those presumed to have existed as the australopithecines evolved to *Homo erectus* and eventually *Homo sapiens*? Why is it that, when Western explorers as colonists encountered the indigenous peoples of

Africa and America, they so often found small bands and tribes without settled governments (or what anthropologists call "stateless societies")?

III. Politics in Stateless Societies

Machiavelli's emphasis on the artificial character of the centralized "state," although confirmed by contemporary evolutionary biology, had long been evident to those who observed so-called "primitive" (or more accurately, pre-literate) peoples. From Plato's image of the "city of sows" or the "healthy" city[35] to Rousseau's graphic account of "savage society" as the condition that was "best for man,"[36] many political philosophers have suggested the advantages of the simpler human communities which preceded the centralized state. If we are to assess Machiavelli's account of the origins and fate of "republics and principalities," it is necessary to consider the politics of "stateless societies."

According to evolutionary theory, individuals in small, face-to-face groups numbering 50 to 100 should engage in a combination of cooperative and competitive behaviors. Individuals who are naturally "selfish" will nonetheless cooperate with close kin on many occasions. More important, as soon as they develop memory, individual recognition of others in the group, and language, it is to be expected that reputations will matter. What Richard Alexander calls "indirect reciprocity"—cooperation with others in a group sharing a web of interactions—can easily extend to bands of the size observed among hunter-gatherers.

One of the principal mechanisms for enforcing social cooperation within such groups is ostracism.[37] If members of a group can identify those who fail to return favors and do not help others, and reject them (even by merely withholding routine social greetings), great pressures for group solidarity are created. While this process can be modeled mathematically as a Prisoner's Dilemma with a number of participants (the so-called "n-person Prisoner's Dilemma"), the practices of actual stateless societies are probably of more relevance.

In the Hobbesian "war of all against all," self-interested individuals compete with each other "excepting the governance of small families, the concord whereof dependeth on natural lust." Although Hobbes claimed that the savages of America illustrated his account of the state of nature, careful descriptions of such societies provide a very different picture. While occasional violence is observed in stateless societies, the evidence does not confirm that nature has "dissociated" men and made them "apt to invade" one another.[38] Stateless societies actually reveal a subtle pattern of competition and cooperation in which the individual resort to aggression is constrained by kinship, by reciprocity, and by custom.[39] Even feuding relationships between groups have a more complex (and cooperative) function than might first appear.

In stateless societies, individuals and kin groups engage in "self-help": that is, what philosophers like Hobbes, Locke, and Rousseau called the "natural right" to self-preservation takes the form of an expected and customary claim to respond, with violence if need be, against anyone whose actions are deemed harmful or unfair. Within the group, however, there are important constraints on fighting or violence. Women tend to be less likely than men to engage in conflict. Much of the appearance of conflict is highly ritualized, consisting more of bluster than actual fighting.[40] And often, if tensions escalate and men do fight, it will lead to a split in the band as each combatant is assisted by kin or friends, with the winning group driving the losers away or the losers fleeing voluntarily.[41]

The most visible conflicts in stateless societies are the feuds and battles *between* bands. Indeed, what Hobbes saw as the "state of war" among the indigenous tribes of North America was the conflict between familial groups or bands, not the relationships within them. Yet even here, the picture is a compound of competitive and cooperative behaviors, comparable in some respects to the social behavior of nonhuman primates, but modified considerably by the emergence of memory, language, and forethought.

In many stateless societies, kinship is reckoned in lineages or clans. Kin-groups or neighboring villages often have lasting relations of feud. In American mythology, we speak of "the Hatfields and the McCoys"; Shakespeare immortalized the Montagues and the Capulets. In relationships of feud, everyone in one group has a lasting enmity with those of the other. Since self-help is the accepted and legitimate mode of behavior, this means that a member of one clan, band, or village can kill anyone from the other clan, band, or village with impunity if it is possible to "get away with it."

In practice, however, there seem to have been two rather different circumstances in which self-help led to violence and death. The first has been well documented to this day among the hill peoples of Montenegro and the Pathans of Kashmir.[42] It can be described as a form of ostracism, in which a contentious member of one band is essentially abandoned by his kinsmen or neighbors, so that the feuding rivals are effectively serving as "executioners."

Appearances to the contrary, in these cases the basic incitation to violence occurs when members of the victim's own group ostracize him. In a world based on self-help, security depends on the continued support of others in one's kin-group or band. If, for example, a young man is badly tempered (a "hot-head") or uncooperative, he may be described as a "bad lot" by his peers. In feuding societies, such a person can cause a great deal of difficulty; those in his group may therefore simply fail to accompany him when he walks in a dangerous place or otherwise indicate that they will not retaliate if the "bad lot" is attacked. In this way, lasting traditions of feud can function to allow members of another group to "execute" individuals who are unsociable or uncooperative.

On most occasions, decisions within the bands or kin-groups of stateless societies depend on consensus. Lengthy discussion is a typical mode of procedure. Hence it is quite misleading to think of feud as evidence of a Hobbesian "war of all" in which concord depends on "natural lust." Confirmation of the *social* nature of feud comes, for example, from Ralph Barton's calculation of the death rate from feuding among the headhunting Ifugao of the Philippines: before the imposition of American law, the death rate from feud was substantially lower than our contemporary rates of automobile fatalities in the United States.[43]

The second form of feud was more collective in nature and seems to reflect intergroup rivalries over limited resources. The primate origins of such conflict can be seen in the violence between two bands of chimpanzees in the Gombe, in which the males of one group effectively hunted and killed those of another.[44]

Ethologists have presumed that these conflicts reflect competition over resources (since in epochs of abundance groups will separate rather than fight). In much the same way, human hunter-gatherer bands often disperse so that their territorial ranges do not overlap, with the possible exception of water-holes or other resources that can be shared. When this is not possible, feuding relations may arise.

Such feuds need not focus on territory. When the horse was introduced among the Plains Indians as a result of Spanish colonization, it transformed social relationships in many ways. Members of one tribe would typically prey on the horses of enemy tribes (and, less frequently, with distant or enemy bands of their own tribe). Westerners in fact misunderstood quite fundamentally what happened when Plains Indians "stole" their horses. In effect, among a stateless people, our concept of property often does not exist. Rather, an individual or group has usufruct over a resource for as long—but only as long—as that resource can be actively defended or controlled. As Aristotle pointed out long ago, what civilized peoples call "piracy" is a settled mode of livelihood among many human populations.[45]

Among such stateless peoples, cooperation and competition thus form a complex system. Bravery and the willingness to fight, which Machiavelli calls the praiseworthy attributes of "spirit" and a desire for "glory," play an essential role, though they are checked by the need to gain consensus within the group. Elders or headmen, known not only for bravery but above all for prudence and an ability to resolve disputes, play a major role in the day-to-day life of the group. Among simpler hunter-gatherers, like the Kalahari San or the Batek, there is a minimal differentiation between males and females; in these societies, the leader may be either male or female, depending on the individual with the most highly reputed qualities.

Where resource competition has become more acute, as in the war-like Yanomamo, leadership becomes a masculine function along with a sharper division between male and female roles. But in all these societies, leadership does not entail the existence of a formal government or state. Since pre-literate groups of this sort survived to the twentieth century, why did the state arise? If formal governments do not occur among other primates and were not necessary during most of hominid evolution, is it appropriate to consider them as a "creation" of human "art" as Machiavelli did?

IV. Collective Goods and the "Tragedy of the Commons"

Before turning to the origin of the state, another property of social behavior needs to be examined. Above, it was noted in passing that the theory of natural selection is generally assumed to operate at the level of individuals. That is, animals are not presumed to act for the "good" of the species or of the group. Rather, most biologists argue that individual animals have evolved to behave in ways that improve their individual "reproductive success," and any benefits that accrue to the species are a consequence of this process of natural selection.[46]

On some occasions, however, all members of a group share a resource or a benefit that is indivisible. If one has it, all have it. One citizen of Los Angeles cannot benefit from clean air unless everyone there does so. Such resources are called "collective goods," and they introduce complexities to the theories of evolutionary biologists. Machiavelli sees precisely this problem, "because all *the arts that are provided for in a state for the sake of the common good of men,* all the statutes made in it so that men will live in fear of the laws and of god, would be vain if for them there were not provided defenses" (*Art of War,* Pref., p. 566).

Even among animals, features of the environment or ecological niche can have the character of collective goods. For this reason, ecologists who study how different species live in the same area often focus on aspects of behavior that generate indiscriminate benefits for all members of a group. If one male hamadryas baboon dies while killing a predator who otherwise might have killed any individual in a band of 50 to 100 individuals, reproductive rivals as well as kin benefit from the "collective good" of greater group security. The juvenile Japanese monkey who began the practice of washing wheat invented a tradition that has become a "collective good" for the entire band.

The nature of collective goods has been studied with some care by theorists who focus on the calculus of cost and benefit. The logic underlying game theory, akin to what has been called Machiavelli's economics of power, can thus be extended to those circumstances in which individuals have a self-interest to invest in resources that will help rivals as much as—or more than—themselves and their own kin.[47] In so doing, complexities are added that cannot be logically derived from a competitive situation in which the only outcomes are individually measured gains and losses.

The central issue arising from collective goods was described by Garrett Hardin as the "tragedy of the commons." The problem arises whenever there is a collective resource (like the common fields on which cows are herded, the fish in the sea, or the atmosphere over a city) that is exploited by a large number of self-interested individuals whose behavior is not externally regulated. Each individual may know of the long-term risks of overgrazing the fields, over-fishing, or polluting the atmosphere. But as long as all individuals determine their behavior in terms of their personal costs and benefits, there is no incentive to avoid destruction of the collective good: my forbearance merely leaves more of the commons to be exploited by my competitors.[48]

Daily experience indicates the numerous situations which resemble the tragedy of the commons. Hardin's conclusion is that the only way to avoid self-destructive behavior is the formation of a centralized government which can establish and enforce rules in the best long-range interests of the community. Although members of the group may be at a relative disadvantage compared to governmental officials, who usually receive in-

Biological Nature of the State   125

dividual perquisites or "side-payments" as an inducement to protect the commons, in many circumstances there do not seem to be alternative restraints likely to protect collective goods. This, obviously, can provide one account of the origins of the centralized state.

While governmental regulation is invoked to deal with situations like the tragedy of the commons, other solutions do sometimes exist. As the ecological disasters of Eastern Europe under communism demonstrate, the organization of a powerful state invoking the common interest need not protect collective goods; rather, the result may merely increase the side-payments exacted by those in power for their services in organizing society. In recent years, therefore, much has been said of "privatization" of economic systems. Do these arguments imply that states are inherently evil and ultimately could be done away with?[49]

A number of devices have been proposed to limit the need to rely on state regulation. It is useful to survey these arguments, for they will clarify the issue of the rise and fall of states which is at the center of Machiavelli's theory:

- ○ In some cases, it is possible to divide what appears to be a commons into privately owned shares, so that individual owners gain a self-interest in limiting overexploitation of natural resources. If each herdsman owns and fences part of the prairie, the incentive to overgraze disappears.[50] In other cases, as with the fish in the sea and the air over our cities, this solution is impossible. As with other forms of property in market economies, however, there need to be some rules enforcing the nature and limits of ownership.

- ○ When privatization is technically impossible, the costs of exploiting the commons can be directly imposed by means of taxes, fees for polluting the environment, or other means of increasing the costs of using the commons.[51] The atmosphere cannot be divided up into private plots, but factories can be allowed to "buy" the right to pollute—at a fee that then discourages polluting. Like privatization, however, policies of taxation or licensing require enforceable legal rules that would not function well in a stateless society.

- ○ Technological innovations can sometimes create sufficiently great increases in resources so that what seemed to be fixed limits of collective goods disappear. If fishermen are depleting stocks in the seas, one can develop fish hatcheries to increase the supply. Because investments that expand collective goods usually produce lower immediate returns than comparable expenditures in the private sector, however, governments typically have to support scientific and technological research that generates collective benefits. Since the nineteenth century, this has been particularly the case for "pure science," whose long-term contributions to economic development are generally indirect. Other examples include public education, basic transportation networks, and other elements of the infrastructure.

○ Educate people in the dangers of overexploiting the commons. If people know of the long-term costs, hopefully they will avoid them. Difficulties arise because short-term self-interest often outweighs knowledge of ultimate benefits; those who benefit most from unfettered access to the commons can justify themselves by claiming to have counter-evidence (the earth can recuperate from pollution, global warming is a myth, the fish population will regenerate itself). Because scientific methods legitimate the challenge to purported findings, deception and self-deception can easily occur on both sides of issues concerning collective goods.

○ Ostracize those who do not restrain themselves from overexploiting the commons. The process by which small face-to-face groups control deviance can be used, even in larger societies, to shame individuals who violate informal norms. But these constraints will not work against people whose "nature" is to be "grasping" or "greedy" (to use Machiavellian terms).[52] Ultimately, there is a demand to use legal punishment to enforce the norms protecting the collective goods.

Historical evidence shows periodic cycles, shifting from market processes which privatize costs and benefits to state regulation to protect common resources. Consider attitudes toward the environment in the United States. During the late nineteenth century, there was an extraordinary reliance on private self-interest: homesteading the "wild west" was a classic example of "privatizing" a commons. Then, with the emergence of the conservation movement led by Gifford Pinchot and Theodore Roosevelt, and more massively during FDR's "New Deal," the focus shifted to governmental regulation. During the 1980s, under Reagan, opinion shifted back toward privatization. Although the dominant strategy in each period was based on overwhelming popular approval, strong voices of dissent insisted that prevailing policies were pernicious; usually, the justification of preferred policies is deduced from theoretical principles (social Darwinism; equal rights; freedom of opportunity, etc.).

Ultimately, the question concerns the proper mixture of state control and private initiative. That the dream of a stateless society in an industrial society is a dream can easily be verified: while stateless societies existed throughout the longest period of human evolution, they coincided with the epochs when, as Machiavelli put it, the world's "inhabitants were few" and "scattered"—and hence could have little impact in degrading the environment. Hardin's tragedy of the commons is a product of population growth, itself the consequence of the successful exploitation of natural resources.

The necessity for some degree of centralized governmental power in an industrialized society is confirmed by observation of very large flocks or "colonies" among birds or mammals. Such populations, which are the closest approximation to the size of the industrial nation-state among vertebrates, have been explained as a response to two factors: exploiting natural resources (equivalent to the "commons" of Hardin), and external predation. Defense against outside attack is a very different kind of "common good" than environmental protection. In large human societies, neither can be achieved without some governmental role.

One of the ironies of modern politics is that individual leaders or party platforms seeking private solutions to environmental degradation have often exaggerated the need for state intervention to provide for military defense against foreign threats. Conversely, those who emphasize the need for state intervention to protect the environment have ridiculed the focus on defense spending.

The difficulty of establishing the proper mixture of private and state activity leads to unending political controversy. Because there are no clear answers, there is always an excuse for those who seek to overexploit common resources. The logic of preferring immediate benefits to long-term investment in collective goods applies to the humanly constructed infrastructure (roads, highways, hospitals, and schools) as well as to the natural environment. And these pressures also work against the law itself, which functions as a "collective good" by providing a common set of rules which individuals can take for granted.[53]

Because successful provision of collective goods produces population increase, wealth, and the illusion of a secure future, all centralized states have fallen due to pressures of this sort.[54] Machiavelli understood the process well. As he summarized the process in the *Florentine Histories*:

"virtue gives birth to quiet, quiet to leisure, leisure to disorder, disorder to ruin" (V, 1; p. 185). For this reason, Machiavelli insists in an important chapter of the *Discourses* that "a religious institution or a state" must "frequently be restored to its original principles" (III, 1; pp. 385–390).[55]

> For at the start religious institutions, republics and kingdoms have in all cases some good in them, to which their early reputation and progress is due. But since in the process of time this goodness is corrupted, such a body must of necessity die unless something happens which brings it up to the mark. (Ibid., p. 386)

Compared to the historical chaos—the "flood" of the allegory in chapter twenty-five of *The Prince*—human institutions devoted to the common good "have *in all cases some good in them,*" but the very success of these institutions recreates the pressures that made states or religions necessary in the first place.

This *persistence* of the problem most obvious at the founding of a state explains Machiavelli's emphasis on the "entirely new" prince or founder: *The Prince* is focused on a perennial problem in all regimes, not merely a topical concern of the Medici or of Italian politics. In contemporary evolutionary theory, the process by which successful adaptation establishes the opportunity for counter-strategies by competitors (whether parasites on hosts, predators on prey, or some members of a species on others) has been called the "Red Queen" effect, since like Lewis Carroll's character of that name, it is necessary to keep running merely to stay in place.[56]

The role of the state is thus to control the natural propensity to overexploit collective goods. Contemporary science confirms that this tendency is both a logical necessity from the perspective of evolutionary biology and an empirically observed characteristic of human history. It is hard to deny that Machiavelli's theory is an astute if sometimes cynically phrased assessment of the human condition.

V. The Common Good and Leadership

Was Machiavelli correct to assert that, given human nature, the very success of political institutions will lead to their downfall unless corrective measures are taken? Since Machiavelli argues that both the rise and fall of the state are part of a single process, it is illuminating to analyze the pres-

sures that undermine political institutions in terms of the theories explaining the origins of states.[57]

Three principal explanations have been given for the origin of political
institutions. For some, it is war and threat of external attack that leads to
the emergence of the state; for others, the management of technology and
money—internal economic institutions and practices, like the irrigation
systems at the origin of the states of Mesopotamia, Egypt, and Mesoamer-
ica, that provide great collective benefits—came first. According to a third
view, leadership is necessary whether as a response to external threat or to
internal economic needs.

Empirical evidence shows that the evolutionary pressures against very
large human communities are so pervasive that no one of the three theories can fully explain the rise and functions of centralized governments.
Population pressure and competition between communities typically do
generate both the need and the justification for developing powerful
governments. But archaeological studies of "pristine" states—that is, institutions arising without pressure from or experience of foreign states—
show that they often began to develop in peaceful contexts as a means of
exploiting natural resources that were otherwise unavailable.[58]

The historical record shows that both processes of internal economic
development and external defense occurred. Whichever one came first,
moreover, it necessarily elicited the other. Where states began to form because conflict between groups became too intense to be controlled by
the mechanisms observed in stateless societies, in general not only had economic innovations already led to population growth, but further investments in collective economic development were justified in the name of
self-defense. Where technological or market innovations made possible
hitherto unknown increases in productivity, they either attracted "predation" from less "advanced" peoples at the margins of society or they spread
to produce fearsome rival powers.[59]

In either case, however, the organization of states *also* requires leadership. Intelligent planning and coordination is obviously needed in order to
mount effective military defense or successful attacks on rivals. Even
among nonhuman primates, one function of dominance is security against
predators; in hunter-gatherer bands or stateless societies, although formalized governments and bureaucracies do not exist, there is typically a
headman or chief who excels in leading young males to fight outsiders.
Such leaders often have different skills than those needed for resolving

domestic disputes and coordinating activity within the group. Hence, prior to the emergence of governments, human leadership roles were often situation-specific, with one chief for the hunt, another for war, and yet another for mediating familial, social or economic disagreements within the village.

While defense against outsiders requires a leader, so does the organization of new, collective economic enterprises. The coordination of a large labor force was necessary to build the irrigation systems along the Tigris, Euphrates, or Nile (not to mention the Ganges River in India, the Yellow River in China, or the water basins among the low-land Maya). Once built, of course, these constructions made possible increased agricultural yields. But the economic benefits could not have occurred until several years *after* the construction began.

Whether contributions to the common effort were based on coercion or voluntary effort, they would hardly have been possible without intelligent and energetic leaders. And, indeed, we have thousands of pictures of these leaders in the iconography of ancient Mesopotamia and Egypt, as well as in the statues, pictographs, and artifacts of other early civilizations. The popular veneration for heroes credited with founding or preserving states confirms the psychological importance of individuals in history, even though the frequent failure of heroic enterprises demonstrates that individual leadership by itself does not guarantee success.

The likely explanation for the origin of states is therefore a complex feedback of internal collective enterprises, external threat to the group, and intelligent leadership to meet both domestic and foreign needs.[60] More parsimonious explanations do not account for the millions of years during which hominids survived without states, the rapidity of the process of state formation, and the frequent breakdowns of centralized governments once formed. Political institutions are both more complex and more fragile than most of us like to believe.

Leonardo da Vinci's projects for scientifically engineered urban planning epitomize the modern approach to the creation of collective benefits through the initiative of enlightened political leadership. When working for Duke Ludovico Sforza in Milan, Leonardo designed several plans for radically new cities. Not surprisingly, they involved using dikes and dams to redirect rivers, in part to control the flow of sewage and thereby provide a healthy environment for its inhabitants.[61] In 1493, when describing such a proposal to redevelop Milan, Leonardo outlined more fully the modern project of a community based on property and material interest rather than kinship—and promised Sforza that he would gain personally by instituting it:

> All communities obey and are led by their magnates, and these mag-nates ally themselves with the lords and subjugate them in two ways: either by consanguinity, or by fortune [*roba* = property]; by consan-guinity, when their children are, as it were, hostages, and a security and pledge of their suspected fidelity; by property, when you make each of these build a house or two inside your city which may yield some reve-nue and he shall have . . . 10 towns, five thousand houses with thirty thousand inhabitants, and you will disperse this great congregation of people which stand like goats one behind the other, filling every place with fetid smells and sowing seeds of pestilence and death;
>
> And the city will gain beauty worthy of its name and to you it will be useful by its revenues, and the eternal fame of its aggrandizement.[62]

By abandoning communities based on the limited principle of kinship, and expanding the city to all those sharing the same economic interest, Leonardo foresaw not only a collective good, but a means of increasing the power of its leader.

A similar view of political leadership is evident in *The Prince*. Machi-avelli's own frustrations when the Signoria abandoned the attempt to redirect the Arno in 1504, and later when attempting to develop an effec-tive citizen army, must have reinforced his understanding of the critical role of individual leadership in taking advantage of historical opportuni-ties.[63] Even those who question whether Leonardo and Machiavelli knew each other closely can hardly deny that their common experiences cast new light on the discovery of the power to be derived from a unification of science and leadership in the construction of new political institutions providing collective goods to large populations.

Machiavelli's political theories are not only historically significant as milestones in the emergence of the modern state, but are also consistent with contemporary scientific evidence and hence still relevant. Today as in the sixteenth century, centralized states seem vulnerable to both domestic overexploitation of collective goods and foreign attack. The search for le-gitimate reasons to stimulate obedience to the law by self-interested individuals is as insistent today as it was when Machiavelli wrote Vettori in December 1513. And the appeals—to religion, to nationalism, or to en-lightened self-interests—are essentially the same as those described in *The Prince,* the *Discourses,* or the *Florentine Histories.*

At the outset of the *Discourses*, Machiavelli reminds us that he "always" had the "natural desire" to labor for "the common benefit of all" (I, Pref.; p. 97). There *is* such a thing as the "common good"—and some such "goodness" inheres in any stable religion or state. Although human institutions that generate lasting collective benefits are sometimes the result of accident, as apparently was the case in Rome, Machiavelli warns that it is extremely foolish to rely on luck or fortune.

> [T]here is nothing more necessary to a community, whether it be a religious establishment, a kingdom or a republic, than to restore to it the prestige it had at the outset, and to take care that either good institutions or good men shall bring this about rather than that external force should give rise to it. For though this on occasion may be the best remedy, as it was in Rome's case, it is so dangerous that in no case is it what one should desire. (*Discourses*, III, 2; p. 390)

Since a combination of law and leadership is needed to secure the common good, it will never be possible to dispense with the reliance on enlightened leaders ("good men"). We can now see more clearly why the most accessible and effective presentation of Machiavelli's principles is found in *The Prince*.

Chapter Six

*P*olitical *L*eadership, *E*motion, and *C*ommunication

There will be eternal fame also for the inhabitants of that town, constructed and enlarged by him . . .

Leonardo da Vinci[1]

*L*eadership is necessary for the origin and survival of civilized political systems. Even in bands of nonhuman primates or human hunter-gatherers, where there is a minimal differentiation of status and authority, some individuals (whether males or females, depending on circumstances of species and situation)[2] exercise dominance in dispute settlement and other leadership roles. Typically, though not always, dominant members of the group get prior access to food, mates, or useful resources; sometimes dominant males actively risk their lives in defense of others in the band.

Leadership became far more important—and the differences between leaders and led greatly increased—with the emergence of large-scale societies with centralized governments.[3] From Sargon in Sumer or Akhenaton in Ancient Egypt to Augustus Caesar in Rome, the rise of centralized states was associated with the immense power and prestige of individual leaders. The powers of those who control the state are the result of laws, conventions, and customs. Some regimes are what Machiavelli calls "republics" (in contemporary terms, we would probably say "constitutional democracies") in which the "people" have a direct or indirect control over affairs; others, either "ordered" monarchies or "disordered" tyrannies, are ruled by a single individual.

For Machiavelli, the organization and character of lasting regimes ultimately depends on individual leaders. Over the last two centuries, however,

133

the focus of political theory has shifted from leaders to the societies they govern. In the liberal tradition stemming from John Locke and the Glorious Revolution of 1688, political institutions are founded on the rights of individuals; because all have equal rights to "life, liberty, and property" which are the foundation of the social contract, leadership is a secondary factor in the origin and survival of the state. In the socialist tradition epitomized by Marx, the primary factors are socio-economic classes and the productive forces that generate them; in this tradition, particularly since the state itself is a necessary evil that will be transcended in the future, leadership is also of secondary importance.

As long as history seemed the story of leaders like King Charles V of Spain, King Louis XII of France, or King Henry VIII of England, Machiavelli's theory of leadership could claim to focus on the central phenomena of politics. In more recent times, Machiavelli's works have either been viewed as primarily of historical interest or, at most, as an analysis of the tactics appropriate to astute and amoral, if not immoral, political manipulators. In an age of mass politics, "Machiavellianism" became a term of opprobrium.[4] To what extent, then, can Machiavelli's understanding of human life claim to have scientific relevance in our own time?

To answer this question, we must focus more sharply on the role of the "prince" or leader. Three key issues need to be discussed:

- First, what is leadership? All political theories make assumptions about human nature which claim to be true. Is Machiavelli's "economy of power" consistent with contemporary scientific knowledge about animal and human social behavior?
- Second, are the natural foundations of leadership relevant in contemporary industrial civilization? In the age of television, do Machiavelli's categories of analysis correspond to important features of politics that have been ignored by conventional political theories?
- Finally, has the "effectual reality" of power changed in the centuries since Machiavelli wrote *The Prince?* Machiavelli's approach to life appeared evil if not anachronistic after the revolutions of the late eighteenth century. Can an understanding of the media explain this reputation as well as why his thought seems more topical today than in the last two centuries?

The answers to these questions challenge the conventional assessments of Machiavelli's thought. By focusing on the triad of love, hate, and fear,

Machiavelli identifies the natural elements on which all political life is founded. This approach to leadership casts new light on the character and limitations of "modern" political institutions and the theories on which they rest. As a result, Machiavelli should not be seen merely as a teacher of immorality, as a child of his age, or at best as a "republican" precursor of modernity. Rather, Machiavelli deserves attention as a political philosopher of the first rank whose understanding of human life, while not beyond question on some points, is superior to that of successors from Hobbes and Locke to Hegel, Marx, and Nietzsche.

I. The "Nature of Princes" and the Economy of Power

Machiavelli's economy of power corresponds to the nonverbal behaviors and emotions that organize primate social behavior. Experimental studies of the responses of humans when watching leaders reveal the importance of these nonverbal cues (part of what Machiavelli called the way of the "beast"). Transformations in the means of communication, moreover, help explain the renewed interest in Machiavelli's theories, which analyze the relationship between leaders and followers more fully than the works of Locke, Marx, Mill, or later moderns. Before reconsidering Machiavelli's understanding of political leadership in the light of evolutionary biology, however, it will be necessary to restate in more detail his understanding of the "nature of leaders" and what I have called the economy of power.

Machiavelli seems to use the word "prince" [*il principe*] in three rather different meanings. Often, "the prince" refers to the ruler of a "principality" (whether a "kingdom" governed by law, or a "tyrant" not so limited). Sometimes "the prince" is the "founder" of a regime, whether a principality or a republic; this meaning is the focus of the important discussion of "entirely new" princes in chapter six of *The Prince*. And finally, on occasion Machiavelli will use the word to refer to any leader in a republic, as in the phrase "the prince in a republic" [*il principe della republica*], which we find in the *Discourses* (e.g., I, 10; p. 136); in *The Prince*, this usage appears most notably in chapter nine on "The Civic Principality."[5]

When Machiavelli speaks of "the nature of princes" (e.g., *Prince*, Dedicatory Letter; p. 4; *Discourses*, I, 58; p. 254), which of these three meanings is involved? Does the last of the three suggest that Machiavelli's concept of "the nature of princes" can apply to political leaders today? To see whether this is the case, it is necessary to reconsider Machiavelli's distinction between "republics" and "principalities" as well as the difference between "king" and "tyrant."

According to the first line of *The Prince*, "All states, all dominions that have held and do hold empire over men *have been and are either republics or principalities*" (ch. 1; p. 5). This twofold distinction covers a deeper triad of "republic," "principality" or "kingdom," and "tyranny" which is spelled out more extensively in the *Discourses* (especially I, 10; pp. 134–138). A prince "who does not regulate his conduct by laws" is sharply different from one who governs "in accordance with the law" (*Discourses*, I, 58; pp. 252–257). This distinction between the praiseworthy rule by one man in a mode that provides lasting "order" and rule by a single individual whose acts are blameworthy is also found in *The Prince*, although it is not introduced until chapter eight (pp. 34–38).[6]

Although these different forms of government were brought about by "chance" (*Discourses*, I, 2; p. 106), there are "objective" criteria which permit us to distinguish better from worse. Machiavelli's preferences are explicit: "government by the populace is better than government by princes," and kings whose government is "regulated by law" are better than those of "bad princes" or tyrants (*Discourses*, I, 58; pp. 252–257). These preferences are relative to the situation, not absolute: *a republic is better than a monarchy, a monarchy better than a tyranny, and a tyranny better than the slavery arising from defeat by a foreign power.*

Because the standards of judgment are relative to circumstances, Machiavelli does not formulate his republican preferences in terms of the "best regime." Although many philosophers developed an elaborate picture of "the best regime," such "imagined principalities"—which were rarely hereditary monarchies, as Plato's *Republic* illustrates—did not prevent the ravages of fortune and the loss of human control over political events. Machiavelli's writing seems focused, therefore, on the need to train those "who know how to govern" and hence "deserve" to be "princes" (*Discourses*, Dedicatory Letter; p. 94).

The function of leaders is to help the community choose the "least bad as good"; even a republican regime requires leadership. One might well ask why some form of direct democracy would not be possible for Machiavelli. His answer is twofold. On the one hand, a "multitude" or crowd is "useless" as long as it "is without a head" (*Discourses*, I, 54; p. 219); only with a leader is the assembled public, and even more so a dispersed citizenry, capable of taking a position. Secondly, and perhaps even more important, "men make quite a number of mistakes about things in general, but not so many about particulars" (*Discourses*, I, 57: p. 225); because events are constantly changing, yet follow regular patterns that can be discerned by a knowledge of history, someone must have the prudence to decide *which* "particulars" to present to the public. Even in the context of praising the populace, Machiavelli emphatically asserts that "princes are superior to populaces in drawing up laws, codes of civic life, statutes, and new institutions" (*Discourses*, I, 58; p. 256).

The need for leadership is especially evident at the moments when a regime is founded or needs to be brought back to its "first principles." At these times,

> it is essential that there should be but *one person upon whose mind and method* depends any similar process of organization. Wherefore the prudent organizer of a state *whose intention it is* to govern not in his own interests but for the *common good*, and not in the interest of his successors but for the sake of that fatherland which is common to all, should contrive to be *alone in his authority*. (*Discourses*, I, 9; p. 132)

Paradoxically enough, it is *especially* necessary for the founder of a republic to exercise leadership as an individual, for only in this way will it be possible to establish consistent "modes and orders."

This is not to say that leaders are, in general, reliable. On the contrary, Machiavelli explicitly defends a position which, he says, "*all* writers attack" by asserting that the "multitude" or populace is "more knowing and more constant than is a prince" (*Discourses*, I, 58; p. 252):

> I claim, then, that for the failing for which writers blame the masses, any body of men one cares to select may be blamed, and especially princes; for *anyone who does not regulate his conduct by laws will make the same mistakes* as the masses are guilty of. This is easily seen, for there are and have been any number of princes, but of good and wise ones there have been but few. (Ibid.)

This passage is not intended to endorse the notion of direct democracy, for Machiavelli goes on to exclude from criticism kings who "governed in accordance with the law" in Egypt, Sparta, and "France in our own times, for the kingdom of France is better regulated by laws than is any other of which at present we have knowledge" (ibid., pp. 253–254).[7]

Machiavelli's goal, then, is somehow related to effective leadership in a society that is "well-ordered." What I have described in chapter two as the economy of power concerns the mechanisms used by any leader, not just a prince in the sense of a king or a tyrant. This is underscored by Machiavelli's examples in chapter seventeen of *The Prince*. Immediately after stating the general rule that "the prince" should "make himself feared in such a mode that if he does not acquire love, he escapes hatred" (p. 67), Machiavelli contrasts two cases: the cruelty of Hannibal and the mercy of Scipio. And to be sure that the thoughtful reader recalls that both were leaders in republican regimes, he stresses the fact that excessive "mercy" did not undermine Scipio's "fame and glory" uniquely because "he *lived under the government of the Senate*" (p. 68).

Broadly speaking, leaders can relate to the public in one of three ways. They can be "loved," usually by being "liberal" and "merciful." They can be "hated" because they are too "rapacious" in taking the "property and women" of citizens or are perceived as "effeminate" by the military. Or they can be "feared" without being hated, as is the case when "greatness, spiritedness, gravity, and strength are recognized" in their "actions" (*Prince*, ch. 19; pp. 71–72).

Is Machiavelli's analysis of the techniques of power still relevant? Since the seventeenth century, political theory has focused on the "rights" of individuals rather than the skills and responsibilities of leaders. Do contemporary studies of political leadership throw new light on his understanding of the emotions of followers, particularly in what Machiavelli called "republican" regimes? In the age of representative government and elected leaders, works like *The Prince* and *Discourses* have often seemed of limited relevance. To what extent does Machiavelli's science of power illuminate contemporary politics?

II. *The Primate Behavioral Repertoire and Human Leadership*

Machiavelli's analysis of the strategies available to leaders is clearly not unreasonable. For example, his distinction between the positive effects of the "cruelty" of Hannibal and the "mercy" of Scipio in chapter seventeen of *The Prince* (pp. 67–68) seems directly parallel to the experiences of this century. In constitutional regimes during times of relative peace and prosperity, what Machiavelli calls "liberality" and "mercy"—and even "excessive mercy"—seem consistent with success: electoral politics in normal times depends on positive ratings in the public opinion polls (or, in Machiavelli's terms, being "loved"). The means to this end, moreover, are usually policies that provide benefits for one's supporters: lower taxes, better public services, government subsidies. One thinks of President Eisenhower, who—like Scipio—was successful both in war and in politics because of his apparently "agreeable nature"; Eisenhower's program was "peace and prosperity"—and his supporters responded "I like Ike."[8]

In contrast, the totalitarian regimes of Nazi Germany and Soviet Russia maintained themselves by "fear" until they were overthrown, in the first case by foreign conquest and in the second by domestic "hatred" or "contempt" for the communist party. The founders of these regimes treated their subjects the way Hannibal treated his army: since Hitler and Lenin did not "care about a name for cruelty," they used "inhuman cruelty" to become "venerable and terrible in the sight" of the masses (*Prince*, ch. 17; p. 67).[9] The success of Stalin illustrates how "being feared and not being hated can go together very well" as long as the populace is primarily concerned about security and obeys "by a dread of punishment" (ibid.).

Events in Eastern Europe since 1985 seem to underline the difference between being "feared" and being "hated." Neither Hitler nor Stalin was "disturbed by conspiracy," whereas Gorbachev was challenged by a coup when he appeared "contemptible" to hard-liners who thought him "variable, light, effeminate, pusillanimous, irresolute" (*Prince*, ch. 17; pp. 72–74). While Gorbachev was saved temporarily by the support of Yeltsin and the popular backing for reform, the disintegration of the Soviet Union in 1991 was one of the "many revolutions involving a change from freedom to tyranny or the other way about" in which almost "nobody at all gets hurt" because a new "form of government has been brought into being by the common consent of the whole people" (*Discourses*, III, 7; p. 425).[10]

Where do the categories of "love," "hate," and "fear" come from? And why do these three emotions, which we think of as characteristic of private life, seem to form the basis of the differences between regimes and the causes of change? Recent research on the social behavior of primates suggests an answer: Machiavelli's science of power rests on a repertoire that is deeply embedded in human nature. In chapter three, I presented the evidence supporting Machiavelli's conception of the "ways" of "man" and "beast" underlying political behavior. Here, it is necessary to look with more detail at the categories of social behavior in nonhuman primates and their role in human political leadership.

As Darwin had noted, animals need to have easily distinguished cues that signal the likely future behavior of each other. The evolution of emotions and their visible expression seems to be due to the benefits of such displays. As a result, mammals—and especially primates—have well-developed repertoires of nonverbal behavior which both express inner feelings and signal emotion to others.[11]

Darwin's study of this phenomenon emphasized what he called "the principle of antithesis." To be effective, cues need to be sharply different from their opposites. For instance, a display of reassurance, signaling the absence of an intent to fight, needs to be as far from that animal's attack behavior as possible. As Darwin noted, the elements of a reassuring cue are not fixed: dogs wag their tails and crouch when showing reassurance and bonding, whereas cats making a comparable display hold their tails still and arch their backs. In each species, the behavior is the "antithesis" of the movements that precede an attack, since cats crouch before leaping at their prey whereas dogs show themselves as large as possible before initiating a fight (see Figure 4.3).

Two hypotheses follow from Darwin's principle of antithesis. First, competitive behavior should be sharply different from reassurance displays. And second, within competitive encounters, animals need to have strikingly different ways of showing a willingness to attack and to flee. As a result, three easily distinguished sets of nonverbal displays should be associated with emotions of happiness and signals of reassurance, with anger and threat, or with fear and evasiveness.

A survey of the nonverbal behavior of primates shows distinct facial displays for these three kinds of behavior; the facial expressions of the corresponding human emotions share features inherited from nonhuman primates.[12] The point is easy to verify. Watch one of Jane Goodall's films of chimpanzees or visit a monkey colony at the zoo. Note how often you can intuit the body language of the animals you are watching (Figure 4.4). Many social displays are virtually identical in chimpanzees and humans (Figure 6.1).

For over a decade, I have been engaged with colleagues in experimental studies of the way facial displays influence the relationship between leaders and followers. In the age of television, viewers can see close-up images of heads of state and political rivals on a nightly basis. To classify the nonverbal expressions of leaders, we used objective features defined in studies of nonhuman primates and of humans. Starting from a survey of all cues observed, three major types of facial display—associated with the categories of bonding, attack, and flight—appeared to be particularly important.

Because these facial gestures both *express* an inner emotion and *signal* a likely behavior, each display has been given a compound name: happiness/

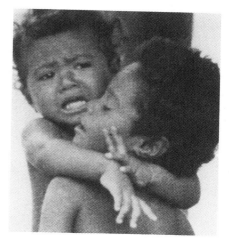

Figure 6.1. "Similarities in Primate and Human Social Displays. (A) Rhesus monkey mother with infant. Young Old-World monkeys seek comfort with their mothers. They clasp them firmly and are protectively embraced by them. Drawing: H. Kacher after a photo from I. Eibl-Eibesfeldt. (B) Anxious small girl from Kaleuna (Trobriand Islands) embracing her older sister. From a 16mm film. Photo: I. Eibl-Eibesfeldt. (C) A four-year-old chimpanzee female beneath the hand of chimpanzee male. Drawing : H. Kacher after a photograph by Jane van Lawick-Goodall. (D) A young American protectively embraces his girl friend. Drawing: H. Kacher after a photograph taken in Disneyland (California) by I. Eibl-Eibesfeldt." Reprinted with permission from Eibl-Eibesfeldt, Irenäeus, *Human Ethology* (New York: Aldine de Gruyter). Copyright © 1989 by Irenaeus Eibl-Eibesfeldt.

Table 6.1   Criteria for Classifying Facial Displays

	Anger/ Threat	Fear/ Evasion	Happiness/ Reassurance
Eyelids:	Opened Wide	Upper Raised/ Lower Tightened	Wide, Normal or Slightly Closed
Eyebrows:	Lowered	Lowered and Furrowed	Raised
Eye Orientation:	Staring	Averted	Focused then cut off
Mouth Corners:	Forward or Lowered	Retracted, Normal	Retracted and/or Raised
Teeth Showing:	Lower or none	Variable	Upper or both
Head Motion:			
Lateral	None	Side-to-Side	Side-to-Side
Vertical	Upward*	Up-Down	Up-Down
Head Orientation:			
To body	Forward from Trunk	Turned from Vertical	Tilted from Vertical**
Angle to Vertical	Down	Down	Up

Revised from Roger D. Masters, Denis G. Sullivan, John T. Lanzetta, Gregory J. McHugo, and Basil G. Englis, "Facial Displays of Leaders: Toward an Ethology of Human Politics," *Journal of Social and Biological Structures* 9 (1986): 319–343, Table 2.

*Earlier versions of this table show "None." Further research has shown that an upward movement of the head is associated with a "signature" and "challenge" displays in many species: see Paul MacLean, "A Triangular Brief on the Evolution of Brain and Law," in *Law, Biology, and Culture*, ed. Margaret Gruter and Paul Bohannan, 2nd edition (New York: Primis-McGraw Hill, 1992), 87–88. In objective coding of dyadic interactions between a dominant and a subordinate, while individuals differed in the original position of the head in the vertical axis, subordinates could be observed to challenge the dominant with an upward head movement which invariably elicited a larger upward movement by the dominant individual: Siegfried Frey (unpublished data). Routine observation has confirmed the use of a brief upward head movement as an aggressive display.

** Earlier versions of this table do not include the saggital movement (head *tilt*) as distinct from movement in other orientations. A number of studies have shown that a tilted head is an essential component in such affiliative gestures as mother-infant bonding. See Siegfried Frey, H-P. Hirsbrunner, A. Florin, W. Daw, and R. Crawford, "A Unified Approach to the Investigation of Nonverbal and Verbal Behavior in Communication Research," in *Current Issues in European Social Psychology*, ed. W. Doise and S. Moscovici (Cambridge: Cambridge University Press, 1983), 143–197.

reassurance, anger/threat, and fear/evasion. The specific cues corresponding to each kind of display are summarized in Table 6.1. These three "natural" behaviors, which subsequent studies confirm to be the most frequently observed facial displays of leaders, correspond to Machiavelli's categories of love, hate, and fear. In what sense, then, are these categories innate or natural?[13]

Facial displays and head movements play a central role in the normal relationship between mothers and infants. Even blind infants first smile at about the same time and under the same circumstances as sighted children. Cross-cultural studies confirm that the basic system of our facial expressions is similar (though its performance varies slightly) in different human cultures: images of a smiling face are decoded as expressing happiness in virtually every known human population. It is for good reason that such nonverbal behavior has often been described as a "natural language."[14]

Experiments show that nonverbal cues of love, fear, and hate immediately elicit physiological reactions of which people are often unaware. Despite differences of custom, habit, personality, or gender in performing and responding to nonverbal behavior, displays of happiness/reassurance, anger/threat, and fear/evasion are associated with characteristic muscle activations that are elicited, even without being visible, when we experience feelings of joy, anger, or fear. Muscle reactions that mimic these displays occur unconsciously while viewers watch the faces of leaders. Other physiological reactions, such as differing changes in body temperature and arousal (as measured by the electrical charge of the skin), are also triggered when seeing facial expressions of emotion and social interaction.[15]

These often unconscious physical reactions to the nonverbal behavior of others are associated with emotions that can influence our judgments of others and modify attitudes toward leaders. Experiments in both France and the United States show that, whatever a viewer's attitude toward a particular leader, a display of happiness/reassurance elicits more positive emotional reactions and judgments than one of fear/evasion. Culture also matters—for example, a leader showing anger/threat elicits more positive feelings in French viewers and more negative ones in the United States— but each of the three types of facial display has significantly different effects than the others.[16] Machiavelli's theory of the economy of power can apparently be based upon a natural or innate system of nonverbal behavior that humans share with other primates.

The system of nonverbal communication between leaders and follow-ers, while based on the primordial triad of love, hate, and fear, is highly complex. While the basic cues seem universal, people of different cultures have diverse ways of moving their bodies and expressing emotion. Ob-jective analysis of body movements reveals that native speakers of German, French, Spanish, or English have distinct styles of behavior. Indeed, when students learn a foreign language, they accompany the words with their native body language rather than the nonverbal cues that accompany the same verbal message for native speakers.[17]

These differences can have important political implications. In a recent study, for instance, adults saw videotapes showing a representative se-lection of facial displays by German, French, and American leaders. When the images were seen without the sound, so that the nationality of the leader was not known, viewers expressed negative feelings and negative judgments toward the foreigners. With the sound, so that viewers were aware of each leader's nationality, the ethnocentric prejudice disappeared.[18] Machiavelli had reason to emphasize the question of whether people "are either of the same province and same language, or not" (*Prince*, ch. 3; p. 9); what we today call nationality or ethnicity is a crucial factor in the re-lationship between a "prince" and those he governs.

Other factors also enter into the picture. Not only is our "natural" rep-ertoire of nonverbal behavior performed in subtly different ways in each society, but a gesture that is appropriate in one context may be culturally unacceptable in another. In comparable experiments, French viewers felt warm emotions when they saw their leaders expressing anger/threat facial cues, whereas Americans reacted as negatively to anger/threat as to fear/evasion. But in 1985, when then Prime Minister Laurent Fabius dis-played unprovoked threats during a debate with his election rival, Jacques Chirac, public reaction was uniformly negative.[19]

Previous attitudes also influence perceptions and reactions to a specific event. When people watch a leader, supporters are more likely to respond differently to his varied nonverbal displays and feel more positive emotion when seeing a happiness/reassurance display. Critics are less likely to react differently to displays of various kinds, and it is their negative feelings that are disarmed by the leader's happiness and reassurance. Hence a smiling leader makes his supporters more enthusiastic and his critics less hostile; in Machiavelli's terms, reassuring displays increase "love" among partisans and decrease "hate" among enemies. These differences are enhanced when rivals are seen competing with each other, a setting that makes one's prior attitude to each of the rivals more salient.[20]

Many other factors enter into the way people are influenced by watching leaders. Nonverbal displays have stronger effects when seen without hearing the voice (as when a television viewer sees the picture with the sound turned off); such a silent image in the background of a newscast can actually change people's attitudes.[21] Gender matters: although women and men perceive the same cues, they seem to integrate nonverbal behavior and conscious information in somewhat different ways.[22] In the United States, blacks and whites integrate emotion and cognition differently even when they perceive similar behaviors on the part of politicians.[23]

Finally, but of particular importance, the observer's personality seems to be an important factor distinct from culture or political opinion. Individual differences in what Machiavelli calls our "natural inclinations" (see above, p. 55) influence both leaders and led. Among viewers, perceptions of the same display seem to depend on one's personality: some people look at the world through rose-colored glasses, as it were, seeing more reassurance where others do not perceive the same cues. Hence, in our studies, the viewer's personality predicts differences in response that cannot be accounted for by the other factors just described.[24]

Among leaders, similar personality differences affect the performance of the same nonverbal behavior. We all know this intuitively of course: our judgments of "character" often depend on the way people "look" and the "feel" of their nonverbal behavior. In experimental studies, the more homogeneous or pure a leader's expression of happy/reassuring displays, the warmer and more positive the observer's reactions. Mixed or confused behavior, such as a tense smile combining reassurance and fear, obviously produces a bad effect. Some leaders (Ronald Reagan was an exceptionally good example) tend to perform nonverbal displays very homogeneously whereas others (like Walter Mondale) typically blend fear or anger in their happy/reassuring expressions.[25]

The system just described may seem puzzling in its complexity. Recent research in neuroscience indicates, however, that multiple cues are processed simultaneously in parallel by localized "modules" or neuronal structures in the brain. Much of our thinking is preconscious or unconscious, reflecting the integration of these multiple perceptive and emotional processes.[26] As a result, it is perhaps not surprising that our innate responses to emotional display behavior often produce strong but unsuspected reactions of the sort Machiavelli described as "accidents" (*accidenti*).

It is worth reflecting a moment on the connection between these findings and Machiavelli's thought. The term "accidents" has two meanings, one colloquial and the other philosophic. In everyday speech, an "accident" is an unexpected event like the one that Cesare Borgia called his "bad luck." In philosophy, "accidents" traditionally referred to the external or phenomenological features of things, as contrasted with "substance" or "essence." In either sense, the term "accident" could apply to the way a leader's appearance, including such apparently irrelevant features as the way he smiles, can unexpectedly be more important than the substance of his actions or policies.

To avoid failures due to such "accidents," training in body language and facial display has long been essential in teaching public speaking. Since antiquity, teachers of rhetoric emphasized the importance of the way a speaker expresses emotion. Indeed, Plato tells us that it was a measure of Socrates' refusal to follow the conventional wisdom that he refrained from attempts at tears to evoke sympathy and pity. Politics is more a matter of feelings or "gut reactions" than of reason, which may explain the disdain that many practicing politicians feel for intellectuals and "egg heads."[27]

Poets have also been fully aware of the importance of nonverbal cues and associated it with what Machiavelli called the way of "the beast" in politics. Shakespeare gives us a vivid indication of how the ambitious leader can counterfeit facial expressions as a means to power. When the hunchback Duke of Gloucester—the future Richard II—is scheming how to gain the crown in *Henry VI, Part III*, he gives a memorable soliloquy:

> *I can smile, and murder whiles I smile . . .*
> And wet my cheeks with artificial tears,
> And *frame my face to all occasions . . .*
> I can add colours to the chameleon,
> Change shapes with Proteus for advantages
> *And set the murderous Machiavel to school.*[28]

More recently, of course, we hear of presidential candidates learning how to smile. How dangerous is this system? And how does television, which makes it possible for our entire population to see its leaders on the nightly news, change the impact of the "natural" system of nonverbal displays?

To answer these questions, it is necessary to put the communication of facial cues of "love, hate, and fear" in the context of the development of Western political institutions.

III. Individual Leadership, the Media, and the Decline of Reason

Compared to contemporary political science, which has stressed such factors as political parties, economic policies, and the extent to which the centralized state should regulate the market economy, Machiavelli's political thought puts more emphasis on leadership. Political issues today are often discussed in terms of the "rights" of individuals or groups, a concept that seems to make *The Prince* and *Discourses* primarily of historical interest. Paradoxically, however, recent events suggest that the Machiavellian perspective is both more accurate scientifically and more prudent politically than the ideological doctrines that seem embedded in the dominant modern political theories.

To understand contemporary politics, we need to reconsider the history of Western democracy in the light of what is now known about verbal and nonverbal communication. How has politics changed since Machiavelli wrote *The Prince* in 1513? Marx thought that social institutions, ideas, and laws were ultimately determined by the *mode of production.* Now, it seems that it is *the mode of communication* that counts.

Television has obviously changed American politics. A simple example was described recently by Professor Katherine Hall Jamieson of the University of Pennsylvania's Annenberg School of Communications. Before the 1988 presidential campaign, a man named William Horton, Jr., was involved in a prison furlough program. The famous anti-Dukakis television ad referred to him as "Willie," a name he had never used and is not found in court records. Shaped by the force of this Bush campaign tactic, journalists, politicians, and scholars started referring routinely to "Willie Horton" rather than William Horton, Jr.[29]

The image projected by the flickering tube became the reality of our public discourse. Even newspaper commentators and Democrats critical of the Bush television ad nonetheless adopted its way of packaging information. People still talk about "Willie Horton." Although it is easy to blame television anchorpeople or network policies for these changes, television has had similar effects in other countries. Television, with its omnipresent images, has unconsciously formed the way we think and feel.

This may explain why the leadership of Jefferson, Lincoln, or Teddy Roosevelt seems a world apart from the Reagan-Mondale debate of 1984, sound bites, talk shows, negative ads, and thirty-second commercials. Money has always played a large role in electoral politics, but in the old days, it was used to create a machine—and if need be, to buy voters' allegiance with patronage. Today, money buys television time. The result weakens political organizations and shifts the focus to the individual leader. The transformation is symbolized by the presidential election of 1992, in which Ross Perot used wealth and television exposure to gain about one-fifth of the vote, even though he had entered politics from private life, left the campaign, and returned to it under puzzling circumstances.

Once upon a time, presidents had "coat-tails"; now they seem to wear T-shirts. Political parties and their programs, once the life-blood of politics, are clearly secondary to personalities and their images. The so-called "Reagan revolution" is a good illustration. In 1984, many voters said they agreed with Mondale but voted against him. While Reagan claimed a mandate to change many public policies, his landslide victories had little effect on voters' behavior in Congressional or state election campaigns. Reagan's personal popularity seems to have been associated with a decline in party identification as much as with an increase in support for the GOP.

In 1988, Bush's triumph involved a complete reversal of popular images in the course of a few short months. We have forgotten that when Dukakis was nominated in July of that year, he led Bush in the opinion polls—among men by 46 to 43 percent, among women by a whopping 56 to 26 percent. Over the next month, image-manipulation transformed a "wimp" into the tough exponent of a "kinder, gentler" nation, associating the images of the flag and the "Willie Horton" ad with the verbal rhetoric of "a thousand lights" of concern for the unfortunate.

Politics has become a sequence of "media opportunities." The "sound bite" replaces the speech. Television ads have taken on a new role, as Katherine Jamieson points out, often setting the agenda for journalistic commentary. The continuous coverage available on CNN transforms the statements of political leaders and candidates into rival forms of "packaging." Since image manipulation counts more than party platform or programs, we have entered an age of personalized politics.

Nowhere are these changes more evident than in the way we nominate presidential candidates. In the heyday of party politics, the national conventions brought together local elites for days of party-making in the literal as well as figurative sense. Leaders drank together, smoked cigars together, trading stories and favors while deciding who would run for the White House. Since the 1960s the nomination process has been reformed, ostensibly to increase public control and party responsiveness. Actually, the spread of primary elections and the insistence on open conventions may just reflect the power of television. Deals in smoke-filled rooms make for bad visual images. The result: interminable campaigns dominated by stock speeches, media opportunities, and negative advertisements.

Let it not be thought that the situation is unique to America. Similar trends are visible in Europe. Everywhere, party organizations and programs seem to have been reduced in importance. Everywhere, television has led to a politics of image, of symbols, and of superficiality. Germans complained that Chancellor Kohl never had to explain the costs of reunification. The French Socialist Party came to have little to do with socialism and everything to do with its role as the basis for François Mitterand's presidency. Scandals in Japan succeeded each other without producing basic political change.

Everywhere in the industrialized world, such changes have occurred. One simple fact illustrates the way television has changed communication between leaders and the led: the frequency of visual images of leaders on television. A recent study revealed that the face of a political leader was visible in television newscasts during 14 percent of the time in France, 17 percent of the time in the U.S., and 30 percent of the time in Germany. When we see the news, pictures of our leaders are often used to give meaning to the story.[30]

These "visual quotes" are typically quite short. The average image of a leader is on the screen for less than six seconds, the minimal time usually thought necessary to process a verbal message. Television doesn't show leaders so that we can hear them. If anything, we hear leaders so that we can see them, identify them, and thus agree or disagree with the principles or positions they symbolize. The result has been the success of media candidacies like those of Zhirinovsky in Russia or Berlusconi in Italy.

This omnipresence of leaders is particularly evocative because our brains have specialized structures for observing the faces of other people. In one key portion of our brain, the inferior temporal lobe, Edmond Rolls of Oxford found that 10 percent of the neurons only fire on the sight of a human face. Moreover, he has shown that some cells are specialized to react to very specific nonverbal cues, such as the upward movement of the head that signals threat and dominance.[31]

In short, television exploits our brain's capacity to respond emotionally to images, and especially to the sight of others. It gives us the impression of being face-to-face with national leaders. In addition to hearing their words—and, often, *instead* of hearing them—we see facial expressions and other symbols or images that trigger strong emotional responses. And these emotions in turn organize what we remember and how we remember it.

Can it really be said that television led to the changes described above? It seems far-fetched to claim that television is responsible for an extensive transformation of our political life. Is the medium really the message? If not, how has this electronic messenger changed the way people think and behave?

More and more, events are designed for television. Whereas newspapers tried to record what happened in the world, now the world and its leaders pose for the television camera. As commentators have noted, the signs carried in mass demonstrations from Vilnius and Zagreb to the West Bank are often in English because the real audience is now CNN, not the protesters' compatriots.

The efforts devoted to creating television images reflect their power to move us. The human brain responds to visual cues more strongly than to complex combinations of sound and picture. These responses are often highly emotional. And since emotional arousal is the basis of learning and attitude change, visual information is both easy to process and highly effective.

In the age of print media, politics was often equated with the written word. Such a view made it easy to think of political dialogue as a matter of ideas and thoughts in which emotion is secondary (unless dangerous demagogues have been at work). Even today, it is hard for newspaper journalists to admit the primacy of visual images and emotional responses as determinants of voting behavior and public opinion.

A simple measure of the misunderstanding is the ubiquitous use of public opinion polls. Little matter that, in 1988, a Roper poll showed a five-point difference depending on whether people were asked if they preferred Dukakis to Bush or if they preferred Bush to Dukakis. It is easy to forget that respondents often try to please the pollster, and in any event are reacting to something very artificial when presented with an abstract verbal question.

Polls are, of course, supposed to measure likely behavior. But the rapid changes in poll results should give us pause. The candidate that people say they support today may not receive their vote on election day. In the 1988 campaign, between July 28 and August 23 support for Bush rose from 43 to 46 percent among men—and from 26 to 44 percent among women.

Why do such changes occur—and how do they relate to the immense power of television?

Experiments over the last decade in both Europe and the U.S. demonstrate that emotional responses play a principal role in the way citizens respond to the information presented to them. Television has immense power in this respect because it is so easily understandable and highly evocative. Pictures not only make it easier to process abstract verbal information; they are more likely to be remembered as images or symbols that organize our thinking.

Recall the 1988 campaign. Can you see Bush's "Willie Horton" ad or remember the position he took in the debates? Do you recall the image of Dukakis looking like Snoopy in a tank—or the text of his acceptance speech? And when something a candidate said does come to mind, isn't it often associated with an image, such as Dukakis's emotionless response to a question about the death penalty for someone who had attacked his wife?

The focus on visual symbols, the personalization of politics, and the resulting decline of party organizations can be observed in the democracies of Western Europe. Everywhere, television coverage leads to negative images of those in power, weakening party attachments and discrediting traditional elites. These trends were epitomized by the Italian election of 1994: after television had transformed routine Italian political practices into unforgivable corruption, Sergio Berlusconi forged a winning coalition just three months after entering politics, using his ownership of the three major commercial networks to develop an overwhelming media blitz. Similar trends can be seen in the collapse of communism in Eastern Europe and the Soviet Union, the challenges to the Liberal Democratic Party in Japan, and the end of the dominance enjoyed by the Congress Party in India.

Can all these events be associated with changes in the mode of communication between leaders and led? McLuhan proclaimed "the media is the message"; it may seem an exaggeration to go further, implying that the media is the *regime.* Yet the alternative explanation, which assumes that the influence of television is due to the way the medium is used, is increasingly contradicted by the scientific evidence. Many of the critical effects of television are due to the medium itself, not its content.

Studies of the political effects of television show that what the journalist says is often (but not always) secondary. As Shanto Iyengar of UCLA and Donald Kinder of the University of Michigan demonstrated in an elegant series of experiments,[32] television news sets the agenda of politics. What is covered is what we think about. Increasingly, issues that are not covered on television do not penetrate to the public's awareness.

In part, this is due to the role of emotions in learning and memory. Politics is about gut reactions. Because television can elicit such strong feelings, it is highly effective in producing lasting memories. And because the human brain processes positive and negative emotions separately before bringing them together, television can generate either positive feelings of comfort and support, or negative ones of hostility toward the images we see.

The unexpected of course attracts our attention. Negative information can often get attention quickly, particularly if directed toward a candidate or policy about which little is known or attitudes are unstable. Hence the increasing importance of negative appeals, not only in political campaigns but also in commercial advertising. Even when positive images predominate, they are processed quickly as symbols and color our judgments of more complex verbal images.

Today, anyone who watches the nightly news has the impression of being directly in contact with national and international events and leaders. The feelings and judgments elicited by televised images are so strong that leaders who are highly effective on television can overcome the opposition of traditional party organizations. The professional insiders who dominated politics in the age of print have everywhere been challenged by individuals skilled in manipulating the media. Oddly enough, this explains not only the success of Ronald Reagan or Newt Gingrich, but the rise to power of Mikhael Gorbachev, his replacement by Boris Yeltsin, and the subsequent challenge of Vladimir Zhirinovsky.

Television has thus produced the politics of personality and image-making. The decline of political parties has coincided with the triumph of visual over printed information. Direct appeals to the mass of society are now possible, and they tend to reduce the difference between the well-informed elite and the public at large. We all watched coverage of the first air raid on Baghdad at the same moment.

Such a profound change in the means of communication cannot fail to have extensive results. Some might question whether every disagreeable feature of contemporary politics can be attributed to television. Probably not. But we have been far too reluctant to consider how much television has changed contemporary politics. Before reassessing the contemporary and future relevance of Machiavelli, it would be well to consider the extent to which the politics of the last two centuries marked a unique episode in human history.

IV. The Newspaper, Political Parties, and the Rise of Constitutional Government

McLuhan spoke of the creation of a "global village." After scenes of the Persian Gulf War, Yeltsin braving the hard-liners' coup, or the siege of Sarajevo, it is hard to deny the truth of his prediction. Such television coverage has an immediacy and emotional power that goes far beyond the conscious intentions of broadcasters and network executives. What is this global village like and how does it affect our traditions of constitutional government? To answer this question, it is necessary to see why, after two centuries during which Machiavelli's focus on individual leadership and passionate violence often seemed anachronistic, recent trends show the perennial relevance of his view of human nature and politics.

In the eighteenth century, two great revolutions transformed the political life of the West. In the American colonies of 1776, as in the France of 1789, monarchical power was destroyed once it became possible to mobilize public support and activity on a broad scale. Earlier political institutions depended on what happened at the royal court or in face-to-face situations. How is it that modern politics touches the entire population of the nation-state in a direct way unheard of in the sixteenth century? More than is generally realized, it may have been the newspaper that destroyed the old regime.

For Machiavelli, the basic choice in regimes was between a monarchy and a republic; he defined the basic conflict as the perpetual struggle between "few" or the "nobles" as opposed to the "people." Modern politics has seen the disappearance of the aristocracy as an autonomous political force, the rise of egalitarian norms, and the appearance of the representative or legislative assembly and elected leaders as the central institutions of constitutional government. Written constitutions establish competitive frameworks within which political controversies are transformed into legal enactments. The dynamic feature permitting this change has been the rise of the political party, organizing rivalry during election campaigns and forming coalitions within the institutions of representative government.

These changes would not have been possible without the emergence of printing as an essential mode of communication. Ironically, it was Richelieu who in 1631 instituted the first major political newspaper, the *Gazette de France*. He saw the need for informing a broader national elite about events at the court. While the strategy of bringing the nobility to Versailles had been a means to extend royal power, the modern state required better and more regular communication. The printing press provided the means.

From the outset, therefore, journalism has had a political dimension. Even the king himself wrote anonymously in Richelieu's *Gazette*. Before long, of course, critics found they could use printing presses too. French *philosophes* like Diderot used books, pamphlets, and the great *Encyclopedia* to spread radically new ideas to the regional nobility and clergy, thereby paving the way for the events of 1789. Broadsides and popular newspapers followed, both on the continent and in the New World.

Constitutional democracy was thus, to a great extent, the creature of the printing press and the newspaper. It is no accident that the classic statement of American political principles, *The Federalist Papers*, is a series of newspaper articles. To secure ratification of the American constitution, Hamilton, Madison, and Jay needed to convince the voters of New York—and newsprint was the most effective means to this end.

These seemingly elementary facts have some not-so-evident implications. As the basis of political communication, print media focus on ideas that can be communicated to literate readers. In the eighteenth century, this meant a bias of social class. More important, print media until recently were focused on words. And a politics of written communication has at least three important consequences.

First, reliance on the printed word was a departure from the means of communication that had dominated human society and politics for millennia. From the early hunter-gatherer band to the princely courts or urban assemblies, leaders engaged in face-to-face dialogue with each other or gave speeches to selected audiences. Spoken language was the medium of politics.[33]

The printing press, and its use to produce newspapers for mass distribution, thus represented a vast change in the scale of what we today call the public. As recently as the eighteenth century, a serious thinker like Rousseau could assume that a democratic government was only possible in a community small enough to hear its leaders speak.[34] Representative government in the nation-state—a mass society based on an informed citizen body—is a modern invention dependent on the novelty of printed news.

Second, a politics based on newspapers made possible—and reinforced—the institution of the political party. The press by its nature focuses on verbal descriptions, proposals, and analysis. A political point of view requires a language or discourse that is understood by leaders and followers in the same way. And when deep disagreements arise, the resulting ways of talking about issues produce political parties. When Machiavelli thinks about "parties" and "sects," he has in mind the divisions of Guelph and Ghibelline: deeply entrenched, mutually hostile social allegiances that differ from either the competitive political parties of today's electoral democracies or the politics of propaganda, terror, and hero-worship of the totalitarian parties of Hitler and Stalin.

As is well known, the American constitution does not provide for political parties in their modern sense. Although our Founders understood the importance of passionate disagreements based on self-interest, they apparently did not see the link between the press and partisanship. But even though they did not deliberate about this connection at Philadelphia, supporters of the new American republic discovered it quickly enough: the battle for ratification became a controversy between "Federalists" and "anti-Federalists"—and the American party system was born.

Constitutional government based on newspapers thus became an arena for party politics. Nominating conventions, platforms, the emergence of national leadership, big-city machines, reform crusades from the abolition of slavery to civil service reform and prohibition: the life-blood of American politics throughout the nineteenth and into the twentieth centuries reflected a competition between political parties based on print journalism. Much the same could be said of European politics since the middle of the last century.

This points to the third implication of printing as the principal mode of political communication. Mass politics based on writing involves what has been called the "two-step" flow of information. Leaders speak or write messages to an elite. The elite then reads and interprets events, spreading the word to the less-informed members of society. Machiavelli focused on the relation between the leader and the society at large; the development of the printing press as a political institution inserted the *media* in this relationship.

Specific political events like the Lincoln-Douglas debates had their impact through this two-stage flow. Newspapers provided detailed and complex arguments to well-informed partisans. At the local level, civic and party leaders used these arguments to mobilize broad-based support. Democracy did not mean that everyone had equal access to information. Party politics was the politics of smoke-filled rooms.

This explains why, a hundred years ago, newspapers were so highly partisan yet American politics was so competitive. It also explains why conspiratorial leaders like Lenin also formed organized political parties and used them to disseminate a two-step flow of information.[35] The totalitarian systems of Hitler and Stalin rejected our tradition of the free competition of ideas, but their ideology and propaganda machines used the same mode of communication found in Western democracies—and hence relied on the institution of a political party that had been developed as a means of political competition.

Almost everything that has been said and thought about politics in the last century thus takes the primacy of printing for granted. Like water for the fish, print media have been the invisible but omnipresent world of the political life of democracies. So much so, that we don't realize how unusual this mode of communication actually is or how profoundly it transformed the world that Machiavelli observed and knew. In fact, printing represents a radical break with the social processes that characterized millions of years of hominid evolution.[36]

To understand the impact of television, we need to realize that the apparent eruption of visual images and emotionally arousing mass appeals involves a return to modes of communication that humans used from the Stone Age to the Renaissance. Politics in McLuhan's "global village" may be more like the prehistoric hunter-gatherer band or the Italian *città* than the nation-states of the last two centuries.

V. The Return of Machiavellian Politics

Machiavelli's advice to leaders has, in a sense, always been topical. But in the world of party politics, "Machiavellianism" came to be a term of unqualified evil. Politics was the politics of partisanship; partisanship was the politics of platforms or principles. Citizens knew of course that deception was involved and that platform promises weren't realities. But the conflicts of life and death, rich and poor, friend and enemy were filtered and transmuted through *principles* like the "rights of man," "national self-determination," or the "welfare state."

Today we see two radical changes. First, the eruption of direct violence in national, ethnic and religious conflicts that remind us more of Machiavelli's "sects" than of traditional political parties, willing to compromise and govern. And second, the emergence of individual leaders as the incarnation of policy alternatives. Both trends make good television, of course. But both also coincide with the replacement of complex verbal programs and lengthy speeches by direct expressions of the repertoire of anger/ threat, happiness/reassurance, and fear/evasion.

Consider again the two-stage information flow that characterized the political era dominated by print media. Before television, leaders were usually only seen by a few. If their body language influenced anyone, it was the reporter whose story might reflect the feelings at the time. But in Peoria or Albuquerque, it was the story (at most accompanied by a still photo or a cartoon) that was read. For a large part of the electorate, information came by word of mouth from a friend or neighbor who read it in the newspaper or, by the 1930s, heard it on the radio.

Television creates the appearance of a direct link between the leader and every citizen. What it took Hitler massive theatrical preparations to stage at Nuremberg is achieved routinely on the nightly news of every country in the world. But instead of being massed in one place, visibly choreographed by flags and bands, contemporary citizens watch television at home. And instead of seeing leaders live but at a distance, we typically see videotaped or produced close-up images of their faces.

Three things follow. First, a leader can no longer show the anger and high arousal that "work" when speakers address huge crowds. When we see a leader on television, it is as though he were in our living room. One doesn't shout and flail one's arms while sitting on a friend's couch. Politics now requires the reassuring behavior of face-to-face interaction even when a leader is addressing millions of citizens all around the world. To see the difference, you need only look at old newsreels of politicians in the 1930s.

Second, while leadership often must be presented in bland, reassuring terms, television paradoxically generates great negativity toward politics and politicians. News must attract attention. Departures from expectation are most likely to do so. Good news is boring—and more likely to be emphasized by government-controlled media than by a free press. It isn't news if the president holds a successful cabinet meeting, but it is newsworthy if he gets ill and throws up during a state dinner in a foreign capital. The result is a predominance of negative stories, generating negative images and judgments of those in power.

Finally, watching television can elicit very strong emotions in viewers, emotions that lead to lasting changes in attitudes. One study showed that some viewers' attitudes could be changed merely by inserting silent images of President Reagan in the background of routine news stories. In a follow-up, one day after the study, men with little previous opinion who often saw a smiling Reagan in the background were more favorable to him than those who had seen stories accompanied by angry or neutral images of the president. Since the viewers heard and saw otherwise identical newscasts, the only factor producing these changes was the silent nonverbal behavior accompanying the story.[37]

Other images and symbols obviously have similar effects. The revolving turnstile of the "Willie Horton" ad was easy to decode and to remember. That Ronald Reagan as governor of California had supported a furlough program similar to the one in Massachusetts was not visible. Such information, like statistical evidence of the effectiveness of various forms of parole, is harder to process than the picture of a revolving turnstile.

It may be objected that such deceptive uses of television are due to the practices and political choices of the American media and politicians. Without seeming to underestimate their responsibility, a cross-cultural study of the way television news is produced in Germany, France, and the United States suggests otherwise. It is true that many aspects of the televised image of politics presented to the public are different in each country. But analysis of these differences reveals that the formative role of television in the United States need not result from malevolent intentions.

Many of the differences in television production techniques reflect national culture or language rather than conscious choice. For example, the speech rhythms of the television anchors are sharply different in the three countries studied—and these differences are paralleled at another temporal scale by rhythmic differences of the visual images of leaders on the screen.[38] Topics covered in newscasts differ in each culture: in France, for instance, the leading subjects of news coverage are culture and sport, whereas in Germany most attention was given to politics and the weather; in the United States, in contrast, attention tends to be paid to economics or business and to human interest stories.[39]

Within the domain of political news coverage, American television news is more likely to show leaders in close-up images outside of the places where they work (be it the legislative assembly or an administrative office); American political figures are less likely to be shown on the screen with each other than are Europeans. In Germany, as in many other countries, the anchor or announcer often visibly reads a text (unlike their American counterparts, who appear to be looking directly at the viewer as they read from an unseen teleprompter).

The result of such production techniques is that Americans have the illusion that the political leader or journalist speaks directly to each individual viewer. This feature of production is, however, not "real": the networks have artfully generated an impression of directness that is suited to American culture. A number of features reinforce this deceptive sense of a democratic relationship between viewers and leaders.

In the three countries studied, the frequency with which different leaders are shown on television news mirrored the power structure: that is, the most powerful individuals were always seen most often. But beyond this, American television showed more different people than television in France or Germany, creating an impression of "democracy" that evaporated when total amounts of coverage were analyzed. At least in this study, American presidents dominate our television to a degree not found in either Germany or France.

Combined with the more frequent use of close-ups of the leader's face (a shot called "*l'américaine*" by the French), such production techniques mean that the viewer is less likely to see American leaders in their "natural" political environment. Settings, especially in the studio, are contrived. Or a normal activity is transformed into a predictable pseudo-event, as when journalists shout questions at the American president as he goes to his helicopter en route to Camp David.

To put it another way, the extent to which television news has been *manufactured* is often less visible to the American viewer. By comparison, European television production, especially in Germany, Italy, or Switzerland, long seemed more "primitive" or more "naïve." As a result, the European viewer was somewhat less likely to be manipulated by the choice of shots and the verbal coverage than an American who is lulled into ignoring the fact that "media opportunities" have been produced with as much care as television ads. Little wonder that, in our campaigns, the television ads become the reality.

These features exaggerate the universal tendency of television to personalize politics. Political parties, already weaker in the United States than in Europe, have probably been further reduced in importance by the way American television generates the images on our screens. Whatever the dangers of the "global village" elsewhere, it should therefore not be surprising that intellectuals complain about the superficiality and shallowness of political debate in the United States.

These changes are tantamount to a reversal of the transformations introduced by the political revolutions of the seventeenth and eighteenth centuries. We find ourselves, more than is generally realized, in a world suddenly akin to that of the Renaissance. Assassination, violence, and deception seem everywhere. From Bosnia to Rwanda, ethnic or religious attachments are pressed with a violence akin to that described by Machiavelli. Often it seems that history has become a flood, out of the control it once seemed possible to exercise over human passions. Machiavellianism seems more a descriptive term than an epithet of unbridled opprobrium.

One example should suffice. Washington insiders now speak of the "CNN effect." Scenes shown live from a foreign location often elicit strong emotions in viewers, feelings that throw policy plans into disarray. For instance, in the last days of the Persian Gulf War, televised scenes of Iraqi troops being killed on what television announcers called "the highway of death" were factors in the decision of the Bush Administration to end the war before achieving its goal of destroying Saddam Hussein's elite republican guard. Similarly, intervention in Somalia in 1993 and Haiti in 1994 may have been due in good part to the highly emotional responses to televised scenes of suffering in each country.

To assess how these changes might properly be related to a theoretical understanding of politics, it is necessary to reconsider the emergence of modernity from the perspective of political theory. The means of communication is obviously not the only factor that has shaped modern society. Exactly what distinguishes the epoch we call "modern" from ancient or medieval life? Did Machiavelli's self-proclaimed novelty contribute to the emergence of these changes—and if so, was his experience of working with Leonardo relevant? If Machiavelli's theory of human nature is broadly consistent with contemporary science, why or how was it eclipsed? What led to the domination of political discourse by the doctrines of "natural right" elaborated by Hobbes, Locke, or Rousseau, and the theories of history of Hegel and Marx?

It often seems that modern society faces a crisis of confidence. To assess the problems of our time, it is particularly useful to return to the origins of modernity in the Renaissance. Exactly how did Machiavelli and Leonardo contribute to the emergence of a novel approach to human life and society? What is the difference between their thought and the full articulation of modern principles by Hobbes? Why has the Machiavellian view of politics been dismissed for so long as simply immoral? Does the impact of television justify a return from Locke's ideals of constitutional democracy to Machiavelli's practical strategies of leadership? To answer these questions, we must reconsider the rise of modernity from a historical as well as a philosophical perspective.

Chapter Seven

Machiavelli, Leonardo, and the Emergence of Modernity

Science is the captain and practice the soldiers.

Leonardo da Vinci[1]

*T*he modern conception of politics has coincided with the unprecedented political and military success of Western European civilization, which has used the innovations of science and industry to conquer the planet, destroy older feudal or primitive political systems, and develop technological wonders hitherto only imagined by dreamers. In antiquity, Icarus was a symbol of human folly; in our times, Neil Armstrong walked upon the moon. Yet despite this success, modern political and social systems confront a deep crisis of self-confidence.

To understand this paradox, it is necessary to explain why for the last five centuries "modern" life has been said to differ from "antiquity." Conventional accounts of Western political thought often identify the origins of modernity with Machiavelli. There are good reasons for this practice, for Machiavelli is unusual in describing his approach to human life and politics as "new" or a "departure" from the "ways" of "others."[2] Why then do so many commentators stress the "premodern" elements of Machiavellian political thought and date the modern period from Bacon, Hobbes, or Descartes, seeing in works like *Leviathan* and *Discourse on Method* the first fundamental departure from the theories of human nature, society, and history accepted in classical Greece or Rome and medieval Europe?[3]

To evaluate Machiavelli's role in the emergence of modernity, one must focus on his claim to integrate both "long experience with modern things and a continuous reading of ancient ones" (*Prince*, Dedicatory Letter; p. 3). While this remark implies that "modern" writings, as distinguished from "ancient" ones, are useless, the phrase also suggests that if Machiavelli is an innovator, the source of that innovation is related to his "long experience" in Florentine politics. In reassessing Machiavelli's teaching, therefore, I have emphasized his dispatches from the court of Cesare Borgia (1502/3), and especially his relationship with Leonardo da Vinci, apparently begun at Cesare's court and continued in Florence (1503–1508). These events, which have been ignored by virtually all commentators, put Machiavelli's writings in a new light.

Machiavelli claims that humans sometimes have the capacity to control chance and attempts to develop theoretical understanding toward this end. Leonardo's understanding of the relationship between science and technology, epitomized by his role as consultant on the attempted diversion of the Arno River, provides an important example of this new perspective on human knowledge and activity. Whether one interprets the facts and documents in chapter one as evidence of a close friendship between Machiavelli and Leonardo, or merely as signs of parallel development, both thinkers use theoretical knowledge as a guide to the transformation and improvement of human life.

Although this novel understanding of theory and practice is a major step toward modern politics and thought, Machiavelli saw theory as an incomplete guide for practice, leading to the necessity for prudent statesmen or legislators. Without denying the role of Bacon and other transitional figures, I suggest that the fullness of modernity was not revealed until the seventeenth century, when Hobbes constructed a deductive theory of politics based on a combination of Euclidean geometry and Galileo's physics. Hobbes's claim that a geometric or scientific mode of reasoning will overcome the tension between theory and practice ushers in the specifically modern age, in which ideology or political religion comes to replace statesmanship. One key element in this further change is a reduction of Machiavelli's complex view of human nature to a simpler calculus of pleasure and pain, permitting the substitution of formal models and abstract concepts for the prudential rules developed in works like *The Prince* and *Discourses*.

This reanalysis of Western intellectual and political history has substantive implications. When contrasted to Machiavelli, let alone the thought of antiquity, moderns from Hobbes and Locke to Hegel, Marx, and Nietzsche appear to base their understanding of human life on oversimplified concepts, erroneous assumptions, and biased interpretations of the facts. More than has been realized, the crisis of modernity may be traced to the tragic flaws of political philosophy and science in the three and half centuries since Hobbes.

Before reaching such a radical conclusion, it is essential to demonstrate that its premises are sound. First, then, we need to agree on the description of "modern" thought and society. Once modernity has been shown to entail a new relationship between theory and practice, it will be necessary to reconsider how the joint legacy of Leonardo and Machiavelli contributed to the perspective that came to dominate the West. Then, by describing more precisely why Machiavelli's political theory as well as Leonardo's scientific technology differ from modernity after Hobbes, the dangers of a total integration of scientific knowledge and political life will become more obvious.

I. Modernity and the Integration of Theory and Practice

To assess the fundamental problems confronting our civilization, it is first necessary to define it. This is more difficult than might appear: many substantive features that seem at first typical of "modernity" (e.g., equal rights of all individuals, popular sovereignty, secular science) do not distinguish our epoch from others without excluding some cultural experiences that also deserve to be called "modern."[4] Although I do not claim to have a solution to this definitional problem, I suggest that three related features deserve particular attention in defining the "modern" epoch: 1) the new relationship between theory and practice, which gave rise to the uniquely modern conception that humans can "control" or "conquer" nature for the "relief of man's estate" (to use Bacon's famous phrase); 2) the new scientific theories of nature and of human nature, which transformed human knowledge and technology; and 3) the resulting integration of scientific knowledge and practical wisdom, giving rise to political religions or ideologies in place of the dual realms of secular and divine authority which had characterized medieval Europe. Before describing the role of Machiavelli and Leonardo in the emergence of modernity, it will be helpful to explore these three defining features of our civilization in more detail.

The cultures that emerged in Western Europe with the Renaissance and extended their power to create global economic interdependence have various names: industrialized societies (though some—like New Zealand—are heavily dependent on agriculture), constitutional democracies (though some—like Nazi Germany and Stalinist Russia—were totalitarian dictatorships); secular or materialist economies (though some—like the Ayatollah Khomeini's Iran—are based on theological fundamentalism).

No single set of political and social principles seems to define the universe of modern systems. For example, Rousseau's *Social Contract*—the work often said to present the principles underlying the French Revolution—asserts that the principles of a free society can be reduced to "equality" and "freedom."[5] The American Founders would seem to have agreed, since the Declaration of Independence begins with the ringing words: "We hold these truths to be self-evident, that all men are created equal, that they are endowed with certain rights, and that among these are the rights to life, liberty, and the pursuit of happiness." But the American revolutionaries did not extend the equality of rights to women, not to mention Native Americans and Blacks (groups which have only begun to gain equal status under the law in this century), and the French revolutionaries ultimately found it convenient to deny religious freedom to the Catholic Church and free speech to monarchists.

Indeed, when the history of modern political systems is considered from an outsider's perspective, it is hard to deny that the "effectual reality" has been far from the supposed principles underlying constitutional governments. We are told that the English developed a government of law and representative institutions based on the extension of freedom and property rights to the individual—but in fact, this system was established by the forcible destruction of the independent cultures and social systems of both the Scots and the Irish (who were denied rights of self-government, forcibly removed from their land, and exploited economically as well as militarily in founding the British Empire). From the terror under the First French Republic to the repression under the Second Empire, France rose to political power and economic success at the expense of the feudal aristocracy and the disadvantaged poor. In the United States, the regional tensions of the Civil War were overcome by destroying the habitats and the populations of Native American tribes, forcibly removing the surviving remnants to "reservations" in order to open western lands to settlement and economic development. An even greater gap between principle and reality would, of course, be evident in the history of the Soviet Union (where the pretense of building communism was a mask for forcibly destroying the old peasantry and enriching the Communist Party elite), not to mention other modern totalitarian or authoritarian regimes.

In short, equality and freedom are absent in many modern political and social systems; political principles, whether stated or real, seem not to be the defining characteristic of modernity. Perhaps we will be on stronger ground if we begin by listing a set of cultural and social *aspirations* that might set modern societies apart from those of antiquity, the Middle Ages, or the so-called "Third World." None of the following characteristics is perfectly realized in any modern society, but the combination of these goals has typically been present in modern cultures with varied political institutions and beliefs. To an unprecedented degree, all individuals—as individuals—expect to enjoy security, predictability, mobility, comfort, and progress. These attributes can be said to characterize the politically diverse versions of modernity of totalitarians and democrats; liberals, conservatives, and socialists; secular rationalists and religious fundamentalists.

Security. Modern societies seek to provide safety from both foreign attack and natural disaster for their elites—if not for all their members. The symbol of this transformation might be found in the word "enlightenment," which stood for the movement to dispel the prejudices and vices of pre-modern life. In fact, the rise of modernity coincided with a more literal "enlightenment": the installation of lights on city streets, making it possible to move safely among strangers in urban centers. Although never perfect, the promise that citizens can find their security in obeying the law renders obsolete the reliance on kinship or clan for self-defense. Individual security became the foundation of a market economy, in which valued goods can be offered for sale in the expectation that even when the poor have no money, they will not loot and steal.

Insecurity or violence is seen as a deep challenge to the basic principles of modernity, as is evident in the universal condemnation of uncontrolled criminal behavior by contemporary regimes. To be sure, those viewed as outsiders—whether Jews in Nazi Germany, kulaks and "bourgeois" in Stalinist Russia, or Native Americans, Blacks, Chinese, and other minorities at times in nineteenth-century America—have often been the target of organized violence or spontaneous harassment. Even so, modern regimes of the most diverse political principles have typically sought to establish a kind of "law and order" not found in primitive or feudal society. The best evidence of this is the uniform policy of repressing violent self-help, clan feuding, or aristocratic privilege—all of which provided security to selected groups at the cost of undermining universalistic norms.

Mobility. In pre-modern social systems, individuals or groups were often psychologically if not legally tied to a specific geographical place or social status. In the market economy, individuals need to be able to move through time and space in order to produce and consume goods and services; even where centralized planning and governmental ownership replaced free markets, some degree of geographical mobility was instituted (unless purposed "security" threats were used as a justification for denying them). This feature of modernity may explain the immense importance of systems of transportation and communication in contemporary life. Modern governments devote enormous resources to the construction of highways, bridges, railroads, seaports, and airline terminals, subsidizing the infrastructure for moving goods, people, and information—and, when technologies are being developed, sometimes subsidizing the introduction of new means of communication and transport.

Predictability. Moderns seek the predictability of economies that guarantee survival, laws whose provisions can be foreseen, and governments whose procedures will remain in place. The hyperinflation of Weimar Germany is widely viewed as the critical event destroying the legitimacy of that regime. Similarly, the catastrophe of Chernyobl destroyed the myth of the devotion to the common good by the Communist Parties of Eastern Europe (whose elites imposed secrecy and distributed gamma globulin to their own children before allowing the media to report the explosion). More recently, demands for "guaranteed" access to health care, full employment, and the safety of bank deposits—not to mention the attention paid to weather forecasts—reflect the characteristically modern desire for predictability.

Comfort. Security and predictability make it possible to devote resources to immediate consumption. Although the Welfare State was long challenged and, in some quarters remains controversial, its goal can be restated as the provision of material comfort to all fully eligible members of a modern society. This goal is shared by free market exponents hostile to the Welfare State as well as by Socialists for whom income redistribution and social equity are the principal goals of government. Modern technology provides, of course, the means by which physical discomfort and bodily disease can be remedied; insofar as individuals have "rights," they are typically associated with a claim on access to the means of comfortable life.

The emphasis on comfort seems at first materialistic and this-worldly, for it leads to the use of resources to facilitate the daily routines of life. But comfort and the consumer durables facilitating it are desired by religious believers and atheists alike. The focus on convenience seems to have a rather different principle: the minimization of the time and difficulty separating an individual for the realization of desires or wishes. Typically modern inventions, from the flush toilet to the computer, have this common principle: reduce the obstacles to the completion of any task, whether necessary or frivolous.

Progress. Security, predictability, and comfort imply that the future will be better than the present. To make possible a continued expansion of the economic system, new technologies and scientific discoveries are indispensable. The promise of a continued sequence of benefits is the condition of allegiance to anonymous, heterogeneous communities in which individuals from diverse backgrounds can cooperate in safety and predictability.

Although the goals of security, predictability, mobility, comfort, and progress are elusive, these typically modern aspirations suggest the underlying principle that defines modernity. In one of the earliest explicit formulations of this principle, Sir Francis Bacon spoke of the "conquest of nature" for the "relief of man's estate." In Bacon's view, it was necessary to organize science and technology for the end of political power; by integrating knowledge and technical ability, it would become possible to create "new natures upon old" and thereby direct the course of events.[6]

Why, one might ask, is the relationship between theory and practice a central defining characteristic of the modern epoch? However one distinguishes this stage in the history of Western thought—or, for that matter, in the development of human civilization more broadly—a simple fact comes to mind: only one civilization has come to conquer, both physically and culturally, virtually the entire planet. No culture, prior to that of the industrialized and commercial West, gave rise to a truly global economy, a global communication system, and even global (albeit embryonic) political institutions. In no other epoch have humans exploded nuclear weapons, developed in vitro fertilization, or placed artificial satellites in orbit, whereas in our time such technological capabilities have not only been developed, but—due to the character of our science and technology—they routinely transcend social or national frontiers.

This fact suggests that the relationship of theory to practice is characteristic of our civilization for a number of reasons. First, conceptualizing nature and human society in abstract or scientific terms—and then using these theories as the guide to political or economic practice—is not found in most civilizations: along with many other features of our own historical context, it is more problematic than it might first appear.[7] The typically modern attempt to base political practice on principles that claim scientific truth has given rise to ideology, allowing leaders or elites to use popularized belief systems as a mechanism of social control and power.

Second, to develop a "theory" which can effectively guide practices or beliefs, it is necessary to establish an epistemological difference between statements that are scientifically demonstrable (facts) and those which express contingent preferences or goals of human action (values). When only the former came to be considered worthy of assent, modern *science* emerged as a new way of discovering and transmitting knowledge about the world. Such scientific knowledge, which changes even purely theoretical science from understanding to a kind of making, claims a universality not limited by language, belief, or social practice while serving as the foundation of technological transformations barely imagined before the Renaissance.[8]

A concrete example from cosmology will be useful. Recently, astronomers have been confronted with new observational evidence that the structure of the cosmos is highly uneven, with galaxies clustered in a way that was not predicted by established theories of the origin and evolution of the universe. The situation was reported in *Science* as follows: "The structures revealed by this celestial coverage are certainly sowing confusion. 'We see these large-scale features and *we don't know how to make them*. We don't *know how to make* the structure of the universe,' says Geller [Professor Margaret Geller of the Harvard-Smithsonian Center for Astrophysics]. For instance, minor energy fluctuations that cosmologists argue existed in the early universe appear to be insufficient seeds to give rise to such prodigious clusters of galaxies. 'Gravity can't, over the age of the universe, amplify these irregularities enough,' Geller explains."[9]

Whereas the layman—like the ancient philosopher—would speak of an inability to *understand* events which obviously surpass the human creative power, today's physicists think they understand something only when they know how the causal forces *make* it. In a field like cosmology, using these terms sounds a little odd. In molecular genetics, in contrast, the equation of knowing and making takes the form of what has come to be called "genetic engineering": to understand a gene, it must be cloned and its activity demonstrated in practice by experimental means.

Third, this new relationship between theory and practice has challenged beliefs and traditions concerning the gods or God. For most human peoples, the political and the theological—the domains of the sacred and the profane—have not been sharply divided: one need merely glance at Leviticus to see that the Mosaic Law does not make a sharp division between what we call the secular and the religious spheres of life.[10] Ancient pagan philosophy inaugurated a profound dualism between scientific knowledge (*episteme*) and public opinion or belief (*doxa*), which Christian theology transformed into the equally profound dualism between faith and reason. Scientific theories claiming universal validity and practical applicability challenged such premodern approaches to the world, introducing a this-worldly or secular arena of social life whose government is a matter of human agency rather than divine will, and whose policies favor religious toleration. While science as we know it first appeared among the ancient Greeks, its social importance was therefore transformed by the claim that such knowledge could and should guide a technological and political transformation of the world.[11]

To be sure, all philosophy or science must to some extent differentiate between theory and practice. Since the Renaissance, however, a view arose that was not adopted even by those in antiquity who sought universal or rational knowledge of nature and of human nature: the typically modern conception of a successful conquest of nature and a definitive solution of human problems. In place of the ancient tension between philosophic knowledge and conventional opinion, moderns have seen the rise of ideologies derived from science (or pseudoscience).

I suggest that Machiavelli's self-proclaimed novelty lies in a self-conscious adoption of this new approach to theory and practice, influenced by his personal encounters with Leonardo da Vinci between 1502 and 1508. Machiavelli's political thought, when illuminated by the scientific and technical perspective developed by Leonardo, therefore symbolizes the beginnings of modernity. Even so, however, neither Leonardo's artistic projects, engineering skills, and scientific theories, nor Machiavelli's attempt to transform the norms and values of Christianity exhibit the fully modern characteristics epitomized by such seventeenth-century thinkers as Bacon, Galileo, Hobbes, Locke, and Descartes. In this view, modernity in the precise sense presupposes theories which claim to provide universal political guidance in the construction of an "eternal" and beneficent commonwealth here on earth, replacing the dream of a *City of God* with the construction of a city of men.[12]

II. The Legacy of Leonardo da Vinci: The Integration of Science and Technology

What role did Leonardo da Vinci play in the emergence of modernity? This question would be important whether Leonardo influenced Machiavelli directly or was merely a leading representative of the intellectual transformations in the first years of the sixteenth century. The brief summary of Leonardo's life and work in chapter one suggests the astounding variety of his activities; equally astonishing is the novelty of his understanding. In almost every field of his endeavors, Leonardo was an innovator. In many areas, these innovations were so radical that it took centuries for Western science, technology, and art to develop fully Leonardo's initiatives. To be sure, scholars often point to similar developments by others in the Italian Renaissance.[13] Without ignoring continuities, however, Leonardo's innovations are often unusually radical, going well beyond anything attempted by his contemporaries or even his immediate successors. Even more important, Leonardo seems unique in the way his artistic, scientific, and technological innovations relate to each other.

In this interpretation, Leonardo's principal legacy was the *scope* and the *interrelatedness* of the new ways of thinking he sought to introduce to virtually every human endeavor. To show this, it is important to survey—even briefly—some of his innovations in the arts (notably painting and sculpture), in science (relating mathematics to a new view of motion in nature), and in technology (including not only military weapons and productive machines, but large-scale projects of urban design and waterworks). In so doing, we will see that Leonardo's frequent failure to complete specific commissions and projects was the inevitable price he had to pay for the awesome intellectual achievement of inventing the relationship between theory and practice that was to develop into modernity. It is fitting that his motto was *ostinati rigore* ("obstinate rigor").[14]

FINE ART

Leonardo's achievements are most evident in the fine arts, for his paintings are among his best-known legacy. Even here, however, the specificity of his contribution is not fully understood unless the works that have become familiar icons of Western culture, like the *Mona Lisa* or *The Last Supper,* are situated in a broader context. It is important to go beyond conventional "art history" when analyzing Leonardo's works because he himself viewed art as a scientific activity. For Leonardo, painting is "more intelligible and beautiful" than poetry: "If poetry deals with moral philosophy, painting deals with natural philosophy. Poetry describes the action of the mind, painting considers what the mind may effect by the motions [of the body]."[15] The primacy of art is its scientific status as an activity illustrating the potential of human making as contrasted to the mere description or observation of events.

Leonardo's preference for painting over poetry thus mirrors the difference between the modern science as an activity of *making* and therefore *controlling* nature, and the ancient approach to science as merely understanding nature. This active view of art as a way of demonstrating knowing is evident in his *Treatise on Painting* as well as in a number of specific artistic innovations, each of which has been noted by historians as important in its own way. When considered together, Leonardo's contribution to the artist's representation of perspective, form, movement, light, and technique form a coherent initiative toward a radically different type of art than had ever existed before. Consider each of these five artistic domains separately.

Perspective. Much has been written about the role of three-dimensional perspective and its "humanistic" implications. What is fascinating in Leonardo's art is the transcendence of Renaissance humanism through the invention of a radically new perspective which might almost be called surrealist: the aerial view, as if the artist and viewer are already flying in Leonardo's imagined airplane or even a contemporary satellite. This new perspective first appears in Leonardo's maps, such as the plan of Milan from the 1490s (Figure 1.4) or the plan of Imola drawn when he was in the service of Cesare Borgia in 1502 (Figure 1.5). Even more striking—particularly in the context of the argument of this book—are some of the maps intended to facilitate the rechanneling of the River Arno (Figures 1.6 and 3.2).

Looking at these maps, we see at once either direct aerial views (sometimes with the geographic detail of a satellite photograph, as in the map of Imola) or views from an angle (showing topography as well as physical location, as in the map of the Arno). Since both views are present in the map of Milan, which seems to be the earliest of the series, both innovations would seem to be part of the same break with tradition: moving the human observer through space at will to produce the point of view that is *useful* under the circumstances.

There were, of course, neither airplanes nor space satellites in the early sixteenth century. No human being had ever actually perceived space as it is presented in these maps. Yet for Leonardo, this new point of view immediately became a resource in painting. There is no better example than the most famous of his paintings—indeed, perhaps the most famous painting ever executed in the history of art: the *Mona Lisa* (Fig. 3.1).

Because this famous image has been rendered trite through over-familiarity, it is necessary to make an effort to look at it with a fresh eye. Consider the *background*, which Brizio calls "not a real landscape" but a "stratification of centuries."[16] How could a woman be so situated with relationship to the environment? The background appears to be seen from an airplane, much like the perspective in the map of the Arno (Figure 3.2). Somehow, then, Mona Lisa is solidly placed at an altitude which is not on the earth (unless she is standing on top of Mount Everest!). That is, there is something *divine* about the aerial perspective of Leonardo.

The importance of this new perspective concerns not only its artistic consequences, but its implication for the artist and his relation to the viewer. Classical perspective could be called "humanist" because it places the naturalistic visual perception of the painter before the observer: visually, both are on the same level, giving rise to the realism of the image. Look again at Leonardo's *Ginevra de Benci* (Figure 1.1): the face is at eye level, and its "realism"—the sense that we would perceive the same thing if, instead of the painting, we were seeing Ginevra de Binci "in person"—rests on the equivalence of our visual experience when looking at the picture and the artist's perception when painting it. The difference between the background of *Ginevra de Benci* (the bush, a juniper, being a verbal play on the subject's name) and the aerial perspective behind the face in *Mona Lisa* is telling: no viewer can approximate the standpoint achieved by Leonardo. Rather, he raises us above our "natural," earth-bound point of view. In this sense, the artist becomes a creator, in the image of the creative God of Genesis.

This interpretation is confirmed by Leonardo's explicit statement in the *Treatise on Painting* that the "painter is lord of all types of people and of all things"; at that point, before the sentence from this passage cited above in chapter two, Leonardo adds:

> If the painter wishes to see beauties that charm him *it lies in his power to create them,* and if he wises to see monstrosities that are frightful, buffoonish, or ridiculous, or pitiable *he can be lord and god thereof;* if he wants to produce inhabited regions or deserts or dark and shady retreats from the heat, or warm places in cold weather, *he can do so.*[17]

This assertion of the painter's superiority as the "universal" human being suggests that the novel perspective emphasized here is no accident, but rather Leonardo's visual realization of what he saw as the essential characteristic of painting.[18]

Form. On the surface, it would seem that the naturalistic presentation of form is characteristic of the Renaissance in general: one need only look at Michelangelo's *David* to see the rediscovery of the tradition of Praxiteles and the ancient Greek sculptors. But Leonardo went beyond his contemporaries in at least two ways. First, he sought to discover hitherto unknown natural structures underlying the visible form; second, he was insistent that the functional or dynamic characteristics of things were essential to a presentation of their outer shape.

As he put it elsewhere, "Truly painting is a science, the true-born child of nature, for painting is born of nature, but to be more correct we should call it the grandchild of nature; since all visible things were brought forth by nature and these her children have given birth to painting."[19] Whereas Plato views manmade images as the lowest stage of the divided line, at the farthest remove from the forms, Leonardo inverts the hierarchy, asserting that "he who despises painting loves neither philosophy nor nature."[20]

This attempt to go beyond his contemporaries illuminates aspects of Leonardo's behavior that otherwise may seem inexplicable. As an illegitimate son of a Florentine notary, Leonardo did not have the status or wealth to engage in what today would be called scientific research and experimentation. In his time, for example, dissection was forbidden by the church. By using his interest in the nature of things to become a military engineer and urban planner, Leonardo was able to find patronage; he then used the power of his patrons to authorize such experiments as his research into the structure and function of the human body.[21]

Among the many examples of Leonardo's radical quest to know the inner reality of outward form, one will suffice. Leonardo seems to have been the first human being to draw an unborn fetus (Figure 1.8). It takes but little reflection to realize the moral as well as religious obstacles that had prevented other artists from giving us this image. And as this drawing implies, Leonardo's invention of a god-like perspective does entail scientific discovery as well as an artist's image that transcends the "realistic" depiction of a pregnant human woman.

Leonardo's *Notebooks* contain evidence that this radical use of art was completely intentional. For what was intended to be a book of anatomical drawings, he wrote:

> I wish to work miracles. . . . And you, who say that it would be better to watch an anatomist at work than to see these drawings, you would be right, if it were possible to observe all the things which are demonstrated in such drawings in a single figure, in which you, with all your

cleverness, will not see nor obtain knowledge of more than some few veins, to obtain a true and perfect knowledge of which I have dissected more than ten human bodies, destroying all the other members, and removing the very minutest particles of the flesh by which these veins are surrounded, without causing them to bleed, excepting the insensible bleeding of the capillary veins; and as one single body would not last so long, since it was necessary to proceed with several bodies by degrees, until I came to an end and had a complete knowledge; this I repeated twice, to learn the differences.[22]

Techniques for presenting form can therefore no longer be viewed merely as trial-and-error practices or artisanal secrets. The artist needs to know the inner nature of a thing ("complete knowledge") in order to create an adequate image of its external shape or form. As will be evident, much the same is true of Leonardo's radical innovations in the representation of motion.

Motion. Another element of Leonardo's art struck his contemporaries and continues to astound art historians: images that portray both animate and inanimate *movement.* In his paintings and sketchbooks, we have visual evidence of an unusual ability to communicate the experience of motion, based on Leonardo's insistence on understanding how nature works.

Leonardo's radical innovations concern inanimate nature as well as living beings, both animal and human. Two instances of this ability will suffice here; each can be associated with activities during the period between 1503 and 1506, when Leonardo's work was most likely to have brought him into personal contact with Machiavelli.

Leonardo's fascination with water is evident in the repeated projects of rechanneling rivers, draining marshes, and redesigning urban environments. For example, his work at the port of Piombino required knowledge of the natural movements of water. While Machiavelli seems to have sponsored this project as Florentine technical assistance to ensure the political loyalty of Jacobo Appiani, Leonardo used the occasion to study the dynamics of inanimate nature in motion. Similarly, the projects to change the course of the Arno, as well as a later plan to create a canal from Milan to Lake Como, gave rise to drawings of the dynamics of moving water.[23] Similar images of storms and other natural phenomena have a character unparalleled for their ability to seize the movements of nature.[24]

Leonardo's use of scientific study as the basis of uniquely successful pictures of motion is even more notable with animate figures. As one art historian notes, "no one could rival him at rendering" a rearing horse.[25] In representing the human form, Leonardo was even more explicit, criticizing his contemporaries for confusing the existence of muscles with their role in movement. As André Chastel put it:

> Leonardo and his rival Michelangelo were both masters of the nude. Michelangelo's figures were sculptural, revealing the play of every muscle. . . . But Leonardo, switching from anatomy to art, wanted his muscles to suggest the 'movements of the soul.' Perhaps with Michelangelo in mind, he writes in Codex Madrid I, "Do not make all the muscles of your figures apparent, because even if they are in their right places they do not show prominently unless the limbs in which they are located are exerting great force or are greatly strained. Limbs which are not in exercise must be drawn without showing the play of the muscles. And if you do otherwise, you will have imitated a bag of nuts rather than a human figure."[26]

This new approach to depicting the movements of horses and humans was nowhere more evident than in the ill-fated *Battle of Anghiari*. Consider what the art historian Anna Maria Brizio writes of this mural on the wall of the Palazzo della Signoria:

> *The Battle of Anghiari* belongs to a totally different cycle of experiences and concepts [than Florentine art in the first years of the sixteenth century]. A new dynamism breaks into it with shattering vehemence. Here again the protagonist is man, but a savage ferocity is present. The figures whirl around in a vortex of motions, as if the forces dominant in nature were unleashing the elements in an attempt to absorb man himself. An abyss separates Leonardo's conception from the battles of Paolo Uccello, for example, of just 50 years before, in which every gesture and attitude is frozen in posture and every single part surrealistically composed and fixed within the network of the abstract and unchangeable relationships of specular perspective. With the *Battle of Anghiari* there is a violent break away from the perspective syntax of the 15th century; the group turns and rushes forward like a hurricane unleashed. Leonardo's mind becomes increasingly more removed from humanism and passes on to consider in an ever wider and more cosmic sense the forces, motions, and elements 'of heaven and earth'.[27]

Today, of course, we cannot see the original the way Machiavelli would have seen it every time he entered the Salla del Gran Consiglio. But we can see Rubens's copy in the Louvre (Frontispiece), which "caught its meaning, its violence, and its confused fury, interpreting it with incomparable immediacy and authority."[28]

Light. Leonardo's innovations in representing perspective and motion would have been impossible without a radical innovation in the understanding of light. For example, he points out that the aerial perspective on a landscape requires that the tops of mountains be darker than their lower slopes (see Figure 3.2).[29] More profoundly, Leonardo realized that to understand perspective, particularly in large paintings like *The Battle of Anghiari,* one had to understand how humans see—and that to understand the eye, one had to understand light.

The result of these investigations is not only visible in Leonardo's paintings, but accessible to us in his *Treatise on Painting.*[30] Although that work was not published until 1651, Leonardo left the manuscripts to his associate Melzi with the clear instructions and intention that it be published (not unlike Machiavelli's action in leaving *The Prince* and *Discourses* to be published posthumously). That is, Leonardo clearly intended to transform the art of painting by making publicly known the science on which it rests. And that science seems to be part of an integration between theory and practice that is otherwise unknown in the history of art.[31]

Technique. Leonardo's repeated attempts to develop radical innovations in the technique of painting and sculpture need to be seen in the context of his novel view of the relationship between theory and practice. Two examples will suffice, each a major political commission: the equestrian statue of Francesco Sforza, often called *Il Cavallo,* sculpted in Milan between 1482 and 1499 but never cast in bronze, and *The Battle of Anghiari,* painted in Florence between 1503 and 1506 but subsequently destroyed. The failure of each of these projects reveals, to its clearest extent, Leonardo's attempt to use his scientific and technical knowledge to produce artistic innovations beyond the limits of known possibilities.

When Leonardo went to the court of the Sforza in 1482, Duke Ludovico (il Moro) wanted to erect an equestrian statue of his father Francesco that had been projected by his elder brother. Leonardo at first proposed a design on which Sforza is riding a *rearing* horse in life-size—a dynamic image of unheard of difficulty, for the statue would not have support for either of its front legs. The duke, ambitious and desiring permanent evidence of the legitimacy of Sforza rule in Milan, sought a bronze monument larger than had ever been cast. The biggest equestrian statue from antiquity—Marcus Aurelius in Rome—measures 4.24 meters (horse and rider combined); the monument in Venice to Colleoni by Leonardo's teacher Verrocchio, completed in 1488 after a decade of work, is 4.0 meters (again, horse and rider combined). For the Sforza monument, the horse alone was to measure 7.2 meters. And, of course, since sculpture is three-dimensional, the increases in surface and weight are the cube of a linear measure.[32]

The enormity of the task made existing casting techniques impractical. Brugnoli says of the notebook containing Leonardo's notes for the project:

> Leonardo the innovator—this is perhaps the greatest significance of the Codex Madrid II folios on *Il Cavallo*. The problem that Il Moro presented to Leonardo, to cast a bronze horse four times greater than life size, could not be solved to the satisfaction of a perfectionist like Leonardo with the then existing methods of casting bronze. In this codex he clearly outlines a new method of casting bronze in a single operation. Once again Leonardo the innovator proved himself to be years ahead of his contemporaries: in fact we find the first reference to his new method of casting in the treatise on 'Pyrotechny' written between 1530 and 1535 by Vannoccio Biringucci. . . . Only two centuries after this new method was developed by Leonardo was it to be used for a large-size monument like the one planned for Francesco Sforza: the equestrian statue of Louis XIV of France.[33]

Ultimately, Leonardo's sculpture was not cast due to the financial and material difficulties of Ludovico, who diverted Leonardo's attentions to court pageants, and finally used the bronze for the statue to make cannon. When Sforza was driven from power in 1500, French soldiers destroyed the sculpture by using it for target-practice.

A second illustration of Leonardo's use of innovative technique in the arts is *The Battle of Anghiari*. In addition to the novelty of its composition, Leonardo sought to use new materials for the wall mural in order to provide a more lasting and more vivid image. The mixture of oil and pigment that Leonardo apparently based on a text in Pliny proved faulty (some say due to adulterated linseed oil, others to the technique of heating the wall after painting, which had worked properly on a small-scale test but failed on the painting itself). For whatever reason, the entire painting was never completed and even the portion actually painted was eventually covered with plaster and repainted by Vasari during renovations of the building in 1560.[34]

The failure of these artistic projects is explained by the boldness of Leonardo's attempt to integrate making and knowing, radically new techniques with daring artistic conceptions based on scientific studies of the objects represented. Despite the relatively small number of artistic works that he had completed, this close linkage of theory and practice had already established Leonardo's fame by 1500, when he returned to Florence after the fall of Ludovico Sforza.[35] Such works as were completed—especially those publicly visible, like *The Last Supper* or *The Battle of Anghiari* before its destruction—were not, however, Leonardo's only legacy. Indeed, they were probably far less important than his manuscripts and the oral traditions they spawned among philosophers and scientists as well as artists.

MATHEMATICS AND PHYSICAL SCIENCE

Over the last century, many historians of science have explored and debated Leonardo's role in the emergence of modern science. It is not possible here to resolve the detailed controversies involved.[36] For present purposes, it will be more important to show the importance of the innovations proposed by Leonardo in his *Notebooks*. In no single case can we prove definitively that his ideas were the seminal contributions that actually changed the course of scientific inquiry: though manuscripts circulated and had great importance even if never published (as we know from the case of Machiavelli's works), the essential point is the new temper and articulation of theory and practice which Leonardo everywhere epitomized.

Modern science is often traced to the discovery of the calculus by Newton and Leibnitz, which made possible a mathematical formulation of Galileo's discovery of inertia and hence a true science of motion. Leonardo's view of mechanics was based on a concept of "impetus" that fell short of Newtonian understanding of the laws of attraction between bodies on which classical mechanics was ultimately based. But Leonardo does seem to have discovered many of the key steps toward the scientific foundations of modern physics.

In the *Notebooks*, Leonardo makes it clear that mathematical knowledge is necessary for science of nature: "Let no man who is not a Mathematician read the elements of my work."[37] In itself, this is hardly an innovation, since it echoes the motto said to have been engraved over the portals of Plato's Academy. For Leonardo, as for Plato, this is not merely a pedagogic prerequisite, but rather a basic characteristic of knowledge itself: "There is no certainty in sciences where one of the mathematical sciences cannot be applied, or which are not in relation with these mathematics."[38]

Leonardo's originality lies in the way he uses mathematics, and particularly in relation to other domains of scientific activity. Three points stand out: first, his emphasis on experimentation and observation; second, his departures from the substance of ancient mathematics and physics—paving the way for the modern sciences of motion; and finally, his constant awareness of the linkage between pure science and applied technology. A word on each.

That Leonardo emphasized experimentation and observation should be obvious from what has been said of his studies of vision and anatomy as the basis of innovations in painting. "All true sciences are the result of Experience which has passed through our senses, thus silencing the tongues of litigants. Experience does not feed investigators on dreams, but always proceeds from accurately determined first principles, step by step in true sequences to the end; as can be seen in the elements of mathematics."[39] While sharing the priority of mathematics in the Platonic tradition, Leonardo thus broke with the speculative—not to mention theological—form of much Renaissance Platonism.

The substantive innovations in Leonardo's scientific notebooks repeatedly demonstrate his break with tradition. One example will have to suffice here. In ancient mathematics, there is a fundamental distinction between number (as in the whole numbers 1, 2, 3—or ratios 1:2, 1:3, 1:4) and measure. As a result, the ancients confronted the problem of incommensurability (e.g., the measure of the hypotenuse of a right triangle cannot be reduced to or made commensurable with a number). Perhaps more important, the ancients had difficulty with the mathematics of motion and acceleration, since they had no way of calculating continuous acceleration over time.[40]

Modern mathematics, and especially the infinitesimal calculus, require the notion of a point which is indivisible and has no measure. While not fully articulated in number theory until the nineteenth century, this conception was clear to Newton as the foundation of the mathematics of continuous or accelerating motion. Yet it was already articulated by Leonardo:

The point, being indivisible, occupies no space. That which occupies no space is nothing. The limiting surface of one thing is the beginning of another. 2. That which is no part of any body is called nothing. 1. That which has no limitations, has no form. The limitations of two coterminous bodies are interchangeably the surface of each. All the surfaces of a body are not parts of that body.[41]

The break with tradition is clear if one consults Aristotle's *Physics*, which challenges virtually all of Leonardo's statements (e.g., *Physics*, IV.211a–212a; VIII.261b–265a).

That Leonardo is working toward a new understanding is evident in a reflection on the number zero (*nulla*) that had been discovered by the Arab mathematicians.

> Amid the vastness of the things among which we live, the existence of nothingness holds the first place; its function extends over all things that have no existence, and its essence, as regards time, lies precisely between the past and the future, and has nothing in the present. This nothingness has the part equal to the whole, and the whole to the part, the divisible to the indivisible; and the product of the sum is the same whether we divide or multiply, and in addition as in subtraction; as is proved by arithmeticians by their tenth figure which represents zero; and its power has not extension among the things of Nature.[42]

In place of the ancient approach to "nothingness" as a qualitative problem, we see here Leonardo focusing on issues of pure mathematics and geometry, searching for operational rules which can utilize a point of zero magnitude for computations in either time or space.

While the philosophical implications of pure mathematics might be left to specialists, the consequences of Leonardo's radical break with the past are evident everywhere. To take the most obvious, long before Galileo's observations with the telescope, Leonardo abandoned the geocentric view of the world upheld by tradition and the church.

> The earth is not in the center of the Sun's orbit nor at the centre of the universe, but in the center of its companion elements, and united with them. And any one standing on the moon, when it and the sun are both beneath us, would see this our earth and the element of water upon it just as we see the moon, and the earth would light it as it lights us.[43]

While other such examples could be catalogued, it is evident that Leonardo was as radical in the substance of his scientific views as in his approach to art.

Even more important is Leonardo's explicit insistence on the integration of pure or theoretical natural science and applied technology. I have emphasized the importance of the project to redirect the Arno and Leonardo's view that water has been the principal agent of historical change. Throughout his career, Leonardo was fascinated with the dynamics of water, seeking a scientific understanding of the form and power of waves, rivers, and other examples of moving liquid.

In the *Notebooks*, Leonardo projects a scientific work on this topic. Following in the tradition of Verrocchio and other painters, he presumed that assistants—in this case, probably Melzi—would complete the editing of his manuscripts. The notes directed to his editor therefore tell us much about how Leonardo intended his ideas to be brought together: "When you put together the science of the motions of water, remember to include under each proposition its application and use, in order that this science may not be useless."[44]

This does not mean that Leonardo failed to see the difference between theory and practice. On the contrary, in the notes for rechanneling rivers—the example of Leonardo's new science with which Machiavelli was most likely to have been familiar—the instructions are clear:

Of digging a canal. Put this in the Book of useful inventions and in proving them bring forward the propositions already proved. And this is the proper order; since if you wished to show the usefulness of any plan you would be obliged again to devise new machines to prove its utility and thus would confuse the order of the forty Books and also the order of the diagrams; that is to say, you would have to mix up practice with theory, which would produce a confused and incoherent work.[45]

The development of theoretical science presupposes its potential utility for human application; the development of technology presupposes its reliance on theoretical science. Theory and practice, fundamentally distinguished in pagan antiquity, are here cast in a radically new interactive relationship which was to emerge as the hallmark of modern society and the basis of its unprecedented material power.

The technological examples of Leonardo's inventiveness—the submarine, the repeating canon, the automatic tool-making machine, the novel clock, etc.—are legion. It would be trivial to catalog them here. Nor is it essential to point out how many have been realized only in the twentieth century. Rather, it should be enough to note that his plans for the airplane mark the decisive intermediate step between the ancient symbol of Icarus (the desire to fly as the epitome of tragic *hubris*) and the modern reality of Neil Armstrong walking on the moon (the construction of flying machines leading to the utterance "One small step for man, a large step for mankind").

HUMAN NATURE, ARCHITECTURE, AND POLITICS

Leonardo's innovative genius touched many other areas of science and applied technology. For present purposes, it is most important to mention his attention to animal and human behavior, scientific fields that provided the basis for his concerns with the design of civil and military technologies to improve the quality of social life. In his art, Leonardo was particularly interested in the diversity of human faces—and the way they seem to symbolize differences in character and behavior. For example, when painting *The Last Supper* in Milan, he walked the streets to find the face that perfectly suited Christ and each of the disciples; his sketches depict all manner of grotesque as well as normal faces and gestures.[46]

In observing the varieties of human nature, Leonardo was disgusted by "rough men, of bad habits and little intelligence" and remarked on the many who were "mere channels for food, producers of excrement, fillers of latrines, for they have no other purpose in this world; they practice no virtue whatsoever."[47] Perhaps for this very reason, Leonardo seems committed to the spread of scientific knowledge and technology, believing that publication of his discoveries would have beneficial results. The mathematical study of light in the science of perspective "preeminently (tends to) elevate the mind of the investigator"; whereas "those men who are inventors and interpreters between Nature and Man" should be "esteemed" as "something in itself," others—"boasters and declaimers of the works of others"—are little more than "herds of beasts."[48] Leonardo's projected treatise on anatomy promises the reader "a true and complete knowledge of all you wish to learn of the human figure"; he will "speak of the function of each part in every direction," so that "if it please our great Author, I may demonstrate the nature of men, and their customs in the way I describe his figure."[49]

The claim to move from form to function implies that Leonardo can identify principles of behavior from the exterior evidence of the sense impressions of other living things. This is precisely what Leonardo sets out to do in a "Bestiary," in which diverse traits are associated with different animals. For example, he finds "love of virtue" in the goldfinch, "sadness" in the raven, "gratitude" in the hoopoe, "avarice" in the toad, and "generosity" in the eagle. Unlike Machiavelli's use of animals like the "lion, fox, and the wolves" to symbolize traits of human behavior, Leonardo seeks the corresponding traits in the life of other animals themselves.[50] Hence, of the lion (Machiavelli's exemplar of courage), Leonardo writes:

"This animal, which is so terrible, fears nothing more than the noise of empty carts and likewise the crowing of cocks."[51]

Such objective knowledge can be used for applied technologies in human affairs, not only in military and civil architecture, but in public health, politics, and urban planning. Leonardo's innovations in the design of weapons and fortifications have been discussed in chapter one (see especially Figures 1.2, 1.9, and 1.10). Having discovered the parabolic trajectory of a cannon shell, he realized it would be necessary to develop forts with thick walls that were curved or angled—so that the attacker's shells would ricochet harmlessly while the defense could fire over the fortified wall. Even with these discoveries, however, Leonardo also realized that massed firepower could inevitably give the offensive forces an advantage, reversing the balance favoring a well-entrenched defense that had characterized the entire history of medieval warfare.[52] This explains Leonardo's invention of a fortress with a moat *inside* the outer wall (so that attackers could be trapped and fired upon between the outer fortifications and an inner wall)—an innovation publicly proposed for the first time in Machiavelli's *Art of War*.[53]

Leonardo therefore seems to have been one of the first to see how radically artillery could transform warfare.

> If any man could have discovered the utmost powers of the cannon, in all its various forms and have given such a secret to the Romans, with what rapidity would they have conquered every country and have vanquished every army, and what reward could have been great enough for such a service.[54]

Leonardo apparently did not assume, however, that military technology would have the same efficacy in any hands; on the contrary, he sees the need to combine "means of offence and defense" with political institutions that permit "communities" to "maintain their good and just Lords."[55]

Leonardo's schemes for urban planning and the development or re-channeling of rivers for economic purposes have already been mentioned. These plans had a political and legal dimension that was essential to their conceptualization. For example, on the map of the diversion of the Arno for economic development, which Leonardo drew in the 1490s, he noted:

> The law which establishes that those who want to make mills can conduct water through any land, paying twice its value.[56]

Even when drawing a map to show how water could be diverted for agricultural development and commerce, Leonardo reminds himself that legis-
lation will be needed to finance the project and control its use.

It is obvious, particularly from the remarks concerning the importance
of controlling sewage for reasons of public health, that such projects
were viewed as the means of unifying scientific knowledge and political
benefit. Such an interpretation is strengthened by the remarks indicating
that Leonardo's projects were intended to secure "revenue" and ensure
political support: "even if he should not wish to reside in Milan he will still
remain faithful in order not to lose the profit of his house at the same time
as the capital."[57] In place of the principle of kinship or "consanguinity,"
which characterized medieval societies, Leonardo wishes to substitute
"property" as the link by which "communities obey and are led by their
magnates."[58]

Leonardo's civil architecture—notably his designs for palaces for Governor Charles d'Amboise in Milan and for King Francis I in Romorantin—shows this same quest for a scientific view of a peaceful, economically
prosperous life in which military danger has been removed to a distance.
Having recognized that the new technology of cannon gave offensive
armies a decisive advantage over medieval fortresses, Leonardo also seems
to have sought the foundation of political success in economic prosperity,
replacing the traditional ties of blood and native birth with self-interest.
Consider the following:

> And nothing is to be thrown into the canals, and every barge is to be
> obliged to carry away so much mud from the canal, and this is after-
> wards to be thrown on the bank.

> Blessed is that possession which is watched by its owner's eyes. Love
> conquers everything.

> The ascending subjects are to their lord as the ivy is to the wall over
> which it climbs.[59]

The first of these suggests combining the self-interest of the barge-owners
with the public need to maintain clean canals for reasons of health and
transportation; the second can be interpreted to refer to the essential
role of private property (establishing "love" of one's own as the legitimate
social bond); the last indicates that upward social mobility will enhance the
external reputation of rulers without challenging their power.

The implication that Leonardo has in mind something like the emerging modern state is reinforced by another maxim written at the same time:

"To order is an aristocratic act; to work is a servile act."[60] Indeed, like Machiavelli, Leonardo sees the need for strong rule to control and channel the potential "beast" in human nature:

Justice requires power, insight, and will; and it resembles the queen bee.

He who does not punish evil commands it to be done.[61]

Leonardo is thus clearly opposed to an egalitarian political and economic community, apparently suggesting to a ruler like Duke Ludovico that he can easily maintain his status by enriching his subjects under conditions that make them more dependent on his rule.

This survey of Leonardo's legacy confirms that his capacity to imagine technological wonders was derived from a coherent and revolutionary perspective on human art, human thought, and human action. No one before Leonardo ever attempted such an integration of theory and practice. Perhaps more important for our purposes, Leonardo extended his understanding of science and technology to outline a radically new vision of human society and politics—a vision which intimates the future of modernity in the West.

As indicated by the historical facts noted above, Machiavelli must have known about many of the projects in which Leonardo's new articulation of theory and practice was revealed: the project for redirecting the Arno (including the maps illustrating a new aerial perspective), *The Battle of Anghiari* (with its novel artistic composition as well as problematic material techniques), the attempt to build a flying machine (which Leonardo apparently pursued actively while in Fiesole during 1504/5), and even *Il Cavallo* (the ill-fated statue of Sforza, whose grandiose dimensions were visible before the uncast model was destroyed at the fall of Ludovico). Even if Machiavelli had never met Leonardo personally, he would have been aware of these innovations from his everyday experiences and his circle of friends and acquaintances.

Although Machiavelli is silent about Leonardo's art, for example, documentary evidence proves he was aware of the open controversy between Leonardo and Soderini (with whom Machiavelli was so closely associated) concerning payments to the artist and his failure to complete *The Battle of Anghiari*.[62] The dedication to *The Prince*, where Machiavelli compares his analysis of the nature of princes and of peoples to an artist's perspective on mountains and valleys,[63] echoes a passage in Leonardo's *Notebooks*,[64] suggesting that Machiavelli may have known Leonardo's manuscript on *The Art of Painting*—or at least the ideas it contains.

Any one similarity of this nature could readily be dismissed as fortuitous. In chapter three above, however, I have analyzed at length the
famous allegory of fortune as a river in *The Prince*, showing the connection
between the view of history it represents and not only the abortive plan to
redirect the channel of the Arno, but above all its relation to Leonardo's
writings on hydraulics and history.[65] While some authors have assumed that
similar ideas concerning floods and history were "probably arrived at independently by the two men,"[66] in fact Leonardo's theories of hydraulics and
their relation to human affairs were far from commonplace; [67] in the biblical view, as the stories of both Moses crossing the Red Sea and Noah's
construction of the ark testify, floods are part of God's plan—and only
God can control the resulting inundations. The similar novelty underlying
the work of Leonardo suggests that Machiavelli's thought was in some way
influenced by conversations between the Second Secretary and the great
artist-scientist-philosopher. Even if the skeptic rejects all such circumstantial evidence, there remain many striking parallels in the thought of the
two famous Florentine contemporaries.

Machiavelli often speaks of the need for "bold" action at critical moments in history. On the back of a sheet with material for the diversion of
the Arno, Leonardo wrote a common proverb:

> When fortune comes, seize her in front with a sure hand, because behind
> she is bald.[68]

Whatever the historical effects of any single invention or theory of Leonardo, the boldness of this innovator was probably his greatest legacy not
only to Machiavelli, but to Western history more generally.

III. The Legacy of Machiavelli:
Replacing Christian Piety with Human Knowledge and Politics

Like Leonardo, Machiavelli died having left behind relatively few works
available to the public: for both, many practical endeavors ended in failure; for both, the most significant works were not widely accessible.
Leonardo's *Mona Lisa* was not in a museum; he kept it with him when
leaving Florence, and it found its way to King Francis I—and only later to
the Louvre, where it could be seen by millions of visitors; Leonardo's
Treatise on Painting was not published until the seventeenth century, and
most of his *Notebooks* were largely unknown until late in the nineteenth

century. Machiavelli's *Mandragola* had been performed and his *Art of War* and *Florentine Histories* published before his death, but the *Discourses on Titus Livy* and *The Prince* were not published until 1531 and 1532 respectively. Yet, like Leonardo, Machiavelli's historical legacy has been enormous, first by word of mouth and private circulation of manuscripts, and of course ultimately by publication and fame.

To summarize Machiavelli's achievement, it is useful to consider how he changed the understanding of human history and action. For this purpose, it is well to return to *The Prince*. In chapter fifteen, when Machiavelli speaks of "imagined republics and principalities," the thoughtful reader is tempted to recall one exemplar of each of these kinds of regime: the *Republic* of Plato and *The City of God* of Augustine. More broadly, then, Machiavelli is critical both of the "best regime" of the ancient (pagan) philosophers—presumably including Aristotle's *Politics* or Cicero's *De Republica* along with the work of Plato—and of the Christian ideal of the "kingdom of God" (whether in its biblical or medieval formulation). Philosophers and theologians alike have explored what we call "theories" of human nature and political life, but these theories are defective when considered in the light of practice.

Machiavelli's criticism of these defective theories entails a redefinition of the concept of *virtù*. For the ancient pagan philosophers, virtue (*arete, virtute*) meant human excellence either in moral and ethical action or in theoretical wisdom: as Plato's *Republic* illustrates, the four cardinal virtues were courage, moderation, wisdom, and justice. For the Church Fathers and Christian theologians, virtue meant belief in God, submission to his will, and love of fellow-men or, as the New Testament puts it, "faith, hope, and charity."

Although there is debate on the exact meaning that Machiavelli gives the word *virtù*, there can be no doubt that he departs radically from both the Platonic and Christian ideals. For some, Machiavellian virtue is merely "ingenuity" and "astute" manipulation of power; for others, it is prudent and effective political leadership in the founding and maintenance of republican government. What is obvious is that—to risk an anachronistic phrase—Machiavelli engages in a transvaluation of values, converting both pagan and Christian ideals into a practical, this-worldly form of human excellence.

To define Machiavelli's novelty with more precision, it is necessary to consider the practical exemplars or models which replace the "imagined republics and principalities." Machiavelli's two main works, *The Prince* and the *Discourses*, represent the substitution of "realities" in human history for the defective theories of the past. In the *Discourses*, Plato's *Republic* is replaced by the historical example of Republican Rome (as it is known to us through the writings of Titus Livy and other historians); in *The Prince*, Jesus as the "prince of peace" is replaced by the example of Moses as human legislator (with the Old Testament tacitly serving as a historical account equivalent to Xenophon's *Cyropedia* or the works of Polybius, Livy, and other pagan historians who describe Cyrus, Theseus, and Romulus as founders of human regimes).[69]

Machiavelli's teaching is thus a radical attempt to refocus human energy and thought on this-worldly political action. The apparent immorality of his advice to rulers is not, in this view, primarily undertaken with the view of encouraging leaders to exploit their power for narrow selfish ends.[70] On the contrary, as careful readers like Rousseau were at pains to emphasize, Machiavelli seeks to rehabilitate the practice of republicanism as exemplified by pagan Rome.[71]

In this reading, emphasis on the need for individual leadership, which is so obviously a principal teaching of *The Prince*, is necessary for "the common good." Since the chief foundations of all societies are "good arms and good laws," it is necessary to have leaders who combine the way of the "beasts" who do not share human moral standards (the skills of "the lion and the fox") with those of "man" (who governs by law or the standards of praise and blame we associate with morality). The virtuous Machiavellian leader is, therefore, the founder or, to use the phrase of the *Discourses*, the "prince of a republic" who uses power in a tough-minded and unscrupulous manner for the benefit of the community.

Machiavelli's most extensive treatment of the relationship between human knowledge (or science) and action is doubtless his famous allegory of fortune as a river in chapter twenty-five of *The Prince*. In chapter three, this passage was analyzed in the light of Machiavelli's experience in attempting to redirect the Arno River, in which Leonardo was a consulting engineer. Moreover, I have shown that virtually the same image of the floods as the principal agent of historical change is spelled out in detail both in Leonardo's own *Notebooks* and in Machiavelli's *Discourses on Titus Livy*. There is every reason, therefore, to assume that this allegory presents a basic teaching in concise, easily remembered form.

For Machiavelli, human wisdom can respond to the challenges of history. Just as the allegorical "river" of fortune can sometimes be controlled by constructing "dikes and dams," historical accidents can sometimes be controlled by the establishment of "good arms and good laws." This prospect of using scientific knowledge for human betterment, like so many of Leonardo's projects, rests on technical or scientific understanding of all the relevant natural forces. If the effects of floods can be controlled by science and technology, as Leonardo proposed in developmental schemes for the rulers of Milan, Florence, Rome, and France, then the effects of historical unpredictability or fortune should likewise be limited by understanding human nature.[72]

I have argued that, in the allegory of the river in chapter twenty-five of *The Prince*, "water" stands for events, a "flood" or "violent river" is a war or foreign invasion, the "earth" human beings, the "trees" the natural resources, and the "buildings" the arts, sciences, and civilizations made by humans. "Dikes" (representing military forces or "good arms") and "dams" ("good laws") are the technological inventions that can control the "impetus" of potentially dangerous natural forces, but their use requires "virtue" or the effective use of human knowledge, strength, and courage.

Book II, chapter five of the *Discourses* confirms that the river allegory represents Machiavelli's theory of history (and not—as some have suggested—merely a commonplace of Renaissance thought). Three points are worth adding in this regard. First, the "measures which Christianity adopted *vis-à-vis* paganism" are the principal human example of the catastrophic discontinuities in history; the "heads of the Christian religion . . . burnt the works of poets and historians, destroyed images and spoiled everything else that betokened in any way antiquity" (ibid., p. 289).[73] Second, it follows that Christianity is simply one religion akin to others; such religious persecutions destroy the common argument against "those philosophers who want to make out that the world is eternal" and hence reduce the biblical account of God's creation to a human "institution" (ibid., pp. 288–289).[74] Third, the repeated historical or natural catastrophes "obliterating the past" are, for Machiavelli, salutary; "when the craftiness and malignity of man has gone as far as it can go, the world must needs be purged . . . so that mankind . . . may adopt a more appropriate form of life and grow better" (ibid., p. 290).[75]

Machiavelli's analysis of Brunelleschi's failed project of flooding Lucca not only confirms the importance of political prudence when implementing such technical projects, but suggests that attempts to divert a river will fail if they are inconsistent with the code described here. Since the relevant chapter of *Florentine Histories* (IV, 23) is quite short—sometimes a sign of great importance in Machiavelli's works—it is worth citing in full:

In those times there was a *most excellent architect* in Florence, called Filippo di ser Brunelleschi, of whose works our city is full. So great was his merit that after his death his likeness in marble was placed in the principal church of Florence with an inscription on the pedestal that *still gives testimony of his virtues* to whoever reads it. He showed how Lucca could be flooded, considering the site of the city and the bed of the river Serchio, and so much did he urge it that the Ten commissioned the experiment to be made. But nothing came of it other than disorder in our camp and security for the enemy, for *the Lucchese raised the earth with a dike on the side where the Serchio was being made to come and then one night they broke the dike of the ditch through which the water was flowing*. Thus, the water found the way toward Lucca blocked and the dike of the channel open, and it flooded the plain so that not only could the army not get near the town but it had to draw off.[76]

Several things in this chapter deserve mention: first, Brunelleschi is described as a "most excellent" architect, whose "merit" and "virtue" were sufficient to produce lasting fame; the flaw in the project does not seem to have been a faulty understanding of the scientific facts; second, since technological stratagems in warfare are vulnerable to countermeasures, knowledge of the likely human response to their use is absolutely essential to success; scientific knowledge can be pernicious unless guided by political prudence; and finally, because Brunelleschi's attempt inverts the image of *The Prince*—in this case dikes are used to create a flood rather than to prevent one—the failure might be taken as a covert suggestion that pacific uses of technology and law may be more likely to succeed in controlling fortune than military ones.[77]

This allegory of fortune as a river is, moreover, not to be taken too literally: though rivers, harbors and irrigation systems are of immense import to civilized states, the political and military implications of science and technology are not limited to them. But for Leonardo, an understanding of the motions of water (and not, as with Galileo, Newton, and subsequent physicists, the trajectories of falling bodies associated with projectiles) was the critical issue at the foundation of a science of nature.[78] Hence the allegory of the river suggests the project of using science and technology—as Leonardo's *Notebooks* show he thought possible—to transform the human condition to one of hitherto unimagined convenience, security, and plenty. Could the prospect of such a science have played a role in Machiavelli's claim to have opened a "new way" in political thought?

These passages show that Machiavelli's allegory of the river is not simply derived from an attempt to rechannel the Arno (whether the military plan on which the city of Florence consulted Leonardo, or the more pacific and economic design that Leonardo first envisaged a decade earlier). Rather, Machiavelli's allegory is an extended and complex code representing the possibility that human initiative could channel political events if guided by a satisfactory political as well as natural science. And it is precisely this image of human history as well as the potential of a science capable of controlling nature that Machiavelli might have borrowed from Leonardo.

It may be asked whether the several parallels between Leonardo's *Notebooks* and Machiavelli's *Prince* and *Discourses* form the basis of the latter's claim to novelty—and if so, why Machiavelli never discusses Leonardo openly. I suggest that the answer to the second question depends on the first. Machiavelli's novelty must in some way be associated with the reason for his praise of the political life of antiquity. Republican Rome is the exemplar of practical politics because it provides an antidote to the passivity and otherworldliness of Christianity; praise of antiquity is directed to the needs of the present:

> there is nothing more necessary to a community, whether it be a religious establishment, a kingdom or a republic, than to restore to it the prestige it had at the outset, and to that one should desire. (*Discourses*, III, 2; p. 390)

Political success needs to be under human control. It is precisely on this score that Rome—not to mention Christianity—is defective: even Roman greatness was due to accident, not human design. Even the highest examples of human history prior to Machiavelli's time need to be corrected by a science of human nature and political institutions.

While any religion can be dangerous if it discourages human initiative, Christianity tends to be especially pernicious. Humans orient their action to a goal or target, and for Christians, that target is "an imagined principality": the city of God governed by the "prince of peace." Machiavelli repeatedly described himself as seeking to orient the human gaze elsewhere: not to heaven (to gain it), but to hell (to avoid it).

This attempted reorientation and its political intention is clearly stated in the letter to Guicciardini cited in chapter two, in which Machiavelli claims that "*I believe the true way of going to Paradise would be to learn the road to Hell in order to avoid it.*"[79] Political life needs to be reoriented to the practical problem of avoiding such hellish outcomes as foreign invasions and civil wars. To do so, Machiavelli must lead the public at large to think of this-worldly pleasures as legitimate and proper ends of their activity.

In setting forth Machiavelli's theory of history in chapter three, I analyzed Machiavelli's *Mandragola* as an example of this attempt to reorient popular attitudes by an astute use of the dramatist's craft. As will be recalled, the lesson of the play is summarized by the song composed as a prologue: "*let us follow our desires . . . because whoever deprives himself of pleasure . . . doesn't know the tricks of the world.*"[80] Moreover, Machiavelli wrote other works that suggest the same goal of using a combination of political skill and human knowledge to replace Christian doctrine in order to organize and control human fortune. Among these is *Belfagor*, a short tale in which a devil named Belfagor bets Satan that he can control a human woman, comes to earth, and is outwitted by a clever peasant, who gains wealth and pleasure in the process. Like *Mandragola*, this story addressed to the popular reader teaches that this-worldly success is possible for those willing to challenge the traditional image of Christian piety. And like *Mandragola*, the story suggests that—as Mandeville later put it—"private vices" can be the foundation of "public virtue."[81]

Natural science can assist in this process: Callimaco's seduction of Lucrezia in *Mandragola* is based on knowledge of the presumed properties of the mandrake root. But natural science cannot by itself persuade the virtuous Lucrezia to engage unwillingly in adultery: such knowledge can direct humans to control outcomes formerly attributed to chance or fortune, but doesn't provide methods that are certain to succeed. Ultimately prudence and political judgment will be needed to found a new political regime or to liberate people from sterile rules imposed on them.

Machiavelli's new way therefore does not promise certainty of success and a definitive conquest of fortune and natural necessity. At best, he says in chapter twenty-five of *The Prince*, humans could control "about half" of the historical events commonly attributed to chance. Individual leadership and political prudence are—and will always remain—essential to human success. In part this follows because the rules of his new political science are complex, dependent on circumstances or "accidents," and in need of application based on good judgment or what the ancients called "practical wisdom."[82]

The need for leadership and prudence is illustrated by Machiavelli's advice with regard to fortresses (*Prince*, ch. 14). Fortresses are an architectural (material) component of "good arms"; they could be said to

represent the engineering that Leonardo's scientific technology could contribute to human politics.[83] But although Machiavelli says that there is no
simple rule about when to build fortresses, such material forms of power
are less effective than the commitment of a republican citizenry; because
"it is not fortresses but the wills of men that keep rulers in power,"
fortresses are "generally much more harmful than useful."[84] Ultimately, it
is the human dispositions and virtues that are central to political success,
not the technological devices derived from a scientific understanding of
inanimate nature. Prudence or practical wisdom (the *phronesis* of the
ancients) is superior to both theoretical wisdom (*sophia*) and art or technology (*techne*).[85]

According to Machiavelli, most innovations do not change war and
politics in any fundamental way. In the chapter of the *Discourses* devoted
to the military effects of "new devices" as well as "new words," for example, Machiavelli advises that a "good general" should "try to confuse
the enemy" with them, but only if they have "more truth than fiction"
since such innovations often fail if they are "fictitious" or "flimsy"; most of
the chapter concerns "new words" or deceptive tricks, not technology.[86]
Earlier in the same work, when dismissing most technical inventions as
ineffective, as well as in Book IV of *The Art of War*, Machiavelli uses the example of "scythed chariots" (one of the devices drawn by Leonardo) and
indicates countermeasures that were effective both when these devices
were used by the "Asiatics" (the example described in Xenophon) and by
Archelaus against Sulla.[87]

Machiavelli's apparent indifference to military technology may be, however, intentionally deceiving; there has apparently been one technological
change in human history that greatly transforms human politics—albeit
without modifying the primacy of political prudence. Actually, Machiavelli
devotes considerable attention to the effects of "cannon" and "artillery"
on both the effectiveness of infantry and the design of fortifications. In this
case, although Machiavelli insists that the technological transformation
does not diminish the primary importance of the infantry and the *virtù* of
its soldiers, he admits that the innovation has simply superseded ancient
weapons in sieges[88] and necessitates the redesign of fortifications along lines
like those described by Leonardo. For the infantry, in addition to such traditional weapons as the crossbow and bow, Machiavelli advises adding "the
harquebus, a new weapon, as you know, and necessary."[89]

Such innovations apparently have had a transforming effect on the technological component of warfare of the utmost political importance. For

example, artillery inherently favors the offense over the defense, and hence ends the effectiveness of the traditional defensive fortifications.[90] This does not end the decisive role of the infantry in warfare, as some thought; quite the contrary, "any who think artillery all-important must be either of little prudence or must have thought very little on these things."[91] But artillery *does* completely change the *political* dimension of warfare: whereas formerly it was thought that soldiers should be drawn only from those in virtuous occupations ("tillers of the soil, smiths, horseshoers, carpenters, butchers, hunters, and the like"), under the new conditions of warfare, any citizen—including "falconers, fishermen, cooks, pimps, and whoever makes a business of providing pleasure"—can be a good soldier if properly motivated.[92]

Machiavelli's emphatic preference for a citizen army (e.g., *Prince*, ch. 12) is, in part, linked to the effect of modern artillery and military technologies with which Leonardo was expert. But Machiavelli could not openly stress these technological factors without running the risk that readers would erroneously think them "all-important." Machiavelli therefore puts his stress on the human element: it is always prudent to espouse the benefits of a citizen army, motivated by *virtù* to defend its homeland. Moreover, because technological innovations make the courageous and motivated pimp as valuable as the courageous and motivated yeoman farmer, the egalitarian implications of military service flow directly from the effects of artillery.

This exposition not only explains what Machiavelli and Leonardo share, but also may indicate why Leonardo's example is not discussed in Machiavelli's works. The two great Florentines share a focus on the bodily things: *le cosi* (as Machiavelli so often calls "politics").[93] Both seek to improve human existence through knowledge of the movements and functions of bodies. While accepting the impermanence of an individual human life, both seek an art that can achieve lasting excellence that will surpass the greatest works of classical antiquity. But whereas Leonardo's principal endeavors were focused on the arts of painting, architecture, and the science of moving objects, Machiavelli's work concerned human communities more directly, in politics but also in history and in drama or poetry.[94]

This difference may explain the differing role of patriotism in Leonardo and Machiavelli. Leonardo was, so to speak, a citizen of the world: he served not only Cesare Borgia and Republican Florence, but the Milanese, the Medici, and the French; by 1507, he was in the service of King Louis XII—

and, of course, he was ultimately to die at Amboise in the service of Francis I. Machiavelli, in contrast, was by principle as well as by passion a Florentine patriot, as epitomized by the eloquent plea to Italy in the last chapter of *The Prince*. It follows that, by the time Machiavelli started to write *The Prince* and the *Discourses* in 1513, he could well have been reluctant to avow openly his debt to Leonardo's scientific and technical knowledge: on the one hand, Leonardo's expertise did not prevent failure in two conspicuous Florentine projects (the abortive military plan to divert the Arno and the unfinished, ill-fated painting of *The Battle of Anghiari*); on the other, Leonardo served foreign rulers—the Milanese, the Medici, and the French and even Cesare Borgia—thereby demonstrating the defect of technical knowledge that is not in the service of political principle.

While Machiavelli may have opened the route to modernity, his teaching does not envisage the definitive "conquest of nature" for the "relief of man's estate" described by Bacon.[95] Ultimately, Machiavelli's view of human nature is limited by the accidents of time and place, which give rise to parochial attachments and imperfect outcomes. It is otherwise for Hobbes. A century and a half later, as one can see in his *Leviathan*, modernity appears in its fullness as a significant extension of the claims for science and human politics.

IV. Hobbes's Political Theology: The Integration of Reason and Practice

For the purposes of this exposition, it will be necessary to focus on Hobbes's *Leviathan*. From the outset of his best-known work, Hobbes integrates three principal themes: first, a science of nature (more specifically, Galileo's new physics of motion) capable of beneficent technological application; second, a theory of human behavior (based on a logically consistent redefinition of terms) that forms a deductive system of confirmable hypotheses; and third, a transformation of traditional Christian doctrine in order to legitimate the practical application of the resulting political theory. Hobbesian theory is thus both a geometric tautology and a self-fulfilling prophecy, using what is today called the "social construction of reality" to found a peaceful, orderly, and powerful commonwealth.

For Machiavelli, as for Leonardo, a hypothetical-deductive science based on mathematical formalization, capable of explaining the motions of bodies and serving to generate beneficent technology, was little more than a promise. Hobbes found himself in a very different situation. On the one hand, as we know from his biographer Aubrey, the experience of reading Euclid had astonished Hobbes, showing him the possibility of universally valid demonstrative proofs. On the other, the physics of motion developed by Galileo provided a scientific theory generating a consistent system of definitions, principles, and hypotheses capable of empirical verification.[96] Because such a blend of mathematics and physics can be used to guide technological construction, Hobbes can propose a relationship between theory and practice that reaches more optimistic conclusions from premises similar to those of Machiavelli.[97]

The Author's Introduction to *Leviathan* exhibits all of these features. Hobbes begins the Introduction with a comparison between God as maker of the universe and man as maker of the commonwealth: humans are viewed as creators of political order, just as the Christian God is the creator of the world. This creation of political institutions is compared to "automata": self-moving machines, like a watch, which represent successful technological innovations based on scientific knowledge.[98] To this end, however, it is necessary to redefine terms and generate observational means of testing the resulting propositions. Only then can political institutions be designed and implemented so that natural propensities of humans generate political stability and even something approximating the premodern virtues.

Hobbes's procedure is as follows. At the outset, he shows that human behavior is the product of matter in motion. The natural condition of all bodies is the inertia described by Galileo: motion continues until external forces or objects intervene. Applied to humans, this means that all thoughts and ideas are produced by particles or bodies which have communicated an environmental event to the individual brain (*Leviathan*, chs. 1–4; pp. 25–45).

This view has epistemological consequences. If all thought is the result of environmental conditioning on a "blank slate," all concepts are conventional; as Locke argued in the *Essay on Human Understanding*, there are no "innate ideas" and no ways of knowing the "essence" or inner nature of things. It follows that the redefinition of any concept can be undertaken as long as it is consistent with empirical evidence. Hence it is both possible and necessary to redefine all basic terms describing human nature and social behavior, abandoning the natural teleology of Aristotle and the Thomist tradition (*Leviathan*, chs. 5–11; pp. 45–92).

Because inductive categories are limited by the experience of the individuals who use them, the only universal knowledge takes the form of a deductive system based on the model of Euclid's geometry. Only such a system can produce hypothetical statements about the world which are rigorous and capable of demonstration. "Absolute knowledge"—the testimony of a witness in a specific event—is utterly unreliable; instead, hypothetical knowledge (statements in the form "if . . . then") can be the basis of deductive theorems whose descriptive accuracy is tested by experience (*Leviathan*, ch. 9; p. 75).

This approach explains why Hobbes's theory is based on a model of the "natural condition of mankind." Hobbes replaces the historical science of Machiavelli with a quasi-geometrical model of the state of nature based on a formal definition of natural right and natural law. The natural right to self-preservation, understood as the human equivalent of inertia in physics, is an unlimited claim on all things, giving rise to "a perpetual and restless desire of power after power, that ceases only in death" (*Leviathan*, ch. 11; p. 86). So defined, this basic principle of human behavior can readily be confirmed by observing human selfishness. Although Hobbes uses the evidence which served as the basis of Machiavelli's prudential theory, he thus transformed selfishness into an equal "right" of all humans that could be the foundation of a deductive science.[99]

Since all humans have an unlimited right to all things, the basic problem of social behavior is the ubiquity of conflict: the "natural condition of mankind" is a "war of all against all." To avoid a life that is "solitary, poor, nasty, brutish, and short," individuals form a society or "commonwealth" based on a social contract or "covenant" (*Leviathan*, chs. 13–16; pp. 101–136). Because this view of human nature resembles the account in Glaucon's restatement of the Sophist theory of justice (*Republic*, II.358e–360d), Hobbes's premises are hardly novel—but he uses them as the basis of a radically new theoretical system.

According to Hobbes, natural right must be distinguished from the law of nature, which consists of the obligations established by reason. Hobbes completely transforms the traditional or Thomist concept of natural law by converting moral injunctions into a logical tautology. The first law of nature is formulated as follows: "seek peace if you have hope of obtaining it, and enter into war if you do not." Cooperate if you think you can preserve yourself by so doing; compete if you think that you cannot preserve yourself by cooperating. Since each individual is the only judge of which branch of the law of nature applies in any situation, there is no way of disproving this rule of behavior. If humans are obeying the government; they have followed the first branch of the law; if they disobey the government, obviously they are following the second.

Hobbes's commonwealth is thus embedded in—and always risks re-verting to—the state of nature. It is impossible to avoid this outcome merely by exhortation or threat: even if a subject has been justly con-demned for violating the law, the criminal who perceives enforcement of the law as a threat to continued life will return to the state of nature. Because no covenant can entail the surrender of the natural right to self-preservation, individuals can and will resist punishment. More generally, subjects can be expected to obey the sovereign only when they judge that the benefits are greater than the costs.

The apparently authoritarian power of the Hobbesian sovereign is misleading, since Hobbes's carefully redefined terms describe a "represen-tative" government based on the "consent" of the subjects. This paradox can only be understood by considering the problem of applying Hobbes's theory to practice. After spelling out his theory of the commonwealth, Hobbes concludes Part 2 of *Leviathan* with a curious passage:

> And now, considering *how different this doctrine is from the practice of the greatest part of the world*, especially of these western parts that have received their moral learning from Rome and Athens, and how much depth of moral philosophy is required in them that have the administra-tion of the sovereign power, I am at the point of believing this my labor as useless as the commonwealth of Plato. For he also is of opinion that it is impossible for the disorders of state and change of governments by civil war ever to be taken away till sovereigns be philosophers. But when I consider again that the science of natural justice is the only science necessary for sovereigns and their principal ministers; and that they need not be charged with the sciences mathematical, as by Plato they are, far-ther than by good laws to encourage men to the study of them; and that neither Plato nor any other philosopher hitherto has put into order and sufficiently or probably proved all the theorems of moral doctrine that men may learn thereby both how to govern and how to obey—I recover some hope that one time or other this writing of mine may fall into the hands of a sovereign who will consider it himself (for it is short, and I think clear) without the help of any interested or envious inter-preter, and *by the exercise of entire sovereignty, in protecting the public teaching of it, convert this truth of speculation into the utility of practice.* (*Leviathan*, ch. 31; pp. 287–88)

Hobbes here suggests that the empirical adequacy of his theory depends on its successful application by a sovereign. More important, such an application of the theory requires that subjects be taught to claim their natural rights to self-preservation whenever, as subjects, they feel rightly or wrongly that their lives are in question.

Appearances to the contrary, Hobbes does not teach that subjects should be taught to be uncritically submissive and obedient; rather, the implementation of *Leviathan* seems to require a commonwealth in which the subjects are fully informed and aware of their rights. The presupposition of this extension is printing, and the correlative spread of reading.

Hobbes's science is thus radically egalitarian in two senses. On the one hand, all humans have the same natural rights—and, indeed, no one could conceivably abandon the right to self-preservation, since it is the human equivalent of inertia in falling bodies (*Leviathan*, ch. 14; p. 112). On the other, all humans have, at least in principle, the capacity to discover scientific truths. Whereas Machiavelli asserts that political success depends on understanding inevitable differences in human intelligence,[100] Hobbes claims that there is basically an "equality of ability" in matters of the "mind" as well as of the "body."[101]

Machiavelli's prudential rules for the intelligent leader become, for Hobbes, a logical tautology. The Hobbesian commonwealth is entirely manmade. And by building the commonwealth on the basis of a quasi-geometric demonstration, obedience can become a self-fulfilling prophecy (*Leviathan*, ch. 20; p. 170). If all subjects know and insist on the enforcement of their inalienable rights to self-preservation, sovereigns will come to encourage commerce, control monopolies, and establish a powerful government capable of effective punishment where absolutely necessary. It is, in principle, possible for humans to create an "eternal" commonwealth.

Hobbes thus replaces both ancient moral philosophy and traditional Christian teaching as the foundation of political obedience; in their place, he publishes *Leviathan* and encourages a sovereign read it and teach it to an entire society. Unlike Machiavelli's *Prince*, which describes political things much as a painter portrays landscapes, Hobbes's work has a constructive character in which the act of publication is itself central; for the first time, the existence of printing is consciously at the heart of a philosophic teaching.[102]

In his own lifetime, Machiavelli relied on the theater (*Mandragola*), parables (*Belfagor*), and the private distribution of manuscripts as the principal means of popular diffusion for his ideas.[103] In contrast, Hobbes expects that the sovereign can command his book to become a printed text that rivals the Bible as the basic educational text of a society.[104] Whereas Machiavelli and Leonardo were particularly influenced by the transformations in military technology introduced by artillery, Hobbes's thought seems to have been shaped by the parallel (but slightly slower) diffusion of the transformation of communicative technology introduced by printing.

Printing is essential because Hobbes seeks to replace obedience based on the biblical teaching ("Obey the powers that be") with his Christianized mathematical physics of human nature. When reading *Leviathan*, the reader himself is supposed to test the premise that the natural right to self-preservation is the principal motivation for behavior whenever individual life has been threatened (*Leviathan*, ch. 13; p. 107). If all members of a society were taught to do this, the political problem would be transformed into the self-fulfilling prophecy of a new political situation in which the sovereign, "authorized" by the members of the commonwealth, represents them.

This "liberal" conception of the state follows from the practical application of Hobbesian theoretical principles. All citizens have an inalienable natural right to self-preservation. Even if the government has legitimately taken steps to punish a criminal, that criminal can resist arrest or punishment by force—and in doing so, is merely following the law of nature. What is true of one citizen is true of groups of citizens. Hence the sovereign can interfere in the private lives of subjects only to the extent that the latter consent. In addition to suggesting prudential reasons for limiting state intervention in private matters, this principle shows the utility of transforming the ubiquitous competition for power into competition for economic success and wealth.

The resulting order is not merely authoritarian. While the subjects of the commonwealth are to read *Leviathan*, it is to be put in practice only after the sovereign has done so—and has become sufficiently convinced of the benefits of Hobbes's theory to teach it throughout the community. And from the sovereign's perspective, the principles outlined above required a limited government under law—or, in modern terms, a constitutional government based on the conception that the individual should be free wherever possible.

Serious interpreters as different as Jean-Jacques Rousseau, Karl Marx, Leo Strauss, Carl Schmitt, and C. B. MacPherson have therefore noted that Hobbes provides the foundations for the liberal or capitalist framework of political life which came to dominate the Anglo-Saxon nations and provided the foundation of modernity in the West. To be sure, the main features of Hobbesian theory were more effective when presented in more palatable form in Locke's *Second Treatise*. Whether one considers the utilitarian thought of Bentham, John Stuart Mill, or the American constitutional tradition, however, we find the principal features of an individual rationality based on the belief in a socially constructed community in which law becomes the framework for economic progress and contentment.

While Hobbes's theory presents itself as "secular" or this-worldly, moreover, its practical application entails a theological dimension of the greatest importance. Most readers are content to read the first two books of *Leviathan*, ignoring the last half of the work devoted to a "Christian commonwealth." In seeking to avoid this error, however, it is incorrect to conclude that Hobbes's professions of Christianity are sincere if not orthodox.[105] Rather, like Machiavelli—only in a more explicit and formal manner—Hobbes transforms the Judaeo-Christian tradition, absorbing it into his reconstruction of political theory and practice through a thoroughgoing reinterpretation of the texts.

Without entering into all the details, it should suffice to contrast the way Hobbes and Machiavelli utilize the biblical texts. In *The Prince*, the account of Moses in Exodus is used to provide an exemplar of the entirely new prince as a human leader (see esp. ch. 6, pp. 22–23 and ch. 26, pp. 103). In Parts 3 and 4 of *Leviathan*, Hobbes goes to great lengths to show that his theory is consistent with the biblical texts if they are read as humanly written. Hence, in Hobbes, we can see the beginnings of what came to be known as the "higher criticism"—i.e., the use of logic to extract meaning from otherwise puzzling texts.

For example, it is imperative for Hobbes to show that the Pentateuch (Five Books of Moses) could not have been entirely written by Moses himself. To provide evidence of this interpretation, Hobbes cites the passage in which the grave of Moses is described as being unknown "to this day" (*Leviathan,* ch. 33; p. 54). Reading the text with usual canons of interpreting human speech, it seems logically impossible that Moses could have written a description in the past tense of the site of his own grave. Instead of using biblical texts as literal truth or testimony to divine grace (as do theologians) or as metaphor and historical source (as in Machiavelli's *Prince*), Hobbes integrates the Bible into a thoroughly nominalist political teaching.

To summarize, one can describe Hobbes's *Leviathan* as the foundation of a political religion. Irrational belief in biblical Christianity is replaced by a rational understanding of Christianity as an integral part of the common-wealth defined and explained in Parts 1 and 2 of *Leviathan*. As Rousseau put it, Hobbes was the modern writer who first sought to integrate politics and religion, creating a politico-theological teaching in which theory and practice are effectively united.[106]

For practical purposes, this solution entails both a tacit political establishment of religion (in the abstract) and extreme toleration of doctrinal variation. The sovereign must be the sole judge of the religious doctrines to be taught in the community. But as long as subjects do not use religious beliefs as the basis of challenging authority, prudent rulers will limit their enforcement of doctrine to narrowly defined norms which emphasize overt behavior. As in England to this day, the king can well be head of a state church in a commonwealth that encourages religious toleration.

Hobbes's perspective can thus be viewed as a this-worldly political theology based on the fusion of theory and practice as well as the integration of natural science and political thought. The "new way" opened by Machiavelli is very greatly broadened in the process. In place of a perspective that presupposes prudence (and even wisdom) in the leader, Hobbes develops a deductive system with geometric certainty, reminds the reader that its premises can be empirically verified, and then outlines how a lasting regime can be created on the basis of these principles. That the result stands as one of the major landmarks in the history of Western political thought is confirmed well enough by the continued fascination of Hobbes's works not to mention the relationship between his thought and the traditions of empirical research in modern social science.[107]

V. The Legacy of Modernity

In claiming that what we call modern political theory originates in Machiavelli but is fully developed for the first time in Hobbes, I do not mean that all political theory since the Renaissance can be reduced to these two thinkers. Modernity has another variant in continental thought, epitomized by the tradition stemming from Descartes and developed further by Montesquieu, Rousseau, Kant, Hegel, and Marx. In the *Discourse on Method* and *Rules for the Direction of the Mind*, Hobbes's French contemporary showed a rather different method of integrating the new, mathematical sciences of nature with the study of humans; as set forth in the *Meditations*, to which Descartes appended the *Objections* of Hobbes (among others), the differences between this approach and that of *Leviathan* become explicit.

In a fuller account, it would be necessary to spell out in more detail the variants of what has here been called modernity. For the moment, however, it should suffice to indicate the central traits of fully developed modernity as they are developed by Hobbes and can be seen in subsequent thinkers whose approach to theory and practice can be called "modern." Whatever the differences between Hobbes and thinkers in the Anglo-Saxon tradition from Locke to John Stuart Mill, not to mention the parallel continental tradition from Descartes to Marx, several common characteristics can be traced. By summarizing these traits, we can gain a better view of our own situation.

Rational or scientific knowledge of nature can, in principle, explain all things in a manner comprehensible to all. To do so, science must abandon the claim of knowing the essence or purpose of things and limit itself to explaining their movements and changes. In such a science, theories take a hypothetical-deductive form, in which mathematical representations of nature are accepted only insofar as experiments confirm them.

In modern science, concepts therefore need to be defined explicitly so that they will be logically consistent and empirically relevant: "Let x equal . . . ." Explanations need to be couched in hypothetical manner so that any trained scientist can produce the predicted effects: "If x, then y." Scientific theories are therefore constructive insofar as they take the form of rules or instructions that permit the observer to reproduce visible things in principle if not in practice.

To know something, therefore, is to know how to "make" it—even if the construction is theoretical.[108] Such a natural science continually gives rise to technologies that control or redirect natural necessity. In turn, these technologies permit an ever-increasing extension of scientific theories to explain things too distant, too minute, or too complex for naïve observation. Theories therefore have practical applications, and practice is the test of theoretical knowledge.

Because humans are natural things, modern science can focus on social or political things as well as on inanimate or animate nature. Since the hypothetical-deductive method cannot derive primary terms from experience or custom, political or social theories approach human behavior from an objective standpoint (as if the theorist were outside society much as a watchmaker is outside the watch being made or repaired). This perspective makes possible theories claiming to explain the motive forces and history of human affairs, but not the best way for an individual to live.

The result is a paradox. Although a thoroughly modern science cannot claim to know the essence or goal of human life, its theories can and should guide practice. Prior to the Renaissance, such practical guidance was, in part, sought in religious doctrine and belief. Hence science, while focusing on the visible world and the material experience of humans, necessarily has theological implications.

If modern science can explain all things, it can change things: theories in the natural sciences are the foundation of technology. If science and technology can change or control things, humans can replace prayer to God or the gods by activity using power in the quest for desired outcomes. Because science, technology, and their practical fruits claim to be understandable to all humans, scientific theories of human society can be the foundation of systems of belief. The scientific temperament provides satisfactions on earth in place of otherworldly faith—but in politics, the success of this endeavor entails the transformation of political philosophy into political religions or ideologies.

Before the emergence of such political religions or ideologies, political leadership entailed prudence or good judgment. Only some individuals, endowed with talent and educated to achieve their natural potential, were capable of effective rulership. Modernity, by ushering in the age of ideology, points to the replacement of prudence by a science of public policy. The design of effective "development" or progress is thus made possible by a combination of technical expertise among the elite and political belief among the citizenry. At most, there is disagreement concerning the advisability of public controversy concerning policy proposals and belief systems: for modern "liberals" and "democrats," regimes must be open or free, whereas in the authoritarian versions of modernity, public debate concerning policies and principles is a luxury that cannot be tolerated.

Whatever other differences are found within the Anglo-Saxon and continental traditions of modernity, this epoch of history represents an attempt to integrate theory and practice, science and belief, religion and human affairs, national patriotism and the interests of the human species as a whole. It remains to be seen, however, whether this attempt is feasible. The failure of Marxism and the eruptions of violent nationalism, racism, and religious fundamentalism both within and outside the West, which mark the last years of the twentieth century, suggest that the modern epoch may be approaching its end.

Today, many have recognized this "exhaustion of the West" by speaking of post-modernism. Those who use this term often seem to espouse a highly relativist or subjective view of knowledge, attributing established modes of thought to the social forces that are dominant in our society. The foregoing exploration of the origins of modernity suggests a rather different set of questions. Most of the traits here associated with the modern epoch are shared by post-modernists. As we witness the collapse of global communism, the emergence of nationalistic irredentism, and the resurgence of religious enthusiasm, the expressions of post-modernism appear as one version of modernity rather than a true challenge to its fundamental assumptions.

Looking ahead to the twenty-first century, the technological and practical dreams of Leonardo and Bacon now appear to be within reach. It seems but a matter of time until techniques of in vitro fertilization and intensive neonatal care are merged to permit industrialized production of human beings.[109] The advances in the human genome project, molecular genetics, and neuroscience—not to mention technologies from supercomputers and fiber optics to genetic engineering, nitrogen-fixing plants, and other technological revolutions—loom on the horizon precisely at a time when many have become deeply skeptical of science and the modern project itself.

The issue can be put simply. Soon, *Brave New World* will be technologically feasible: institutions introduced as comic impossibilities in Plato's *Republic* and as horrible dystopia in Huxley's novel are likely to become practicable in coming generations. For the first time since the opening of a new epoch of Western thought by Machiavelli, Leonardo, and Hobbes, we need to question whether our civilization should return to the horizon that these early moderns sought to transcend. Put in nutshell, can theory be a complete guide to practice? If not, should we return to the ancient view that human politics is ultimately limited by what is just according to nature?

Conclusion

The difference between Plato and Aristotle is that Aristotle believes that biology, as the mediation between knowledge of the inanimate and knowledge of man, is available.

Leo Strauss[1]

Contemporary Western civilization offers a paradox: societies of hitherto unparalleled power and wealth seem to be in cultural disarray and uncertainty. One hundred years ago, the end of the nineteenth century was marked by an optimistic belief that the benefits of science, industry, and commerce were virtually unlimited; as we approach the twenty-first century, the mood is more often doubt, fear, or anger. Why the current predicament? Can a better understanding of Machiavelli's thought explain the frustrations and unexpected failures of industrial civilization?

To gain a fresh perspective on the problems of our time, I have suggested, it is useful to reconsider the origins of modernity in Renaissance Italy. This book argued that the modern epoch is principally defined by an unprecedented integration of theoretical science, technology, commerce, and politics. Before the Renaissance, the inventiveness of artisans and artists was usually separated from philosophic or theological inquiries into nature and human history. How, then, did humans imagine that rational or scientific understanding of the world could give rise to continuous transformations of material technology and social practice, producing what Shakespeare named a "brave new world"?

The ancient Greeks and Romans developed rational theories of nature and secular political regimes—but relegated technology to a secondary status; medieval Europe slowly developed technological abilities—but did so in the context of theological doctrine and religious belief. In the Renaissance, the rediscovery of classical antiquity was combined with a focus on this-worldly success. Such terms as "secularism" and "humanism," often used to describe the change, do not fully explain the origins of modernity: self-reliant human achievement can be found in both pagan antiquity and the Middle Ages. Nor can modernity be equated with secular republicanism, a tradition that scholars have traced from classical antiquity and Florence in the early fifteenth century to the generation of Savonarola and Machiavelli.[2]

What changes were needed to produce societies that could develop the internal combustion engine, organize concentration camps to industrialize the murder of millions, and send a man to the moon? The origins of this civilization can be illuminated by a careful study of Machiavelli and Leonardo da Vinci for three reasons: first, these two extraordinary men openly proclaimed their novelty; second, they have often been viewed as originating important aspects of modernity; and finally—though not generally appreciated—their experience of working on at least three common projects in Florence during 1503/4 illustrates the interaction between science, technology, and politics which is the hallmark of modernity and its crises.

I. Machiavelli's Theory of Human Nature

I have argued that Machiavelli and Leonardo represent a break with the perspectives of medieval Christendom and pagan antiquity. Whatever the role of other factors, these two thinkers were among the first to articulate the modern combination of theory and practice in the service of human emancipation. Machiavelli claims his theory of human nature is based on combining a study of ancient writings with his personal experience as a statesman. Most scholars emphasize only his literary sources and contribution to political ideas. Although Machiavelli does not explicitly describe the experience of working with Leonardo between 1503 and 1506, Leonardo's unparalleled attempt to integrate scientific knowledge, technical innovation, and social utility makes it particularly important to reconsider Machiavelli from the perspective of science and technology.

Machiavelli reminds his readers that the ancients wrote about politics with "covert" meanings; as soon as his works are compared to each other, Rousseau's assertion that Machiavelli used the same techniques becomes evident. Anyone who considers Machiavelli's experience of torture after the Medici took power in 1512 can see why he was forced to hide his republican "intention" (chapter one). Because many of the controversies concerning Machiavelli's political thought can be traced to superficial or hasty reading,[3] *The Prince* is examined closely to see why Machiavelli claimed to have opened a way "as yet untrodden" by any other writers (chapter two). Reread in this manner, Machiavelli was not merely an exponent of immoral selfishness and the arrogant exercise of power. On the contrary, Machiavelli's political theory does indeed open the way toward modern political life by combining the "way of the beast" (self-interested force, fraud, and cleverness) with the "way of man" (law and virtuous leadership in the common good). Throughout Western Europe, Machiavelli's goal of "republican" government under laws became, after the revolutions of the seventeenth and eighteenth centuries, one of the basic themes in modern political practice.

Machiavelli's comparison of fortune and a river in chapter twenty-five of *The Prince* is a powerful image of the transformation in attitudes that was needed at the outset of modernity. The belief that human action can alter historical outcomes is clearly symbolized by the construction of "dams and dikes" to channel the "river" and control "floods." I have argued that this passage, often described as an *allegory*, also reflects the Florentine project of redirecting the Arno River in 1503/4, directed by Machiavelli and using the technical expertise of Leonardo. While this attempt to use technology failed, it symbolizes not only Leonardo's other plans to rechannel rivers and control water for peaceful political ends, but the broader potential of harnessing science and technology to the goals of human action.

In this interpretation, Machiavelli learned from both the potential *and* the failure of Leonardo's scientific and technological projects. On the one hand, the promise of this experience led Machiavelli to see a new way of integrating theory and practice, abandoning the stance of philosophic judgment in order to enhance the human control of nature and history. On the other hand, the lack of success in redirecting the Arno and the failure of Leonardo's technical innovations on other projects taught Machiavelli to stress the primacy of politics over technology and abstract science (see chapter seven and Appendix III).

Hidden in Machiavelli's writings, therefore, is the proposal that humans use natural science and technical expertise to imitate the creative power of the Judeo-Christian God. The resulting development of industry and commerce as the basis of political power is, of course, a hallmark of modernity. For Machiavelli himself, however, the quest for what Bacon later called "the conquest of nature" for the "relief of man's estate" can never be completely attained. Neither science nor technology, but human excellence (*virtù*) is the critical need: "discipline can make up where

Nature is lacking."[4] Politics remains the master science, for technical solutions can never attain total control over the "accidents" of human nature and history. Aware of the dangers of Leonardo's science and the ease with which it could be used by unscrupulous men like Cesare Borgia, Machiavelli (like the ancients) feared the popular teaching of science at the same time that he saw the promise of using technology to achieve human ends.

The self-conscious use of science and technology as instruments of human betterment and political power is a basic characteristic—indeed, I argue, *the* basic characteristic—of modernity. Given Machiavelli's contribution to the spread of this new perspective, the study of his ideas can illuminate our current situation. But to do so, it is necessary to go beyond merely historical or literary study by asking: is Machiavelli's theory of human nature true? In chapters three, four, and five I have confronted Machiavelli's assumptions about human nature with the findings of contemporary natural science.

The evidence shows an extraordinary congruence between Machiavelli's views and the research of evolutionary biologists, ethologists, and neuroscientists. Human nature is not merely a poet's symbol or philosopher's assumption: it is a subject of scientific inquiry.[5] Unlike many later political theorists, Machiavelli presents, albeit in literary form, an account of humans as combining elements of "beast" and of "man" that is generally confirmed by the latest scientific studies of nonhuman primates and hominid evolution. As if to confirm this view, some contemporary biologists use the term "Machiavellian intelligence" to describe the social competence of monkeys and apes which characterizes the evolution of primates generally and hominids more specifically.[6] In this light, Machiavelli's theory of human nature and history deserves the respect and analytical scrutiny given to the more systemic writings of Plato, Aristotle, Hobbes, or Hegel.

For Machiavelli, human social organization is based on the interplay of three passions: love, fear, and hate. As recent studies of animal behavior show, this triad corresponds to the fundamental behavioral repertoire of social bonding, threat, and flight found among mammals (and especially among nonhuman primates). Unlike later moderns from Hobbes to Rousseau, moreover, Machiavelli places stress on social *inequality,* emphasizing the necessities—and demands—of leadership as an inescapable feature of stable social life. Here again, studies of animal dominance and subordination show that Machiavelli's view of human nature is broadly consistent with the scientific evidence for species whose environment and behavior resemble the life of our hominid ancestors.

Even more important may be Machiavelli's analysis of the origins and vulnerability of political institutions like the modern nation-state. Universal traits of human nature cannot explain the rise—or fall—of centralized governments; evidence of human evolution has confirmed that, for the longest portion of our species' existence, our ancestors lived in small groups like those found among monkeys and apes. This perspective suggests that, whatever the role of competition between groups and economic development within them, the emergence of governments and states was heavily dependent on the intelligence, ability, and courage of individual leadership. Here too, Machiavelli's theories point to factors that were given only secondary importance by Locke, Marx, and the ideologies they inspired.

This analysis reveals a puzzle. Modern politics in the West has long been dominated by the ideological traditions of Lockean liberalism, Marxian socialism, and Burkean conservatism. Yet Machiavelli's understanding seems more accurate, on *scientific* grounds, than the theories of Locke, Marx, or Burke. When or how was Machiavelli's complex and subtle theory of human nature and leadership transformed into the simplistic ideologies that have dominated the politics of the last two centuries? The civilization of the West can be defined primarily by its integrated view of natural science, technology, and society, yet Machiavelli's contribution to this historical change led to an intellectual climate in which "Machiavellianism" became a word of opprobrium. Can the problems of contemporary modern society be attributed to Machiavelli's vision of a "new" mode of social life, or did subsequent events somehow modify modernity in a way that helps to explain the current predicament?

In chapter seven, I have explored this question. First, it was necessary to return to the historical origins of the unification of theory and practice by reconsidering the thought and work of Leonardo da Vinci. Machiavelli's contemporary, Leonardo worked in and for Florence between 1503 and 1506, sometimes under circumstances that necessarily involved Machiavelli. A survey of Leonardo's contributions to art, to science, and to technology reveals the same emphasis on innovation and the same commitment to overcoming the traditional gap between theory and practice which are evident in Machiavelli's writings. Even more surprising, we learn of Leonardo's political project, developed as early as the 1490s, clearly outlining something like the fully modern state based on property, technology, and law. Whatever the extent of personal friendship and communication between the two Florentines, therefore, they represent the critical moment in the emergence of modernity.

This analysis confirms the account of Machiavelli presented earlier, suggesting that there were critical events in the transformation of Western history subsequent to the time of Machiavelli and Leonardo. Chapter seven focuses on but one: the theoretical difference between Hobbes and his predecessors. At the outset of the sixteenth century, the two Florentines foresaw a complex and challenging possibility of innovation, technical mastery of nature, and political change. In the middle of the seventeenth century, Hobbes sought to reduce this conception to geometric certainty. My thesis is that it was this reduction—and its subsequent redefinition by thinkers as diverse as Locke, Rousseau, and Marx—which lies at the root of the current intellectual malaise throughout the modern world.

II. The Contemporary Predicament

Machiavelli's understanding of human nature and society helps us to clarify the reasons for the mood of uncertainty that has spread through the West at the approach of the twenty-first century. Even a generation ago, most reasonably prosperous Americans and Europeans imagined that their children would be at least as secure and prosperous as their parents. The coming period of history was still viewed as offering the potential for progress. Today, such optimism has been replaced by doubt, fear, and anger.

Within industrial societies, problems of unemployment, education, crime, health care, and environmental degradation often seem intractable. Frustrated voters often support leaders who use television and other mass media to broadcast simplified proposals and condemn the impotence of established parties and institutions. As a result, even in the wealthy societies of Western Europe and North America, there is widespread popular cynicism and disenchantment with the traditional institutions of constitutional government. In the former communist societies of Eastern Europe, not to mention the less fortunate countries of Africa, Asia, and South America, the problems are even worse. For example, one journalist has recently written a gloomy assessment of the way "scarcity, crime, overpopulation, tribalism, and disease are rapidly destroying the social fabric of our planet."[7]

Underlying a growing sense of impotence and fear is the feeling that our civilization is in a trap. We cannot go forward, we cannot go back. Modernity has been predicated on progress—but the most likely arenas of progressive improvements in standards of living, wealth, and scientific achievement have been largely exploited. Ancient societies had a different ethic, in which technological progress and universal emancipation were never central components, but it is impossible to return to the economics, culture, and politics of the Greek or Roman city-state. After the last century of industrialization, scientific progress, and technological advance, how can one propose a return to societies based on slavery, artisanal technology, and pagan polytheism?

Throughout the nineteenth century, one of the principal foundations of economic and social progress was the availability of "empty land" for colonization, settlement, and economic development. European imperialism and the American frontier played a similar role: superior technology and military force were used to take control of resources of land and raw materials in areas inhabited by less highly developed peoples. Today, however, the benefits of settling the frontier and colonizing Africa and Asia have been exhausted. No longer can the "huddled masses" of Europe, "yearning to breathe free," find homes, work, and prosperity in the New World. And no longer can industry exploit a politically passive labor force and pollute the environment within the most powerful states in the world. Opening a global market in the computer age necessarily entails increasing the tensions associated with ethnic and religious conflict; guaranteeing the protections of the welfare state necessarily requires limits on immigration.

Throughout the nineteenth century, nation-states were established, using public schooling, patriotism, and economic growth as the basis of political commitments and moral values. Conflicts between progressives and conservatives within each European society concerned how much of the wealth and power of the more fortunate citizens should be distributed to the "have-nots." Today, a global economy makes it impossible for a single nation-state to isolate itself from the world-wide flow of information, material goods, and disease, while the global population explosion poses an insoluble problem. Today, many are beginning to fear that the growing numbers of "have-nots" exceed the productive capacities of global economic development or the political will for equitable redistribution of resources.

Within the nation-state over the last two centuries, problems of inequality have been solved—at least in favorable times—by economic growth: as the pie increased, it became possible for a higher and higher proportion of the population to gain access to the fruits of industrial civilization. On a global scale, explosions of violence from Somalia to Bosnia are making many fear that the epoch of progress may be over. Today, it is difficult for leaders to promise a rosy, uncomplicated future with equal freedom and prosperity for everyone (or what the French call *les lendemains qui chantent*).

To these fears of the future needs to be added a threat from the recent past. Over the last century, Western civilization has observed the dangerous mixture of ideology and technology engendered by fears of anarchy, poverty, and loss of self-respect. When a modern society is confronted with blocked hopes, demagogues can now use the instruments of totalitarian rule beyond the wildest dreams of ancient tyrants. From the Stalinist myth of "socialism in one country" to Hitler's "thousand-year Reich," the failure of a government of law has given rise to a kind of industrialized terror that makes Cesare Borgia seem childishly primitive. If the future is fearful, the failures of the past greatly increase that fear.

A century ago, such observations were characteristic of traditionalists. From Burke to Ruskin, critics of commerce, industry, and utilitarianism claimed that the best fruits of Western civilization were being lost to crass leveling and materialistic equality. Today, there does not seem to be a secular past to which we can return. Religious belief is fractured into churches and sects, with the most militant—generally described as "fundamentalist"—often willing to use violence to extirpate the evils of godlessness. Only a society which can make plausible claims to homogeneity could even pretend to use such religious views as a means of restoring social self-confidence. The Ayatollah Khomeini's Iran is hardly the regime that either Burke or Ruskin had in mind.

Modernity seems unable to continue its promise of economic development, political equality, and social justice. This dead end can be traced to a theoretical principle: the error of Hobbes's dream of deductive certainty, based on the reduction of human nature to a simple calculus of pleasure and pain. In place of Machiavelli's complex theory of human nature, the inalienable "right of self-preservation" became the essential premise of political thought. In place of Machiavelli's view of leadership, for Hobbes and liberals following Locke, all people are by nature equal. That equality is manifest in the equal "natural right" of all to "life, liberty, and the pursuit of happiness" (to use Jefferson's famous phrase). But when there are too many humans to find food, water, or shelter, what do these universal "human rights" mean?

The problem is evident in Locke's formulation of the limits of the natural right to self-preservation. According to Locke, without the existence of a settled government, humans are in a "state of nature." In this condition, for Locke (as for Hobbes or Rousseau) individuals "are in a state of perfect freedom to order their actions and dispose of their possessions as they see fit."[8] To be sure, Locke argues that the "natural right" to all things needed for survival is limited by the "law of nature": because reason teaches us that all people are "the workmanship of one omnipotent and infinitely wise maker," it follows that individuals ought not to harm others uselessly: "Everyone . . . when his own preservation comes not in competition, ought he, as much as he can, to preserve the rest of mankind."[9]

Locke's doctrines seemed to have progressive implications as long as "the plenty of natural provisions" far exceeded the potential of human overpopulation. Locke bases a title to property on labor. Indeed, had money not made it possible for some to claim title to more property than suffices for an individual, Locke boldly claims that "the same rule of property, viz. that every man should have as much as he could make use of, would hold still in the world, without straitening anybody, since there is land enough in the world to suffice double the inhabitants."[10] To solve the problem introduced by money, Locke proposes that private property, supported by representative governments, will make possible increases in productivity and thereby allow the survival of a growing population.

Today, the global population threatens to double each generation. While rates of population growth are stabilizing, the global population continues to grow in absolute numbers. The resulting pressure on resources makes it absurd to think of the issue in terms of an *individual* versus another *individual*. Everywhere ethnic and religious groups seek control over resources for their members. The Serbs were not concerned with "the rest of mankind"; their goal of "ethnic cleansing" was directed at the Bosnian Muslims. The same dynamic is evident everywhere. Under these circumstances, Locke's principles seem at best impossible to enforce, and at worst an ideological defense of private property.

Similar difficulties can be found in the Marxian tradition. Common ownership of the means of production proved totally incapable of resolving the economic and social problems of industrial societies. The "vanguard of the proletariat" became the cult of personality and a means of securing advantages for party functionaries. While the isolated individual seems powerless at the end of the twentieth century, the homogeneous social classes of Marx's theory of history turned out to be nonexistent. "Workers of the world" have not united—rather, they have become either small-scale bourgeois homeowners or impoverished ethnic rivals. Religion, the "opiate of the masses," has had more staying power than Marxist ideology.

Modern theories that promised to guide political, social, and economic practice have thus turned out to be a mask for privilege and power. As Machiavelli would have predicted, those without resources easily come to hate those who have wealth but refuse to share it. Little wonder that, in the streets of cities as diverse as Miami, Hamburg, Cairo, or Belfast, individuals—be they drug-addicts, skinheads, religious fundamentalists, or national extremists—take matters in their own hands, acting with unpredicted and uncontrolled violence. Although for a Marxist such behavior reflects "false consciousness" and ideological error, a careful observer of the racist violence of German skinheads noted that most often the source is rather an inarticulate "chaos in the head."[11]

If my suspicions are correct, we confront historical transformations as great as those that marked the end of feudalism and the emergence of modernity. In the last half of the fifteenth century, two developments simultaneously revolutionized war and domestic politics. On the one hand, artillery and other firearms (which, as both Machiavelli and Leonardo realized, provided a technological advantage to the offense) ended the age of the fortresses, castles, and armor on which feudal lords relied for invulnerability. On the other, printing made identical information equally available to a broad population dispersed in time and space, ending the superior knowledge of clerics and aristocrats.[12] Both of these innovations undermined the feudal aristocracy; together, they provided the foundations for the modern nation-state.

While printing overcame the gap between the medieval elite and some segments of society at large, it did not produce a rigorously egalitarian society; oddly enough, however, the political effects of the new mode of communication may have been mediated through military technology. Because, as Machiavelli argues, success in warfare ultimately depends on the citizens' willingness to fight in the infantry,[13] printing had the effect of creating larger bodies of citizens who could be motivated by a common cause. This meant that the critical technology in domestic life had, as one of its byproducts, the capacity to form large and very effective citizen armies, thereby providing an advantage for the defense capable of counteracting the technological benefits that cannon conferred on the offense.

In this view, the medieval world finally crumbled when technologies simultaneously inverted the military balance of forces (by ending the feudal advantage of defenders) *and* the civilian balance of forces (which, in ending the domestic advantages of the nobility, made it possible to enlarge the scale of a modernizing state to encompass entire linguistic and cultural communities). Throughout the emergence of industrial society, a series of ambitious leaders—including Oliver Cromwell in the seventeenth century, Napoleon in the eighteenth, and Lincoln in the nineteenth—progressively exploited these interacting transformations of military and civilian technology.

I now believe that the combination of nuclear weapons and electronic media is reversing these dual technological relationships. Nuclear-armed missiles paradoxically provide an advantage to the *defense*: given the fearsome nature of an invulnerable retaliatory force, it is little wonder that the first critics of Cold War strategy in the United States called for a "fortress America." Simultaneously, the electronic media—notably telephones and television, computers, fibre optics, satellites, and what has erroneously been called the "information superhighway"—interact to produce worlds that are totally distinct within a single human society.

The new military and civilian technologies are radically inegalitarian. Many potential soldiers do not have the intelligence or self-control to operate the high-technology weapons of contemporary military services. Many citizens, without education and skills, cannot utilize the powerful tools of computer software and interactive networks of communication. Whereas the end of the feudal era was marked by the emergence of egalitarian technologies in both warfare and socio-political relations, this suggests that the simultaneous eruption of inegalitarian technologies in both spheres will inevitably contribute to the end of modernity.

Even if the effects of new technology are not this profound, our predicament cannot be attributed solely to a lack of will, of moral commitment, or of theoretical wisdom.

It follows that neither a return to the theoretical principles of pagan antiquity nor a religious revival offers the promise of a global solution. Elsewhere, I have argued that ancient philosophers had a more profound understanding of human society than the moderns since Hobbes, whose thought seems adequate only in the special case of modern societies.[14] Most contemporaries would reject the claim that Plato, Aristotle, or Cicero present theories of human nature that are *scientifically* superior to the thought of Hobbes, Locke, or Marx. Even if we accept the classic theories of human nature and politics, however, it would not follow that we should adopt the practices and institutions of the ancient city-states.

Whatever the depth of ancient philosophy, contemporary societies cannot go back to the *polis* and its principles. Not only were these city-states based on a pagan polytheism inconsistent with Judeo-Christian monotheism, but the scale of modern societies does not admit of institutions like those of ancient Greece and Rome. Even more significant, the world-view of pagan antiquity provided no basis for the continued interactions between commerce, technology, and knowledge. Although the global economy of personal computers, jet airplanes, and interactive cable television may not resolve problems of political and social conflict, such technological transformations present material obstacles to reactionary nostalgia.

Plato, Aristotle, and other ancients may well be invaluable for their understanding of the human condition, but their thought in itself is unlikely to dispel the sense of doubt among our contemporaries. Today, biologists are on the brink of industrializing genetic engineering. It will soon be possible to design and create not only new agricultural products, but different kinds of humans. The promise of such fantastic technologies calls for moral principles guiding their use—but modern science, unlike that of the ancients, has no settled principles other than utility and popular sovereignty.

Earlier in this essay, I remarked that the difference between the ancients and the moderns is symbolized by the transition from the myth of Icarus to the reality of Neil Armstrong walking on the moon. Leonardo, planning the first realistic aircraft, obviously represents the transitional innovators of the Italian Renaissance. Elsewhere, I have tried to show in detail that our civilization needs to accept the necessity of living with a tension between the world-views of pagan antiquity, medieval religious faith, and modern scientific technology.[15] The very power of ancient science and its claim to continued attention lies in its approach to human knowledge as a mode of pattern-matching, profoundly different from the constructive principles of modern science or the intuitive belief of religion. All three approaches to knowledge can have validity; we will need to learn to live with the tension between them. If this is so, Machiavelli's thought may be uniquely relevant to the contemporary situation.

III. Machiavelli and the Creative Tension

Because Machiavelli wrote at the moment of transition to modernity, his thought retains important elements of ancient thought. He teaches that humans can *sometimes* control chance, but does not promise an "eternal" commonwealth (as does Hobbes). For Machiavelli, human nature is complex (as Plato taught), rather than reducible to a simple pleasure-pain calculus of Bentham, the utilitarians, and modern economics and behaviorist psychology. For Machiavelli, history is unpredictable (as Thucydides knew), rather than the unfolding of a knowable pattern of development as claimed by Hegel, Marx, and modern ideologies of left and right. Thus, for Machiavelli, prudent leadership is a principal requisite of political success (as Xenophon taught), not the secondary factor ignored by Lockeans and Marxists alike. Politics remains the "master science," determining which other activities should or should not be pursued in the city (as it was for Aristotle), and not a product of economics or history (as it is in Hobbes, Locke, or Marx).

Because Machiavelli foresees the basic principles of modernity without abandoning the wisdom of the ancients, we can turn to Machiavelli as someone who can *teach* us. Instead of adopting the stance of historians and political scientists for whom Machiavelli is primarily an interesting historical figure, we need to treat him as a systematic philosopher or scientist. In doing so, we will learn several uncomfortable but necessary lessons. The most important of these may concern social equality and popular enlightenment.

Natural Equality, Inequality, and Government under Law. Hobbes, Locke, Rousseau, and the modern liberal tradition begin from the "self-evident" truth, proclaimed in the Declaration of Independence and the revolutions it inspired, that "all men are created equal." Enshrined in the concept of equality before the law, this principle is essential to a republican government which provides justice and opportunity to the poor as well as to those with power and wealth. Although equality of right does not mean equality in every respect, many contemporary liberals have concluded that differences in intelligence, in skill, or in status are entirely the product of education, social class, and individual experience. As a result, one tradition of modern thought rebels at claims that "nature" could ever produce significant differences between one individual and another; for those in this liberal, egalitarian tradition, such a premise legitimates hierarchy and makes injustice inevitable.

Plato, Aristotle, Cicero, and the ancient philosophical tradition teach that humans differ in intelligence, character, and skill; though education is needed to realize natural potential, civilized societies inevitably depend on recognition of these natural differences in talent and taste. In particular, this tradition assumes that since complex societies will always have leaders, the task of political education is to foster ability, virtue, and a sense of responsibility among the elite. In this view, expressed most emphatically by Aristotle, while standards of merit vary from one society to another, the just regime respects—and rewards—those differences necessary to the excellence of a stable human community.

For the moderns, therefore, natural equals are shaped by convention or history, whereas for the ancients, natural unequals need to be trained and educated to fulfill their potential excellence. Machiavelli shares elements of both traditions: on the one hand, he treats standards of praise and blame as conventions relevant to time and place; on the other, he emphasizes natural differences of intelligence, character, and skill. Because societies can be shaped by their founders, humans cannot look to nature for a single standard of excellence that would be accepted everywhere; because humans inevitably differ, an egalitarian society is no longer possible as soon as simple hunter-gatherer societies have been replaced by large communities with centralized governments and a complex division of labor.

Contemporary evolutionary findings show that our species evolved in highly egalitarian, loose social systems, more akin to Rousseau's "savage society" than to other versions of the state of nature. Machiavelli had, however, already suggested that humans originally lived "dispersed" like "beasts." Recent studies of personality show that genetics, fetal development, early childhood experience, social class, and current situation all have an effect on an individual's behavior. Machiavelli insisted that men differ in their "natures" with respect to temperament (the "bold" versus the "cautious"), intelligence (some learn by themselves, some only when taught, and some not at all), and virtue (some are devoted to the "common good," others only to narrow self-interest). Primatology and ethology confirm that leadership can be observed even in highly egalitarian species. Machiavelli focuses one of his principal works on the need to train the exceptional leader.

In short, Machiavelli's teaching points to the possibility of combining the competing traditions in Western thought. To do so, however, will require recognition of what Jefferson called the "natural aristocracy." Those who use the inevitability of social inequality to defend established power and wealth are subject to Machiavelli's criticisms of the nobles, whose claim on status must always be balanced by the demands of the people. Those who use the natural equality as a ground for arbitrarily redistributing wealth or rely on populist democracy to solve social problems are subject to Machiavelli's criticisms of demagogues, whose appeal to the people needs to be constrained by a government of law. Only by taking from outsiders can the "liberality" of promising wealth to all be realized within a lasting community.

Machiavelli's republicanism—like the republicanism of pagan antiquity—avoids the worst extremes of the ideological politics of fascists, communists, and populists alike. A government that combines law and force must, therefore, accept differences of status and ability. Machiavelli would have scoffed at the liberal dream of equality not earned by performance, viewing it as a luxury that cannot be afforded in times of conflict and uncertainty. Insofar as we are approaching such times again throughout the West, we will need to return to the traditional view that insofar as inequalities of status are inevitable, the rewards of power must be balanced by the duties and obligations of serving the common good.

Science and Popular Enlightenment. Hobbes, Descartes, and their followers proposed the dream of a universal enlightenment as the basis of political stability. The sheer complexity of contemporary science makes such a dream absurd. The ancients viewed higher education as the preserve of a narrow elite in societies based on slave labor, artisanal manufacture, and small-scale agriculture. The sheer complexity of contemporary technology would make such a restriction of educational training economically untenable and politically disastrous.

Machiavelli proposes a more complex view. He teaches, openly, a science that challenges the popular pieties: as he wrote Guiccardini, rather than describing the way to heaven in hopes of achieving it, he would rather teach men the way to hell in order to avoid it. At the same time, however, Machiavelli teaches, "covertly," a lesson he borrowed from ancient political theorists: leaders need to know truths that they cannot share with the masses. As Rousseau put it, sharing Machiavelli's view of the legislator, "there are a thousand kinds of ideas that are impossible to translate into the language of the people."[16] Once the transparency and equality of the primitive hunter-gatherer society has been lost, the scientific knowledge needed to govern complex communities cannot be understood by the entire populace.

The relationship between education, public opinion, science, and politics thus needs to be reconsidered. In the last century, modern societies developed hitherto unknown systems of popular education, achieving widespread if not universal literacy. An economic system based on commerce and industry requires such popular enlightenment: the worker must read instructions, the salesperson must make change, and the businessman must understand the terms of legal contracts. A return to societies in which only a narrow elite can read, write, and understand the daily news is un-thinkable. At the same time, traditional education has everywhere been transformed by television and the mass media, undermining the standards of "classical" education. Only two generations ago, one could not attend an elite university without having studied Latin, and scholars could not attain the doctorate without demonstrating a working knowledge of at least two foreign languages. Today, many articles and books delight in cataloguing popular ignorance of elementary facts in geography, history, and government.

Again, we confront the paradox that the full realization of modern goals is impossible, yet a return to traditional practices is also out of the question. The only possibility consistent with a government of law would be a natural elite, capable of understanding the complexities of modern science yet restrained in its willingness to use this knowledge for self-aggrandizement and narrow benefit. Recognition of the need to foster leaders who work for the "common benefit of all" is another lesson we can learn from Machiavelli.

It will be recalled that, for Machiavelli, there are three kinds of intelli-gence: "one that understands by itself, another that discerns what others understand, the third that understands neither by itself nor through others" (*Prince*, ch. 22; p. 92). Scientists like Leonardo are "most ex-cellent" because they understand things by themselves; unlike Plato, Machiavelli does not think it necessary to encourage their education. Most people, understanding neither by themselves or "through others," cannot understand such scientific knowledge; such an individual is "useless" as an advisor and dangerous whenever "looking for something useful to himself" (ibid., pp. 92–93).

Universal enlightenment cannot therefore function effectively in an age of complex science. While Machiavelli describes "letters" and "philosophy" as an "honorable leisure," he points out that it encourages "disorder" and undermines devotion to the common good (*Florentine Histories*, V, 1; p. 185). Instead, Machiavelli seems to counsel a middle way: the education of an elite that "discerns what others understand." Only if society has such leaders will it be able to control the scientific and technological develop-ments constantly discovered by such natural geniuses as Leonardo.

For Plato, the best regime would be ruled by a philosopher-king, trained in the entire range of scientific disciplines; for Hobbes, all that is necessary is the universal public teaching of his own doctrines—but such universal education is an indispensable prerequisite to a lasting commonwealth. Machiavelli requires neither total wisdom for the prince nor universal education for the public, but rather a class of rulers (those "deserving" to be a prince or leader of a republic) capable of understanding the requisites of natural science, technological innovation, and political prudence.

Western civilization confronts the awesome potential of genetic engineering, the inevitability of the diffusion of nuclear weapons, and the disintegration of the stability provided by the cold war. Neuroscientists have learned more about the biology of the human brain in the last decade than was discovered in the five centuries since Leonardo drew the first realistic sketches of its structure; today we can shape personality and character with medications like Prozac instead of relying on exhortation, punishment, and self-control. Geneticists have learned more about the biology of inheritance in the last decade than was discovered in the previous 10,000 years of agriculture and animal husbandry; soon we will genetically engineer plants, animals, and even people, replacing the trial and error processes of domestication with techniques of unquestioned power and danger. Ecologists have learned more about the complexities of the environment in the last decade than was discovered in the previous million years of hunting and gathering; whereas political theorists and governments long ignored natural limits on productive technology, now we know that there are unsuspected interactions between our own behavior, the lives of other species, and the physical environment.

These discoveries are said to promise unparalleled benefits, but often bring immeasurable risks to health, welfare, and to the very survival of life on earth. Some, following Rousseau, might dream of returning to the day when the public was entirely insulated from the existence of the sciences and arts.[17] Alas, if we can't go forward to universal enlightenment, we can't go back to rigid elitism or the slave society of the pagan Greeks and Romans. Once again, Machiavelli offers a third way, intermediate between the exaggerated hopes of modern optimists and the limited world of ancient pessimists.

In a modern, highly technocratic society, we will need a class of potential leaders whose training parallels the experience Machiavelli describes for those who "deserve" to be in power. Such an elite needs to "discern" what the scientists and technocrats "understand." Such an elite needs to learn how to judge and apply scientific or technical advice: "good counsel, from wherever it comes, must arise from the prudence of the prince, and not the prudence of the prince from good counsel" (*Prince*, ch. 23; p. 95).

In short, such an elite can no longer rely on ideologies or popular recipes if our civilization is to avoid self-destruction.

In advising a prince on what he must learn, Machiavelli outlines an educational program that differs markedly both from that of Plato's self-less philosophic-ruler and Hobbes's enlightened, self-interested citizen. At first, this educational program seems remarkably narrow: "a prince should have no other object, nor any other thought, nor take anything else as his art but the art of war and its orders and discipline; for that is the only art which is of concern to one who commands" (*Prince*, ch. 19; p. 58). As we have seen above (see chapters one and two), however, first impressions on reading Machiavelli's text are often misleading—and he is most likely to have a "covert" teaching when presenting his view of the very subject, the education of leaders, on which he reminds us that the ancients had a covert teaching (*Prince*, ch. 28; p. 69). Before concluding that Machiavelli's educational advice to the potential prince is irrelevant to our own time, it is worth looking at it most carefully.

In the second paragraph of chapter nineteen, Machiavelli makes it clear that his educational advice is directed to "a private individual" who becomes a powerful leader (like Francesco Sforza) as well as to a powerful leader who inherits power rather than earning it through his own ability and virtue (like Sforza's "sons," including Ludovico "il Moro," the patron of Leonardo da Vinci). He suggests that "a prince who does not understand the military" is not likely to keep power (the example of il Moro's defeat by the French in 1499 comes to mind). To use the classification of intelligence in chapter twenty-two, leaders need to "understand," either on their own ("very excellent") or by "discerning" what "others" understand ("excellent"). But *what* is the substance of this educational curriculum described here as "the art of war"?

Machiavelli indicates "two modes, one with deeds, the other with the mind" (*Prince*, ch. 14; p. 59). The deeds comprise "keeping his armies well ordered and exercised"—an action obviously only relevant to those already in power—and to "always be out hunting, and through this accustom the body to hardships" (ibid.). Then, as if it is part of the deeds or actions of hunting, Machiavelli adds with nonchalance:

> and meanwhile *he should learn the nature of sites, and recognize how mountains rise, how valleys open up, how plains lie, and understand the nature of rivers and marshes—and in this invest the greatest care.* (Ibid.)

Even a private citizen, of course, can "learn *the nature of sites*"—and even a powerful ruler can "*in this invest the greatest care.*"

In considering Machiavelli's first educational requirement, one is reminded of the passage of the dedication of *The Prince*, in which Machiavelli compares himself to an artist who can "sketch landscapes" (p. 4). In the parallel passage in Leonardo's *Notebooks*, the artist himself claims he is "lord" of mountains, valleys, and plains because he knows their "nature" well enough to make them; for Leonardo, art as a form of philosophic understanding. Machiavelli counsels that in order to "learn the nature of sites," the future leader must also *"understand the nature of rivers and marshes"*—an injunction reminding us of the comparison between fortune and a river in chapter twenty-five.

In the guise of training in the "art of war," Machiavelli thus suggests that the future leader acquire a "skill" that is useful because one not only "learns to know one's own country," but to "comprehend with ease every other site that it may be necessary to explore [lit. speculate on] as new" (*Prince*, ch. 14, p. 59). That this may be a covert symbol for learning the natural sciences is reinforced by the sentence that follows: "For the hills, the valleys, the plains, the rivers, and the marshes that are *in Tuscany*, for example, have a certain similarity to *those of other provinces*, so that *from the knowledge of a site in one province one can easily come to the knowledge of others*" (ibid.). In contrast, standards of praise and blame for human actions vary; hence the *"Tuscan"* word *misero* differs from *avaro "in our language"*—but not in other languages (*Prince*, ch. 15; p. 61). If, as Leonardo also suggests, the artist drawing "the hills, the valleys, the plains, the rivers, and the marshes" represents the natural sciences, the potential prince or leader needs to have a practical "knowledge" of those scientific facts not only for defense of his own country ("one can better understand its defense") but for attacking "other provinces," when it will be necessary to "find the enemy, seize lodgings, lead armies, order battles, and besiege towns to your advantage" (*Prince*, ch. 14; p. 59).

The remaining educational proposal in chapter fourteen is explicitly called "the exercise of the mind," as if Machiavelli had not already described an area of "knowledge" to be acquired. In addition to the "nature of sites" (or natural science), the future leader should study human history (or what we today call the social sciences):

a prince should *read histories and consider in them the actions of excellent men, should see how they conducted themselves in wars, should examine the causes of their victories and losses.* . . . Above all he should do as some excellent man has done in the past who found someone to imitate who had been praised and gloried before him. . . . And whoever reads the life of Cyrus written by Xenophon will then recognize in the life of Scipio how much glory that imitation brought him, how much in chastity, affability, humanity, and liberality Scipio conformed to *what had been written of Cyrus by Xenophon.* (*Prince*, ch. 14; p. 60)

Although it sometimes appears that Machiavelli totally rejected ancient thought, especially in the Socratic tradition, this praise of Xenophon's *Cyropedia* suggests otherwise. It is, however, the utility of Xenophon's book that recommends it rather than the excellence of its contents. The test of a book is whether a great man like Scipio was successful because he read it.[18] In the study of human history, Machiavelli is not interested in general pronouncements and universal theories, but specific cases that teach the intelligent and ambitious leader how to make prudent decisions.

Machiavelli's curriculum for elite education is far more practical and pragmatic than the political theories of Plato and Aristotle in antiquity, or of Hobbes, Locke, or Marx in more recent times. Books like Xenophon's *Cyropedia*—historical accounts of a single leader or event—symbolize the social sciences, just as studying "the nature of sites" in one's native country symbolizes the natural sciences. Descriptions of concrete particulars need to be presented in a way that leads the student to develop good judgment and prudence. Since the "most excellent" leader needs to be able to discover the truth on his own, scientific generalizations or "laws of nature" are less useful than case studies.

This curriculum is also directed to *republican* leaders, as is shown in Book III, chapter thirty-nine of the *Discourses* ("That a General ought to be acquainted with the Lie of the Land"). In this chapter, Machiavelli argues that "knowledge of terrains and of countries" is "essential" for *any* "army commander," and proposes "a good deal of practice" in "the sport" of hunting on the authority of Xenophon's *Cyropedia*. Bodily exercise (what the ancients called "gymnastic") needs to be focused on a practical activity ("going to lay snares on the ridges" and "rouse a wild beast from its lair") combined with knowledge of applied natural science and history. Indeed, the principal difference between *Prince,* chapter nineteen and *Discourses,* III, chapter thirty-nine is that the latter uses the example of Publius Decius "when he was a tribune in charge of troops which the consul, Cornelius, commanded" (pp. 511–512) whereas the former describes "Philopoemen, prince of the Achaeans" (pp. 59–60). In place of *theoretical wisdom*, the heart of the educational program set forth in Plato's *Republic*, Machiavelli emphasizes "practice."[19]

Unlike most political philosophers, both ancient and modern, Machiavelli does not believe it is salutary to teach abstract political *theories*, whether they concern the just regime, the logic of obligation, or the course of world history. His writings are primarily concerned with the need for training effective leaders. While the education he proposes is suited to republics as well as kingdoms, Machiavelli addresses an elite which will need to make prudent judgments on grounds that other citizens will not understand. In place of universal abstractions taught to everyone—one thinks of Kant's "categorical imperative"—Machiavelli sets his sights on the "effective reality" of governing complex societies under uncertain conditions.

At no time has such a view of statesmanship been more appropriate. While Machiavelli, unlike the ancients, sees the capacity of using the science of nature to resolve human problems, he adopts the ancient distinction between the beliefs of the majority and the knowledge needed by an elite. In an age of complex science of even greater power than Leonardo da Vinci imagined, dare we ignore the wisdom of this advice? Now that it is evident how easily popular opinions can be molded by television and the mass media, those with responsibility need to learn how to think on their own.

Since Rousseau, political leaders have been taught that their function is to represent the "general will." Although the founders of the American constitution shared the older, Burkean view that representatives govern according to their own judgment of the common interests, today we live in an age of public opinion polls and mass opinion. Leaders have come to believe that choices need to be shaped to meet the passing mood of the public. It is but a short step to the use of media techniques to *create* that mood—and as Hitler taught, such propaganda techniques are easily used to establish vicious tyranny.

The practical problem can be traced to a theoretical principle. Modern political thought has come to focus on "rights." Everywhere, people express their preferences in terms of a "right" that supposedly justifies a public policy: the "right to life" and the "right to health care"; the "right to choose" and the "right to property"; the "right to national self-determination" and the "right to work." Machiavelli teaches us that such universal abstractions are dangerous in the extreme. Perhaps, as the West faces the uncertainties of the twenty-first century, we would follow his advice by focusing on the practical needs of governance in a violent world. Perhaps, as Machiavelli claimed, the quest for perfect justice on earth is more dangerous than knowledge of the way to hell.

Western civilization has been built upon a creative tension between religious faith, ancient philosophy, and modern science. For the last two centuries, however, moderns have pretended that their ideas reflect a historical *progress*, making both religion and classical thought obsolete. The result has been a dangerous belief that we can control history and achieve universal freedom, equality, wealth, happiness, and stability. Machiavelli's prudence provides a useful antidote to such "imagined republics and principalities." After two centuries of relying on the power of science, whose fruits now threaten civilization itself, it is time to study once again the science of power. Given the dangers of ideological pretensions from the right and the left, it is time to return to the "effectual truth" based on knowledge of nature and an understanding of human nature.

Documents from Machiavelli's Association with Leonardo da Vinci

1. The Legations to Valentino— Correspondence of 1–3 November 1502

In the summer of 1502, Cesare Borgia captured Urbino and, for a short time until expelled by the French, held Arezzo and other towns in the Val di Chiano deemed essential to the security of Florence. To ensure Borgia's neutrality toward Florence, Machiavelli was sent to his court in Imola. Concern about Cesare's actions was heightened when a group of his condottieri met in Perugia on 9 October and agreed to challenge him openly. Throughout the remainder of the fall, while Cesare was engaged in negotiations with his rebellious captains, the Florentine Signoria sought information from Machiavelli on Cesare's plans: was the Duke intending to attack his former allies with troops provided by other European powers, or would he conclude an agreement with them? In late December, Cesare was to trick his condottieri into meeting with him in Sinigaglia, where he captured and killed them.

A. MACHIAVELLI TO COMMITTEE OF TEN, 1 NOVEMBER 1502

In the first dispatch reproduced here, started on 31 October 1502, Machiavelli reports on a draft agreement that Cesare planned to submit to the rebels. After describing in detail conversations with Messer Agobito, one of Cesare's key advisors who is described as a "friend," on the morning of 1 November Machiavelli added a passage indicating that to "verify" this account he has just "talked to another [*uno altro*] who is also acquainted with this lord's [Cesare's] secrets." Although Machiavelli is careful to name other informants, using a cipher to designate Agobito, his silence on the identity of this "other" person makes it impossible to know whether or not it was Leonardo.

Magnifici Domini Decemviris etc.,

Magnificent Lords, etc., through my last letters of the 29th and 30th, which I sent through Zerino, messenger for your Lordships, in reply to your letter of the 28th, you have been informed of what has been happening to me, and also of what I have been able to know, both from the mouth of the Duke, and from others, about Signor Paulo's conduct and the agreements drawn up between the allies and this Lord. And since the Duke promised to have a copy given to me, I insisted on Messer Agabito giving it to me but finally he told me: "I want to tell you the truth: these agreements are not yet completely finalized, but a rough draft has been made, approved by both the Duke and Signor Paulo, with which Signor Paulo left. And as soon as the allies approve it, Signor Paulo will be able to approve it in the name of the Duke: and to this end Signor Paulo has been appointed fiduciary by the Duke. After Signor Paulo had left, while examining the agreements, it seemed to the Duke that one section was missing, that concerning the state and honor of the King of France; and he wanted that section to be created; and the Duke made me ride after Signor Paulo in order to tell him that he [the Duke] was not going to draw up any agreement without that section; and, when I reached him, he refused to accept it and then he said that he would take it to the others but that in his opinion they would not accept it. For this reason the Duke does not want any copy to be given away; and it has not been given either to the Chancellor of Ferrara or to any others." Then Messer Agabito added: "These agreements will be accepted or not: if they are accepted, a window will be opened through which the Duke can escape at his pleasure; and if not, a door will be opened to him; but concerning these agreements, even children should laugh at them, since they were made by force with so much injury to the Duke and so much danger for him." This speech made him [Messer Agabito] grow very fervent. And what I wrote to your Lordships concerning this matter was told me in secret; and if you put it together with what I wrote yesterday, you, Wise Lordships, will come to the conclusion that you will consider more proper; I only want to remind you that Messer Agabito belongs to the Colonna party and is a supporter of that faction.

Your Lordships, through the Postscriptum to your letter of the 28th, point out that the auxiliary troops that this Lord is expecting from France are not in sufficient number and have not yet arrived; for this reason you can suppose that this Lord, finding himself in a weak position and pressed by his enemies, will stipulate some agreement that will be unfavorable to him and dangerous for his neighbors. I believe that your Lordships have received reliable information from Milan and France as to the quality of the men that are in one place and the other; and yet I will tell you what I have seen here, so that your Lordships can have a better understanding of the events and consequently judge them more properly. One citizen of yours, Guglielmo di Niccolò di Piero di Bonaccorso, came back yesterday. As I wrote, he accompanied the French lancers that arrived, all of which he has quartered in the countryside around Faenza. He told me that these lancers consisted of five companies, that is Montison, Fois, Miolans, Dunais, and Marquis of Saluzo, and having inspected all the troops that were lined up, 7 lances were missing of the 250 that were supposed to be there but he now thinks that there are more of them than was necessary because they were joined by a few mercenary troops; and as I said, these troops are currently here. At the same time, yesterday a Spaniard, Pietro Guardaroba, who had been sent to France by this Lord, came back as well; and this Guglielmo, who along the road had a long talk with him, said to me that Pietro informed him of having arranged with His Majesty the King the arrival of three companies; and that at his departure from Milan the company of Monsignor [of Ciamonte] of Lignì had already left; and concerning the other two companies, Monsignor of Ciamonte had not decided yet which ones will arrive.

In my letter of the 9th, if you remember correctly, I wrote to your Lordships that, among other preparations organized by this Lord after the rebellion of the Orsinis, he had sent a son of the General of Milan in order to put together 1500 Swiss and to give accommodations to fifty or a hundred of the best soldiers among those who were already at the service of the Duke of Milan and to bring them under him; and the expenses necessary to transfer these people will be met by the General because of his wish to have his son elected cardinal. Guglielmo told me that the Swiss are already in Pavia and that the soldiers were almost drawn up.

Moreover he said that the son of Monsignor Le Pret is passing again through Italy with a hundred soldiers for his brother-in-law, which, if it was true, would be honorable in spite of its delay. And Guglielmo, who gave me this piece of information, is as far as I know a sensible and honest person.

As far as the Italian people are concerned, the conduct of the Count of Mirandola is ascertained: a few days ago he received money. It is said that he is still giving soldiers to Fracassa and that he received money from one of the Palavisini, his gentleman. The evidence for what I am saying rests in the fact that he is giving hospitality to any soldiers that have deserted their troops and that happen to go to his house; and two days ago a fellow, Piero Bolzano, arrived there with

40 crossbowmen on horses, after having escaped from Messer Giovanni Bentivogli, and as soon as he arrived he received money.

I cannot tell you anything else about what is happening here, because after the rebellion in Camerino I have not heard anything either from there or from Bologna. Neither did Protonotary Bentivogli come here as it had been ordered and as I wrote to you Lords. But if I had to tell you in brief what is happening here, I would say that one side is discussing peacefully, and the other is preparing for war [what is until here was written on 31st]. Your Lordships, who receive advice from any side, can judge better of what your enemies are doing or might do, and if this Lord will surrender to you or not, than if you had to form your opinion aided by a single thing.

[What is until here written on the 31st.] Today is November 1st: since I was eager to send the treaty to your Lordships and to verify what the friend had told me, according to what I wrote you above, I talked to another who is also acquainted with the Lord's secrets; and while we were discussing the same question, he told me the same thing my friend had told me; neither could I draw any particular conclusion from this further conversation, other than that it concerns the honor of France; and again, he maintained that nothing had been mentioned about your Lordships. He underlined that in the agreements there was a section that stated that not all the Orsinis and the Vitellis were obliged to serve the Duke personally, but only one at a time; and while laughing he said: "look what agreements these are." I will not consider this last piece of information as separate from the rest so as to see in it something different from what it actually is; and in order not to keep your Lordships waiting, I will send this letter through a messenger, Giovanni Antonio from Milan, who promised me to be there at the latest by tomorrow, and your Lordships will have him paid one florin in gold.

November 1, 1502, midnight., Imola

E. V. D.   Your servant,

Niccolò Machiavelli

While I was concluding this letter Tommaso Spinelli arrived and informed me that he had left Protonotary Bentivogli at Castel Sampiero and that he will be here tomorrow morning.

Source: Niccolò Machiavelli, *Legazioni. Commissarie. Scritti di Governo,* ed. Fredi Chiapelli (Rome: Gius. Laterza & Figli, 1973), 2.260–264 (Archivio di Stato di Firenze, X di B., Cart. Resp. 119, cc 13r–14v, 21r–v). Translation by Francesca Roselli.

B. COMMITTEE OF TEN (MARCELLUS) TO MACHIAVELLI, 3 NOVEMBER 1502

Writing for the Committee of Ten, responsible for Florentine policy, Marcellus instructs Machiavelli to seek a postponement of the agreement Cesare is negotiating with his rebellious condottieri and to keep them informed of any actions that might be directed against Florence.

Dear Sir, that man that you sent with your letter of the 1st has served us very badly because he did not get here until this morning at dinner time; in spite of this, in order not to give a bad opinion of us in case he might come here again, we paid him as you had written us and we sent him back tonight so that he can arrive there tomorrow in the early morning: and we would be glad if he would serve you better than us, which thing he promised.

We do not need to write a long reply to your letter: here nothing new has happened, except that we are waiting for an Archdeacon of Celon, a Frenchman who had already been to Rome for the King, sent by the Pope and according to the information we have, on commission of His Majesty the King; the reason for it would not be other than to urge us to do what the Pope has been wishing for a long time. The Pope is shown to us, through Sir Alexandro, to wish more than ever that the agreement will not take place—a wish of which there are many indications—and he relies a lot on us. You will be able to use your friendship with this Lord to defer the agreement: although we rather wish that you express what we are telling you: that we cannot declare our intentions before having enough troops; that here we are engaged in gathering money and soldiers. Of these, we do not know yet how we will employ the people of Mantova; since he is in France and we have not received any news about his intentions; to certify to his Lordship always that this city is with him and that, with respect to his forces, he can have as great hopes as that of any other [city].

We do not know how to consider the agreement concluded between this Lord and the others since there are so many different opinions about both sides; but we urge you to keep us informed about any detail and to point out anything that could reveal the existence of preparations from one side or the other.

We also consider it proper for you to talk about that with the Duke, and to suggest to him that it is necessary that his Excellency support our good intentions and think, if not of anything else, at least that it does not cost anything either to his Excellency or the Pope to support us, since it be for the advantage of his Excellency. You should mention to him the Church tithes which will help this city to support so many expenses and that this city could not hope to obtain the same results if it had to do everything by itself.

Enclosed with this letter you will find a safe-conduct, of which we have already written to you. It will be valid one year and cannot be prolonged, according to our laws, with the exception of the city of Pisa because we are at war with it. You will communicate these two things to his Excellency, and will clarify them in the way you may judge more appropriate; we do not need to remind you of anything else in this letter, except of writing us conscientiously about anything that happens there.

Farewell

Ex Palatio Fiorentino, die III Novembris MDII
Decemviri Libertatis et Balie Reipublicae Florentinae
M<arcellus>

Source: Niccolò Machiavelli, *Legazioni. Commissarie. Scritti di Governo,* ed. Fredi Chiapelli (Rome: Gius. Laterza & Figli, 1973), 2.264–265 (BNF: CM III, 84; copy Archivio di Stato di Firenze, X di B., Cart. Miss. L.C. 26, cc. 169v–170r). Translation by Francesca Roselli.

C. MACHIAVELLI TO COMMITTEE OF TEN, 3 NOVEMBER 1502

Machiavelli reports that "one of the First Secretaries" of Cesare has promised him a copy of Cesare's draft agreement with the condottieri as soon as it is available. After listing by name the French captains with whom he has met, Machiavelli remarks that he cannot report a crucial conversation between Cesare and the papal envoy Bentivogli because "the person that used to inform me of such things"—probably Agabito—left with Bentivogli; instead, Machiavelli reports a conversation with "one of those who is acquainted with this Lord's [Cesare's] business," adding that he "had to be more careful in writing this letter." In the last paragraph, Machiavelli describes the difficulty of dealing with Borgia, since "nobody talks to him except three or four of his ministers or some stranger who has important questions to deal with him" and his daily routines are highly unusual.

Magnificis Dominis Decemviris etc.,
Magnificent Lords,

I wrote to your Lordships my last news of the 31st of October and the 1st of November; and I was able to know about the agreements and the reason why I had not received them. Even today I talked to one of the First Secretaries, who confirmed everything I wrote in my other letters; he says that he expects the Chevalier Orsino to come back and, depending on his report, the agreements will be made public or not. He promised me that the copy will be given to no other than me; and I will give a report of it to others. Other than this, I did not notice anything that could point to something to the contrary, nor did I hear anything concerning your Lordships, except I heard you condemned for not having done anything to put a stop to this Lord.

Concerning what is happening here, I wrote extensively in my letters all I know; and since I have not kept anything to myself, nor having anything new happened, I have nothing to write, except for repeating this to you: if words and documents point towards an agreement, nonetheless orders and preparations indicate war; and as I wrote in another letter, five companies of French soldiers have been quartered for four days in the countryside around Faenza, and yesterday their captains visited this Lord and conversed with him for a while; after they had left, I visited Monsignor of Montison, the supreme leader, in the name of your Lordships; he welcomed me very warmly and was ready to offer you help and wanted to know from me if at the moment he could do anything for your own benefit. I visited the Baron of Bierra, Monsignor Lo Grafis, and Monsignor of Borsu, lieutenants of Fois, Miolans, and Dunais; I introduced myself and they recognized me for having been on familiar terms with them. They were all pleased to see me and, according to what I noticed, they are your supporters and praise highly your Lordships: which thing is considerably positive. Your Lordships will give me directions about what I have to discuss with these Lords.

Today about 300 more Gascons arrived, while the Swiss are expected within four days. It is believed that at their arrival here what has to be accomplished will have a start.

In my last letter of November 1st I wrote that Protonotary Bentivogli was supposed to arrive yesterday morning by virtue of safe-conduct; and he arrived at about seven p.m. He had dinner with the Duke and after that he remained with him for about half an hour, after which he left immediately for Bologna; neither could I receive information about their conversation because the person that used to inform me of such things left with him. By talking to one of those who is acquainted with this Lord's business, I understood that he is to come back soon and that if Messer Giovanni is willing to support him against the Orsinis and the Vitellis, he should offer him every promise of peace and security; and about the way in which he could, with regard to the coalition, etc., he answered that he would arrange that the King of France would give him dispositions; and we discussed together about how this thing, if successfully conducted, would be favorable to the Duke, to your Lordships, and to Messer Giovanni and added that this Duke supported it warmly. In fact it was evident to him that it was safer for his state to keep Messer Giovanni in his position and establish a friendly relationship with him than to send him away and take possession of a land that would be impossible to keep and that with time would represent the beginning of his ruin. Moreover, he said that the Duke of Ferrara had never wanted to promise any help to this Lord, nor is he willing to offer him any if he does not come to an agreement with Bologna. I did everything that was in my power to strengthen his opinion concerning all this and I added to what he said whatever reasons I considered necessary. It seems certain to me that this agreement will be concluded both by the Duke and by the Duke of Ferrara; I inform your Lordships of this because I consider it as opportune and even though I had to be more careful in writing this letter, nonetheless I want to have your Lordships receive it and I will send it through my own messenger. I hope you will be grateful for the common benefit derived from it and will consequently honor me.

A man [Guicciardini] who is a citizen of yours and your commanding officer, currently an independent soldier for this Lord, told me that yesterday evening, at about five p.m., finding himself in the lodging of the Count Alexandro from Marciano, brother of Count Rinuccio, he saw this Lord passing by that place at that time and call Count Alexandro outside. He stayed with him for an hour; and left him afterwards, told him that the Duke had discussed many things with him, which, taken all together, showed that his Lordship had more a feeling of vengeance against those who put his state in danger than a wish or intention of peace.

The letter of your Lordships of November 1st does not need other reply than what I wrote above; I did not try to talk to the Duke since I have nothing new to tell him and he would be annoyed if my report concerned things he already knows. You have to remember that nobody talks to him except three or four of his ministers or some stranger who has important questions to deal with him; and he does not leave his antechamber except from five or six in the morning on: and for this reason it is never possible to talk to him, except by private audience. And if he knows that one has only words for him, he does not grant him audience. I write you this so that your Lordships will not be surprised of my decision not to see him and also for the future, in case I should write you that I could not obtain an audience from him.

Farewell,

Ex Imola, die III November 1502
E. V. D   Servitor
Nicolaus Machiavellus

Source: Niccolò Machiavelli, *Legazioni. Commissarie. Scritti di Governo,* ed. Fredi Chiapelli (Rome: Gius. Laterza & Figli, 1973), 2.266–268 (Archivio di Stato di Firenze, X di B., Cart. Resp. 119, cc 15r–16v). Translation by Francesca Roselli.

2. Leonardo's Consultation on the Diversion of the Arno, July 1503

After Leonardo's return to Florence in 1503, his first major commitment was the agreement to paint *The Battle of Anghiari* in the Grand Council Hall of the Palazzo Vecchio. The following documents, however, demonstrate conclusively that he played a critical role as a consulting engineer on the feasibility of the diversion of the Arno. Having drawn maps and plans for a diversion of the Arno for peaceful purposes in the 1490s, Leonardo was well qualified to assess the proposed military project, and since Leonardo is the only "expert" named, his judgment was presumably considered particularly important. But Leonardo had only recently arrived in Florence from Cesare's court. How, then, was his expertise in this matter known to the Signoria? While we cannot know, conversations with Machiavelli while both were in Cesare's court are at least one plausible explanation.

Because of the importance of the following documents, the translations are preceded by the original Italian text.

A. FRANCESCO GUIDUCCI TO COMMITTEE OF TEN, 24 JULY 1503

Report of Leonardo's visit to the field:

Ex Castris, Franciscus Ghuiduccius, 24 Jul. 1503. Appresso fu qui hieri con una di V. Signoria Alexandro degli Albizi insieme con Leonardo da Vinci et certi altri, et veduto el disgno insieme con el ghovernatore, doppo molte discussioni et dubii conclusesi che l'opera fussi molto al proposito, o si veramente Arno volgersi qui, o restarvi con un canale, che almeno vieterebbe che le colline da nemici non potrebbono essere offese; come tucto referiranno loro a bocha V. S.

Ex Castris, Franciscus Ghuiduccius, 24 Jul. 1503. Yesterday one of your Signoria, Alexandro of the Albizi, was here together with Leonardo da Vinci and some others, who examined the plan in the presence of the Governor and, after many discussions and doubts, they concluded that the work was very appropriate, whether Arno turned there or remained with a channel; in any case it would provide that the hills could not be attacked by the enemies; they will tell you everything in person V. S.

Source: Leonardo da Vinci, *Notebooks*, ed. Jean-Paul Richter (New York: Dover, 1970), 2.229 note (Archivio di Stato di Firenzi, Lettere alla Balia; previously published by J. Gaye, *Carteggio inedito d'Artisti* [Florence, 1840], 2.62). Translation by Francesca Roselli.

B. ACCOUNT BOOKS OF SIGNORIA, JULY-AUGUST 1503

The following entry in the accounts of Florence confirms Leonardo's visit to the field.

Andata di Leonardo al Campo sotto Pisa. Spese extraordinarie dieno dare a di XXVI di Iuglio L. LVI sol, XIII per loro a Giovanni Piffero; e sono per tanti, asegnia avere spexi in vetture di sei chavalli a spese di vitto per andare chon Lionardo da Vinci a livellare Arno in quello di Pisa per levallo del lito suo.

Leonardo's trip to the camp below Pisa.
Extra expenses, of the amount of 50.56 "soldi," must be paid for the 26th of July, 13 of them to Giovanni Piffero. This money has been spent to provide six-horse coaches and to pay the board expenses for the expedition with Leonardo in the territory of Pisa to divert Arno from its course and take it away from Pisa.

Source: Leonardo da Vinci, *Notebooks*, ed. Jean-Paul Richter (New York: Dover, 1970), 2.229 note (Archivio di Stato di Firenze, Libro d'Entrata e Uscita di cassa de' Magnifici Signori di liuglio e agosto 1503, 51 T; previously published by Milanesi, *Archivio Storico Italiano*, Serie III, Volume XVI). Translation by Francesca Roselli.

3. *Decision of the Signoria of 4 May 1504 Concerning Leonardo da Vinci.*

When Leonardo seemed to delay in starting to paint *The Battle of Anghiari*, the Gonfalonier Soderini was greatly upset. The formal agreement between Leonardo and the Signoria, co-signed by Machiavelli, is the only text explicitly linking the names of Machiavelli and Leonardo da Vinci. The cartoon—i.e., the preparatory drawing for the painting itself, made of sheets of paper stuck together—was ultimately completed and Leonardo began the painting itself on 6 June 1505. For the history of the painting and the controversy surrounding it, see Bramley, *Leonardo*, 336–349.

Item ditch Domini simul adunati etc. servatis etc. deliberaverunt etc. infra-scriptas deliberationes infra vugari sermone descriptas videlicet: the Magnifi-cent and Excellent Lordships, the Priors of Liberty and the Gonfalonier of Jus-tice of the Florentine people, considering that: several months ago Leonardo of Sir Piero da Vinci, Florentine citizen, began to paint the Hall of the Great Council; that Leonardo had already painted a preliminary drawing of it on a cartoon and that he had received 35 large golden florins for this work; that these Lords wish that the work will be completed as soon as possible and that the above mentioned Leonardo will be given at different times a certain amount of money; nonetheless, the Magnificent Lords servatis etc. resolved that Leo-nardo will have to finish the entire cartoon completely by next February 1504, no exception or excuse accepted, and Leonardo shall be paid 15 large golden florins for each month, counting from the 20th of April. And in case Leonardo should not have finished the cartoon within that time, then the Magnificent Lords can compel him in whatever way they consider more opportune, to give back the entire amount of money earned for that work until that day, and to hand over, without compensation, that part of the cartoon which he has man-aged to finish; in the meanwhile Leonardo has promised to finish the cartoon.

It could be the case that Leonardo would consider it proper to begin paint-ing on the wall of the hall the part he had drawn on the cartoon, in which case the Magnificent Lordships will be pleased to give him the wage they will con-sider as proper for each month of his work and on the day agreed between Leonardo and them. And since Leonardo is engaged in painting the wall, the Magnificent Lords will be pleased to extend the period of time allowed [to him to finish the cartoon], during which Leonardo is obliged to finish the cartoon in the way agreed between the Lords and Leonardo. And since it could also happen that Leonardo, during the time he is engaged in finishing the cartoon, should not have the opportunity to paint the wall but went on with the car-toon, according to the agreement subscribed, the Magnificent Lords will not be allowed to have the cartoon painted by anybody without Leonardo's formal permission. On the contrary, they will let Leonardo finish the painting when it is possible for him and let him paint the wall any month they will agree upon, when it will be considered more opportune. Nonetheless, Leonardo will have to declare his acceptance of 35 large golden florins, and all the money he will re-ceive in the future, as the advance on the money that the Magnificent Lords will declare as total reward for his work. Mandantes . . .

. . . Actum in palatio dictorum Dominorum presentibus Nicolao Domini Bernardi de Machiavellis Cancellario dictorum Dominorum, et Marco ser Ioannis de Romena cive fiorentino, testibus etc.

Source: Denis Fachard, *Biagio Buonaccorsi: Sa Vie—Son Temps—Son Oeuvre* (Bologna: Boni, 1976), 259–260 (Archivio di Stato di Firenze, Signori e Collegi, Deliberazioni fatte in forza di ordinaria autorità, 106, cc. 40v–41r). Translation by Francesca Roselli.

4. Diversion of the Arno—Correspondence September 1504

Although scholars have expressed various opinions concerning who was responsible for implementing the decision to divert the Arno, the texts demonstrate that Machiavelli wrote incessantly to the field, overseeing the project for the Ten of War; in the field, the leading engineer was Colombino. Since Leonardo was primarily engaged in working on *The Battle of Anghiari* at this time, it is not surprising that he did not play a central role. It may be, however, that Machiavelli consulted Leonardo between the letters of 20 and 21 September 1504.

A. MACHIAVELLI TO ANTONIO GIACOMINI, 3 SEPTEMBER 1504

In this memorandum, Machiavelli clearly designates Colombino as responsible for the completion of the work and suggests that it is necessary to stimulate him to action. As the result indicates, Machiavelli's fears were well grounded.

Et chircha à casi di Colombino, li farai intendere che attende ad fare che la opera si tiri innanzi et che la riescha, perché non se li è manchare di remuneratione conveniente, così in suo premio come in suo honore.

With regard to Colombino, you will urge him to make the work proceed and come to an end, if he does not want to lose an opportune compensation, intended both as reward and as praise to his honor.

Source: Denis Fachard, *Biagio Buonaccorsi: Sa Vie—Son Temps—Son Oeuvre* (Bologna: Boni, 1976), 128 (Archivio di Stato di Firenze, X di B., Miss. 78, cc. 110r.-111r). Translation by Francesca Roselli.

B. GIULIANO LAPI TO COMMITTEE OF TEN, 10 SEPTEMBER 1504

Giuliano Lapi was one of the two General Commissioners in charge of the Florentine camp; Machiavelli, as Secretary to the Committee of Ten, was the presumed recipient of the letter. As Fachard points out, this letter shows that as of 10 September, "Colombino was not yet being held responsible for the slowness with which the project was advancing."

. . . che Colombino non può essere in ogni lato egli, et so auanato harebeno rispiarmato questa opera se ce ne fussi suti 4, che qui ce ne è carestia di simili homini, poiché votre Signorie non gli vogiando mandare si farà el meglio si potrà, o manderò per epsi dove crederò ne sia, ché quando non facessino altro che etter gl'homini in sul lavoro innanzi iet indrieto dove fa bisogno, non farebbono poco . . .

. . . Colombino cannot be held responsible for everything, and I know how much time we would have saved if we had four of them, because we are in urgent need of such men, but since your Lordships do not want to send any more of them, we will do as much as we can. I will send the men we have where I believe it is needed, because even if they did not do anything more than place the workers where it is more necessary, this would already be an achievement.

Source: Denis Fachard, *Biagio Buonaccorsi: Sa Vie—Son Temps—Son Oeuvre* (Bologna: Boni, 1976), 142–143, note 34 (Archivio di Stato di Firenze, X di B., Resp. 79, c. 368r.-v). Translation by Francesca Roselli.

C. MACHIAVELLI TO ANTONIO GIACOMINI, 11 SEPTEMBER 1504

Machiavelli writes to the camp before Pisa, indicating his judgment of Colombino's ability and character.

Colombino è huomo intendentissimo di cotesto mesteiro delle adque, ma è persona rimessa et che in tanta moltitudine di huomini et di faccende facilment pare che non comparischa; ma è necessario, conosciute le qualità sua, animarlo et non li torre quore. Diciamooti questo acciò che conoscendolo tu come noi, possa seondare la natura sua et metterli animo quando bisogna.

Colombino is an excellent expert on this hydraulic engineering but as a person he is so reserved that he does not stand out among such a multitude of men and preparations; anyway, after knowing his qualities, it is necessary to support him. We are telling you all this so that, by knowing him as well as we do, you can understand his natural inclination and encourage him when it is needed.

Source: Denis Fachard, *Biagio Buonaccorsi: Sa Vie—Son Temps—Son Oeuvre* (Bologna: Boni, 1976), 128 (Archivio di Stato di Firenze, X di B., Miss. 79, c. 119r-v). Translation by Francesca Roselli.

D. MACHIAVELLI TO GIULIANO LAPI, 20 SEPTEMBER 1504

Informed of a change in the way the work is being conducted, Machiavelli clearly refers to a first plan ("primo disegno") that "we" prefer. The plan he is criticizing corresponds to the design reproduced by Buonaccorsi in his *Sunmario* (reproduced in Figure 1.11); Machiavelli's own preference corresponds with Leonardo's drawing (Figure 1.6). Since Machiavelli often speaks in his own name in correspondence when referring to his private opinion, we ("noi") seems to refer either to a preference of the Committeee of Ten—which would not be likely to be consulted on technical matters—or to Machiavelli and someone else informed about the project (which, under the circumstances, could easily be Leonardo). Given Soderini's controversies with Leonardo, represented by the decision of 4 May 1504 and the stories reported by Vasari among others, Machiavelli may well have preferred not to name Leonardo as the source of his technical advice. Fachard leaves the question in doubt: "Machiavelli makes a personal judgment on the new project designed by Giovan Berardi, which corresponds exactly to the map reproduced by Buonaccorsi, and refers to a design that had previously been executed—but is this enough to conclude that it is a question of Leonardo's design?" (p. 143). While Fachard is obviously correct that we cannot be certain, he does not consider the parallel evidence of other contacts between Machiavelli and Leonardo—not to mention the map of the Madrid Codex (Fig. 1.6), which is the only other plan of the diversion that has survived.

Per questa tua ultima di hieri intendiamo quello che tu ci di' del fosso: et se questo dì dopo mille promesse di dì e' sarà sboccato, ci fia grato; quanto che no, sanze starne in altra speranza, crederreno ad ogni modo che voi habbiate facto et facciate el possibile. Et perché tu di' che costì si era pensato di sboccare el secondo fosso in quel modo che si sarà sboccato questo primo, et dipoi recare in isola que terreno che fra l'una et l'altra bocca del fosso si era disegnato votare secondo el disegno facto quando era costì Giovan Berardi, havendo in questo caso ad dire l'opinione nostra, ci piaceva più quel primo disegno che questo ultimo, perché entrando Arno per due vie, et l'una et l'altra non molto largha, non crediamo che gli entri con quello impeto che farebbe quando se gli facessi una scarsella secondo el primo modo.

Oltre ad di questo, se venissi accidente veruno che disordinassi la pescaia che si fa,
sarebbe più facile assai a' Pisani el remettere Arno nel corso suo quando havessino
ad riturare solum dua boche, et pichole, che se li havessino ad fare una tura di
quella lughaeza che sarebbe lo spatio fra la bocca dell'uno et l'laltro fosso quando
e' fusti necto; pure quando le difficultà dell'operae o altre cagioni che non s'inten-
dono vi forzassino ad pigliare questo ultimo partito che tu scrivi, ce ne rimettereno
ad voi, et ad noi basterà solo havervene replicato l'opinione nostra.

Your letter of yesterday informed us about the ditch; if today, after so many promises, its mouth will be widened, this will please us; if not, without hoping any longer, we will nevertheless believe that you have done or are doing everything possible. As for what you are saying about its being considered to widen the mouth of the second ditch in the same way as the first, and after- wards to create an island of that part of the land between the two mouths of the ditch which was to be emptied according to the plan made when Giovanni Berardi was there, our opinion concerning this is that we preferred the first plan to this last one; because if the Arno flows through two ways, neither of them very wide, we believe that it would not flow with the same force as it would have if you were to make a little inlet as in the first plan. Moreover, if for any reason the weir thus created should be ruined, it would be much easier for the Pisans to direct the Arno back to its own course when they had to fill up only two small mouths, than if they had to fill up the space between the opening of the one and the other ditch; anyway, if the difficulties of the work or other unforeseen circumstances should force you to undertake this last project you wrote me about, we will trust your decision, and we will be content with having let you know our opinion.

Source: Denis Fachard, *Biagio Buonaccorsi: Sa Vie—Son Temps—Son Oeuvre* (Bologna: Boni, 1976), 143-44, note 42 (Archivio di Stato di Firenze, X di B., Miss. 78, cc. 134v-135r). Trans- lation by Francesca Roselli.

E. MACHIAVELLI TO GIULIANO LAPI, 21 SEPTEMBER 1504

Just a day after writing that the decision of which plan to implement should be made in the field, Machiavelli seemingly realizes that there is a serious problem of the depth of the diversionary canal as compared to the Arno itself; he insists on a definite preference ("noi desiderremo inten- dere") and a specific action ("giudicheremo che fussi bene rimediarvi"). The collapse of the walls leading to the failure and abandonment of the project confirms Machiavelli's fears. The letters of 20 and 21 September not only reveal that Machiavelli followed the technical details of the project with care, but they also could be read to suggest that he informally consulted with a specialist between the two letters; if so, that specialist would probably have been Leonardo.

Facci dubitare questa vostra dilatione che 'l fondo del fosso non sia più alto che 'l fondo d'Arno; il che quando fussi farebbe cattivi effecti et secondo noi non si verrebbe al fine del desiderio nostro. Et in questo caso sarebbe bene da desiderare di sboccarlo con una piena, et da pensare che sboccandolo con l'acque basse e' non facessi molto effecto. Et però noi desiderremo intendere questa basseza come la è, et se el fondo d'Arno è più basso o più alto dels fondo del fosso, et se el fondo del fosso fussi più alto del fondo d'Arno, giudicheremo che fussi bene rimediarvi.

Your delay makes us fear that the bed of the ditch is shallower than the bed of the Arno; this would have negative effects and in our opinion it would not direct the project to the end we wish. In this case it would be good to widen it with a flood, since we think that low waters would not have the same effect. Anyway we would like to know if the bed of the Arno is shallower or deeper than that of the ditch, and in case the bed of the ditch is shallower, we would think it proper to make up for it.

Source: Denis Fachard, *Biagio Buonaccorsi: Sa Vie—Son Temps—Son Oeuvre* (Bologna: Boni, 1976), 142, note 32 (Archivio di Stato di Firenze, X di B., Miss. 78, cc. 139r-v). Translation by Francesca Roselli.

F. TOMMASO TOSSINGHI TO COMMITTEE OF TEN, 28 SEPTEMBER 1504

Two weeks after Lapi's letter exonerating Colombino for the delays, his colleague Tossinghi makes the architect's shortcomings explicit.

. . . et perché loro [i lavoratori] hanno poca fede che questa opera si possi ridurre alla perfectione che vostre Signorie desiderano, ne stanno di mala vogiia, et a Giuliano et a me pare che questo maestro Colombino cominci a invilire di poter dar perfectione a questa opera, dandone cagione a' tempi et all'opere chattive che si sono venute . . .

. . . and since the workers do not seem to believe that this work can be carried out as carefully as your Lordships wish, they are working with a bad disposition. It seems to Giuliano and me that Master Colombino is beginning to doubt that he can carry out this project, laying the blame on the weather and the unfavorable circumstances that accompanied the work . . .

Source: Denis Fachard, *Biagio Buonaccorsi: Sa Vie—Son Temps—Son Oeuvre* (Bologna: Boni, 1976), 143, note 34 (Archivio di Stato di Firenze, X di B., Resp. 79, c. 418 r-v). Translation by Francesca Roselli.

5. *Buonaccorsi's Account of the Diversion of the Arno*

Machiavelli's assistant, Biagio Buonaccorsi, wrote a detailed account of the failed diversion of the Arno. Two versions of the text have been found.

A. *SUNMARIO* OF BIAGIO BUONACCORSI (C. 83R.)

This manuscript version is presumed to be contemporary with the events, and probably written to provide the basis of a report to the Committee of Ten; pasted onto the text is Buonaccorsi's sketch of the actual diversion (Figure 1.11). In this document, Colombino is explicitly named as the architect responsible for the project.

At this time it was considered taking the Arno River away from the Pisans in order to conduct it into the Stagno, for it was shown with good reasons that besides depriving the Pisans of their source of life, those who were undertaking this project were to benefit our town immensely; therefore, the decision to undertake the project being taken, the camp was set up at Riglione after having cut the forage, and a Maestro d'Acque, Colombino, was summoned, who was asked to state what was necessary to complete the undertaking. He asked for two thousand laborers a day equipped with the wood necessary to construct a weir in order to retain the river and divert it into two big ditches through which the Arno was to flow, planned to go all the way to the Stagno; and he promised that the undertaking could be carried out with thirty or forty thousand works, and so, provided with such a hope, the project was undertaken on 20 August, with two thousand works, which were to be paid each a carlino a day, and according to the design which will be shown at the bottom of the page. And the undertaking was not completed because it required too much time and money, and if Maestro Colombino had promised to finish the whole undertaking with thirty or thirty-five thousand works, eighty thousand works were not even enough to bring it half way, nor was the expected fall for waters achieved, because with the river in flood the waters entered strongly through the ditch but as the Arno went back to its regular flow the flood-waters began to subside. The Maestro having completed the first two projected ditches, and the weir begun but not finished, the Arno, being narrowed on account of the weir, was having its bed dug out by the faster waters to a level much lower than that of the ditch, so that the waters were entering the ditch only when the river was in flood. The Maestro maintained that the river itself would have corrected the anomaly once the weir was finished, because the sediment produced continually by the waters would have raised its bed, but in actuality the waters never went through except under flood conditions, and as soon as they diminished they flowed back. This undertaking came to cost seven thousand ducats or more, because in addition to the salary for the workers and other things, it was necessary to keep a thousand soldiers in that place to protect the workers from the attack of the Pisans. And the work was begun at the tower of the Fagiano, which tower was ruined to provide brushwood and other kinds of timber for the weir. The only benefit which was to ensue from this work was that the nearby hills came to be protected by the ditches against the Pisans' raids; furthermore, it came to flood the whole plain of Vettola all the way to S. Pietro in Grado, making farming impossible. Two other Maestri d'Acque were called in from Lombardy and they too stated that the river had a fifteen braccia slope, but as the reason for it was understood through experience, it was decided to abandon the project. The greater of the two ditches was thirty braccia wide and seven deep, the second twenty braccia wide and as deep as the other.

Source: Denis Fachard, *Biagio Buonaccorsi: Sa Vie—Son Temps—Son Oeuvre* (Bologna: Boni, 1976), 127–128 and, for the sketch, Plate III, facing p. 158. Translation by Francesca Roselli.

B. DIARIO OF BIAGIO BUONACCORSI (PP. 92–94)

Buonaccorsi's *Diario de' successi piu importanti seguiti in Italia, & partricolarmente in Fiorenze dall'anno 1498 insino all'anno 1512* was published posthumously in Florence in 1568; on the work as a history, see Fachard, *Biagio Buonaccorsi*, chapter 5. Of particular importance is the replacement of specific mention of Colombino by the general phrase "maestri d'acque," thereby avoiding charges of personal responsibility for the failure.

At this time it was considered taking the Arno River away from the Pisans in order to conduct it into the Stagno, for it was shown with good reasons that besides depriving the Pisans of their source of life, it was to benefit our town,

Figure 1.11. Biagio Buonaccorsi, Plan of the Diversion of the Arno (1504). Courtesy of Biblioteca Riccardiana, Firenze—Ricc. 1920. cc. 83v.–84 r.

and finally, the decision to undertake the project being taken, the camp was set at Riglione, and Maestri d'Acque were summoned. They explained that the undertaking required two thousand works a day [an opera is the labourer considered for the work he can carry out in a day] equipped with the wood necessary to construct a weir in order to retain the river and divert it into two big ditches all the way to the Stagno; and they promised that the undertaking could be carried out with thirty or forty thousand works, and so with such a hope the project was undertaken on August 20, with two thousand works, which were to be paid each a carlino a day. This undertaking took much more time and money, and to no profit, for, in spite of the estimated cost, eighty thousand works were not even enough to bring it half way, nor was the expected fall for the waters achieved, because with the river in flood the waters entered strongly through the ditch but as the Arno went back to its regular flow the flood-waters began to subside. The maestri having completed the first two projected ditches, and the weir begun but not finished, the Arno, being narrowed on account of the weir, was having its bed dug out by the faster waters to a level much lower than that of the ditch, so that the waters were entering the ditch only when the river was in flood. The Maestri maintained that the river itself would have corrected the anomaly once the weir was finished, because the sediment produced continually by the waters would have raised its bed. But in actuality the waters never went through except under flood conditions, and as soon as they diminished they flowed back. This undertaking came to cost seven thousand ducats, or more, because in addition to the salary for the workers, it was necessary to keep a thousand soldiers to protect the workers from the attacks of the Pisans. And the work was begun at the tower of the Fagiano, which was ruined to provide the building material for the weir. A benefit which was to ensue from this work was that the nearby hills came to be protected by the ditches against the enemy's raids; furthermore, it came to flood the whole plain of the Vettola all the way to S. Pietro in Frado, making farming impossible. Two other Maestri d'Acque were called in from Lombardy and they too stated that the river had a fifteen braccia slope, but as the reason for it was understood through experience, it was decided to abandon the project altogether and to damage the Pisans in some other way, above all by preventing them from leaving the town. The greater of the two ditches was thirty braccia wide and seven deep, the second was twenty braccia wide and as deep as the other.

Source: Carlo Pedretti, Literary Works of Leonardo da Vinci (Berkeley, Calif,: University of California, 1977), 2.177–178 (Italian), pp. 178–179 (translation).

Appendix II

Machiavelli's Letters

Two important letters by Machiavelli are worth reproducing in their entirety so that the reader will have them at hand. The first, soon to be available in the forthcoming translation of *Machiavelli's Correspondence* edited by James Atkinson and David Sices (Northern Illinois University Press), is an extraordinary letter written in September 1506 to Piero Soderini's nephew, Giovan Battista Soderini. Outlining clearly the view of fortune and human nature made famous in chapter twenty-five of *The Prince*, this letter shows how deeply Machiavelli's political thought was shaped by his experience in Florentine politics. Perhaps more important, this letter shows Machiavelli's explicit denial that humans could attain the definitive "control" or "mastery" over natural or historical forces articulated by Bacon and his successors. The second letter, justly famous, was written to Machiavelli's friend Francesco Vettori on 10 December 1513. In addition to describing in detail the circumstances surrounding the composition of *The Prince*, Machiavelli presents with exceptional clarity the happiness of philosophic activity, thereby leading us to question the view that he was merely a political actor who turned to writing under the pressure of necessity.

1. Niccolò Machiavelli to Giovan Battista Soderini

Perugia, 13–21 September 1506

Your letter came to me with a mask on; yet, after ten words, I recognized it and can well believe in the crowds at Piombino since I know you; and I am certain of the obstacles you and Filippo encountered because I know one of you is impeded by too little 'light'—the other, by too much. I do not find January a nuisance, as long as I can count on holding onto February's support. I am

249

sorry about Filippo's apprehension and await the outcome in suspense. Your
letter was short, but rereading it I made it longer. (He who does not know
how to fence can entangle one who does.) I was grateful for it because it gave
me an opportunity to do what I was hesitating about doing and what you
remind me not to do—the only part of your letter that I admit is to no purpose. This would surprise me if it were not for the fact that my fate has shown
me so many and such varied things that I am forced rarely to be surprised or to
admit that I have not savored—either through reading or through experience—the actions of men and their ways of doing things (*modi del procedere*).
I know you and the compass of your navigation; even if it could be blamed,
which it cannot be, I should not, since I see what ports it has guided you to
and what hopes it may foster in you. (Hence I think, not according to your
perspective [*spechio*], wherein nothing but prudence is visible, but with the
perspective [*spechio*] of the many, which must see the ends, not the means, of
things.) And I see that steering along a variety of routes can bring about the
same thing and that acting in different ways can bring about the same end—
whatever this conviction may have lacked has been filled in by this Pope's
actions and their outcomes. (In fine, advise no one and accept advice from no
one, except for a general suggestion that each man must do what his mind
prompts him to—and do it with daring.) Take Hannibal and Scipio: in addition to their military training, in which they were equally preeminent, the
former kept his armies in Italy united through cruelty, treachery, and impiety
and made himself admired by the populace who, in order to follow him, rebelled against the Romans (men tire of the good and complain about the bad;
bitter things irritate the taste, sweet things cloy it); the latter achieved the identical result among the populace in Spain with compassion, loyalty, and piety:
both achieved victory upon victory. (To try Fortune, who is the friend of
youth, and to change according to the times. But it is impossible both to have
fortresses and not to have them; it is impossible to be both cruel and compas-
sionate, etc.) But, because it is not customary to bring in the Romans as
evidence, Lorenzo de' Medici disarmed the populace to hold on to Florence,
Messer Giovanni Bentivoglio armed them to hold on to Bologna; the Vitelli,
in Città di Castello, and the current duke of Urbino in his territory (*stato*) tore
down fortresses in order to hold on to those territories (*stati*), Count
Francesco in Milan and many other constructed fortresses in their territories
(*stati*) in order to secure them for themselves. The Emperor Titus believed
that he would lose his realm (*state*) on any day that he did not do good to
someone; another person might believe that he would lose his on any day
when he did do good to someone. Many people [do not] succeed in their

plans because they calculate and deliberate everything. (When Fortune slacks off it follows that a man, a family, and a city crumbles; each person's fortune is based upon his way of doing things (*modo del procedere*), and each person's fortune slacks off; when it is slack, it must be regained by some other means.) This Pope, who has no scales or measuring stick in his house, obtains through chance—and disarmed—what ought to be difficult to attain even with organization and with weapons. We have seen, and continue to see, in all the examples mentioned above—and in countless other examples that could be brought in as evidence in analogous instances—that kingdoms are conquered, or are subdued, or have fallen, as unforeseen events would have it. Sometimes the way of doing things (*modo del procedere*) that was praised when it led to conquest is vilified when it leads to defeat and sometimes when defeat comes after long prosperity (the comparison of the horse and bit concerning fortresses), people do not blame anything of their own, but rather indict heaven and the will of the Fates. But the reason why different actions are sometimes equally useful and sometimes equally detrimental I do not know—yet I should very much like to; so, in order to learn your view, I shall be presumptuous enough to give you mine. I believe that just as Nature has created men with different faces, so he has created them with different intellects (*ingegno*) and imaginations (*fantasia*). As a result, each man behaves according to his own intellect and imagination. And, on the other hand, because times change and the pattern of events differs, one man's hopes may turn out as he prayed they would. The man who matches his way of doing things (*modo del procedere*) with the conditions of the times is successful; the man who actions are at odds with the times and the pattern of events is unsuccessful. Hence it can well be that two men can achieve the same goal by acting differently: because each one of them matches his actions to what he encounters, [and] because there are as many patterns of events as there are regions and governments (*stati*). But because times and affairs often change—both in general and in particular—and because men change neither their imaginations (*fantasie*) nor their ways of doing things (*modi del procedere*) accordingly, it turns out that a man has good fortune at one time and bad fortune at another. And truly, anyone wise enough to adapt to and understand the times and the pattern of events would always have good fortune, or would always keep himself from bad fortune; and it would come to be true that the wise man could control the stars and the Fates. But such wise men do not exist; in the first place, men are shortsighted; in the second place, they are unable to master their own natures; thus it follows that Fortune is fickle, controlling men and keeping them under her yoke. I want the examples mentioned above to suffice as proof of this view; I have based it on them and so I should like the one to support the other. Cruelty, treachery, and impiety are effective in providing a new ruler with prestige in that region where human kindness, loyalty, and piety have long been common practice just as human kindness, loyalty, and piety are effective where cruelty, treachery, and impiety reigned for a while; for just as bitter things irritate the taste and sweet things cloy it, so men become impatient with the good and complain about the bad. These causes, among others, opened Italy up to Hannibal and Spain to Scipio and thus each one made time and affairs consistent with his pattern of doing things (*procedere*). In those days a Scipio would have made less progress in Italy and a Hannibal would have made less progress in Spain than each did in his own area.

2. Niccolò Machiavelli to Francesco Vettori

Florence, December 10, 1513[1]

Magnificent ambassador:

"Never were divine favors late."[2] I say this because I appear to have lost, no, mislaid your favor, since you have gone a long time without writing me, and I was doubtful whence the cause could arise. And of all those that came to my mind I took little account except for one, when I feared you had stopped writing to me because someone had written to you that I was not a good warden of your letters; and I knew that, apart from Filippo and Pagolo,[3] no one else had seen them on account of me. I regained your favor by your last letter of the 23rd of last month, where I was very pleased to see how orderly and quietly you exercise this public office;[4] and I urge you to continue so, for whoever lets go of his own convenience for the convenience of others, only loses his own and gets no thanks from them. And because Fortune wants to do everything, she wants us to allow her to do it, to remain quiet and not give trouble, and to await the time when she allows men something to do; and then it will be right for you to give more effort, to watch things more, and for me to leave my villa and say: 'Here I am.'[5] Therefore, wishing to return equal favors, I cannot tell you in this letter of mine anything other than what my life is like, and if you judge that it should be bartered for yours, I will be content to exchange it.

I stay in my villa, and since these last chance events occurred, I have not spent, to add them all up, twenty days in Florence. Until now I have been catching thrushes with my own hands. I would get up before day, prepare traps, and go out with a bundle of cages on my back, so that I looked like Geta when he returned from the harbor with Amphitryon's books; I caught at least two, at most six thrushes. And so passed all September; then this pastime, though annoying and strange, gave out, to my displeasure. And what my life is like, I will tell you. I get up in the morning with the sun and go to a wood of mine that I am having cut down, where I stay for two hours to look over the work of the past day, and to pass time with the woodcutters, who always have some disaster on their hands either among themselves or with their neighbors. And regarding this wood I would have a thousand beautiful things to tell you of what happened to me with Frosino da Panzano and others who want wood from it. And Frosino in particular sent for a number of loads without telling me anything, and on payment wanted to hold back ten lire from me, which he said he should have had from me four years ago when he beat me at *cricca* at Antonio Guicciardini's. I began to raise the devil and was on the point of accusing the driver who had gone for it of theft; but Giovanni Machiavelli came between us and brought us to agree. Batista Guicciardini, Filippo Ginori, Tommaso del Bene, and some other citizens, when that north wind was blowing, ordered a load each from me. I promised to all, and sent one to Tommaso which in Florence turned into a half-load, because to stack it up there were himself, his wife, his servant, and his children, so that they looked like Gabbura with his boys when he bludgeons an ox on Thursday. So, when I saw whose profit it was, I told the others I had no more wood; and all have made a big point of it, especially Battista, who counts this among the other disasters of Prato.

When I leave the wood, I go to a spring, and from there to an aviary of mine. I have a book under my arm, Dante or Petrarch, or one of the minor poets like Tibullus, Ovid, and such. I read of their amorous passions and their loves; I remember my own and enjoy myself for a while in this thinking. Then I move on along the road to the inn; I speak with those passing by; I ask them news of their places; I learn various things; and I note the various tastes and different fancies of men. In the meantime comes the hour to dine, when I eat with my company what food this poor villa and tiny patrimony allow. Having eaten, I return to the inn; there is the host, ordinarily a butcher, a miller, two bakers. With them I become a rascal for the whole day, playing at *cricca* and *tric-trac*, from which arise a thousand quarrels and countless abuses with insulting words, and most times we are fighting over a penny and yet we can be heard shouting from San Casciano. Thus involved with these vermin I scrape the mold off my brain and I satisfy the malignity of this fate of mine, as I am content to be trampled on this path so as to see if she will be ashamed of it.

When evening has come, I return to my house and go into my study. At the door I take off my clothes of the day, covered with mud and mire, and I put on my regal and courtly garments; and decently reclothed, I enter the ancient courts of ancient men, where, received by them lovingly, I feed on the food that alone is mine and that I was born for. There I am not ashamed to speak with them and to ask them the reason for their actions; and they in their humanity reply to me. And for the space of four hours I feel no boredom, I forget every pain, I do not fear poverty, death does not frighten me. I deliver myself entirely to them. And because Dante says that to have understood without retaining does not make knowledge, I have noted what capital I have made from their conversation and have composed a little work *De Principatibus* [On Principalities], where I delve as deeply as I can into reflections on this subject, debating what a principality is, of what kinds they are, how they are acquired, how they are maintained, why they are lost. And if you have ever been pleased by any of my whimsies, this one should not displease you; and to a prince, and especially to a new prince, it should be welcome. So I am addressing it to his Magnificence, Giuliano. Filippo Cassavecchia has seen it; he can give you an account in part both of the thing in itself and of the discussions I had with him, although I am all the time fattening and polishing it.

You wish, magnificent ambassador, that I leave this life and come to enjoy your life with you. I will do it in any case, but what tempts me now is certain dealings of mine that I will have done in six weeks. What makes me be doubtful is that the Soderini are there, whom I would be forced, if I came, to visit and speak with. I should fear that at my return I would not expect to get off at my house, but I would get off at the Bargello, for although this state has very great foundations and great security, yet it is new, and because of this suspicious; nor does it lack wiseacres who, to appear like Pagolo Bertini, would let others run up a bill and leave me to think of paying. I beg of you to relieve me of this fear, and then I will come in the time stated to meet you anyway.

I have discussed with Filippo this little work of mine, whether to give it to him[6] or not; and if it is good to give it, whether it would be good for me to take it or send it to you. Not giving it would make me fear that at the least it would not be read by Giuliano and that this Ardinghelli[7] would take for himself the honor of this latest effort of mine. The necessity that chases me makes me give it, because I am becoming worn out, and I cannot remain as I am for a long time without becoming despised because of poverty, besides the desire I have that these Medici lords begin to make use of me even if they should begin by making me roll a stone.[8] For if I should not then win them over to me, I should complain of myself; and through this thing, if it were read, one would see that I have neither slept through nor played away the fifteen years I have been at the study of the art of the state. And anyone should be glad to have the service of one who is full of experience at the expense of another.[9] And one should not doubt my faith, because having always observed faith, I ought not now be learning to break it. Whoever has been faithful and good for forty-three years, as I have, ought not to be able to change his nature, and of my faith and goodness my poverty is witness.

I should like, then, for you to write me again on how this matter appears to you, and I commend myself to you.

Be prosperous
10 December 1513
Niccolò Machiavelli, in Florence

Why Doesn't Machiavelli Speak of Leonardo?

*T*here is an obvious objection to the claim that Leonardo's work and thought influenced Machiavelli in some way: if Leonardo was as important as I have claimed, why doesn't Machiavelli ever mention him? Why Machiavelli's silence on the abortive plan to rechannel the Arno during the war on Pisa? And, given Leonardo's extraordinary achievements in scientific and technological innovation—some of which were directly relevant to politics, why does Machiavelli say so little about science and technology?

To this obvious question, however, needs to be added a subtler one: why is Machiavelli silent about so many of his own experiences as Second Secretary of the Florentine Republic? True, he tells us in a celebrated chapter of *The Prince* of his conversation with Cesare Borgia on the day Pope Julius II was elected—but that conversation took place when both were in Rome in the fall of 1503, and Machiavelli's account contradicts the dispatches he sent from Cesare's court a year earlier.[1] When he argues that "detached forts outside the city" being defended will "invariably" be taken as the "beginning and cause" of defeat, why does he not cite his insistence on the capture and fortification of La Verrucca in 1504, a prelude to the ultimate defeat of Pisa by Florence?[2] Above all, why is the comparison between fortune and a river, with its reference to "dikes and dams" to prevent floods, not explicitly related to the attempt to divert the Arno?

Although Machiavelli's correspondence provides extensive evidence of his close personal involvement in this project, after mentioning the diversion of the Arno in the *First Decennale* (written in 1504), he never again speaks of it. At most there are indirect references, such as the discussion of sieges in *The Art of War*: "Many generals have poisoned waters and *turned rivers aside in order to take cities*, even though *in the end they might not succeed*."[3] With regard to public events in which Leonardo is known to have been involved, Machiavelli hides *his own* role as well as that of Leonardo.

This pattern cannot be interpreted as Machiavelli's disavowal of decisions in his political career. Although the dangers of using mercenary and foreign troops are strongly emphasized in both *The Prince* (ch. 12) and *Discourses* (II, 20; pp. 339–340), Machiavelli does not tell us of his long practical efforts to provide Florence with such a civilian army.[4] In the *Discourses* (I, 39; p. 209), he explicitly defends the conduct of military affairs by "The Ten of War" without indicating his service for over a decade as the Committee's Secretary and chief administrator. Later in the *Discourses*, Machiavelli discusses "the dangers incurred by citizens or by those advising a prince to take the lead in some grave and important matter in such a way for the whole of this advice they may be held responsible" (III, 35; p. 500). These "dangers" describe his own situation, especially after the failure of the diversion of the Arno in 1504 and the defeat of the Florentine militia at Prato in 1512, yet Machiavelli neither admits making mistakes nor openly refers to his own response to criticism.[5]

The earliest readers of *The Prince* and *Discourses*, such as those to whom Machiavelli dedicated these works (Giuliano or Lorenzo di Piero de' Medici as well as Zanobi Buondelmonti or Cosimo Rucellai), would have known many of the historical details at first hand. For such readers, Machiavelli's silence about his own career and his contacts with Leonardo would have been intentional. Beyond the general silence concerning his own role in events discussed in his works, were there specific reasons for Machiavelli to be secretive concerning his relationship with Leonardo?

The Problem

We can be certain that Machiavelli knew of Leonardo's military expertise as a designer of fortresses and a specialist in waterworks, if only from the documents showing that Leonardo visited the site of the diversion of the Arno on 24 July 1503—and that his consultation was essential in the decision to pursue a project which Machiavelli personally followed with great care.[6] Even if there were personal reasons to be silent about Leonardo himself, if the argument set forth is correct, one might expect Machiavelli to discuss at length the issues of the emerging science and technology of which Leonardo was the harbinger. Yet *The Prince*, the *Discourses*, and Machiavelli's other major works say almost as little about these issues as about the events relating Machiavelli and Leonardo.

It is an old maxim of law and scholarship that the absence of evidence is not the evidence of absence. Machiavelli may remain silent on some matters by choice rather than by lack of information or knowledge. For example, there is good reason to believe that Machiavelli was not a sincere Christian believer, and that he viewed Christianity as one of a long cycle of human religions, albeit with particularly evil consequences for society; behavior that seems to contradict this anti-Christian attitude can clearly be justified on the grounds of prudence. Above all other thinkers, Machiavelli could be expected to use deceit when he deemed it necessary for his purposes.[7]

Prudence and deception were obviously in order when Machiavelli wrote dispatches from the court of Cesare Borgia, whose reputation was not savory even before he murdered his own generals at Sinigaglia in December 1502. While naming many of those he met in Imola, Machiavelli—like any diplomat in a sensitive foreign post—would have attempted to "protect his sources." More generally, his correspondence as a public official makes clear that Machiavelli—like his assistant Buonaccorsi and others—habitually used ciphers, codes, ambiguities, and vagueness; the rare case of an extant letter that names names explicitly ends with the instruction: "tear up this letter."[8]

After Machiavelli's fall from power and torture in 1512, as is witnessed by his correspondence with Vettori in 1513–1514, Machiavelli wrote in a manner that continued to rely heavily on obscurities, indirectness, and puzzling silences. Consider Machiavelli's exchange of letters with Vettori recalling the arrest and expulsion of Piero Soderini when the Florentine Republic fell, an event in which they participated together to save the Gonfalonier's life. Machiavelli fails to mention his presence when Soderini was convinced to abdicate; Vettori answers this letter with one explicitly describing their role in taking Soderini and getting him out of the country.[9] Machiavelli was well practiced in silence and deception. Sometimes he simply preferred not to talk about things or people. But why?

To explain Machiavelli's failure to mention Leonardo, it is well to recall what happened to the two men after Leonardo left Florence in 1506. Although he returned temporarily from Milan in 1507–1508 to win the court case on an inheritance from his uncle, Leonardo never completed *The Battle of Anghiari* as he had promised the Signoria. Since Machiavelli witnessed the agreement between the Signoria and Leonardo that established the terms for the painting—and according to some played a role in negotiating it—it is highly improbable that Leonardo's actions were unknown to Machiavelli.[10]

After Leonardo returned to Milan in 1508, his career contrasts sharply with that of Machiavelli. During the last years of Machiavelli's role as Second Secretary, Leonardo was in Milan serving the French King Louis XII and his governor, Charles d'Amboise. After 1512, when the Florentine Republic fell and the French were expelled from Milan, Leonardo returned briefly to Florence, but promptly left in September 1513 to go into the service of Giuliano de' Medici in Rome, to whom Machiavelli decided to send the manuscript of *The Prince* in late 1513. After Giuliano's death in 1516, Leonardo served his nephew Lorenzo as well as the French king, leaving Italy altogether to spend his last years in France. In short, after 1506 Leonardo's patrons were the French (whose invasion of Italy Machiavelli criticized)[11] and the Medici (who were approached unsuccessfully by Machiavelli in 1513, at the same time that Leonardo was working under the patronage of Giuliano de' Medici in Rome). In Leonardo's last years, he was a feted figure in the court of King Francis I, whereas Machiavelli was reduced to marginal status with little influence on those in power despite some minor military commissions by Guiccardini and the Medici.[12]

In the absence of evidence, we can only speculate about the impression left by these events. I can suggest five different interpretations consistent with the evidence presented above. First, perhaps Machiavelli was angry with Leonardo for leaving Florence and his silence can be viewed as criticism. Second, it is possible that Machiavelli preferred to remain silent because the events in question cast a poor light on his own judgment. Third, perhaps the silence was required by the tactical circumstances, since Leonardo was living and working under the patronage of Giuliano de' Medici in Rome at the moment Machiavelli told Vettori he was sending his "little book" to Giuliano; when Giuliano died in 1516 and Machiavelli changed the dedication to Lorenzo di Piero de' Medici, Leonardo was associated with the new addressee of *The Prince*. Fourth, Machiavelli may have known Leonardo well enough to be quite familiar with the conception of politics described in chapter seven; if so, he would have found that Leonardo's plans sought a technological conquest of nature which, in Machiavelli's view, would be impossible to realize and dangerous to attempt. Finally, the expectation that Machiavelli should have written about Leonardo may itself be anachronistic, misunderstanding the canons of writing and record-keeping in the Italian Renaissance. While any one of these five explanations might be correct, all might have an element of truth—and, of course, others might be offered.

Hypothesis #1

When writing *The Prince* in 1513 Machiavelli might have thought of Leonardo as someone with great scientific and technical ability who had failed to devote himself to Florence and was willing to put his knowledge in the service of the highest bidder. Just as Machiavelli attacks mercenary soldiers, he would have been critical of Leonardo as a mercenary military architect and scientist. According to this hypothesis, by 1509, when Pisa finally fell, Leonardo could have been a very *bad* memory for Machiavelli—and someone he no longer wanted to associate with or to have others remember he had trusted and supported.[13]

Evidence for this hypothesis might be the peculiar way that Leonardo's patrons are treated in the opening chapters of *The Prince*. During Leonardo's first extended stay in Milan, his most flamboyant project—and indeed the one which was instrumental in Duke Ludovico Sforza's decision to employ him—was *Il Cavallo*, the immense bronze monument to il Moro's father, Francesco Sforza. That memorial was, of course, never erected. Could this explain the favorable reference to Francesco in chapter one of *The Prince?*[14] Sforza is discussed four times later in the book; perhaps Machiavelli wanted to symbolize the fact that, in writing, *he* could produce a more lasting monument to Francesco Sforza than Leonardo had achieved after sixteen years of extensive labor.

Another indirect criticism of Leonardo might be inferred from the discussion of King Louis XII of France in chapter three of *The Prince* (pp. 13–16). When Leonardo left Florence for Milan, he began to work for King Louis, who described him in 1507 as "our dear and good friend . . . our painter and engineer in ordinary."[15] In chapter three of *The Prince*, as evidence of the mistakes made when the ruler of one country invades another with a different language and culture, Machiavelli lists no less than five mistakes made by Louis. Knowing the events that had occurred between 1506 and 1512, this passage could be read as criticizing Leonardo's decision to serve a ruler with bad judgment.

There are two other passages that could be read with similar hidden meaning. In *The Prince*, Machiavelli reports on two face-to-face conversations with political figures of status and power: Cesare Borgia in chapter seven (p. 32), and "Rouen"—Cardinal Georges d'Amboise, minister of King Louis XII—in chapter three (p. 16). Both men remind us of Leonardo's patrons: Cesare himself from 1502 to 1503, Charles d'Amboise, the Cardinal's nephew, as Governor of Milan after 1506. Machiavelli ends chapter seven by telling the reader that Cesare made an "error," and he says explicitly in chapter three that he told "Rouen" to his face that "the French do not understand the state." Again, these passages could be taken as implicit criticisms of Leonardo's choice of Cesare Borgia and the French kings (or their ministers) as patrons.

There is one other passage in Machiavelli's work which would support this hypothesis. In Book V, chapter thirty-three of the *Florentine Histories*, Machiavelli gives an account of the Battle of Anghiari—the event which served as the subject of Leonardo's unfinished painting that was the source of ill-feeling between the artist and Piero Soderini, Machiavelli's patron. In describing the battle, Machiavelli asserts contrary to the texts of other histories, that despite the violence of "so long a battle that lasted from twenty to twenty-four hours, only one man died, and he not from wounds or any other virtuous blow, but, falling off his horse, he was trampled on and expired."[16] Historians have long been puzzled by the discrepancy between the other sources and Machiavelli's account.

One solution to the perplexity may have been on the walls of the Signoria. When Machiavelli wrote, anyone who entered the Council Hall would have seen Leonardo's version of a violent battle, in which it seems quite evident that soldiers are being killed. Machiavelli's version of the event therefore implies that Leonardo's picture is not to be trusted. Although this interpretation is purely speculative, no other coherent account seems to be accepted by historians.[17]

Hypothesis #2

On the second hypothesis, it is conceivable that Machiavelli was primarily motivated by a desire to remain silent on the specific events on which he had collaborated with Leonardo between 1503 and 1506. Some scholars believe that the plan to redirect the Arno as a means of defeating Pisa could have been adopted by the Signoria before Leonardo was asked to provide technical expertise in its execution;[18] in this case, the project would be an example of Machiavelli's own poor judgment. Similarly, neither the commission to paint *The Battle of Anghiari* nor Leonardo's mission to Jacopo Appiani in Piombino was a lasting success. Hence any specific mention of these events would redound to Machiavelli's own disadvantage.

Although Machiavelli does not mention the plan to defeat Pisa by rechanneling the Arno River or the fortification of La Verrucca, *The Prince* contains a detailed account of the relationship between Florence and Pisa. Indeed, the references to Pisa can be viewed as a brief summary of Machiavelli's theories. Any reader who wonders about how he thought about the events associated with the abortive project on which he consulted with Leonardo would find the following:

When Louis XII came into Italy, the Pisans were among those who "came to meet him so as to be his friend" (*Prince*, ch. 3; p. 13). Pisa is thus an example of the rule that once a city is "used to living free . . . unless the inhabitants are broken up or dispersed, they will not forget that name [of liberty] and those [ancient] orders, and will immediately recur to them upon any unforeseen event as did Pisa [in 1494] after having been kept in servitude a hundred years by the Florentines" (ch. 5; pp. 20–21). "The Florentines took as their captain Paolo Vitelli, a most prudent man who from private fortune had secured very great reputation. If he had captured Pisa [before the Florentines condemned and killed him in 1499], no one would deny that the Florentines would have had to stay with him" (ch. 12; p. 51). "The Florentines, who were entirely unarmed, brought in ten thousand French to Pisa to capture it [in 1500]" (ch. 13; p. 54). Then Cesare Borgia, in establishing his power, "had taken Pisa under his protection. And as soon as he did not have to pay regard to France . . . he would have jumped on Pisa [in 1503]" (ch. 7; p. 31). Ultimately, therefore, Pisa illustrates the rule that "when a prince acquires a new state that is added as a member to his old one, then it is necessary to disarm that state . . . so that the arms of all your state are only with your own soldiers, who live next to you in your old state. Our ancients, and those who were esteemed wise, used to say that it was necessary to hold Pistoia with parties and Pisa with fortresses; and because of this they nourished differences in some towns subject to them, so as to hold them more easily. In times when Italy was in balance in a certain mode, this would have been good to do, but I do not believe that one could give it today as a teaching" (ch. 20; p. 84).

In short, Pisa illustrates the political and military elements of Machiavelli's teaching—as well as its novelty. This account emphasizes the priority of *political* considerations over *technological* ones: in chapter twenty of *The Prince* and elsewhere, "fortresses" seem to be Machiavelli's metaphor for all innovations in military technology. Whether or not this is an indirect reference to Leonardo's mission to Piombino in 1504, where the main purpose was the redesign of Jacopo Appiani's fortifications, is impossible to say. What does seem evident is that Machiavelli *learned* from his experience with Leonardo.

Actually, there appear to be *two* lessons that Machiavelli learned. The first is the primacy of political knowledge and statecraft. There are a number of examples of the importance of this lesson. After mentioning the plan to divert the Arno in *the First Decennale* (written in the fall of 1504), Machiavelli never speaks of it again, but in the *Florentine Histories* (IV, 23), he does discuss a similar plan by Brunelleschi which also failed. Brunelleschi's plan failed because it did not take into consideration countermeasures from the enemy. The general lesson of the primacy of politics would apply equally well to Machiavelli's own experience when working with Leonardo, since their plan failed due to poor implementation in the field as well as insufficient support and money from the Signoria. If you cannot control the humans involved, knowledge of technology is useless.[19]

The treatment of fortresses in Machiavelli's works would be another case in point. While Leonardo's innovations in the design of fortifications seems to have been adopted by Machiavelli in *The Art of War*,[20] the use of such technologies is subject to serious limitations. In chapter twenty of *The Prince*, Machiavelli argues that to know when to use a technical device or innovation, one needs to know the situation; in *Discourses*, II, 24, he more openly criticizes the reliance on fortresses by both republics and principalities.[21] These lessons from experience point to political science as a "master science" in the Aristotelian sense. Most innovations are really little more than "tricks" intended to confuse or deceive the enemy.[22] The outcome of working with Leonardo seems to have taught Machiavelli not only that scientists can easily defect to the other side (taking their knowledge to the highest bidder), but that technical knowledge is dangerous without understanding the primacy of politics.

This negative lesson might have led Machiavelli to remain silent on Leonardo and anything positive he had learned from him. Leonardo would symbolize the dangers of scientific or technical knowledge without political wisdom—and hence Machiavelli would not want to remind a reader that he himself had trusted Leonardo in the Arno project and had been committed to a technological solution that didn't work. (Such a reminder would have been particularly unwelcome insofar as Machiavelli sought employment from the Medici.)

The second lesson—the positive one—is associated with how much one can change things if it is possible to combine knowledge and power at the right moment. The potential of Leonardo's science might well have been another reason for Machiavelli's reticence to mention it. At one place in his *Notebooks*, Leonardo refers to an invention so dangerous he will not divulge it to anyone.²³ If Machiavelli knew of the scope of Leonardo's inventions, he would have every reason to prefer to keep this knowledge secret for, just as Rousseau—following the ancients—would later warn in the *Discourse on the Sciences and Arts*, Machiavelli worried of the moral corruption that could result from the public teaching of science.²⁴

This positive lesson is implicit in the echo of Leonardo in the reference to the painter's ability to depict both mountains and valleys in the dedication to *The Prince* (p. 4).²⁵ Leonardo's maps of the Arno River are unusual in the innovative "bird's eye view" which is neither on the top of the mountain looking into the valley, or in the valley looking to the top of the mountain. Leonardo's perspective is, rather, like a god on a heavenly throne, looking down on human events. Machiavelli implies, in his own dedication, that he too has such a point of view. One thing that separates ancient from modern thought is the stance—especially evident in the writings of Hobbes, Newton, Locke, and ultimately Hegel or Marx—of being "above" history and human events, looking at the world from a detached, quasi-divine perspective.²⁶ Hence unlike the negative lesson of Leonardo, which was well known to Plato and other ancients, Machiavelli's positive lesson may help explain his contribution to modernity.

Hypothesis #3

The third possibility concerns concrete circumstances. As noted above, when Machiavelli wrote Vettori on 10 December 1513 that he intended to dedicate (and send) *The Prince* to Giuliano de' Medici, Leonardo was living and working under Giuliano's patronage in Rome. Machiavelli could have known of this fact, for Leonardo had been in Florence before moving finally to Rome with Giuliano.

In this case, Machiavelli could not cite his collaboration with Leonardo for several practical reasons. First, if indeed Machiavelli had done Leonardo favors, such as gaining him commissions, supporting him when Soderini was frustrated with slow progress on *The Battle of Anghiari*, or helping Leonardo secure the inheritance from his uncle, Machiavelli may have hoped for a measure of reciprocity and assistance in persuading Giuliano to look favorably on his book. Obviously, Machiavelli could not cite Leonardo's failures without embarrassing Leonardo (if they were still on good terms in 1513), or undermining his own credibility (if they were not friends—and hence assuming that Leonardo might be angry to have his patron reminded of past failures).

The hypothesis of continued friendship after Leonardo left Florence in 1506 would be supported if it could be shown that Leonardo's letter to "Messer Nicolo" was addressed to Machiavelli in 1507. Even if this letter was written to someone else at a later time, relations between Machiavelli and Leonardo might have persisted. This would explain a major puzzle: the dedication of *The Prince*. In all the editions we know, the Dedicatory Letter is addressed to "Il Magnifico Lorenzo," despite the fact that Machiavelli himself stated in 1513, when writing Vettori, that the manuscript was being sent to Giuliano de' Medici. It is widely assumed that after Giuliano's death in 1516, Machiavelli changed to dedication to the younger Lorenzo. But why the change, since in the period from 1519 (the death of the younger Lorenzo) to Machiavelli's own death in 1527, the author found no need to change the manuscript?[27]

Could it be that, after 1515 when Lorenzo became ruler in Florence, Machiavelli made yet a second attempt to have his book read by the Medici through the intervention of Leonardo?[28] This would explain the change in addressee of the Dedicatory Letter—and Machiavelli's decision to leave the book unchanged after both Lorenzo and Leonardo had died in 1519. But even if Machiavelli's refusal to mention Leonardo in his *Prince* or other writings is explained by the awkwardness that the Medici were Leonardo's patrons, other factors doubtless entered between 1519 and Machiavelli's death in 1527. Hence this third explanation might reinforce either—or both—of the first two hypotheses.

Hypothesis #4

Machiavelli's silence about Leonardo could well have been a matter of theoretical principle. This hypothesis, while related to the first explanation, presupposes that Machiavelli and Leonardo became close friends—close enough for Leonardo to share with Machiavelli his plans for rebuilding Milan or for the peaceful development of the Arno, both of which were developed in the 1490s. As outlined in chapter seven, these projects reflect the vision of a society in which natural necessities are controlled through science and technology, using laws to channel the "love" of private property and profit into obedience to a ruler devoted to "freedom."

Like Prospero in *The Tempest*, Leonardo tried to use science to produce "miracles" that would resolve human pain and conflict; like Shakespeare, Machiavelli expresses the gravest doubts concerning Leonardo's dream of a planned society, akin to Sir Francis Bacon's *New Atlantis,* in which conflict is replaced by commerce and technological progress.[29] For Machiavelli, this project would be another "imagined principality," as dangerous as those known from the past. Since Leonardo's projects were not known—and had failed in practice—why even mention and therefore draw attention to ideas which are seen as pernicious?

Machiavelli makes his rejection of the goal of a total "conquest of nature" explicit in both *The Prince* and *Discourses*. Introducing the allegory of fortune in chapter twenty-five of *The Prince*, Machiavelli insists that humans can control only about "half" of fortune. In the *Discourses,* he puts it somewhat differently: "So in all human affairs, one notices if one examines them closely, that it is impossible to remove one inconvenience without another emerging" (I, 6; p. 121). Machiavelli had clearly stated this principle as early as September 1506 in a crucial letter to Giovan Battista Soderini, the Gonfalonier's nephew:

> And truly, *anyone wise enough to adapt to and understand the times and the pattern of events would always have good fortune,* or would always keep himself from bad fortune; and it would come to be true that the wise man could control the stars and the Fates. But such *wise men do not exist:* in the first place, men are shortsighted; in the second place, they are unable to *master their own natures;* thus it follows that Fortune is fickle, controlling men and keeping them under her yoke.[30]

At precisely the time Machiavelli, under my hypothesis, would have been most familiar with Leonardo's ambitious projects, Machiavelli not only denies the possibility of a definitive conquest of fortune or nature, but emphasizes that the crucial obstacle is the inability of leaders "to master *their own natures.*"

The ultimate limits on humans arise from politics, not from the limits of scientific understanding. Leonardo's most ambitious and visionary projects were not generally known, his advice on the diversion of the Arno had not been successful, and even his innovative technical methods in *The Battle of Anghiari* had failed to work. Under these circumstances, Machiavelli could well have felt it imprudent to mention and therefore draw attention to ideas which Machiavelli himself felt potentially dangerous.

Hypothesis #5

The expectations of today's scholars rest on an anachronistic view of writing. For Machiavelli and Leonardo, printing was as new an invention as computers have been to my own generation. For them, most writing was of a private nature: letters, governmental memoranda not intended to see the light of day, notebooks; printing was a public version of such documents, avoiding the costs of copying a text by hand, but not yet a well-established means of communicating to broad audiences.

We know that in private correspondence, Machiavelli and his contemporaries often wrote with obscurity and indirectness. Letters could easily fall into the wrong hands, not only when reporting from the court of Cesare Borgia, but even in routine work in governmental offices. Because one's addressee could usually decode an ambiguous reference, it would sometimes be safer to speak of an unnamed "friend," for example, than to name the individual involved. Machiavelli applied similar constraints to his theoretical works. Hence we find many events in Machiavelli's own career are described in such an indirect and allusive manner that few readers of *The Prince, Discourses,* or *Art of War* even realize the nature of the reference. These practices, clearly demonstrated in Najemy's study of the correspondence between Machiavelli and Vettori,[31] are amply confirmed in the documents of Buonaccorsi, Leonardo, and other contemporaries cited throughout the current volume.

Whatever the conclusion, the facts seem to turn the original question on its head. What needs to be explained is not whether Machiavelli knew his famous contemporary, since it now seems impossible to deny that he was personally acquainted with Leonardo even if they were not close friends as some have claimed. Rather, we need to understand why Machiavelli remained silent about one of the most striking people encountered in his political experience. Ultimately, such an explanation depends less on the facts than on an understanding of the theoretical intention underlying Machiavelli's writings.

Notes

Introduction

1. Letter, Leo Strauss to Alexandre Kojevnikoff (Kojève), 22 August 1948, in Leo Strauss, *On Tyranny, Including the Strauss-Kojève Correspondence*, ed. Victor Gourevitch and Michael S. Roth (New York: Free Press, 1991), 237.

2. The answer to this question depends to some degree on Machiavelli's motives for remaining silent with regard to Leonardo. As I show, this reticence extends to Machiavelli's refusal to mention *his own role* in the projects on which he consulted Leonardo. For the detailed hypotheses explaining their relationship, see Appendix III.

3. This question is especially important because Machiavelli seems to use each animal in a very different way than Leonardo, who compiled a "Bestiary" of traits observed in various animal species: see Leonardo da Vinci, *Notebooks*, ed. Jean Paul Richter (New York: Dover, 1970), 2.315–334, and below, chapter 7.

4. For a fuller justification of this claim, see Roger D. Masters, *The Nature of Politics* (New Haven, Conn.: Yale University Press, 1989).

5. Adam Kuper, *The Chosen Primate* (Cambridge: Harvard University Press, 1994); Leon Kass, *The Hungry Soul* (New York: Free Press, 1994).

6. The question of selfishness and its relationship to power is more complex than is usually thought. On Machiavelli, see Russell Price, "Self-love, 'Egoism' and *Ambizione* in Machiavelli's Thought," *History of Political Thought* 9 (1988): 237–261. For the relationship between the traditional and contemporary scientific concepts, see Roger D. Masters, "Is Sociobiology Reactionary? The Political Implications of Inclusive Fitness Theory," *Quarterly Review of Biology* 57 (1982): 275–292.

7. For the deepest expression of this view, see Leo Strauss, *Thoughts on Machiavelli* (Glencoe, Ill.: Free Press, 1958).

Chapter 1

1. "Decision concerning Leonardo da Vinci," 4 May 1504, in Denis Fachard, *Biagio Buonaccorsi: sa vie—son temps—son oeuvre* (Bologna: Massimiliano Boni, 1976), 259–260. This document, which concerns the Signoria's actions to ensure that Leonardo finish painting *The Battle of Anghiari* on the walls of the Grand Council Hall, was witnessed by Machiavelli and provides evidence that the careers of Machiavelli and Leonardo intersected, though it leaves the nature of their interaction open (ibid., 129–130). For a translation of the full text, see Appendix I.3.

2. Letter from Machiavelli to Giuliano Lapi, 20 September 1504 (Fachard, *Biagio Buonaccorsi*, 143). For the text, see Appendix I.3 D. One of ninety-five letters that Machiavelli wrote between August and October 1504 concerning the projected diversion of the Arno, this text proves that Machiavelli was directly concerned with the engineering aspects of this attempt to defeat Pisa through technology rather than force. For the new design of the project by Berardi, which Machiavelli criticizes, see Figure 1.11. While it cannot be proven definitively that the "first diagram"—which Machiavelli prefers—was drawn by Leonardo (Figure 1.6), this letter as well as another cited in Fachard (p. 142) demonstrate that the comparison of fortune to a river (*Prince*, ch. 25) reflects Machiavelli's political experience as an official in the Florentine Republic. On the importance of the discovery that the so-called "allegory" of dikes and banks can also be read as synecdoche, using an actual engineering project to stand for all human efforts to control nature through technology and science, see chapter three below.

3. For the distinction between "modern" and "ancient or medieval" epochs in the West, see Roger D. Masters, *Beyond Relativism* (Hanover, N.H.: University Press of New England, 1993). It is worth noting, at the outset, that the words "*antichi e modernj*" were used in a similar way by both Leonardo and Machiavelli (Carlo Pedretti, *Literary Works of Leonardo da Vinci* [Berkeley: University of California, 1977], 1.350). Like Machiavelli in politics, moreover, in his *Treatise on Painting* Leonardo recommends the imitation of ancient examples rather than modern ones (*Notebooks*, ed. J. P. Richter [New York: Dover, 1970], 1.244).

4. See the collection of essays in *Leonardo da Vinci: Aspects of the Renaissance Genius*, ed. Morris Philipson (New York: George Braziller, 1966). On science, perhaps the most valuable single study is Ernst Cassirer, *The Individual and the Cosmos in Renaissance Philosophy*, trans. Mario Domandi (New York: Barnes and Noble, 1963). See also Pierre Duhem, "De l'accélération produit par une force constante," *Congrès Internationale de Philosophie*, 2nd session (Geneva, 1904), 3.514ff. and *Etudes sur Léonard de Vinci*, vol. 3 (Paris: Herman, 1913); Paul Valéry, *Introduction to the Method of Leonardo da Vinci*,

trans. Thomas McGreevy (London: John Rodker, 1929); Boris Kouznetsov, "The Rationalism of Leonardo da Vinci and the Dawn of Classical Science," *Diogenes* 69 (1970): 1–11; John Herman Randall, Jr., "The Place of Leonardo da Vinci in the Emergence of Modern Science," *Journal of the History of Ideas* 14 (1953): 191–202; Jacob Klein, *Lectures and Essays* (Annapolis: St. John's University Press, 1985); Alexandre Koyré, *Galileo Studies*, trans. John Mepham (Atlantic Highlands, N.J.: Humanities Press, 1978), esp. Part 2.

5. On the premodern elements in Machiavelli, see J. G. A. Pocock, *The Machiavellian Moment: Florentine Political Thought and the Atlantic Republican Tradition* (Princeton, N.J.: Princeton University Press, 1975); Jack H. Hexter, *On Historians* (Cambridge, Mass.: Harvard University Press, 1979); Anthony J. Parel, *The Machiavellian Cosmos* (New Haven, Conn.: Yale University Press, 1992); Jacob Burkhardt, *The Civilization of the Renaissance in Italy*, vol. 1 (New York: Harper Torchbooks, 1958); Sebastian de Grazia, *Machiavelli in Hell* (Princeton, N.J.: Princeton University Press, 1989); Sammy Basu, "In a Crazy Time the Crazy Come Out Well: Machiavelli and the Cosmology of His Day," *History of Political Thought* 11 (1990): 213–239. On Machiavelli's own claim to radical novelty, see *Discourses*, I, Preface, ed. Bernard Crick (Harmondsworth: Penguin, 1970), 97; *The Prince*, ch. 14, ed. Harvey C. Mansfield, Jr. (Chicago: University of Chicago Press, 1985), 61; *Florentine Histories*, trans. Laura F. Banfield and Harvey C. Mansfield, Jr. (Princeton, N.J.: Princeton University Press, 1988), 8; *Mandragola*, trans. Mera J. Flamenhaft (Prospect Heights, Ill.: Waveland, 1981), 9, all of which are analyzed in detail in chapter two below. Cf. Machiavelli's assertion that he is "departing from the usual practice of authors" (*Discourses*, Dedicatory Letter, ed. Crick, 94–95). Citations in the text will be to these editions. Throughout this book, I take the liberty of adding italics in order to capture Machiavelli's intonation and emphasis.

6. My analysis is based on a preliminary study of Leonardo's *Notebooks* and a sampling of the immense secondary literature on Leonardo; the account that follows can hardly claim to be definitive. In the edition of Leonardo's *Notebooks* edited by Irma Richter (New York: Penguin, 1980), for example, Machiavelli is referred to in editorial notes (pp. 348, 350), but nowhere do these notes refer to specific texts. As I will show below, however, there does exist the draft of a letter to "Messer Niccolò" that some scholars believe was intended for Machiavelli.

7. This absence is particularly notable in Machiavelli's dispatches to the Signoria of 1502/3—the so-called *Legazioni al Duca Valentino* (for the most extensive English excerpts, see Machiavelli, *Chief Works,* trans. Allan Gilbert [Durham, N.C.: Duke University Press, 1965], 1.121–60; for the complete text, Machiavelli, *Legazioni, Commissarie. Scritti di Governo,* ed. Fredi Chiappelli [Rome: Gius. Laterza & Figli, 1973], 2.192–401; for selections, *Opere,* ed. Mario

Bonfantini [Milan: Riccardo Ricciardi, 1958], 438–446; Machiavelli, *The Prince*, ed. Robert M. Adams [New York: W. W. Norton, 1977], 83–92). Machiavelli also describes these events without mentioning Leonardo in the *Descrizione del Modo tenuto dal Duca Valentino nello ammazzare Vitellozzo Vitelli, Oliverotto da Fermo, il Signor Pagolo et il Duca di Gravina Orsini* (*Opere*, 457–464; translation in *The Prince*, ed. W. K. Marriott [Everyman's Library; London: Dent, 1938], 219–239 or *Chief Works*, 1.163–169) as well as in the famous chapter seven of *The Prince* (ed. Mansfield, 25–33). I will return to the puzzle of Machiavelli's silence concerning Leonardo, which may be clarified by the diplomatic reports from Cesare's court in which Machiavelli refers to one of Cesare's "chief secretaries" and an unnamed "friend," either of whom could have been Leonardo.

    8. Vasilii Zubov, *Leonardo da Vinci* (Cambridge, Mass.: Harvard University Press, 1968), 90, 166–167, 229, 225–226; Cesare Laporini, *Le Mente di Leonardo* (Firenzi: G. C. Sansone, 1953), 5, 30, 55, 137, 160, 174. One scholar has even noted similarities in their writing: Girolamo Calvi, *I Manuscritti di Leonardo de Vinci* (Bologna: Nicola Zanichelli, 1928), 3–4, 7.

    9. On the relationship between Machiavelli and Leonardo, see E. Solmi, "Leonardo e Machiavelli," *Archivio storico lombardo* 17 (1912): 231, and the critique by Fachard, *Biagio Buonaccorsi*, 129–130: "il n'est pas à exclure que Leonardo et Machiavelli aient eu quelques contacts occasionels . . . mais . . . le manque de preuves . . . nous font fortement douter d'une étroit collaboration entre les deux hommes." Cf. Carlo Pedretti, *Studi vinciani* (Geneve: E. Droz, 1957), 17: "Nessun documento può con sicurezza i rapporti di amicizia fra Machiavelli e Leonardo, ma le circostanze sono favorevoli per avvalornarne l'ipotesi." In later works, it should be noted, Pedretti provides considerable evidence of a close friendship: see Pedretti's *Leonardo da Vinci: The Royal Palace at Romorantin* (Cambridge, Mass.: Harvard University Press, 1972), 32–33, 39, 297–301; *Leonardo: A Study in Chronology and Style* (London: Thames and Hudson, 1973; reprint, N.Y.: Johnson Reprint, 1982), esp. ch. 1; *Leonardo: Architect* (New York: Rizzoli, 1981), esp. 15, 55, 174, 179, 188, 205. On the milieu, see Felix Gilbert, "Florentine Political Assumptions in the Age of Savonarola and Soderini," *Journal of the Warberg Cultural Institute* 20 (1957), and *Machiavelli and Guiccardini: Politics and History in Sixteenth-Century Florence* (Princeton, N.J.: Princeton University Press, 1965); John H. Najemy, *Between Friends: Discourses of Power and Desire in the Machiavelli-Vettori Letters of 1513–1515* (Princeton, N.J.: Princeton University Press, 1993).

    10. Giorgio de Santillana, "Man without Letters," in Philipson, *Leonardo da Vinci: Aspects of the Renaissance Genius*, 190; Kenneth Clark, *Leonardo da Vinci: An Account of His Development as an Artist* (New York: Macmillan, 1939), 133–134. For the final judgment of Carlo Pedretti, see *Literary Works*, 2.51: "In 1502 Leonardo was in the service of Cesare Borgia with the title of 'Architecto e Ingegnero Generale', and with the task of supervising the forti-

fications in Romagna. He must have had frequent occasions to talk with Machiavelli, especially in the autumn of 1502 in Imola." At this point, Pedretti also notes the parallel between Leonardo's innovative conception for fortifications that could withstand the new artillery and the designs proposed by Machiavelli in *The Art of War* (ibid., esp. note 1).

11. For a thoughtful comparison of the two that does not rest on evidence of personal acquaintance, see Giovanni Gentile, "The Thought of Leonardo," in *Leonardo da Vinci*, ed. Istituto Geografico d'Agostino (New York: Reynal, 1956), 163.

12. Written documents from the early sixteenth century often fail to provide evidence of people or events we know occurred. Leonardo da Vinci's notebooks apparently nowhere mention his teacher Verrocchio, though Leonardo spent his formative years working in Verrocchio's *bottega* and was greatly influenced by him. See Serge Bramly, *Leonardo: Discovering the Life of Leonardo da Vinci*, trans. Siân Reynolds (New York: Edward Berlingame Books, 1991), 69. Conversely, Biagio Buonaccorsi, Machiavelli's friend and assistant in the Signoria, "n'est jamais cité dans l'oeuvre littéraire de Machiavelli" (Fachard, *Biagio Buonaccorsi*, 13, 157). Moreover, Machiavelli fails to mention *his own* role in events which, in at least two cases of his probable relationship with Leonardo, are cited in Machiavelli's published works. Critics need to take into account Machiavelli's extraordinary caution in naming individuals and events in which he himself was involved. In the famous correspondence between Machiavelli and Vettori, for example, compare Machiavelli's oblique description of the fall of Soderini in 1512 with Vettori's explicit mention of his own role in saving Soderini's life (Najemy, *Between Friends*, 89–90). For specific reasons that could explain Machiavelli's silence about Leonardo, see below, especially Appendix III.

13. Although de Grazia notes correctly that "from the beginning to the end of his career, the Florentine Secretary is immersed in military affairs" (*Machiavelli in Hell*, 93), and cites Machiavelli's statement that the art of war is "the sole art that one expects of he who commands" (272), de Grazia's own analysis of *The Art of War* is limited to a few scattered remarks (e.g., 65, 82, 93, 97, 210, 284, 367).

14. The best biography is Bramly's *Leonardo*. I have relied for additional perspectives on a number of more specialized works cited in the following notes; in a number of places, I have followed Pedretti's *Leonardo: A Study in Chronology and Style* in clarifying or correcting otherwise problematic dates. It is also useful to consult the fictionalized but carefully researched biography by Dmitri Merejkowski, *The Romance of Leonardo da Vinci*, trans. Bernard Guilbert Guerney (New York: Random House, 1928). The most famous contemporary account is Vasari's brief summary, though it is focused on Leonardo as an artist and specialists often question its accuracy: see Giorgio Vasari, *Lives of*

Seventy of the Most Eminent Painters, Sculptors and Architects, ed. E. H. and E. W. Blashfield and A. A. Hopkins (New York: Charles Scribner's, 1917), 2.367–407.

15. Bramly, *Leonardo*, 117. Like some other commentators, Bramly takes this event—along with Leonardo's relations with Salai and Melzi—as evidence of Leonardo's homosexuality. Granted that there is no evidence that Leonardo ever formed a heterosexual relationship, however, this conventional interpretation need not follow: Leonardo might have been impotent rather than homosexual—a hypothesis which could explain his adoption of Salai as well as his anatomical interest and drawings of male genitalia (ibid., 117–119). Some might assume that Leonardo's extreme discretion with regard to sexuality was imposed by the social norms, since male homosexuality was legally punishable with death (though in practice tolerated) in Florence. Even when a man like Machiavelli's friend Donato del Corne was known as a homosexual, however, references tended to be indirect and symbolic (Najemy, *Between Friends*, 111–112n). In this as in many cases, therefore, one cannot prove which of two reasonable hypotheses describes private events in Leonardo's life; much the same is true of Machiavelli.

16. Although Vasari dates this painting from Leonardo's return to Florence in 1503, most contemporary scholars question this date on the grounds that Ginevra would have been too old for the beautiful image (Nello Tarchiani, "Leonardo in Florence and Tuscany," in Istituto Geografico d'Agostino, *Leonardo da Vinci*, 100). As a result, some date the painting as a wedding portrait from 1474, although Bramly suggests, for plausible reasons, that the work was done—or at least begun—in 1479 (*Leonardo*, 148–151). Pedretti suggests "mid-1470s" but does not discuss the dating in detail (*Leonardo: Chronology and Style*, 54). Since Leonardo often kept paintings for years, working on details from time to time, it is entirely possible that Vasari correctly remembered that Leonardo was still working on the portrait when he returned to Florence in 1503. It is perhaps worth mentioning this question not only to illustrate the extreme complexity of the historical details, but because this remarkable work in the National Gallery of Art in Washington is the only painting by Leonardo that can be seen in the United States.

17. Bramly, *Leonardo*, 171–183; Pedretti, *Leonardo: Chronology and Style*, 54; Maria Costantino, *Leonardo: Artist, Inventor, Scientist* (New York: Crescent Books, 1993), 14. The reasons for Leonardo's departure from Florence have never been fully elucidated. Although Leonardo was recommended to Sforza by Lorenzo de' Medici and brought him a musical instrument as a gift from Lorenzo, it is not entirely clear whether he originally went as an emissary of some sort or primarily on his own initiative. In the notebook listing his possessions at the time, in addition to many works of art, Leonardo indicates "some machines for ships" and "some machines for waterworks" (ibid., 15),

whereas in a remarkable letter to Sforza in which Leonardo offers to "reveal my secrets," the list of inventions and skills emphasizes military technology (Bramly, *Leonardo*, 174–176). It may be, however, that the most important skill Leonardo promised Sforza was the ability to cast the enormous (but never completed) equestrian statue of Ludovico's father Francesco Sforza which came to be known as *Il Cavallo.*

18. Other paintings from the period 1482–1485 include *Madonna of the Rocks, Portrait of a Musician, Lady with an Ermine,* and *La Belle Ferronière* (probably Sforza's mistress Lucrezia Crivelli). See Costantino, *Leonardo,* 18–19; Bramly, *Leonardo,* ch. 6.

19. On this period, see Maria Vittoria Brugnoli, "Il Cavallo," in *The Unknown Leonardo,* ed. Ladislao Reti (New York: McGraw Hill, 1974), 86–95; Pedretti, *Leonardo: Chronology and Style,* 55–77; Pedretti, *Leonardo: Architect,* 32–115. On the theoretical significance of the aerial perspective, which can be related to the passage about "those who sketch landscapes" in the dedication to *The Prince* (ed. Mansfield, 4), see below, chapter six.

20. When confronted with an alliance of Venice and France, Sforza had invited King Louis XII to send an army to Italy (an invitation Machiavelli condemns in *The Prince*). After the French occupied Milan in 1500, Leonardo met Cesare, who was serving as Louis XII's military aide, as well as the king himself (Costantino, *Leonardo,* 24); interestingly enough, both would become in time Leonardo's patrons. Machiavelli refers directly to this event near the outset of *The Prince* (ch. 2; pp. 8–9) when discussing how it was difficult for Louis XII to hold Milan the first time he entered it (in 1499, when Leonardo, in fear, fled the city) but succeeded easily in so doing the second time (in 1500, when Ludovico Sforza was defeated and captured at Novara).

21. On Machiavelli's early life and political career, see de Grazia, *Machiavelli in Hell,* chs. 1–2; Najemy, *Between Friends,* ch. 2; Charles Tarlton, *Fortune's Circle: A Biographical Interpretation of Machiavelli* (Chicago: Quadrangle Books, 1970); Fachard, *Biagio Buonaccorsi,* esp. chs. 3–4, 7; Gilbert, *Machiavelli and Guicciardini;* Nino Borsellino, *Machiavelli* (Roma: Editori Laterza, 1973); Francesco Nitti, *Machiavelli Nella Vita e Nelle Dottrine* (Napoli: Società Editrice il Mulino, 1991). Machiavelli's posts were of what today would be called cabinet rank, and he was often charged with diplomatic missions and military responsibilities of the highest importance.

22. *The Prince,* ch. 3; p. 16. Since Machiavelli always refers to Georges d'Amboise as "Rouen" or "the cardinal of Rouen" (cf. *Prince,* ch. 7; p. 33), his usage obscures the fact that he was the king's minister—and that, after 1500, his nephew Charles d'Amboise was the French governor in Milan responsible for defending the French position in Italy. Between 1506 and 1508, when Leonardo went to Milan, one of his main activities was designing a new castle for Charles d'Amboise (see Pedretti, *Leonardo: Royal Palace at*

Romorantin, 41–52; Pedretti, *Leonardo: Architect*, 210–217; Costantino, *Leonardo*, 29–30).

23. Bramly, *Leonardo*, 324–25. This text announcing Cesare's appointment of Leonardo served as a passport to his military commanders, and thus confirms that Leonardo's position was concerned with fortifications and military technology.

24. Ludwig H. Heydenreich, "The Military Architect," in Reti, *Unknown Leonardo*, 138. In 1500, when Cesare first offered him a position, Leonardo preferred to travel to Mantua (where he visited the court of Isabella d'Este, sister of Sforza's wife Beatrice) and then to Venice (where he consulted with the government on methods of defending the city against the Turks). From Machiavelli's dispatches of 1501, it is clear that Borgia was already feared by the Florentine government by this time (Fachard, *Biagio Buonaccorsi*, 131–132).

25. See *Machiavelli's Correspondence*, trans. and ed. James Atkinson and David Sices (DeKalb, Ill.: Northern Illinois University Press, in press), letters #29–68. Because the private correspondence of Machiavelli brings these events to life in an extraordinary way, I was fortunate to be able to consult the manuscript of this forthcoming edition, which translates the extant letters to and from Machiavelli into English for the first time; future scholars will find the edition invaluable. For example, shortly after Piero's election, Francesco Soderini wrote "my dearest Niccolò" thanking him for his "affection for the fatherland and for my family" and indicating that Machiavelli's support for the new Gonfalonier was especially welcome because he is "second to none in ability (*virtute*) and affection" (#31, Francesco Soderini to Machiavelli, 29 September 1502). Shortly thereafter Niccolò Valori wrote of Machiavelli's dispatch of 8 October that it "could not have been more appreciated, and people recognize what I in particular have always recognized in you: a clear, exact, and sincere account upon which one can rely completely. . . . Your judgment is desired here about the affairs over there, and your description of the French ones, and the hopes the Duke has about them" (#32, 11 October 1502). Similarly, Piero Guicciardini wrote that "you are giving satisfaction to everyone" (#36, 20 October 1502). The mission was complex, for Machiavelli needed to keep Cesare from adopting a hostile policy toward Florence without making the more substantial commitments Borgia wanted; Piero Soderini found the finances of Florence in a deplorable state and there was difficulty even securing funds for the ambassador's living expenses; Machiavelli himself repeatedly indicated his desire to return to Florence, since he originally thought he would be in Cesare's court for a short time and his wife chafed at his absence. For these reasons, the Gonfalonier himself wrote Machiavelli frequently, often thanking him for his work and confirming that, when possible, he would be relieved; e.g., #40, 22 October 1502; #54, 14 November 1502; #59, 28 November 1502; #60, 4 December 1502; #64, 21 December 1502.

26. Bramly, *Leonardo*, 326–329; *Notebooks*, ed. I. Richter, 342–350. For Kenneth Clark, however, it is likely that they met earlier in the summer (*Leonardo da Vinci*, 133). "Leonardo took the surprising step [in 1502] of entering the service of Cesare Borgia as 'architect and general engineer'. . . . Cautious Florence had 'bought,' so to speak, the good will of the dangerous and powerful neighbor through a treaty that made Cesare a condottiere of the republic, with an annual income of 30,000 gold ducats. No less a person than Machiavelli was delegated repeatedly and over long periods as chargé d'affaires at his [Cesare's] court, and he had no other assignment than that of political observer. His task was to report on the favorableness or the unfavorableness of the general situation" (Heydenreich, "Military Architect," 138).

27. Bramly, *Leonardo*, 326. According to one story, this meeting took place in Nuvarola on the night of 2 November 1503: "After Leonardo had joined Cesare [in 1502], he went everywhere with him in the duchies. . . . By chance he met Macchiavelli [*sic*] in an inn at Nuvarola and offered to share his room with him when the innkeeper insisted on Macchiavelli's surrendering his to a famous courtesan. Leonardo did a sketch of the bony, aquiline, thin-lipped ambassador of the Florentine treasury, as Macchiavelli was at that time. They travelled on to Fano together, where Leonardo was to meet up with the Duke, and when they arrived, he invited Macchiavelli to join him in his splendid apartment close to Cesare's palace" (Maurice Rowdon, *Leonardo da Vinci* [London: Widenfeld and Nicolson, 1975], 164). A fictionalized version of the scene, which may be the source of Rowdon's statement, is presented in Merejkowski, *Romance of Leonardo*, 392–400. It is highly unlikely, however, that this story is true. Machiavelli wrote official dispatches dated from Imola on both 1 November and 3 November (see Appendix I.1 A–C). It is over sixty-five miles from Imola to Nuvarola, a town only four miles from Fano on the coast, and Machiavelli reports that it took a group of soldiers four to six days to travel from Imola to Fano (letter of 13 November 1502; *Legazioni*, 2.288). There is no evidence that Machiavelli traveled extensively but continued dating dispatches from Imola; on the contrary, he responds rapidly to the flow of messages sent from Florence to Imola, which would have been impossible had he been traveling himself. From the dates on Machiavelli's dispatches, it is probable that this meeting took place in Imola (see below).

28. Machiavelli's well-known description of his personal conversation with Cesare after the death of his father, Pope Alexander VI (*Prince* ch. 7; p. 32), needs to be compared to Machiavelli's handwritten dispatch to the Signoria from Rome on 1 November 1503, the day Julius II was elected pope (for the text and a reproduction, see de Grazia, *Machiavelli in Hell*, 119–120) and his letters of 4, 6, and 7 November 1503 (*Chief Works*, 1.143–146). Moreover, Machiavelli had written the Signoria a year earlier that an anonymous "friend" told him that Cesare "knows very well that the Pope can die any day and that

he needs to think before his death of laying for himself some other foundation" (Letter of 8 November 1502; *Chief Works*, 1.130; *Opere*, ed. Bonfantini, 450).

29. The complete text of messages to and from Machiavelli is available in *Legazioni*, ed. Chiappelli, 2.192–401. (For other editions, see note 7 above). Despite the importance often given to the analysis of Cesare Borgia in chapter seven of *The Prince*, few scholars have consulted these texts, which give us Machiavelli's observations and opinions of Borgia as events unfolded. The picture that emerges, as we will see, is totally at variance with the view of Borgia uncritically accepted by most readers of *The Prince*.

30. For the relevance of Erasmus's view that, in "letter-writing . . . one may . . . make use of obscure allusions, ambiguities, hidden connotations, proverbs, enigmas, and abrupt endings," see Najemy, *Between Friends*, 55. That code was used in Machiavelli's correspondence from Cesare's court is proved by the extant replies of his assistants in Florence. In addition to the reference to letters as "onions"—letters from Biagio Buonaccorsi of 26 November and 21 December 1502 (*Machiavelli's Correspondence*, #58 and 65), see the frequent reference to "cloth" as well as "velvet," "black satin," "damask," and items of clothing ("a cloak," "the mantle," "the velvet hat," "the hat . . . of several colors," "doublet") (letters of Agostino Vespucci, 13 October 1502 [#33]; of Biagio Buonaccorsi, 15–18 and 21 October [#35, 37], 1, 3, 5, 12, and 15 November [#47, 48, 49, 52, 55] 22 December [#66]; and of Alamanni Salvalti, 23 December [#67]). When writing other documents for circulation, moreover, it was not unusual to omit names to avoid controversy: for example, in the private account of the failed diversion of the Arno, Machiavelli's collaborator Buonaccorsi named the architect in charge (Colombino), whereas in the *Diario* which circulated in manuscript—and was posthumously published, Buonaccorsi deleted this reference and speaks only of anonymous *Maestri d'Acqui* (see Appendix I.5 A–B).

31. Dispatch of 7 October 1502 (*Opere*, ed. Bonfantini, 443), translated in Adams's edition of *The Prince*, 87. This letter is also interesting for its lengthy account of Machiavelli's first interview with Cesare Borgia.

32. *Legazioni* 2.266–69. Machiavelli's use of the word "secretari" may have misled some readers into thinking the contact was with a subordinate official; as Machiavelli's own title of "Secretary" to the Committee of Ten indicated, the word meant then much what it means today in the title of Secretary of State or Secretary of Defense in the United States. On the story that a meeting between Leonardo and Machiavelli took place at Nuvarola, see above, note 27.

33. "Mi occorre, oltre a quello che per l'alligata si scrive, fare intendere a vostre Signorie un ragionamento avuto con quell'amico, il quale nei dì passati" (ibid., 274). Najemy, in analyzing the letter of 8 November, suggests that Machiavelli imagined the "friend" as a device to go beyond instructions, communicating his own judgments and recommendations instead of simply

reporting the facts: "it is difficult to avoid the impression that Machiavelli's 'friend' was a rhetorical device . . . that allowed him to speak his mind" (Najemy, *Between Friends,* 62). This is also Gilbert's conclusion (*Chief Works,* 1.132, citing Machiavelli's later advice to Raffaelo Girolami (*Chief Works,* 1.118). This interpretation is, however, contradicted by repeated letters from Florentine officials, asking Machiavelli for his "judgment" as well as his "descriptions" of fact and praising him for the excellence of his reports. Just two weeks before the letter in question, Valori had written: "Truly, your reports and discussions could not be better, or more appreciated" (*Machiavelli's Correspondence,* #42; Valori to Niccolò Machiavelli, 23 October 1502), a judgment that Valori repeats in two additional letters the following week (ibid., #45, 28 October 1502; #46, 31 October 1502). Just the day before Machiavelli's dispatch of 8 November referring to the unnamed "friend," Marcello Berti had written urging him to remain in Cesare's court: "The Gonfalonier told me this morning that it does not seem right in any way to him that you should depart . . . since he would have to send someone else there, he does not know who could be more suitable, in respect to many things." The letter from Buonaccorsi which is the basis of Najemy's view that the unnamed "friend" is imagined, should probably be interpreted in the light of requests that Machiavelli write more often and of policy differences within the Signoria (ibid., #44, Biagio Buonaccorsi to Machiavelli, 28 October 1502). See also the passages cited above in note 25. Najemy admits that on "other occasions," including Machiavelli's letter to the Signoria on 26 November, "he took the risk openly" and cites the report of 26 December in which Machiavelli refers anonymously to Borgia's "chief secretaries" (Najemy, *Between Friends,* 62, 66).

34. *Legazioni,* ed. Chiappelli, 2.365; *Chief Works,* 1.142.

35. To support the hypothesis of a meeting between Machiavelli and Leonardo, it is, of course, not necessary that the latter be cited anonymously in official dispatches to the Signoria: many of the common interests of the two concerned interests of human nature and military strategy rather than the practical issues of Cesare's intentions and the strength of his military forces. For example, during his service with Cesare, Leonardo was charged with reviewing the effectiveness of Borgia's fortifications and other questions of military technology which were ultimately important to Machiavelli but not discussed in his *Legazioni.* See chapter seven below.

36. Heydenreich, "Military Architect," 140. Leonardo's map of Imola (Figure 1.5) is in such extraordinary detail that it must have required the artist's presence in that town for a number of days during the time Machiavelli was also there. As the map shows, moreover, Imola was not a large city like Rome, in which these two well-known and inquisitive men from Florence might easily have avoided meeting each other. On Leonardo's work in Imola, see Pedretti, *Leonardo: Architect,* 154–169. Leonardo's plan for a breakwater at

the port of Piombino is recorded in sketches for his notebooks that confirm
his fascination with and expertise in engineering projects relating to water. See
Costantino, *Leonardo*, 27.

37. Machiavelli's dispatches indicate he was in Imola from 7 October 1502
until 11 December; in Cesena from 14 to 26 December, Sinigaglia on 31 December,
and then traveling as follows: Corinaldi, 1 January 1503; Saxo Ferrato,
4 January; Gualdo, 6 January; Asciesi [Assisi], 8 January; Torsiano (four miles
from Perugia), 10 January; Castello della Pieve, 12 January; Castiglioni Aretino,
21 January (*Legationi*, 2.192–401). Leonardo was probably also in Cesena the
day Remirro de l'Orca was cut in two and left in the public square; this scene,
explicitly praised in *The Prince* (ch. 7; pp. 29–30), was apparently seen by
Machiavelli, who reported it to the Signoria as an eye witness in his dispatch of
26 December 1502. Moreover, both may have been at Sinigaglia the day Borgia
assassinated his *condottieri* (ibid.). On these parallels, compare Machiavelli's
dispatches to the Signoria of 26 December 1502, 31 December 1502, and 1 January
1503 (reproduced in the Adams edition of *The Prince*, 88–92) with Bramly,
Leonardo, 328–329. Leonardo's sudden return to Florence in the spring of 1503
could have been the result of fear that he might suffer the fate of Vitellozzo,
Oliverotto, and the other *condottieri*—or of a realization that Cesare suspected
his famous military architect for other reasons.

38. *Machiavelli's Correspondence*, #75 (Luca Ugolini to Machiavelli, 11 November
1503). The key phrase—*Lionardo da Vinci non l'arebbe retracto
meglio*—is mistranslated by de Grazia, *Machiavelli in Hell*, 124.

39. One scholar has argued that "the language used . . . indicates no intimacy
of M's with the painter, but simply that L was known by reputation as a
great master. He is not called 'Lionardo nostro,' or 'vostro,' or even 'maestro
Lionardo,' and the inclusion of the phrase 'da Vinci' renders the comment
quite impersonal" (William Connell, personal communication). Although this
is a reasonable argument for the absence of a personal relationship between
Machiavelli and Leonardo *before* 1502, it is conceivable that the presence of
Leonardo in Borgia's court was known to (and perhaps even authorized by)
the Florentine government. In the latter hypothesis, the formal reference in
the letter to Machiavelli could have been necessary to avoid casting suspicions.
On the possibility that Leonardo was a secret informant, consider also the frequent
remarks about cloth and items of clothing in letters from Machiavelli's
assistants in Florence (see above, note 30); could these obscure passages be
coded references to Leonardo? In this as in other circumstances, it seems impossible
to prove definitively how close the relationship between Leonardo
and Machiavelli actually was.

40. For the details of this project, see Pedretti, *Leonardo: Architect*, 170–94.
On the theoretical implications of the aerial perspective, see below chapter
seven. Although Machiavelli refers to the Florentine fortifications around Pisa

(*Discourses* 2.24), he says they were "useless" and does not name La Verruca (*Chief Works*, 1.396). In contrast, Machiavelli does name La Verruca in *Mandragola* (Act I, scene 2), though without indicating its historical significance (ibid., 2.782). For Machiavelli's dispatches concerning the capture and refortification of La Verruca, see *Legazione*, 2.522, 524, 530, 531, 533, 535, 538–539, 540, 545, 547, 548, 556. Machiavelli does not name the technical expert who is working on the detailed plans—see the letters of 1 July (p. 547) and 5 July (p. 548)—but Leonardo is the only architect known to have produced designs for the fortifications.

41. Bramly, *Leonardo*, 329–333. "Leonardo's exact position in this scheme is very difficult to determine. The facts that he was appointed adviser by the government and that he accepted the task lead us to conclude that he must have been entrusted with the plan. But his own judgment is unknown, and from the new material that has come to light in the Madrid notebooks we must deduce that he was not, as some have believed, the originator of the idea, but rather that he remained undecided and certainly very critical" (Heydenreich, "The Military Architect, 143–144). Compare *Notebooks*, ed. I. Richter, 350–353; Tarchiani, "Leonardo in Florence and Tuscany," 104. Although Bramly argues that it was one of Machiavelli's assistants, Biagio Buonaccorsi, who "followed the matter closely" (*Leonardo*, 331), the evidence in Fachard's *Biagio Buonaccorsi* settles much of this debate, showing Machiavelli's direct involvement; see notes 43–46 below and Appendix I.

42. See Carlo Zammattio, "The Mechanics of Water and Stone, " in Reti, *Unknown Leonardo*, 192–196; Heydenreich, "Military Architect," 144–145. The report on the visit to the camp to assess the feasibility of the project reads: "Yesterday came here accompanied by one of the Signoria, Alessandro delgi Albizzi with Leonardo da Vinci and others and after seeing the plan and after many discussions and doubts it was decided that the undertaking would be very much to the purpose" (cited in Leonardo, *Notebooks*, ed. I. Richter, 350). According to Kenneth Clark, these events were accompanied by a close friendship between Machiavelli and Leonardo: "on Leonardo's return to Florence [from Cesare's court], they seem to have become intimate" (Clark, *Leonardo da Vinci*, 133).

43. See de Grazia, *Machiavelli in Hell*, 119–120 and *The Prince*, ch. 7; p. 32. Machiavelli's correspondence indicates that the conversation reported in chapter seven of *The Prince* is plausible. If so, commentators should have wondered about the singular example of *fortuna* that it illustrates, since it is such "bad luck" that a man of twenty-six would die on the same day as his father. In fact, as any encyclopedia tells us, Cesare Borgia did not die until 1507; Cesare would have been exaggerating the cause of his own failure—as ambitious men often do—if he claimed he was "on the point of dying," and his excuse seems to confuse the election of Pope Pius III in September with

that of Pope Julius II at the end of October. These anomalies should lead us to examine the reasons for that singular "bad luck": what was the cause of Alexander's death? Is there any reason it would have been associated with an unexpected illness that would lead Cesare to say he was dying? In point of fact, the probable cause of Alexander's death was common knowledge in Rome in 1503: after describing the poison used by the Borgias to kill many rivals ("a white powder of an agreeable taste . . . which did not work on the spot, but slowly and gradually"), Burckhardt adds that "at the end of their career father and son poisoned themselves with the same powder by accidentally tasting a sweetmeat intended for a wealthy cardinal" (Burckhardt, *Civilization of the Renaissance in Italy*, 1.132). Given this contemporary rumor, Machiavelli's presence in Rome at the time, and his failure to include the conversation quoted in *The Prince* in his diplomatic dispatches of 4, 6, or 7 November, the praise of Cesare in chapter seven needs to be reassessed: not only had Cesare known for a year that his father could die at any time, but the cause of Alexander's death may have been Cesare's own action. Because these puzzles would have been more evident to contemporaries (like Giuliano de' Medici), Machiavelli's report of his presence in Cesare's court may suggest the importance of that experience in other regards. Among the lessons of Cesare's failure, did Machiavelli want to imply that Leonardo's presence as military architect and advisor was ultimately of no use (as, for that matter, it had been of no avail to Ludovico Sforza)? See chapter three below for a more detailed analysis.

44. Vasari, *Lives*, 397–400; Bramly, *Leonardo*, 336–340; Anna Maria Brizio, "The Painter," in Reti, *Unknown Leonardo*, 44–50; *Notebooks*, ed. I. Richter, 352. Because students of political theory tend to ignore the arts, it is perhaps not surprising that these events have not been mentioned by commentators on Machiavelli's works. Michelangelo, who seems to have been hostile to Leonardo at this time, was awarded the contract to do a companion painting in the Council Hall in August 1504 (ibid., 356; Bramly, *Leonardo*, 343–346). Several additional details are relevant to the political pressures that might have been involved. On the one hand, by 1503 Leonardo would have been known to have failed to complete a number of previous commissions, including not only those left undone in Florence when he moved to Milan in the 1480s, but the equestrian statue of Sforza on which he worked for well over a decade. On the other hand, according to Vasari, Leonardo's reputation on returning from Milan was awesome, with many Florentines anxious to commission a major work. The *Last Supper* revealed his ability for extraordinary painting on the requisite scale—and at the time of the decision Leonardo was engaged in a crucial military project. Although Machiavelli was a close friend of Piero Soderini in this period (see de Grazia, *Machiavelli in Hell*, 95), because Soderini favored Michelangelo and both Soderini and Michelangelo were often critical of

Leonardo, Machiavelli was probably very much the "man in the middle" of a personality conflict not unusual in the world of art and politics.

45. Pedretti, *Leonardo: Royal Palace at Romoratin*, 33. Although I am not aware of any mention of this painting in Machiavelli's works, an unfinished poem on "fortune" does refer to such works in general: "all that realm of hers [fortune], within and without, is adorned with narrative painting of these triumphs from which she gets most honor" (*On Fortune*, 127 [*Chief Works*, 2.75]).

46. Bramly, *Leonardo*, 337; Pedretti, *Literary Works*, 1.381–382; 2.298. Pedretti is unambiguous in his identification of the handwriting as is Fachard (*Biagio Buonaccorsi*, 129), but some scholars are still working on the verification (William Connell, personal communication). Pedretti's interpretation is also consistent with the similarity of Leonardo's handwriting elsewhere on this sheet of paper and on his notes studying the fortifications at Piombino (ibid., 1.382), suggesting that the mission to Piombino and the description of the Battle of Anghiari may be linked in time and sponsorship.

47. Bramly, *Leonardo*, 339–40. The decision, which is partly used as the epigraph of this chapter, effectively gave Leonardo an extension to finish the cartoon with a stipulation that he repay the Signoria for each month of delay; in addition to making separate provisions for Leonardo's painting the mural on the wall of the Grand Council Chamber, the terms gave the city the right to the cartoon, but provided that it could not be painted by another artist without Leonardo's permission. For the text, see Fachard, *Biagio Buonaccorsi*, 259–269. Since it is known that Soderini was frequently angry with Leonardo for the delays in painting *The Battle of Anghiari*, this decision seems to reflect Machiavelli's protection of Leonardo's interest in the face of political pressures to force the artist to justify the large down-payment ("fiorini XXXV larghi d'oro in oro") and Leonardo's artistic impatience and anger when criticized for delays (cf. Bramly, *Leonardo*, 340, 353 *et passim*).

48. Fachard, *Biagio Buonaccorsi*, 129–130.

49. Leonardo's trace for the canal is the horizontal line sketched under the winding river in Figure 1.6. For the text of Machiavelli's letter, see Appendix I.3, D. For the nature of Buonaccorsi's *Sunmario*, the source of this account, see Fachard, *Buonaccorsi*, 119–126. Because Machiavelli does not mention Leonardo by name, however, Fachard wonders whether the evidence is "suffisant pour conclure qu'il s'agit de celui [le dessin] de Leonardo?" See the next note.

50. Ibid., 126–30 and notes, as well as Plate III (facing p. 158), reproduced as Figure 1.11. Although Machiavelli's criticism of the plans employed was confirmed by the outcome, the little known of Machiavelli's education and family background confirms the likelihood of humanistic rather than technical training: "The hypothesis advanced some years ago that he had worked as a banker in Rome for much of the 1490s has been abandoned, and the best evidence,

thin as it is, suggests that Machiavelli spent those years in at least some important connection with the world of literary humanism. He wrote a little poetry; he copied a humanist manuscript edition of Lucretius's *De rerum natura*; and from his early writings and chancery letters it is clear that he had an impressive familiarity with many works of classical antiquity and with the conventions of style and language normally expected of chancery officials" (Najemy, *Between Friends*, 58). Fachard's principal evidence that Leonardo did not collaborate extensively with Machiavelli on the diversion of the Arno is "le manque de preuves de sa présence dans les bureaux des Chancelleries" (*Biagio Buonaccorsi*, 130). This is a curious statement given the fact that Leonardo was painting *The Battle of Anghiari* in the Palace, not to mention interacting with the group of intellectuals of which Machiavelli was a part. My own best guess is that Machiavelli, having discussed Leonardo's pacific plans for diverting the Arno when they met in Cesare's court in the autumn of 1502, continued informal consultations with Leonardo outside the Chancery (perhaps among the circle of friends that met in the Rucellai gardens, where Leonardo had designed a fountain and where Machiavelli often met young intellectuals). Like many men in power, Machiavelli would have privately sought technical advice to confirm the arguments of officially appointed "experts." This would explain why, after criticizing the plan being followed for the diversion, Machiavelli concludes his letter to Giuliano Lapi of 20 September 1504 by saying: "if the difficulties of the work or other unforeseen circumstances should force you to undertake this last project you wrote me about we will trust your decision" (ibid., 144). Then, as if he had discussed this answer with a hydraulic engineer, the next day (21 September) Machiavelli again wrote Lapi, this time urgently posing the question of the precise depth of the bottom of the canal as compared to the riverbed of the Arno and specifically asking that the work be corrected to meet technical necessities ("in case the bed of the ditch is shallower, we would think it proper to make up for it"—ibid., 142, reproduced in Appendix I.4 D–E). Although Machiavelli had the technical information that would have been a normal *consequence* of informal conversations with Leonardo, like any good administrator he tried not to micromanage work in the field—but followed it carefully in hopes of correcting dangerous mistakes in advance. Much of the historical debate is clarified by interpreting these recently discovered texts and memoranda in the light of the practices necessary for men of action.

51. Heydenreich, "Military Architect," 144–145; Costantina, *Leonardo*, 27. For Buonaccorsi's account, see Appendix I.5. *The First Decennale*, the poem referring explicitly to the project to divert the Arno, was apparently written in fifteen days and completed on 8 November 1504 (*Chief Works*, 3.1444–45). Was this poem written in self-justification after criticism of Machiavelli's advice in the war on Pisa? With Machiavelli urging the creation of a militia and supervising the campaign, Pisa finally fell in 1509.

52. The description of the events described above is notable for its indirectness: "It gave us great pain that so great an error should have been made in those waters that it seems impossible to us that it should not been through the fault of those engineers, who went so far wrong. Perhaps it pleases God thus, for some better end unknown to us!" (*Machiavelli's Correspondence*, #94; Francesco Soderini to Machiavelli, 26 October 1504).

53. *First Decennale*, 499–504, in *Chief Works*, 3.1456.

54. Bramly, *Leonardo*, 342. On the details of this project, see Heydenreich, "Military Architect," 152–163; Pedretti, *Leonardo: Royal Palace at Romorantin*, 32–40. Leonardo must have brought with him the basic plans, for he is recorded as being in Florence on 31 October, and noted in his diary that he presented the project to Jacopo on 1 November 1504. It is hard to imagine how such a project could have been undertaken without extensive consultation between Leonardo and Machiavelli. For Machiavelli's opinion of Jacopo IV Appiani, see *Discourses*, 3.18, 457.

55. Bramly, *Leonardo*, 342. From the copies and sketches available to us, this painting must have been truly extraordinary. The cartoon from which Leonardo worked along with that for Michelangelo's companion work (also never completed) were described by Cellini as the "school of the world"; on seeing the completed portion, Raphael is said to have changed his entire mode of painting (Bramly, *Leonardo*, 350). The astonishing power of the original is evident in the rarely reproduced "trial panel," on which Leonardo tested his new technique: see Pedretti, *Leonardo: Chronology and Style*, Plate XVII. Given the immediate fame of Leonardo's painting, it is worth noting that the scene—the battle for the standard—presents an image of the battle that does not correspond with Machiavelli's account in the *Florentine Histories* (ibid., 337). See note 16 to Appendix III.

56. The tradition that the *Mona Lisa* was painted at this time is based on the discussion by Vasari, who apparently wrote about the painting by hearsay only; some specialists now believe that the painting actually dates from around 1513—and that the subject is probably the mistress of Giuliano de' Medici, not Mona Lisa Gioconda: see Bramly, *Leonardo*, 361–367; Pedretti, *Leonardo: Chronology and Style*, 132–139. On Leonardo's attempt to fly, see Francesco Cutry, "The Flight of Birds," in Istituto Geografico d'Agostino, *Leonardo da Vinci*, 343–346.

57. The letter reads as follows: "Messer Nicolò my so much greater honorable brother etc: After leaving your Excellency, I went to see the register [to see] if the name of my brother was signed to it. The book was not there. I was sent many places before I found it. Eventually I went to his excellency the Datario and told him that I was begging his honor not having had the petition signed that tomorrow he would have it read and have it signed. His excellency answered me that for him this was a very difficult thing and that

the petition requested too many things which cannot be done and especially since the gain was of little income. And if it were a thing of greater importance it would be signed with little difficulty" (Raymond S. Stites, *The Sublimation of Leonardo* [Washington D. C.: Smithsonian Institution Press, 1970], 321). The text is in the Codex Atlanticus, Folio 229, recto a (reproduced in Stites, 320). Unlike most entries in the *Notebooks*, the draft is written from left to right, suggesting the care and formality of a text Leonardo was about to send or show to someone else, as distinct from his usual private jottings hastily written from right to left. In 1507, when Stites and Beltrami think the letter was written, Machiavelli was in a position to assist Leonardo.

58. Pedretti, *Literary Works*, 2.300–301 (including a different translation of the greeting as "Messer Nicolò, as much as an elder brother to me, and most honourable at that." On Michelozzi, "who had been a Medici secretary for years and associated long since with the literary endeavors of Lorenzo the Magnificent," see J. N. Stephens, *The Fall of the Florentine Republic* (Oxford: Clarendon Press, 1983), 140. One difficulty with Pedretti's identification of the addressee is that there seems no other evidence of a link between Leonardo and Michelozzi, and no explanation of why if Leonardo was in Rome in 1514, he would have written to Michelozzi in Florence. Some critics point out that only a knight or a lawyer would be addressed as "Messer" and "Your Excellency."

59. During this visit to Florence, Leonardo lived in the house of Piero di Braccio Martelli, a scholar and patron of the arts known by Machiavelli (Bramly, *Leonardo*, 357). Martelli was a frequent participant in the activities at the Orti Oricellari, where Leonardo and Machiavelli may well have been present together (Pedretti, *Studi Vinciani*, 17, 34). For evidence that Machiavelli knew of Martelli before 1507, see his dispatch to the Signoria from Cesena dated 26 December 1502, reproduced in Adams's edition of *The Prince*, 89. Leonardo must have known Martelli at about this time, for in his *Notebooks* (British Museum, 202 verso) is the note:

> Where is Valentino?
> Boots, boxes in the customhouse, the monk at Carmine, squares.
> Piero Martelli
> Salvi Borghesini
> return the bags.
> a support for the spectacles.
> the nude of Sangallo.
> the cloak...
> (*Notebooks*, ed. I. Richter, 348–49)

60. Costantino, *Leonardo*, 29–30. Another project on which Leonardo worked at this time involved redirecting the channel of the Adda River between Milan and Lake Como: see Zammattio, "Mechanics of Water and Stone," 201–204.

61. Although there is no explicit mention of Leonardo in the letters Francisco Vettori sent his friend Machiavelli from Rome in 1513–1514, on 24 June 1513, Vettori "alluded to problems he had had or was having with an unnamed 'amico nostro,' in whom Machiavelli had warned not to place any trust" (Najemy, *Between Friends*, 141). Although it is conceivable that this refers to Leonardo, who at the time of Vettori's letter was projecting a move to Rome in order to live in the Vatican and work under Giuliano de' Medici's patronage, about the only thing that this passage actually demonstrates is the frequency with which Machiavelli and his contemporaries *avoided* naming names!

62. On this period, see Emilio Laragnino, "Leonardo in Rome," in Istituto Geografico d'Agostino, *Leonardo da Vinci*, 127–137; Bramly, *Leonardo*, 381–389.

63. On the details of the last years of Machiavelli's life, summarized below, see de Grazia, *Machiavelli in Hell*, esp. 241–385; "Introduction," *The Prince*, ed. Marriott, pp. xiv–xvii; Najemy, *Between Friends*, esp. chs. 3–9. The famous letter to Vettori is reproduced as Appendix II. There is no clear evidence that, while Leonardo was working with Giuliano de' Medici (the original addressee of the manuscript of *The Prince*), there were any direct contacts with Machiavelli. However, on the back of a letter sent to his half-brother Giuliano da Vinci (then in Rome) is Leonardo's notation that "he had given a book (he does not say what: possibly a treatise in his own hand) to Monsignor Branconio dell'Aquila, the 'secret chamberlain of the Pope'" (Bramly, *Leonardo*, 389). The letter, from Giuliano da Vinci's wife Alessandra, concludes with a postscript asking Giuliano to give regards to Leonardo (who until this time had been alienated from his half-brothers in the suits over inheritance). On the hypothesis that Leonardo's letter to "Messer Nicolò" is dated 1514 in Rome (see above, note 57), could the addressee still have been Machiavelli—and "the book" referred to in this letter a copy of *The Prince?*

64. Pedretti, *Leonardo: Architect*, 251–261.

65. Pedretti, *Leonardo: Royal Palace at Romorantin*, 2. Since Lorenzo and Giuliano were in Florence together during 1515 (Pedretti, *Leonardo: Chronology and Style*, 135), Leonardo's relations with the Medici were continuous from his move to Rome in 1513 through his last days in France in 1519.

66. Pedretti, *Leonardo: Royal Palace at Romorantin*, esp. Part 2 (67–278).

67. Vasari, *Lives*, 2.403. While some scholars questioned this account due to a French royal decree signed at St. Germain-en-Laye on 3 May 1519, others point out that the act was signed by the chancellor, not the king himself (Bramly, *Leonardo*, 408). According to Cellini, King Francis I later said that "he did not believe that there had ever been another man born into the world who had known so much as Leonardo, and this not only in matters concerning sculpture, painting, and architecture, but because he was a great philosopher" (Pedretti, *Leonardo: Royal Palace at Romorantin*, 4). Whatever the truth of these stories, there can be no question that Leonardo was in close personal

relationships with a number of rulers and powerful men, including Ludovico Sforza, Cesare Borgia, Giuliano de' Medici and his nephew Lorenzo di Piero de' Medici, and Louis XII as well as François I.

68. Fachard, *Biagio Buonaccorsi*, 158–160.

69. I will argue that Machiavelli's comedy as well as the fable *Belfagor* need to be viewed as popular presentations of his understanding of human nature and politics. (See below, chapter five.)

70. Pedretti, *Studi Vinciani*, 34–42. Note that *The Art of War* is a dialogue set in these gardens.

71. See *Discourses on Titus Livy*, II, 17 (*Chief Works*, 2.367–372); *Art of War*, Book VII (*Chief Works*, 2.703–708); for Leonardo's views, compare Ignazio Calvi, "Military Engineering and Arms," in Istituto Geografico d'Agostino, *Leonardo*, 275–306; Heydenreich, "Military Architect," and Zammattio, "Mechanics of Water and Stone."

72. Machiavelli, *Discourses on Titus Livy*, II, 17 (*Chief Works*, 1.372).

73. Compare Xenophon, *Anabasis*, 1.17, in *Hellencia*, VI & VIII *and Anabasis*, I–III, trans. Carlton I. Brownson, Loeb Classical Library (London, Heinemann, 1921), 1.313, 317 with the sketches reproduced in Costantino, *Leonardo*, 97; Istituto Geografico d'Agostino, *Leonardo*, 288–289. In addition to *Discourses*, II, 17, Machiavelli also refers to scythed chariots in *Art of War*, Book IV (*Chief Works*, 2.652–653), attributing the device to both "Asiatics" against Greeks and King Archelaus against Romans. In Xenophon's account, the Greeks easily avoid the fearsome scythed chariots—and few soldiers are killed in the battle, thereby illustrating one of Machiavelli's main points concerning the ability of a well-trained infantry to resist most technological inventions. I am indebted to James Tatum for the reference to scythed chariots in Xenophon's *Anabasis*.

74. *Florentine Histories*, 5.24 (ed. Mansfield, p. 270). In this chapter, Machiavelli emphasizes the power of the cataclysm by attributing it to divine intention: "when arms had been put away by men, it appeared that God wished to take them up Himself"; after the description, Machiavelli adds, "Without doubt, God wanted to warn rather than punish Tuscany" because the storm did not hit a city, where it would have had vastly more devastating effects. From the outset, the event is described as unique, with "effects unheard of in the past and for whoever learns of it in the future will have marvelous and memorable effects." Finally, as if to justify that his account is based on personal observation, Machiavelli goes on to add that "This terrifying whirlwind, wherever it passed, had unheard-of and marvelous effects; but more remarkable than those anywhere else were the ones that occurred around the fortified town of San Casciano . . . between this town and the village of Sant' Andrea, situated on the same hill, passed this furious storm, not reaching Sant' Andrea and grazing San Casciano so that only some battlements and the

chimneys of some houses were broken off; but outside, in the space between the places mentioned, many houses were destroyed to the level of the ground. The roofs of the churches of San Martino Bagnolo and Santa Maria della Pace were carried entire, just as they had been on the churches, more than a mile away" (ibid., 169–171). Machiavelli's own home, of course, was precisely in this area. For Leonardo's descriptions of violent storms and deluges, see *Notebooks*, ed. J. P. Richter, 1.305–313.

75. *Leonardo: Chronology and Style*, 11–22. It is worth noting that one of the descriptions of such a cataclysm is on a sheet dated around 1515, when Leonardo returned to Florence (*Notebooks*, ed. J. P. Richter, 1.307n). At this time, both Giuliano de' Medici and Lorenzo di Pieri de' Medici were also in Florence. It is thus possible that Machiavelli met Leonardo again at this time at the Rucellai gardens, a hypothesis that is strengthened by a reference to the storm of 1456 in the *Zibaldone* of Rucellai.

76. It is worth citing Pedretti's note in full:

> An echo of Leonardo's activities as a military architect is in a letter of Guicciardini to Roberto Acciaioli of September 25, 1526: 'Scrissi a V. S. a' 13 del presente: gli mandai una lettera del Machiavello del campo di Cremona, uno disegno di quelle trincee, fatto non per mano di Leonardo da Vinci. . .' (F. Guicciardini, *Opere inedite*, ed. G. Canestrini, Florence, 1857–68, Vol. IV, p. 367. See also Beltrami, *Documenti*, no. 253. Solmi, *Scritti Vinciani*, p. 235, note 1, suppresses the 'non', making the text a reference to a drawing by Leonardo. But F. Villari, *Niccolò Machiavelli e i suoi tempi*, Florence, 1877–82, Vol. III, pp. 343–4, had already ascertained in the autograph that Guicciardini writes 'not by Leonardo', as if to imply that the drawing (probably his own) was certainly not as skillful as one by Leonardo." (Pedretti, *Literary Works*, 2.52, note 1)

77. For an analysis of these parallels, see below, chapters three and seven.

78. *Discourses on Titus Livy*, III, 14 (*Chief Works*, 1.464–466).

Chapter 2

1. Machiavelli, *The Prince*, Dedicatory Letter, p. 3.

2. E.g., see Anthony Parel, "Machiavelli's Method and Its Interpreters," in *The Political Calculus: Essays on Machiavelli's Philosophy*, ed. Anthony Parel (Toronto: University of Toronto Press, 1972), 3–32; Leonardo Olschlei, *Machiavelli the Scientist* (Berkeley: University of California Press, 1945); Pierre Manent, *An Intellectual History of Liberalism*, trans. Rebecca Balenski (Princeton, N.J.: Princeton University Press, 1994). Recently, however, this view has been challenged by influential commentators who stressed "premodern"

elements of Machiavellian political thought, or treated him primarily as a reflection of his times. See, for examples of the former critique of Machiavelli's modernity, Pocock, *Machiavellian Moment*; Jack H. Hexter, *On Historians* (Cambridge, Mass.: Harvard University Press, 1979); Parel, *Machiavellian Cosmos*. For the interpretation of Machiavelli as a representative of his time, see Burkhardt, *Civilization of the Renaissance in Italy*, vol. 1; de Grazia, *Machiavelli in Hell*; Basu, "In a Crazy Time the Crazy Come Out Well."

3. While most of the critics cited in the preceding note illustrate the attempt to situate Machiavelli in historical rather than scientific or philosophical terms, others focus on the judgment of Machiavelli's moral teaching: see especially Leo Strauss, "Niccolò Machiavelli," in *History of Political Philosophy*, ed. Leo Strauss and Joseph Cropsey, 3d. ed. (Chicago: University of Chicago Press, 1987), 296–317.

4. *Mandragola*, p. 9. Machiavelli's comedy, which unlike *The Prince* and *Discourses* was performed and published in his own lifetime, may be particularly important as a reflection of Machiavelli's intention to transform political practice as well as political theory: the conceit of a prologue in which the author addresses the audience directly suggests that the text of the play may be a particularly important way for Machiavelli to communicate his ideas, while the concern for teaching the many is also suggested by such fables as *Belfagor*. See Theodore A. Sumberg, "*Belfagor*: Machiavelli's Short Story," *Interpretation* 19 (Spring 1992): 243–250. On the role of "folk metaphors," "proverbs," and other popularly accessible artistic symbols of knowledge in the Renaissance, see Margaret Sullivan's remarkable "Bruegel's Proverbs: Art and Audience in the Northern Renaissance," *The Art Bulletin* 73 (1991): 431–466. While this study focuses on the generation after Machiavelli, it reveals the way the popular art of the Renaissance broadened the audience of those capable of understanding the fruits of ancient or philosophic wisdom. Without such an intention to break down the exclusiveness that characterized philosophic teaching in pagan antiquity, it would be difficult to explain why Machiavelli—unlike Plato, Aristotle, or other ancient political theorists—also wrote popular plays and tales.

5. This is not to say that Machiavelli's devotion to Florence and to Italy is without importance (see the concluding chapter), but only that his patriotism needs to be understood in the context of his purposes in writing. Note also that, in the dedication to the *Discourses* (p. 93), he says that his "intention" should be more important than the "quality" of his book. At the outset of his major works, Machiavelli is unusually insistent in talking about his own "intentions" and the importance of figuring out what they are.

6. Machiavelli's training as a humanist scholar is demonstrated by the erudition of his correspondence with friends like Vettori (see Najemy, *Between Friends, passim*). For the conventional view, Felix Gilbert, *Machiavelli and Guicciardini*, 193: "Machiavelli was not a philosopher. He intended neither to

outline a philosophical system nor to introduce new philosophical terms." My point is that one can accept Gilbert's conclusion (the second sentence just quoted) without agreeing with the premise (his first sentence above).

7. Najemy, *Between Friends*, 58.

8. *Machiavelli's Correspondence*, #37: Biagio Buonaccorsi to Niccolò Machiavelli, 21 October 1502.

9. The following entry in Leonardo's notebooks—dating from 1505, when he was working in Florence—is consistent with this possibility: "Aristotle and Alexander were teachers to each other. Alexander was rich in power, which gave him the means of seizing the world. Aristotle had a great intellect, which gave him the means of seizing the rest of the knowledge contributed by all the other philosophers" (Pedretti, *Literary Works*, 2.251). Could it be that, in this passage, Leonardo was reflecting on his discussions with Machiavelli?

10. *Machiavelli's Correspondence*, #92: Bartolomeo Vespucci to Machiavelli, 4 June 1504.

11. It was not until after giving the Covey lectures that I myself discovered Machiavelli knew and probably worked with Leonardo da Vinci. The preliminary findings of my discovery were presented in "Machiavelli and Hobbes: Theory and Practice at the Origins of Modernity," presented at the 1992 Annual Meeting of the American Political Science Association, The Palmer House Hilton, Chicago, Ill., 3–6 September 1992. At the time of giving that paper and thereafter, I did not encounter a single political theorist who had previously been aware that Machiavelli had encountered Leonardo and probably been influenced by his scientific ideas (even though some historians have debated the extent of this influence for years). Although my own discovery in November 1991—fittingly enough in the bookstore of the Chicago Art Institute while in that city to present a paper on the biology of human social behavior—confirmed the basic assumptions of my original analysis of Machiavelli in the Covey lectures, it expanded them greatly.

12. Rousseau, *Social Contract*, Book 3, ch. 6; ed. Roger D. Masters (New York: St. Martin's Press, 1978), 88.

13. Ibid., note. By "execrable hero," Rousseau clearly means Cesare Borgia.

14. On this form of writing, see Leo Strauss, *Persecution and the Art of Writing* (Glencoe, Ill.: Free Press, 1952). For the argument against Strauss's mode of analysis and its application in *Thoughts on Machiavelli*, see Shadia B. Drury, *The Political Thought of Leo Strauss* (New York: St. Martin's Press, 1988); John G. Gunnell, "The Myth of the Tradition," *American Political Science Review* 72 (1978): 130–131; Stanley Rothman, "The Revival of Classical Political Philosophy: A Critique," *American Political Science Review* 56 (1961): 351–352; and Quentin Skinner, "Meaning and Understanding in the History of Ideas," *History and Theory* 8 (1969): 19–22.

15. Roberto Ridolfi, *The Life of Niccolò Machiavelli*, trans. Grayson (Chicago: University of Chicago Press, 1963).

16. On Machiavelli's early career, see Najemy, *Between Friends*. Machiavelli's relationship to the Gonfalonier was particularly close—so much so that some of the patrician families in Florence saw Machiavelli as "Soderini's puppet" (ibid., 95) or "Soderini's lackey" (Gilbert, *Machiavelli and Guicciardini*, 173).

17. Machiavelli was, it is true, even more strongly hostile to the *optimates*—leading families who sought to undermine the Florentine Republic—than to the Medici family, and in the last days of Soderini's rule, clearly indicated his willingness to serve in a successor government (de Grazia, *Machiavelli in Hell*, 32–33, 161–162; Najemy, *Between Friends*, ch. 3). Whether this indicates a lack of political principle, as many commentators suggest when reading the dedication to *The Prince*, is another of the many questions that demands careful consideration.

18. Najemy, *Between Friends*, 94; de Grazia, *Machiavelli in Hell*, 32. Of the events in Machiavelli's career, the fact of Machiavelli's torture deserves particular emphasis when interpreting the Dedicatory Letter to *The Prince*, most especially because at the time Machiavelli wrote three sonnets to Giuliano de' Medici describing the event and asking for release from prison (ibid., 34–40; *Chief Works* 2.1013–14).

19. For the text of the letter, see the annotated edition of *The Prince* by Robert M. Adams, 128.

20. "I would be glad of your opinion, because to tell you the truth without flattery, I have found you to be sounder in these matters than any other man I have spoken to" (Vettori to Machiavelli, April 1513 [*The Prince*, ed. Adams, p. 142]). For the period and a detailed interpretation of the Vettori–Machiavelli correspondence, see Najemy, *Between Friends*, chs. 4–5.

21. Machiavelli to Vettori, 20 April 1513 (ed. Adams, p. 142).

22. Ibid., 127. See Najemy, *Between Friends*, ch. 6.

23. Machiavelli to Guiccardini, 17 May 1521 (ed. Adams, pp. 133–135).

24. On the role of ambiguity and deception in private letters, see Najemy, *Between Friends*, ch. 1.

25. The full text of the letter, in Mansfield's translation of *The Prince*, will be found as Appendix II.

26. Mansfield notes at this point: "Perhaps a reference to NM's imprisonment and torture in February and March of 1513" (ibid.). That Machiavelli refers to these events is reinforced by the fact that his release was contingent on his not leaving the territory of Florence for one year (see de Grazia, *Machiavelli in Hell*, 45–47; Najemy, *Between Friends*, 93).

27. The paragraph ends with a reference to the "disaster of Prato," the Spanish victory over the army of Italian troops (including the militia formed by Machiavelli himself) which led to the fall of Soderini and the end of the Flo-

rentine Republic. Cf. de Grazia, *Machiavelli in Hell*, 98, 161. It is impossible to say whether this paragraph—with its apparently trivial details—contained some coded information for Vettori or was to be taken literally.

28. Compare this powerful evocation of the joy of contemplative activity with Aristotle, *Politics*, VII.1325a17–b32 and compare *Metaphysics*, I. 982b10–983a11 and XII.1074b15–1075a10.

29. "*Paradiso*, V. 41–42" (Mansfield's note).

30. Prior to starting on *The Prince* and *Discourses* in 1513, Machiavelli's most substantial work was *First Decennial* (1504), "a chronicle in verse of events in Florence and Italy in the decade 1494–1504"; with the possible exception of the so-called "Prison Sonnets," de Grazia argues that even most of Machiavelli's poetry and drama were written after this letter (*Machiavelli in Hell*, 23).

31. "Giuliano de' Medici, the duke of Nemours, son of Lorenzo the Magnificent. He left Florence in September of 1513 and was in Rome at the time of NM's letter. He died in 1516, and NM decided to dedicate *The Prince* to Lorenzo de' Medici, grandson of Lorenzo the Magnificent, who became duke of Urbino in 1516" (Mansfield's note). Machiavelli knew Giuliano as a young man, and before 1494 had even dedicated a poem to him (Najemy, *Between Friends*, 91).

32. That the work originally had the Latin title *De Principatibus* is confirmed by the record book of Machiavelli's assistant and friend, Biagio Buonaccorsi, who notes that Giovanni Gaddi paid him for a copy of "el libro *De Principatu* composto del Machiavello, scritto da me"; there is no date, but the preceding entry is for 15 September 1520 (Fachard, *Biagio Buonaccorsi*, 215). That Machiavelli originally hoped to gain the patronage of Giuliano de' Medici—whose intervention helped secure Machiavelli's release from jail— is evident in Machiavelli's correspondence with Vettori (Najemy, *Between Friends*, chs. 3–4).

33. This sentence uses a rhetorical device we often find in Machiavelli's letters and works: a sweeping generalization, clearly intended to please some expected reader, followed by a specific qualifying remark which effectively contradicts the general formula. A more famous example of this rhetorical device, chapter seven of *The Prince*, will be discussed in detail below (see chapter three, pp. 67–72). Six weeks after the date of this letter would have ended in January 1514, almost a year after Machiavelli's imprisonment. In fact, Machiavelli never did go to Rome to visit Vettori, who gave up his ambassadorial post and returned to Florence later in 1514.

34. The prison where Machiavelli had been incarcerated and tortured (and where the two young men who initiated the conspiracy against the Medici were executed).

35. Filippo is Filippo Cassavecchia, a friend of Machiavelli's (see above); Ardinghelli was Secretary to Giuliano de' Medici. In 1503, Machiavelli addressed official correspondence to Pierro Ardinghelli as Commisario of Burgo

Santo Supulcro (*Legatione*, II, 429, 433, 436, *et passim*). It is not clear whether Machiavelli knew that Leonardo da Vinci, who had passed through Florence after leaving Milan in 1512, had arrived in Rome on 1 December 1513 to work under the patronage of Giuliano de' Medici.

36. De Grazia interprets Machiavelli's letters in the period 1512 to 1517 as reflecting a degree of despair and self-doubt bordering on melancholia (see especially *Machiavelli in Hell*, ch. 2). Even if these passages are not intended for rhetorical effect, they do not justify the conclusion that Machiavelli came to doubt the fundamental principles expressed in his major political works. On the contrary, I believe that a careful reading shows an extraordinary consistency between *The Prince* and the *Discourses*, the *Florentine Histories*, and such plays as *Mandragola*. For *Florentine Histories*, see Gregory Tamkin, *The Florentine Histories*, Senior Honors Thesis (Hanover, N.H.: Dartmouth College, 1991).

37. The sonnets written while Machiavelli was in prison in February–March 1513 and addressed to Giuliano de' Medici had already asked for favor (see note 18 above); later, Machiavelli succeeded in gaining patronage from Giuliano's cousin, Giulio de' Medici, who became Pope Clement VII (1523–1534) and commissioned the *Florentine Histories*. See Najemy, *Between Friends*, ch. 3 *et passim*.

38. Machiavelli died in 1528. The *Discourses on Titus Livy* were not published until 1531, and *The Prince* in 1532, in editions published in Rome and in Florence.

39. Lorenzo di Piero de' Medici (1492–1519), the grandson of Lorenzo the Magnificent, was the son of Piero de' Medici (1471–1503), the member of the family who had been expected to take power in Florence after the overthrow of the Republic; a talented young man, Piero died suddenly after becoming ill during battle. Lorenzo was then expected by his uncle Giovanni (Pope Leo X) to become the active head of state in Florence; to this end, he was named Duke of Urbino in 1516. See Ferdinand Schevill, *The Medici* (New York: Harcourt Brace, 1949). On the relations between Lorenzo and Leonardo, see above, chapter one.

40. Prior to Machiavelli's death, both *The Prince* and the *Discourses on Titus Livy* circulated among Machiavelli's friends in Florence, and even beyond; to cite one important example, Thomas Cromwell was said to have brought a copy of the manuscript to England in 1529 and to have used it in advising Henry VIII (*Prince*, ed. Adams, pp. 227–228). It is generally assumed, therefore, that Machiavelli made specific provisions to see that his manuscripts were published posthumously. While no one knows why the Dedicatory Letter to Lorenzo de' Medici was appended to the published editions (cf. de Grazia, *Machiavelli in Hell*, 49–50), it needs to be stressed that the younger Lorenzo died in 1519 after failing to play the role in Florentine politics that his

family had expected. That is, during a period of some nine years after both Giuliano and Lorenzo had been dead, Machiavelli had occasion to revise or change the way *The Prince* would be published. While we do not know the reason, it is evident that he did *not* use the occasion to remove a dedicatory letter that would obviously no longer be historically appropriate.

41. As Machiavelli's dispatches from the court of Cesare Borgia and his correspondence with Vettori prove, he had experience in writing with caution and diplomatic obfuscation. See *Legations* (*Chief Works* 1.120–160; Najemy, *Between Friends*, esp. chs. 1–2). See also the reference to a letter Machiavelli wrote while at the emperor's court in 1507, "un document chiffré qui . . . contient des passages inintelligibles ou même illisibles; l'envoyé de la Seigneurerie se divertissait à jouer avec les clefs des messages secrets" (Fachard, *Biagio Buonaccorsi*, 157).

42. On possible changes between the version of *The Prince* written in 1513 and the text as it was revised and copied in 1519–1520 (notably, Martelli's hypothesis that chapter twenty-six was added in 1518), see Najemy, *Between Friends*, 175–197.

43. Fachard, *Biagio Buonaccorsi*, 160, 215. Actually, as Fachard notes, there are three surviving manuscripts in Buonaccorsi's handwriting—all with a dedication to Lorenzo de' Medici (157–161).

44. The two men to whom the *Discourses* are dedicated, Zanobi Buondelmonti and Cosimo Rucellai, were among those who frequented the Orti Oricellari in the Rucellai Gardens; both are characters in the dialogue of Machiavelli's *Art of War*. In fact, Book I of *The Art of War* begins with praise for the memory of Cosimo Rucellai: "Because I believe that without censure every man can be praised after his death, since all cause and suspicion of flattery have disappeared, I shall not hesitate to praise our Cosimo Rucellai, whose name I shall never remember without tears, since I have observed in him those qualities strongly desired in a good friend by his friend and in a citizen by his native city" (*Chief Works*, 2.568). Buondelmonti was one of those caught in a republican plot against the Medici in 1522 (J. N. Stephens, *The Fall of the Florentine Republic: 1512–1530* [Oxford: Clarendon Press, 1983], 120–121). There is thus evidence that Machiavelli is sincere in his praise for the addressees of the *Discourses*.

45. As Mansfield points out, the Italian *animo* can mean "spirit" in the sense of "intention," but not "intelligence" or knowledge.

46. It is, of course, conceivable to assume that they were written between 1519 and 1520, after Lorenzo's death: in this case, the irony would be self-evident since Lorenzo died without having engaged in political activity or achieved anything that could be qualified as "greatness." Cf. note 42 above.

47. The importance of considering a dedication in terms of flattery is reinforced by the Dedicatory Letter to *Florentine Histories*. That work is dedicated

to Pope Clement VII, Giulio de' Medici, who had commissioned a history of Florence in 1520 when he was still a cardinal under the papacy of his uncle Giovanni, known as Pope Leo X. Machiavelli presented the work to the pope in 1525. In the Dedicatory Letter, he defends himself at length against the possible charge of "flattery": "But how far I am from flattery may be known from all parts of my history, and especially in speeches and in private reasonings, direct as well as indirect. . . . *Thus no one who correctly considers my writings can reproach me as a flatterer,* especially when they see how I have not said very much in memory of the father of Your Holiness" (*Florentine Histories,* Dedicatory Letter; p. 4). Whether the "writings" mentioned here include *The Prince* and *Discourses,* which in 1525 had circulated in manuscript but were unpublished, is not clear.

48. *The Prince,* ch. 23; pp. 93–94. The direct address to "you" here makes one wonder whether Machiavelli meant this passage to apply most specifically to the figure of Lorenzo as the ruler to whom the book is dedicated. Such a use occurs, of course, in the famous concluding chapter, but it is not usually considered in the otherwise bewildering changes in pronouns which most commentators dismiss as sloppy usage. As a poet who had been imprisoned and tortured because on one occasion he had not been cautious enough in talking about politics in the aftermath of the Florentine Republic (de Grazia, *Machiavelli in Hell,* 49), Machiavelli should be treated as a writer who was careful with language.

49. Note that here Machiavelli does *not* use "you" of direct address.

50. On the implication of Machiavelli's combination of "understanding" (political knowledge or theory) and "utility" (political action or practice), see below, chapter six.

51. Machiavelli's devotion to the "common good of men" is confirmed by the dedication to *The Art of War* (*Chief Works,* 2.566). See also the description of Cosimo Rucellai (ibid., 2.5), cited above in note 44. On the claim of novelty in this passage as an echo of Lucretius's *De rerum natura,* see Najemy, *Between Friends,* 337–338 (as well as 227).

52. For further evidence that Machiavelli knew and used the tradition of deception in writing, see ibid., 53–57, 89–90.

53. As I will argue below, this novelty seems related to Machiavelli's political experience and his relationship with Leonardo da Vinci, whose scientific and philosophic inquiries point to the distinctively modern integration of theory and practice. On the ground for focusing on the relationship between theory and practice as the key to modernity, see Masters, *Beyond Relativism,* ch. 1, as well as "Machiavelli and Hobbes: Theory and Practice at the Origins of Modernity."

54. Rousseau, of course, established his philosophical "system" in the light of this premise: see *Discourse on the Sciences and Arts,* in *Rousseau's First and*

Second Discourses, ed. Roger D. Masters (New York: St. Martin's Press, 1974). On Rousseau's knowledge and use of "esoteric" writing, see especially the "Preface to a Second Letter to Bordes," in *Collected Writings of Rousseau*, vol. 2, ed. Roger D. Masters and Christopher Kelly (Hanover, N.H.: University Press of New England, 1992), 184–185. On Machiavelli's impressive knowledge of ancient philosophy and humanistic learning, see Najemy, *Between Friends* 239, 337–348, *et passim*.

55. Cf. Aristotle, *Metaphysics*, II.995b1–20, *Nichomachean Ethics*, I.1094b12–1095a11, and *Politics*, VII.1323a23–25. According to the important passage in the *Florentine Histories* (V, 1) just cited, Machiavelli shared the view of Cato that "evil could result to his fatherland" from the public teaching of philosophy precisely because it is an "honorable leisure" (p. 185): the principal danger from openly teaching philosophy may be its effects on the listener, not on the speaker.

Chapter 3

1. From Christopher Marlowe's Prologue to *The Jew of Malta*, lines 7–15; ed. T. W. Craik (New York: Hill and Wang, 1966), 9. Written in around 1590, the play attests to—and contributed to—the dissemination of Machiavelli's teachings.

2. For examples of the diverse interpretations, see note 2 to chapter two above. For a summary of the historical role of *The Prince* in the diffusion of Machiavelli's thought, see Robert M. Adams, "The Rise, Proliferation, and Degradation of Machiavellism: An Outline," in *The Prince*, ed. Adams, 227–238. I will return to the question of Machiavelli and modernity in chapter seven below.

3. *Discourses on Titus Livy*, p. 94.

4. *Florentine Histories*, Preface, pp. 6, 8. As Machiavelli puts it: "if every example of a republic is moving, those which one reads concerning one's own are much more so and much more useful; and if in any other republic there were ever notable divisions, those of Florence are most notable" (ibid., p. 6).

5. *The Prince*, ch. 26; pp. 103–104.

6. *Art of War*, Preface; *Chief Works*, 2.566.

7. Unlike his other major works, Machiavelli does not introduce *The Art of War* with a claim of novelty; rather, he says the work will show the error of the "opinion" that "many have held and now still hold" that "no two things are more out of harmony with one another or differ more from one another than civilian life and military life"; according to Machiavelli, it is necessary to return to the "ancient ways" with regard to warfare (Preface; *Chief Works*, 2.566). In other words, in this work, Machiavelli's novelty is the return to the

practice of pagan antiquity, overturning Christian doctrines in the name of political and military prudence.

8. *Mandragola,* Prologue, pp. 9–10.

9. See above, chapter one and the documents in Appendix I. On *The Battle of Anghiari,* which was commissioned by the Signoria on 18 October 1503, see Brizio, "The Painter," 44–50; *Notebooks,* ed. I. Richter, 352.

10. *Notebooks,* ed. I. Richter, 194–195.

11. Ibid. In other regards as well, it needs to be added that Leonardo was famed in his lifetime for the ability to paint a portrait that looked so much like the subject that the viewer could mistake the painting for the person. Cf. chapter one, note 38, citing the letter of Ugolini to Machiavelli of 11 November 1503.

12. For the rules of the aerial perspective, which uses color to imitate three-dimensional effects in space, see *Notebooks,* ed. J. P. Richter, 2.159–166. The *Mona Lisa* was painted in Florence (c. 1505); see also the background of *Ste. Anne and the Virgin* (c. 1508).

13. Heydenreich, "Military Architect," 149.

14. Compare ibid., 146–149 and *Notebooks,* ed. J. P. Richter, vol. 2, Plates CXII–CXIII with the documents in Appendix I.

15. The astute reader should realize, as the Medici and other contemporaries would have known, that Niccolò Machiavelli had more political experience than the man to whom *The Prince* is dedicated. On Lorenzo de' Medici's preference for private life and his refusal to play the public role expected of him by the Medici family, see Schevill, *The Medici.* In the context of this dedication to Lorenzo, Machiavelli's self-deprecatory remark that it might "be thought presumption if a man from a low and mean state dares to discuss and give rules for the governments of princes" (*Prince,* Dedicatory Letter; p. 4) has an ironic connotation.

16. The novelty of this perspective is, as has been noted, implied by the opening lines of chapter fifteen of *The Prince*: "And because I know that many have written of this, I fear that in writing of it again, I may be held *presumptuous,* especially since in disputing this matter I depart from the orders of others" (p. 61). Leonardo drafted the following Proemium for his *Treatise on Painting*: "I am fully conscious (*sic*) that, not being a literary man, certain *presumptuous persons* (*prosuntuoso*) will think that they may reasonably blame me; alleging that I am not a man of letters. Foolish folks! do they not know that I might retort as Marius did to the Roman Patricians by saying: That they, who deck themselves out in the labours of others will not allow me my own . . . they do not know that my subjects are to be dealt with by experience rather than by words; and [experience] has been the mistress of all those who wrote well" (*Notebooks,* ed. J. P. Richter, 1.14). In a note to this passage, Richter points out that the remark attributed to Marius cannot be found in

any ancient text, though a similar statement was made by Meninius Agrippa to the plebes.

17. Hence Mansfield's comment on the first paragraph of the dedication of *The Prince*: "NM switches from a singular to the plural, a device he uses frequently" (*Prince*, p. 3, note). If there is a possibility that a writer is being intentionally deceptive, such stylistic puzzles cannot be ignored or dismissed as carelessness, as some are wont to do. It is especially prudent to assume that Machiavelli used language with care and skill, for he was one of the greatest prose masters of the Italian language, and described himself as a "poet." See de Grazia, *Machiavelli in Hell*, 34–36, 122, *et passim*.

18. In contrast, in many other key passages of *The Prince*, "you" is the formal plural; for example, Machiavelli says in chapter twenty-five: "And if *you* consider Italy, which is the seat of these variations and that which has given them motion, *you* will see a country without dams and without any dike" (p. 99).

19. For example, Machiavelli states the general rule that "*one* should not care about incurring the reputation of those vices without which it is difficult to save *one*'s state" (*Prince*, ch. 15; p. 62).

20. Note also that, in chapter nine, Machiavelli speaks of "*citizens*" and "*everyone*" whereas in chapter seventeen, from the prince's perspective, Machiavelli says "*they*" and "*them.*"

21. This example is surely intended to make one think, since Nabis was eventually assassinated (*Discourses*, III, 6); elsewhere in the *Discourses* (I, 10, 40), Nabis is described by Machiavelli as a tyrant. Indeed, Nabis is one of those who "are dismissed with scorn" (I, 10; p. 135).

22. Note that Agathocles is presented as the archetype of "those who have attained a principality through crimes" (the title of chapter seven).

23. See also the description of Julius II in *The Prince*, ch. 25 (p. 100), and compare *Discourses*, I, 27 (pp. 177–178).

24. Machiavelli's explanation of the inability to adjust "behavior" to fit changed circumstances nicely balances what we today call "nature versus nurture": "There are two reasons why we cannot change our ways. First, it is impossible to go against what nature inclines us to. Secondly, having got on well by adopting a certain line of conduct, it is impossible to persuade men that they can get on well by acting otherwise. It thus comes about that a man's fortune changes, for she changes his circumstances but he does not change his ways" (*Discourses*, III, 9; pp. 431–432). An example is Piero Soderini's inability to abandon his "good natured and patient way" when confronted by the need to counter the imperious Pope Julius II (ibid.).

25. Cf. *Florentine Histories*, IV, 1, p. 146: "for a city based on good laws and good orders has no necessity, as have others, for the virtue of a single man to maintain it. *Many ancient republics endowed with such laws and orders had states with long lives.*"

26. Machiavelli's use of the term "impetus" here deserves mention, since he uses it in the technical sense that Leonardo introduced in physics; as modified by Galileo's understanding of inertia, this concept became the force of Newtonian mechanics.

27. Heydenreich, "Military Architect," 142. None of these events is discussed in de Grazia's biography; for the only mentions of Pisa in *Machiavelli in Hell*, see 16, 98, 188; the only reference to Leonardo, apart from the letter cited in chapter one, note 38, is a passing reference to his painting *Lady with an Ermine* (ibid., p. 137).

28. Fachard, *Biagio Buonaccorsi*, 228–230. Compare Heydenreich's conclusion ("Military Architect," 143–144): "Leonardo's exact position in this scheme is very difficult to determine. The facts that he was appointed adviser by the government and that he accepted the task lead us to conclude that he must have been entrusted with the plan. But his own judgment is unknown, and from the new material that has come to light in the Madrid notebooks we must deduce that he was not as some have believed, the originator of the idea, but rather that he remained undecided and certainly very critical." See also *Notebooks*, ed. I. Richter, 350–353.

29. "Leonardo was sent off in July 1503 by order of the council, to the Florentine camp to examine the work of trench digging which had been undertaken. For over a year the plan to divert the river was worked upon. It made provision for one canal, in the area of the estuary, that was to lead the water of the Arno off into the river Serchio, and for another canal from Vico Pisano to the Stagno di Livorno. The instructions of the Florentine council issued through the letters of Machiavelli to headquarters reveal quite clearly that the project had been planned in detail. Two thousand workmen in 150 to 200 days were to accomplish the enormous shift of earth necessary to dig canals approximately 40 to 60 feet wide, and 16 to 21 feet deep. The calculation proved to be erroneous. Five times as much manpower would have been necessary, according to the more realistic calculations of other experts, to complete the affair. Besides that, the work suffered considerable difficulties. It proved to be impossible to muster the thousands of workers required, or rather to keep them at work, especially since wages were frequently overdue. A completed section of canal did not withstand the mass of water fed into it and collapsed. Because of such setbacks, opinion was split among the commanders. Machiavelli defended his idea in entreating letters and reports to the council until autumn 1504, but in vain. In October the enterprise was definitely broken off—much to the triumph of the Pisans. The Florentines had to fight another five years for Pisa, for only in 1509 did the exhausted city give itself up" (Heydenreich, "Military Architect," 142–143). Compare Buonaccorsi's report, reproduced in Appendix I.5 A–B.

30. Heydenreich, "Military Architect," 144. Accompanying the text are illustrations of the maps and sketches recently discovered in the Madrid codex

as well as the previously known map of the Arno from the collection at Windsor, accessible in *Notebooks,* ed. J. P. Richter, vol. 2, Plate CXII.

31. On one of the maps of the peaceful project, Leonardo wrote: "The law which establishes that those who want to make mills can conduct water through any land, paying twice its value." On another, he wrote: "Prato, Pistoia, and Pisa, as well as Florence, will gain 200,000 ducats a year, and will lend a hand and money to this useful work" (Heydenreich, "The Military Architect," 145). It is difficult to believe that Machiavelli was unaware of the contrast between this visionary (dare one say "utopian") scheme, and the actual reality of the ill-fated efforts during the war between Florence and Pisa: the fact that Leonardo was so familiar with the topography and hydrography would have been essential to Machiavelli's confidence in 1503/4 that the planned diversion from Pisa would succeed. For a fuller analysis, see below, chapter seven.

32. See Zammattio, "Mechanics of Water and Stone," 191–207 (which also describes Leonardo's later project for rechanneling the Adda River between Milan and Lake Como) and Heydenreich, "Military Architect," 152–163.

33. "Tercets on Fortune," lines 151–159 (*Chief Works,* 2.748). This poem is not dated, though a reference to "Caesar and Alexander" in the tercet following the citation above suggests that it was written after 1503 with the fall of the Borgias in mind.

34. "On Ambition," lines 86–87 (*Chief Works,* 2.757).

35. There are, however, additional reasons for Machiavelli's silence on Leonardo and the projected rechanneling of the Arno. On the one hand, if Machiavelli considered Leonardo a friend in 1513, it would have seemed inappropriate to cite the failed project once Leonardo went to Rome to work in the Vatican under the patronage of Giuliano dei Medici (apparently the original addressee of *The Prince*). On the other hand, while Machiavelli seems to have been fully aware of the importance of Leonardo's scientific and technical knowledge, he sought to show the need for political control of science. As a result, it may not be entirely fortuitous that in the *Florentine Histories* Machiavelli discusses the failure of an earlier Florentine project to win a war by rechanneling a river which had been directed by the architect Brunelleschi (IV, 23; pp. 169–170). See below, chapter seven and Appendix III.

36. The "you" used twice in this sentence is the formal plural (*Voi*): the sentence is not addressed to an actual prince like Giuliano or Lorenzo de' Medici, but rather to potential princes, like the addresses of the *Discourses.* Compare chapter two.

37. This equivalence is reinforced in the last chapter of *The Prince* when Machiavelli exhorts "your illustrious house" to end "barbarian domination" in Italy by imitating such founders as Moses, Cyrus, and Theseus. Having stated that "nothing brings as much honor to a man rising newly as the new laws and the new orders found by him," Machiavelli only speaks of the necessity "to prepare such arms for oneself so as to be able with Italian virtue to defend oneself

from foreigners"; he calls this needed reorganization of the military "a change in orders," based on the experiences of the Spanish, French, and German armies (ch. 26; pp. 103–105). In short, the last chapter associates the lessons of the three countries with their military forces, suggesting "dikes" or "orders" represent "good arms" whereas "dams" stand for "good laws" (cf. ch. 12; p. 48, discussed below).

38. As if to reinforce the puzzling character of the image of rape as a means of controlling history, consider the plot of *Mandragola*: Lucrezia is "coaxed and not treated roughly or with violence" by Callimaco, who does not follow Machiavelli's apparent advice "to beat her and strike her down." Successful seduction has more lasting benefits than rape. Leonardo's text is from 1506–1509 and concerns the Arno in Florence; see Leonardo, *Notebooks*, ed. J. P. Richter, 2.230; Pedretti, *Literary Works*, 2.181. For the 1490s as the date of Leonardo's passage on rivers as the "foremost" cause of destruction, ibid., 2.161–162.

39. In other words, whereas the analogy between fortune and a river concerns cities, states, and humans as a species, the metaphor of fortune as a woman concerns the leader as an individual. This distinction corresponds to Machiavelli's deeper distinction between simple and "mixed" or "composite bodies" (e.g., *Discourses*, III, 1; p. 385). For additional evidence, see the verses of "On Fortune" immediately after the description of fortune as a river: "Tercets On Fortune," lines 160–166 (*Chief Works*, 2.749).

40. See *Discourses*, I, 39, p. 208, where Machiavelli attributes the mismanagement of Florence's war against Pisa to the abolition of the "Ten of War," shifting conduct of the war "from the very men who had been administering it wisely" to the Signoria as a result of "complaints by the populace" occasioned by "heavy taxation." Commentators have usually failed to see this remark as a comment on Machiavelli's own experience as Secretary to the "Ten of War," and his frustration on being overruled in 1504. Machiavelli thus implies that if the institutions responsible for military policy are defective, even the best technical expertise and strategy will fail.

41. This priority of politics over the natural sciences is implied by the parallel which Machiavelli sees between the dominance of antiquity in the arts of statesmanship and medicine (*Discourses*, I, Pref.; p. 98). Cf. Aristotle, *Nicomachean Ethics*, I.1094a–b, a passage Machiavelli imitates at the end of the first paragraph of *The Prince*, ch. 6; p. 22. This priority can be found as early as 1509 in Machiavelli's poem "On Ambition," lines 112–114 (*Chief Works*, 2.737): "And when someone blames nature . . . discipline can make up where nature is lacking."

42. "Besides, one cannot maintain a province as inhabited or preserve the inhabitants well distributed within it without this order [of republics or principalities]. For all places in it are not either productive or healthy; hence it arises that men abandon the latter and are wanting in the former, and if there

is no mode of getting men back to what they abandoned or to go where they are wanting, the province will in a short time be spoiled for one part becomes deserted from too few inhabitants, another part poor from too many. *And because nature cannot compensate for this disorder, it is necessary that industry compensate for it: for unhealthy countries become healthy by means of a multitude of men that seizes them at a stroke; they cleanse the earth by cultivation and purge the airs with fires, things that nature could never provide*" (*Florentine Histories*, II, 1; p. 32).

43. Machiavelli is silent with regard to the most striking apparent exception to this rule: Jesus. Could it be that this silence implies that Jesus himself was "ruined" by his crucifixion, but chance (which he had no way of controlling) led to the survival and spread of his beliefs, leading to the adoption of Christianity as the official religion of Rome by the Emperor Constantine? In the *Discourses*, Machiavelli says that, "of all men that are praised, those are praised most who have played *the chief part in founding a religion*. Next come those who *have founded either republics or kingdoms*" (I, 10; p. 134). To receive praise as the founder of a religion, one need only "play the chief part"; to receive praise as the founder of a state, a man must be effectively responsible for the founding (with his own "arms" and "virtue" to use the terms in *The Prince*). The success of Jesus was due to chance, since he had no way to "keep" his disciples "in that persuasion" (unlike Moses when he came down from Mount Sinai). "He who reads the Bible with discernment will see that, in order that Moses might set about making laws and institutions, he had to kill a very great number of men" (*Discourses*, III, 30; p. 486).

44. *Art of War*, Book II (*Chief Works*, 2.623). The sequel is extraordinary: "*Then* [in antiquity] *men overcome in war either were killed or kept in perpetual slavery*, so that they passed their lives wretchedly; conquered cities were either laid waste or the inhabitants driven out, their goods taken from them and they themselves sent wandering through the world. Hence those conquered in war suffered the utmost of every misery. Terrorized by this dread, men kept military training alive and honored those who were excellent in it. *Today this fear has for the most part disappeared*; of the conquered, few are killed; no one is long held a prisoner because captives are easily freed. Cities, even though they have rebelled many times, are not destroyed; men are allowed to keep their property, so that *the greatest evil they fear is a tax*. Hence *men do not wish to submit to military regulations* and to endure steady hardships under them in order to escape dangers they fear little" (ibid.). It is worth reflecting on the possibility that, in the twentieth century, nuclear weapons and other technological revolutions are transforming these pervasive effects of Christian mercy.

45. The "you" in this passage is the formal plural (*Voi*), not the singular (*Tu*). Unlike the passage in chapter twelve, there is no indication in the last phrase that "one" (whether laws or arms) is prior to the "other."

46. In the context of discussing republics in the *Florentine Histories,* Machiavelli describes this duality as "good laws and good orders" (IV, 1; p. 146). Even when the precise words vary, the need for a duality of principles is emphasized.

47. *Social Contract,* 3.6; cited above, p. 33.

48. Machiavelli's precise terms are worth noting: "Therefore the duke, before everything else, should have *created* a Spaniard pope, and if he could not, should have *accepted* Rouen, and not San Pietro ad Vincula." The identity of his father's successor was Cesare's top priority; his best option was to have gained such control that he could effectively name the next pope (in which case he should have chosen a Spaniard), his second best tolerable outcome was to accept a Frenchman (Cardinal Georges d'Amboise, Bishop of Rouen). Machiavelli had firsthand evidence that "Rouen" would not have been able to block Cesare's plans, based on his own personal conversations (*The Prince*, ch. 3; p. 15).

49. On Cesare's mistaken belief that he could control Julius II—and the cleverness with which the new pope outmaneuvered Borgia—see Machiavelli's dispatches from Rome (*Chief Works*, 1.142–160).

50. Could it be that the sentence introducing Machiavelli's summary of his account of Borgia should be read: "I would not know *how* to reproach *him*" (since Cesare is already both infamous and dead)? On the difference between praise and blame of the dead and the living, cf. *Art of War*, Book I (*Chief Works*, 2.568).

51. As Mansfield notes, "NM was in Rome at the time of the conclave that elected Julius II pope in October–December 1503" (p. 32, note 14).

52. Later, Machiavelli adds a further rule showing the error of this calculation: "And above all, a prince should live with his subjects *so that no single unforeseen event whether bad or good* has to make him change" (*Prince*, ch. 8; p. 38).

53. *Chief Works*, 1.128.

54. Ibid., 142. This probability is important: although, as Machiavelli points out in *The Prince*, Cesare might have blocked Julius's election, in actuality Borgia was deceived into supporting his erstwhile and future enemy by promises of personal gain.

55. Ibid., 143–144.

56. This interpretation is further confirmed by Machiavelli's dispatch of 6 November 1502 (ibid., 145), in which he reports speaking personally with Cesare Borgia for the first time after the papal election—but does *not* mention the remark attributed to Cesare in chapter seven of *The Prince*.

57. The parallels between the situation of Cesare Borgia in 1502/3 and Lorenzo de' Medici in 1513–1519 are underscored by the concluding lines of the dedication to Lorenzo, in which Machiavelli expresses "my extreme desire that you arrive at the greatness that *fortune* and your other qualities promise you" (p. 4). Both Cesare and Lorenzo de' Medici are examples of rulers who

came to power through fortune; i.e., both are ultimately bad examples for anyone who wants to found a lasting state.

58. This conclusion does not presuppose the reader's knowledge that Cesare lived until 1507: as Machiavelli tells the story in *The Prince,* the brief tenure of Pope Pius III, who was elected on 22 September 1503 and died on 18 October is omitted, making it seem that his conversation with Cesare at the election of Julius II occurred in the days immediately following the death of Cesare's father, Alexander VI. In fact, almost two and a half months intervened. Machiavelli apparently does not blame Cesare for the choice of Pius III ("Romagne waited for him for more than a month" [*Prince,* ch. 6; p. 32]); had Cesare still been so sick that he couldn't influence the election of Julius at the end of October, he would have had the excuse of "necessity" (for Machiavelli, always a justification).

59. Burckhardt, *Civilization of the Renaissance in Italy,* 1.132. Given Machiavelli's presence in Rome at the time, this contemporary report underscores the deep ironies of the praise of Cesare in chapter seven of *The Prince*—but it also may be intended to suggest the importance of other experiences of Machiavelli at Cesare's court.

60. Lest this seem an absurd suggestion, consider *Discourses* I, 27 (pp. 127–128): entitled "Very Rarely Do Men Know How To Be Either Wholly Good or Wholly Bad," Machiavelli tells the story of Giovampagolo Baglioni, "tyrant" of Perugia, who "thought nothing of incest or of publicly murdering his relatives" but, when presented with the opportunity to kill Pope Julius II and thereby gain "immortal fame," allowed himself to be taken prisoner. In *The Prince,* the only mention of the Baglioni occurs in the chapter on Cesare Borgia, where we learn that, with the Vitelli and Orsini, they "came to Rome" after Alexander VI's death but could not get support against Borgia (*The Prince,* ch. 7; p. 32).

61. Burckhardt, *Civilization of the Renaissance in Italy,* 1.129.

62. Ibid., 129–130. Note that Alexander's plans contradict Machiavelli's own judgment that Cesare needed to ensure that his father's successor was a Spaniard or, if that were impossible, the French Cardinal of Rouen (*Prince,* ch. 7; p 33). For the events discussed here and the possibility that Machiavelli's discussion of Cesare is intended to teach the need for action of precisely this nature, combining patricide with the destruction of the Church as a secular power, see John T. Scott and Vickie Sullivan, "Patricide and the Plot of *The Prince*: Cesare Borgia and Machiavelli's Italy," *American Political Science Review* 88 (1994): 887–900. I am greatly indebted to the authors for discussions of the issues associated with Machiavelli's treatment of Cesare.

63. Compare the discussion of the "virtuous tyrant" in *Discourses,* II, 2; p. 276.

64. Note the difference between "most excellent captains" and "most excellent men" and compare the difference between the "military" and "civilian"

ways of life in the Preface to *The Art of War* (*Chief Works*, 1.566). The "most excellent men" must combine the military and civilian excellences, whereas "the most excellent captains" have only a partial virtue.

65. Machiavelli's silence on the *name* of the "founder" of "the Christian *commonwealth*" is worth noting: was this founder Jesus, Paul, or—most probably of all—Constantine, the first "ruler" to adopt Christianity as the religion of the state or "commonwealth"?

66. As evidence, in over twenty-five years of teaching Machiavelli, I have only encountered one student who remembered Moses doing anything besides breaking the Tablets of the Law after finding the Israelites dancing around the Golden Calf. Cf. *Discourses*, III, 30; p. 486, cited above.

67. See Volume 2 (1756) of Jacob N. Moreau, *L'Observateur, ou Letters de M. Van ** à M. H** de la Haye sur l'état présent de l'Europe*, 8 vols. (La Haye, 1755–1759).

68. The immediate sequel to the passage just cited contains an important textual uncertainty. Mansfield, following several editions, reads: ". . . will be praised by everyone. For the vulgar are taken in by the appearance and the outcome of a thing, and in the world there is no one but the vulgar; the few have a place there when the many have somewhere to lean on" (*Prince*, ch. 18; p. 71). As Mansfield notes, however, one manuscript reads: "the few have no place there..." (ibid., note 5). The sense, seemingly rendered more clearly by the manuscript Mansfield does not follow, is that most humans ("the vulgar") are taken in by "the appearance and the outcome of a thing" and the "few"— those with a brain that "understands by itself" (*Prince,* ch. 22; p. 92)—have no effect "in the world" of politics, where for all practical purposes, "there is no one but the vulgar."

69. See the analysis of this passage by Najemy, *Between Friends*, 190–193. While Najemy identifies Machiavelli's "huge and audacious claim . . . to leap over the pitfalls and ambiguities of everyday speech into a realm of understanding based on direct contact with things" (p. 193), Najemy does not seem to consider that such scientific knowledge of human affairs is possible. As I will argue in the succeeding chapters, this is precisely what is at issue.

70. *Discourses*, I, 11–15; pp. 139–152. "Of all men that are praised, those are praised most who played the chief part in founding a religion" (ibid., I, 10; p. 134). Machiavelli himself symbolizes this by the fact that Moses, the lawgiver who could be said to have founded the Hebrew religion, is the only name included in the list of the "greatest examples" of founders in both *The Prince*, chapter six ("I say that the most excellent are Moses, Cyrus, Romulus, Theseus, and the like"; p. 22) and *Discourses*, Book I, chapter nine ("Moses, Lycurgus, Solon and other founders of kingdoms and republics who assumed authority that they might formulate laws to the common good"; p. 133).

71. This passage should suffice to disprove the thesis that Machiavelli was a Christian (see note 75 below): in the context of a discussion of religion, he flatly denies Paul's claim—e.g., Romans 5:15–20—that the coming of Christ changed the "order" of human life and death. Compare the critique of Christianity in *Art of War*, Book II (*Chief Works*, 2.623), cited above.

72. See the analysis of the "three parts of the soul"—desire or appetite, spirit or *thymos*, and reason—in Plato's *Republic*, IV.436b–441b.

73. That some individuals are willing to bind themselves to friends "by a chain of obligation" is illustrated by Machiavelli's own behavior in dedicating the *Discourses* to Zanobi Buondelmonti and Cosimo Rucellai as a way of "showing some gratitude for benefits received" (*Discourses*, Dedication; p. 93). When Machiavelli says "men are wicked" (or sometimes "men are sad [*triste*]"), he does not mean that *all* humans are irremediably sinful in the Christian sense. See the praise of Cosimo Rucellai at the outset of Book I of *The Art of War* (*Chief Works*, 2.568). The difficulty of "obligations" among "friends" based on "love" would seem to be greater in public or political matters than in private relationships based on "greatness and nobility of spirit." Cf. Aristotle, *Nicomachean Ethics*, VIII, esp. 1156b.

74. E.g., see the account of the origin of the "White" and "Black" parties in Florence in *Florentine Histories*, II, 16–20; pp. 68–73.

75. *Discourses*, II, 2; p. 277. For the argument that Machiavelli was a Christian, see de Grazia, *Machiavelli in Hell*, ch. 5. Although de Grazia claims that Machiavelli believed that "Christianity is the true faith" while criticizing the Church (*Machiavelli in Hell*, 89), it is hard to accept his description of Machiavelli's views as "fairly conventional, paganizing, Christian ideas of the essence of man, his creation and fall, his human nature once fallen, his coming together with other men and their banding into political organization" (ibid., 87). For example, de Grazia simply misreads Book II, chapter five of the *Discourses*, interpreting this text to mean that Machiavelli "doubts that the world is eternal, as some philosophers (possibly those stemming from the Arab, Averroës) would have it, and believes false that it goes back 40,000 or 50,000 years, as the histories of Diodorus Siculus would have it" (ibid., 77). Compare Machiavelli's own words: "One can well believe, therefore, that what Christianity did with regard to Paganism, Paganism did to the religion that preceded it; and, as there have been two or three changes of religion in five or six thousand years, *the record of what happened before that has been lost; or, if of it there remains a trace, it is regarded as a fable* and no credence is given to it; as has happened with regard to the *History of Diodorus Siculus,* which covers a period of some forty or fifty thousand years, but is looked upon as untrustworthy, as I believe it to be" (*Discourses*, II, 5; p. 289). Clearly Machiavelli is pointing to the transformation of prehistory into fable—and uses this as evidence to contradict the biblical account in Genesis. Given Machiavelli's

insistence on the political imperative of religious belief for the many (e.g., ibid., I, 12), his use of the word "God" and other images of both Christianity and astrology need hardly be equated with a personal belief in supernatural or occult forces.

76. *Mandragola*, Prologue, p. 10.

77. Ibid., Act 1; pp. 12–13. The dramatic date of the action (1504) coincides with the year of the diversion of the Arno and Machiavelli's collaboration with Leonardo in fortifying La Verruca and providing technical assistance to Jacopo Appiani of Piombino. Is this intended to suggest the origin of Machiavelli's goal of harnessing scientific knowledge and political prudence in a radically new approach to human life?

78. When pressured to have sexual relations with a man who is not her husband, Lucrezia exclaims: "if I were the only woman remaining in the world and if human nature had to rise again from me, I couldn't believe that such a course would be allowed to me" (ibid., Act III, scene 10; p. 35). Machiavelli's parody of the biblical account of Abraham and Sarah comes to mind.

79. The supervision is direct and graphically described by the triumphant Nicia, who tells Ligurio that he has personally stripped "naked" the disguised Callimaco, examined his skin and "other things," then "pulled him after me, and led him into the bedroom in the dark" and "put him to bed," waiting to see "how the thing was going" before leaving the couple (ibid., Act V, scene 2; pp. 50–51).

80. Ibid., Act V, scene 6; p. 55.

81. Ibid., p. 7.

82. Francesco Guicciardini, Governor of Florence in 1526.

83. Pope Clement VII, who named Guicciardini. In this song, note how the traditional otherwordly symbols of Christian faith are transvalued into earthly pleasure.

84. Letter from Machiavelli to Guicciardini, in *The Prince*, ed. Adams, pp. 133–135.

Chapter 4

1. Letter of Alexandre Kojève to Leo Strauss, 29 October 1953, in Strauss, *On Tyranny*, rev. and expanded edition, 262.

2. Najemy, *Between Friends*, 193. As noted frequently in chapters one and two, Najemy is one of the few interpreters of Machiavelli who seeks to situate him precisely in the context of both his practical experience and his knowledge of the philosophical as well as literary traditions of the Renaissance.

3. Ibid., 58 (citing research by Sergio Bertelli and Franco Gaeta). As Najemy points out, one can find a precursor for Machiavelli's distinction be-

tween the "effectual truth" and "imagination" in Lucretius (ibid., 190, citing *De rerum natura*, 4.51–52): the image of a thing "bears a look and a shape like the body of that from which it is shed to go on its way." On the relationship between Lucretius and contemporary evolutionary theory, see Roger D. Masters, "Gradualism and Discontinuous Change in Evolutionary Biology and Political Philosophy," in *The Dynamics of Evolution: The Punctuated Equilibrium Debate in the Natural and Social Sciences,* ed. Albert Somit and Steven Peterson (Ithaca, N.Y.: Cornell University Press, 1992), 282–319.

4. Leonardo's notes outline an empirical approach to comparative anatomy; this fragment comes from a list dividing the animal kingdom into four categories:

Man. The description of man, which includes that of such creatures as are of almost the same species, as Apes, Monkeys and the like, which are many.

The Lion and its kindred, as Panthers, Wildcats [*Leonza*], Tigers, Leopards, Wolfs, Lynxes, Spanish cats, common cats, and the like.

The Horse and its kindred, as Mule, Ass and the like, with incisor teeth above and below.

The Bull and its allies with horns and without upper incisors as the Buffalo, Stag Fallow Deer, Wild Goat, Swine, Goat, wild Goats . . . Muskdeers, Chamois, Giraffe.

(*Notebooks,* ed. J. P. Richter, 2.118)

On Leonardo's comparative anatomy and biology, see Istituto Geografico d'Agostino, *Leonardo da Vinci,* 363–398.

5. Note, however, that Machiavelli advises the prince to "always be out hunting" and "learn the nature of sites" (*Prince,* ch. 14; p. 59; cf. *Discourses,* III, 39). On this advice, and its relation to the study of natural science (and especially contemporary biology), see the conclusion of this book.

6. For an excellent introduction, see Robert Wright, *The Moral Animal* (New York: Pantheon, 1994). The contemporary understanding of evolution is often summarized as the "neo-Darwinian synthesis"; for classic statements of the theory, see George Gaylord Simpson, *The Meaning of Evolution,* rev. ed. (New Haven, Conn.: Yale University Press, 1958); Theodosius Dobzhansky, *Evolution, Genetics, and Man* (New York: John Wiley, 1955); and Ernst Mayr, *Animal Species and Evolution* (Cambridge, Mass.: Harvard University Press, 1963). This so-called "classical" approach to natural selection was modified by William D. Hamilton's introduction of the concept of "inclusive fitness": see "The Genetical Theory of Social Behavior," *Journal of Theoretical Biology* 7 (1964): 1–52 and, for the work that established the importance of this insight, Edward O. Wilson, *Sociobiology* (Cambridge, Mass.: Harvard University Press, 1975). More recently, Stephen Jay Gould has challenged the

assumption that slow and gradual change by natural selection is the dominant force in evolution: see *Wonderful Life* (New York: Norton, 1989). For a balanced view of the resulting controversy over rates of change, suggesting the diversity of evolutionary processes and the impossibility of reducing the history of living things to any single theoretical principle, see Somit and Peterson, *Dynamics of Evolution*. For the relevance of evolutionary theory to human behavior, see also Richard Alexander, *Darwinism and Human Affairs* (Seattle: University of Washington Press, 1979).

7. For this example, I am indebted to Francisco J. Ayala, "The Mechanisms of Evolution," *Scientific American* 239 (1978): 56–69.

8. For an excellent survey of recent work showing the importance of this distinction, with an emphasis on its relevance to male-female differences, see Matt Ridley, *The Red Queen: Sex and the Evolution of Human Nature* (New York: Macmillan, 1994). Those familiar with neo-Darwinian theory should note that the distinction made in the text does *not* correspond exactly with the conventional distinction between "natural selection" and "sexual selection": whether the selective pressure comes from conspecifics of the opposite sex or from other organisms in the environment, this new research concerns *interactions* between organisms when an adaptive trait in one leads to selection for counteractive adaptations in others. I have called this "relativistic selection": see review of Ridley, *The Red Queen* in *Ethology and Sociobiology* 16 (1995): 173–179.

9. For an introduction, see John Maynard-Smith, "The Evolution of Behavior," *Scientific American* 239 (1978): 176–192. Game theory, in which independent decision-makers are assumed to pick the most favorable strategy on the basis of interaction with other similarly strategic actors, has become a major tool in evolutionary theory. See especially Robert Axelrod and William D. Hamilton, "The Evolution of Cooperation," *Science* 211 (1981): 1390–96 and Jack Hirshleifer, "Evolutionary Models in Economics and Law: Cooperation versus Conflict Strategies," in *Research in Law and Economics* (Greenwich, Conn.: JAI Press, 1982), 4.1–60. Machiavelli does not adopt this kind of mathematical formalization, or the abstract cost-benefit explanation that—since the pre-socratics like Antiphon the Sophist and Thrasymachus—had been used to explain human society as a social contract (see Masters, "Gradualism and Discontinuous Change"). In contrast to Hobbes, Locke, and the modern natural right tradition, Machiavelli sees an irreducible complexity and diversity in the factors that generate positive and negative consequences for an individual; hence, unlike social contract theorists, utilitarians, economists, and behaviorist psychologists, Machiavelli does not treat "pleasure" and "pain" as homogeneous or linear factors whose value can be easily added and subtracted using mathematical precision. Contemporary sociobiologists, whose cost-benefit models concern the transmission of genes to future generations ("inclusive fit-

ness"), find the same complexity at the level of the organism's behavioral responses and strategies. Despite the apparent difference, as I will show below, it is Machiavelli—not Hobbes and the tradition following him—whose perspective is confirmed by recent biological research.

10. Paul Ehrlich, David S. Dobkin, and Darryl Whey, *The Birder's Handbook: A Field Guide to the Natural History of North American Birds* (New York: Simon and Schuster, 1988). On the general issue of behavior and evolution, see David Barash, *Sociobiology and Behavior*, 2nd ed. (New York: Elsevier, 1982); Robert Trivers, *Social Evolution* (Menlo Park, Calif.: Benjamin/Cummings, 1985); and—for an older view—Anne Roe and George Gaylord Simpson, eds., *Behavior and Evolution* (New Haven, Conn.: Yale University Press, 1958).

11. For the analysis in this section, see Wilson, *Sociobiology*; Barash, *Sociobiology and Behavior*; and Trivers, *Social Evolution*. On hamadryas baboons and other primates, the first major contemporary survey was Irven Devore, ed., *Primate Behavior* (New York: Holt, Rinehard, and Winston, 1965); see also Hans Kummer, *Primate Societies* (Chicago: Aldine Atherton, 1971) as well as Robin I. M. Dunbar, *Primate Social Systems* (Ithaca, N.Y.: Cornell University Press, 1988). On the methodological difficulties of establishing adequate scientific explanations of adaptation, see Philip Kitscher, *Vaulting Ambition: Sociobiology and the Quest for Human Nature* (Cambridge, Mass.: MIT Press, 1985).

12. See Glendon Schubert and Roger D. Masters, eds. *Primate Politics* (Carbondale: Southern Illinois University Press, 1991), especially chs. 1 and 5.

13. While it will be necessary to return to this theme, for the moment it should be enough to point out two distinct levels on which the attribution of human behavior to conscious choice can often be questioned. First, at the individual level, neuroscientists have now shown that much human behavior is the consequence of preconscious or unconscious information processing for which conscious statements provide a "rationalization": Michael Gazzaniga, *The Social Brain* (New York: Basic Books, 1985) and Pawel Lewicki, Thomas Hill, and Maria Czyzewski, "Non-Conscious Acquisition of Information," *American Psychologist* 47 (1992): 796–802. Secondly, at the social level, cultures can evolve much like species due to factors that transcend the consciousness of any individual: e.g., Luigi Luca Cavalli-Sforza, "Genes, Peoples and Languages," *Scientific American* 265 (1991): 104–110 and William Durham, *Coevolution: Genes, Culture, and Human Diversity* (Stanford, Calif.: Stanford University Press, 1992).

14. Recent books for a general audience have shown how careful observation reveals unmistakable intentionality in the social behavior of mammals. For lions (and domestic cats), see Elizabeth Marshall Thomas, *The Tribe of Tiger: Cats and Their Culture* (New York: Simon and Schuster, 1994); for wolves as well as domesticated dogs, Elizabeth Marshall Thomas, *The Hidden Life of*

Dogs (New York: Houghton Mifflin, 1992); for mammals generally, Vicki Hearne, *Adam's Task* (New York: Viking, 1987). The phenomena of animal intentionality have often been obscured by academic methods based on theoretical or ideological bias; compare Schubert and Masters, *Primate Politics*, Conclusion.

15. Masters, *The Nature of Politics*, ch. 1, citing David Barash, "The Evolution of Marmot Societies: A General Theory," *Science* 185 (1974): 415–420 as well as Barash, *Sociobiology and Behavior.*

16. In addition to the citations in notes 6 through 9 above, see the applications of this discipline to human social behavior in Napoleon Chagnon and William Irons, eds., *Evolutionary Biology and Human Social Behavior* (North Scituate, Mass.: Duxbury Press, 1979) and Eric Alden Smith and Bruce Winterhalder, *Evolutionary Ecology and Human Behavior* (New York: Aldine de Gruyter, 1992).

17. See the references in note 11. For an example that is more directly relevant to human evolution, see the extraordinary analysis of chimpanzee "culture" in William C. McGrew, *Chimpanzee Material Culture* (Cambridge: Cambridge University Press, 1992) as well as the study of social behavior in the closely related bonobo (or "pygmy chimpanzee"), Takyoshi Kano, *The Last Ape: Pygmy Chimpanzee Behavior and Ecology* (Stanford, Calif.: Stanford University Press, 1992). As McGrew shows by applying the techniques used by cultural anthropologists when comparing human societies to the comparative study of chimpanzees in different environments, there is now incontrovertible evidence of "cultural" variation among chimpanzees.

18. Some critics have been explicitly motivated by political (or "ideological") concerns—e.g., Richard Lewontin, Stephen Rose, and Leon Kamin, *Not in Our Genes* (New York: Pantheon, 1984)—but others have emphasized scientific questions (e.g., Kitcher, *Vaulting Ambition*). For an early selection of texts on both sides of the debate, see Arthur Caplan, ed., *The Sociobiology Debate* (New York: Harper & Row, 1978).

19. For chimpanzees, the strongest evidence is probably the experimental work with learning and communication: see Sue Savage-Rumbaugh and Roger Lewin, *Kanzi: The Ape at the Brink of the Human Mind* (New York: Wiley, 1994). See also Shirley Strum, *Almost Human: A Journey into the World of Baboons* (New York: W. W. Norton, 1987).

20. R. W. Byrne and A. Whiten, eds., *Machiavellian Intelligence: Social Expertise and the Evolution of Intellect in Monkeys, Apes, and Humans* (Oxford: Clarendon Press, 1987) as well as "Cognitive Evolution in Primates: Evidence from Tactical Deception," *Man* 27 (1992): 609–627.

21. Alexander H. Harcourt and Frans de Waal, eds., *Coalitions and Alliances in Humans and Other Animals* (Oxford: Oxford University Press, 1992). On the likelihood that ape social structures are organized around loose

"networks" rather than the more rigid dominance hierarchies observed in rhesus monkeys and other simians, see Alexandra Maryanski and Jonathan Turner, *The Social Cage: Human Nature and the Evolution of Society* (Stanford, Calif.: Stanford University Press, 1992). On the role of extra-pair copulations, and other compensatory behaviors by lower status animals, see Ridley, *The Red Queen.* Cf. Aristotle, *Politics,* I.2.1252b–1253a.

22. For illustrations of these behaviors, see Frans de Waal, *Chimpanzee Politics* (Cambridge, Mass.: Harvard University Press, 1982); Jane Goodall, *The Chimpanzees of Gombe* (Cambridge, Mass.: Harvard University Press, 1986); and the citations in notes 8, 10, 11, and 12. On the extent to which females *choose* mates—and manipulate male behavior in the process, see Meredith F. Small, *Female Choices: Sexual Behavior of Female Primates* (Ithaca, N.Y.: Cornell University Press, 1993); David Buss, *Anatomy of Desire* (New York: Basic Books, 1994).

23. It is worth emphasizing that popularizations using contemporary field studies of animal behavior to illuminate human society appeared before—and without reference to—the specific developments associated with "inclusive fitness theory" and "sociobiology" (references cited in notes 6 through 9 of this chapter): Konrad Lorenz's *On Aggression* (New York: Harcourt, Brace and Row, 1966) was originally published in German in 1961; Robert Ardrey's *African Genesis* (New York: Atheneum, 1963) appeared two years later—i.e., a year before Hamilton's land-mark paper in the *Journal of Theoretical Biology.* Many critics of ethology and sociobiology (see Caplan, *The Sociobiology Debate,* and Lewontin, Rose, and Kamin, *Not in Our Genes*) tend to blur the difference between these quite different scientific approaches. For a more balanced critique, see Kitcher, *Vaulting Ambition.*

24. See *Notebooks,* ed. J. P. Richter, 2.118, cited above in note 4.

25. Irenäus Eibl-Eibesfeldt, *Human Ethology* (New York: Aldine de Gruyter, 1989). See also Mario von Cranach et al., eds., *Human Ethology* (Cambridge: Cambridge University Press, 1979); Schubert and Masters, *Primate Politics*; Maryanski and Turner, *The Social Cage*; and—for ongoing research—such journals as *Ethology and Sociobiology.*

26. Paul Ekman, Wallace V. Friesen, and Phoebe Ellsworth, *Emotion in the Human Face* (New York: Pergamon, 1972) and Paul Ekman and Harriet Oster, "Facial Expressions of Emotion," *Annual Review of Psychology* 30 (1979): 527–554. For a review of this evidence and its relevance to politics, see Masters, *The Nature of Politics,* ch. 2.

27. Mario von Cranach, ed., *Methods of Inference from Animal to Human Behavior* (The Hague: Mouton, 1976). Leonardo was one of the first scientists after Aristotle to attempt a systematic analysis of comparative anatomy, showing similarities and differences in the physiology of humans and other animals

(see Istituto Geografico d'Agostino, *Leonardo da Vinci*, 363–398); for an example of Leonardo's remarkable anatomical studies, see Figure 1.8.

28. See the Preface to the Paperback Edition of Schubert and Masters, *Primate Politics* (Lanham, Md.: University Press of America, 1994) for a survey and bibliography of the most recent work in this area.

29. Charles Darwin, *The Expression of the Emotions in Man and Animals* (Chicago: University of Chicago Press, 1965).

30. Michael R. A. Chance, "Attention Structure as the Basis of Primate Rank Orders," *Man* (1967): 503–518; "The Organization of Attention in Groups," in von Cranach, *Methods of Inference from Animal to Human Behavior*; and Michael R. A. Chance, ed., *Social Fabrics of the Mind* (Hillsdale, N.J.: Lawrence Erlbaum, 1989).

31. Goodall, *Chimpanzees of Gombe* as well as her popular presentation in *Through a Window: My Thirty Years with the Chimpanzees of Gombe* (Boston: Houghton Mifflin, 1990). See also Frans de Waal, *Peacemaking among Primates* (Cambridge, Mass.: Harvard University Press, 1989).

32. Peter Warr, Joanna Barter, and Garry Brownbridge, "On the Independence of Positive and Negative Affect," *Journal of Personality and Social Psychology* 44 (1983): 644–651. Neuroscientific research has, moreover, traced these two systems to different structures and pathways in the brain. See Jeffrey Allan Gray, *The Psychology of Fear and Stress*, 2nd ed. (Cambridge: Cambridge University Press, 1987).

33. See Konrad Z. Lorenz and Paul Leyhausen, *Motivation of Human and Animal Behavior* (New York: Van Nostrand Reinhold, 1973). For the implications of the distinction between analog and digital signals, especially as it relates to human communication by verbal as well as nonverbal means, see Masters, *The Nature of Politics*, chs. 2–3.

34. J. A. R. A. M. van Hooff, "The Facial Displays of Catyrrhine Monkeys and Apes," in *Primate Ethology*, ed. Desmond Morris (New York: Doubleday Anchor, 1969), 9–81 as well as Eibl-Eibesfeldt, *Human Ethology*. For a recent summary of the evidence and its importance in understanding human nature, see Masters, *Beyond Relativism*, ch. 5.

35. In addition to the work of Chance (note 30) and Maryanski and Turner (note 21), see Vernon Reynolds, "Open Groups in Hominid Evolution," *Man* 1 (1966): 441–452 and *The Apes* (New York: Harper Colophon, 1967).

36. That the theoretical approaches of scientists like Chance and Gray are directly relevant to human political behavior is shown by George Marcus and Michael MacKuen, "Anxiety, Enthusiasm and the Vote: The Emotional Underpinnings of Learning and Involvement during Presidential Campaigns," *American Political Science Review* 87 (1993): 688–701.

37. On the danger of this error, see Aristotle, *Physiognomonics*, esp. 805b–806a. While viewed by some scholars as spurious, this Aristotelian dia-

logue provides an early example of the interest in the "signs" that can be used to assess traits of character or "soul" studied by modern ethologists.

38. On the difference between Machiavelli and Hobbes, and its significance for modern thought, see below, chapter seven. For something like a social contract among lions, see Thomas, *The Tribe of Tiger*, 109–186. Like Hobbes, Descartes establishes a similar gap between human and nonhuman species, albeit for somewhat different reasons. As a result, humans are set apart from animals in both the Anglo-Saxon social contract or utilitarian tradition of Locke, Adam Smith, Mill, and modern liberalism, and the continental traditions of Kant, Hegel, Marx, and such movements as socialism, phenomenology, and structuralism.

39. See again the references in notes 14, 21, 25, and 30.

40. In addition to de Waal's *Peacemaking among Primates* and Kano's *The Last Ape*, it is instructive to see recent videotapes of bonobo behavior: Frans de Waal, "Ethogram of Bonobo Social Behavior," VHS Videotape, Wisconsin Primate Center (1993), and Amy Parish, "Female-female Bonding among Bonobo," video presentation to Gruter Institute–Rockefeller Center Seminar, Biological Perspectives in the Social Sciences, Dartmouth College, 2 August 1993.

41. On the importance of this question, compare: Antonio Damasio, *Descartes' Error* (New York: Grosset/Putnam, 1994); Strauss, *Natural Right and History* (Chicago: University of Chicago Press, 1953); Robert McShea, *Morality and Human Nature* (Philadelphia: Temple University Press, 1990).

Chapter 5

1. "Per mantenere il dono principal di natura cioè libertà, trovo modo da offendere et difendere state assediati dali ambitiosi tiranni, e prima dirò del sito murale, e ancora per che i popoli possino mantenere i loro boni e giusti signiori" (*Notebooks*, ed. J. P. Richter, 2.300). Richter's translation obscures Leonardo's use of the word "states" (*state*) to describe the political constructions he projects—and the plural, suggesting he is speaking of a theory useful to all human communities. This passage has been dated between 1487 and 1490 (Pedretti, *Literary Works*, 2.251)—i.e., over a decade before Leonardo and Machiavelli had the occasion to meet in Cesare's court at Imola.

2. For an excellent presentation of this point from the legal perspective, see Margaret Gruter, *Law and the Mind* (Newbury Hills, Calif: Sage, 1991). An insightful analysis of the sociological implications is provided by Lionel Tiger, *The Manufacture of Evil* (New York: Simon and Schuster, 1987).

3. This does not mean that language is the unmixed blessing described by those followers of modern philosophers as diverse as Kant, Marx, and Niet-

zsche, for whom nonhuman animals are essentially inferior because of their "beastly" nature: e.g., Arnold Brecht, *Political Theory* (Princeton, N.J.: Princeton University Press, 1968); Michel Foucault, *Les Mots et les Choses* (Paris: Gallimard, 1966), translated as *The Order of Things* (New York: Viking, 1970); Allan Bloom, *The Closing of the American Mind* (New York: Simon and Schuster, 1986). Compare Leonardo's judgment: "Man has much power of discourse [reasoning power] which for the most part is vain and false; animals have but little, but it is useful and true, and a small truth is better than a great lie" (*Notebooks*, ed. J. P. Richter, 2.296).

4. For a more extended discussion of this issue, see Masters, *The Nature of Politics* esp. chs. 5–6.

5. Ehrlich, Dobkin, and Wheye, *The Birder's Handbook*, 173–177, 615–619.

6. Prior to and independently of such civilizations, there also arose smaller horticultural tribes which, while larger than the hunter-gatherer band, often lacked fully centralized governments; in such cultures, often encountered when Europeans colonized Africa, kinship rather than the centralized state plays the principal role in organizing social life. On the extent to which both horticultural tribes and agricultural civilizations transformed earlier human social life, see Maryanski and Turner, *The Social Cage*.

7. It is worth reflecting on the different meaning of the word "colony" in human history (where it refers to the splitting up of groups due to population pressure and other factors of social division) and ornithology (where it concerns the formation of very large flocks or "communities" of individuals).

8. See Donald T. Campbell, "On the Genetics of Altruism and the Counter-Hedonic Components in Human Culture," *Journal of Social Issues* 28 (1972): 21–37 as well as the references in note 21 below.

9. For Gould's theory of punctuated equilibria, see *Wonderful Life*. Although Machiavelli would have known such a view from Lucretius, he could also have discussed it with Leonardo, who described (and drew images of) cataclysmic events and linked them to a deeper view of nature. For example, Leonardo explained carnivorous species as follows: "Why did nature not ordain that one animal should not live by the death of another? Nature, being inconstant and taking pleasure in creating and making constantly new lives and forms, because she knows that her terrestrial materials become thereby augmented, is more ready and more swift in her creating, than time in his destruction; and so she has ordained that many animals shall be food for others. . . . Nay, this not satisfying her desire, to the same end she frequently sends forth certain poisonous and pestilential vapours upon the vast increase and congregation of animals; and most of all upon men, who increase vastly because other animals do not feed upon them; and, the causes being removed, the effects would not follow. This earth therefore seeks to lose its life, desiring only continual reproduction; and, as by the arguments you bring forward and demonstrate, like effects always follow like causes, animals are the image of

the world" (*Notebooks*, ed. J. P. Richter, 2.311). In contemporary terms, although natural selection operates constantly on the overabundance of life, natural catastrophes periodically have as disastrous effects for entire species as the predator's killing of a prey has for individuals. Pedretti (*Literary Works*, 2.257–258) dates this entry from around 1480.

10. For example, Leonardo asserts that humans should be called "king of the beasts" instead of "king of the animals" because humans commit "one supreme wickedness which does not happen among the animals of the earth": not merely cannibalism, but active hunting of other members of one's own species for food: although the "rapacious animals, as with the leonine species, and leopards, panthers lynxes, cats and the like, who sometimes eat their children; but thou, besides thy children devourest father, mother, brothers and friends; nor is this enough for thee, but thou goest to the chase on the islands of others, taking other men and these half-naked, the [penis] and the [testicles] thou fattenest, and chasest them down thy own throat; now does not nature produce enough simples, for thee to satisfy thyself? and if thou art not content with simples, canst thou not by the mixture of them make infinite compounds, as Planta [Bartolomeo Sacchi, *De arte coquinaria*] wrote, and other authors on feeding" (*Notebooks*, ed. J. P. Richter, 2.130–131). This passage, which refers to Amerigo Vespucci's report of cannibalism by Europeans on the natives of the Canary Islands, has been dated from 1513 (Pedretti, *Literary Works*, 2.114). Due to the "evil nature of men" (*il male nature delli omini*), Leonardo tells us, he will not divulge at least one invention—a submarine which he thought would be used for "assassinations" on a large scale (*Notebooks*, ed. J. P. Richter, 1.11).

11. In addition to the speeches of the Athenians in the Melian dialogue in Thucydides, *Histories* (New York: Modern Library, n.d.) and of Thrasymachus in Book 1 of the *Republic*, see the restatement of the views of "Thrasymachus and countless others" by Glaucon (Book II.358c–360c). The latter—partly cited below—is a powerful formulation of the Sophist position.

12. Antiphon the Sophist, *On Truth*, in Ernest Barker, *Greek Political Thought* (New York: Barnes and Noble, 1960), 95.

13. Ibid., 97. Because all humans have the same nature with regard to the preference for pleasure and aversion to pain—or, as Antiphon puts it, "we all breathe through our mouth and nostrils"—it also follows that humans are naturally equal.

14. Ibid., 95. For a fuller account of the Sophist view, see Roger D. Masters, "Classical Political Philosophy and Contemporary Biology," in *Politikos: Selected Papers of the American Conference of Greek Political Thought,* ed. Kent Moors (Pittsburgh: Duquesne University Press, 1989), 1.1–44.

15. *Republic*, II.358e–359a; ed. Bloom, pp. 36–37.

16. Ibid., II.359b–360b; pp. 37–38. Some might suggest that, since Socrates goes on to rebut Glaucon's case, Machiavelli's assertion that "all writers on

politics" have emphasized selfishness is contradicted by Plato's *Republic*. This would, however, confuse Plato himself with the views attributed to Socrates in the Platonic dialogues. For a great Islamic philosopher's conclusion that Plato sought to combine "the method of Thrasymachus" with "the method of Socrates," see al-Farabi's *Commentary on the Political Philosophy of Plato*.

17. This is evident in both the educational proposals of Plato's *Republic* and the teachings of Aristotle's *Nicomachean Ethics*. Cf. Leo Strauss, *The City and Man* (Chicago: Rand McNally, 1964). As noted earlier, Machiavelli would have known this position from Lucretius, whose *De rerum natura* he copied by hand (Najemy, *Between Friends*, 58); equally important as a source are the works of Xenophon, whose *Cyropedia*, *Hiero*, and *Anabasis* are prominently cited by Machiavelli.

18. See Romans, esp. chapter 8, and compare Augustine, *The City of God* (New York: Modern Library, n. d.).

19. This usage is confusing: in ethical theory, an act of "altruism" usually presupposes conscious intentionality, whereas biologists may use the term to describe the consequences of animal behaviors that are mechanical or instinctive. Such words as "cooperative" or "helping" behavior have the advantage that they leave open the extent to which an individual engages in conscious and avoidable self-sacrifice for others. In the following discussion of evolutionary theories, I will therefore avoid the term "altruism" unless referring to an established theoretical concept that uses the word (such as Trivers's notion of "reciprocal altruism").

20. Hamilton, "The Genetical Theory of Social Behavior."

21. See Wilson, *Sociobiology*, and *On Human Nature* (Cambridge, Mass.: Harvard University Press, 1978). See also Richard Dawkins, *The Selfish Gene* (New York: Oxford University Press, 1976); Alexander, *Darwinism and Human Affairs*.

22. E.g., Lewontin, Rose, and Kamin, *Not in Our Genes*.

23. Masters, "Is Sociobiology Reactionary? The Political Implications of Inclusive Fitness Theory," 275–292. Neither Machiavelli nor Leonardo present a formalization akin to the social contract theories of the Greek Sophists or the modern natural right theorists, probably because both thinkers emphasize the *differences* in human personality and behavior, and hence the variety of human natures (plural) that was emphasized in the last chapter.

24. E.g., Jack Hirshleifer, "Economics from a Biological Viewpoint," *Journal of Law and Economics* 20 (1977): 1–52 and *Economic Behaviour in Adversity* (Chicago: University of Chicago Press, 1987); Robert Frank, *Choosing the Right Pond* (New York: Oxford University Press, 1985); Gordon Getty, "The Hunt for *r*: One-Factor and Transfer Theories," *Social Science Information* 28 (1989): 385–428.

25. See John Maynard-Smith, "Evolution of Behavior." A frequent, but quite trivial, objection to the theory of games is that individuals do not ac-

tively calculate costs and benefits in the manner described by the model. This error, compounded by the tendency to speak of "rational choice theory" in many of the social sciences, ignores the difference between a scientific theory or model and a phenomenological description. As Alexander has emphasized, in using the theory of natural selection to define the problem of social cooperation, it does not matter whether individual behavior is largely learned, tightly constrained by instinct, or some combination of the two: see Alexander's *Darwinism and Human Affairs.* Economic theory, of course, uses the same methodological assumption in developing a cost-benefit theory for the allocation of resources: the economist need not, and usually does not, assume that individuals or firms "in the real world" actually make decisions by using the axioms and formal theories of contemporary economics.

26. It needs to be stressed that the Prisoner's Dilemma is only *one* of many models in game theory. For many specialists, in fact, it is not particularly interesting compared to those games in which a temporal dimension is more explicitly included in the structure of the game. See Martin Shubik, *Game Theory in the Social Sciences* (Cambridge, Mass.: MIT Press, 1982).

27. In what follows, I will assume that natural selection operates primarily on the individual level, as has been argued by a number of leading biologists. That is, natural selection does not lead animals to act for "the good of the species" or for the "group," but rather for their own individual benefits. See George C. Williams, *Adaptation and Natural Selection* (Princeton, N.J.: Princeton University Press, 1966) as well as Dawkins, *The Selfish Gene* and Alexander, *Darwinism and Human Affairs.* It should be emphasized, however, that there are situations in which some evolutionary theorists argue something like "group selection" will occur. Cf. David Sloan Wilson, *The Natural Selection of Populations and Communities* (Menlo Park, Calif.: Benjamin Cummings, 1979). While these situations, such as small populations in rapidly changing or stressful environments, may be rare in evolution generally speaking, they were probably more significant in human evolution. See Wilson, *Sociobiology.*

28. Robert Axelrod, *The Evolution of Cooperation* (Cambridge, Mass.: Harvard University Press, 1983).

29. Robert Trivers, "The Evolution of Reciprocal Altruism," *Quarterly Review of Biology* 46 (1971): 35–57; Richard D. Alexander, *The Biology of Moral Systems* (New York: Aldine, 1987).

30. Maynard-Smith, "The Evolution of Behavior"; Barash, *Sociobiology and Behavior.* From the biologist's perspective, this reflects the distinction between what animals actually do (called "proximate causes") and the effects of natural selection as predicted by evolutionary theory (defined as "ultimate causes"). Cf. note 19 above.

31. Robert Frank, *Passions within Reason* (New York: W. W. Norton, 1988).

32. To repeat, these comments leave "group selection" to one side. For those who stress evolutionary processes at the group or population level, kinship is a subsidiary mechanism that merely reflects proximity. One reason for this emphasis is that many empirical studies have now shown that natural selection at the individual level can explain otherwise paradoxical behavior in many species. See Barash, *Sociobiology and Behavior* and the ongoing empirical studies reported in journals like *Ethology and Sociobiology*. As in many areas of the natural sciences, what were once bitter theoretical debates are clarified by the evidence.

33. The formal models demonstrating the extent to which kinship can lead to cooperation were worked out by William D. Hamilton in his frequently cited paper, "The Genetical Theory of Social Behavior." This reconceptualization of the concept of natural selection, often called "inclusive fitness theory," lies at the bottom of the development of what is often called "sociobiology."

34. This outcome depends on the precise *ratio* of the pay-offs of the four strategic outcomes as well as on the degree of kinship of the players. If the rewards of defection are high enough, for example, even full brothers will compete. For some of the considerations involved, see Masters, *The Nature of Politics*, 165–169. Males are used as an example here to avoid the complexities of the genetic difference between sex-linked chromosomes of females (XX) and males (XY). Cf. Discourses, I, 9; pp. 131–133.

35. Plato, *Republic*, II. 369b–372d (ed. Bloom, pp. 46–49).

36. Jean-Jacques Rousseau, *Discourse on the Origin of Inequality*, Part 1, in *Rousseau's First and Second Discourses*, ed. Masters, 150–151.

37. For the mechanisms discussed here, see Margaret Gruter and Roger D. Masters, eds., *Ostracism: A Social and Biological Phenomenon* (New York: Elsevier, 1986).

38. Thomas Hobbes, *Leviathan*, Part 1, Chapter 13; ed. Schneider (New York: Macmillan, 1958), 104–109.

39. For a review of the anthropological literature, see Roger D. Masters, "World Politics as a Primitive Political System," *World Politics* 16 (1964): 595–619.

40. See Robin Fox, *The Search for Society* (New Brunswick, N.J.: Rutgers University Press, 1989).

41. Compare Machiavelli's account of the origins of the "parties" or "sects" of the Whites and the Blacks in Florence: *Florentine Histories*, II.16 (pp. 68–69).

42. See the chapters by Christopher Boehm and Mustafer Mahdi in Gruter and Masters, *Ostracism*.

43. See Masters, "World Politics as a Primitive Political System."

44. See Goodall, *Chimpanzees of Gombe*.

45. When describing the "many sorts of food" and correspondingly "many kinds of lives both of animals and men," Aristotle describes the variety of

human "ways of life" as follows: "The laziest are shepherds, who lead an idle life, and get their subsistence without trouble from tame animals . . . cultivating a sort of living farm. Others support themselves by hunting, which is of different kinds. Some, for example, are brigands, others, who dwell near lakes or marshes or rivers of a sea in which there are fish, are fishermen, and others live by the pursuit of birds or wild beasts. The greater number obtain a living from the cultivated fruits of the soil. Such are the modes of subsistence which prevail among those whose industry springs up of itself, and whose food is not acquired by exchange and retail trade—there is the shepherd, the husbandman, the brigand, the fisherman, the hunter. Some gain a comfortable maintenance out of two employments, eking out the deficiencies of one of them by another: thus the life of a shepherd may be combined with that of a brigand, the life of a farmer with that of a hunter. Other modes of life are similarly combined in any way which the needs of men may require" (*Politics*, I, viii.1256a–b; *Complete Works of Aristotle,* ed. Jonathan Barnes [Bollingen Books; Princeton, N.J.: Princeton University Press, 1984], II, 1993). Note that piracy ("brigands"), mentioned three times in this passage, is treated on a par with fishing or game hunting. For a vivid evocation of the functioning of such a system among the Blackfeet Indians in the late nineteenth century, see James Welch's powerful novel, *Fools Crow* (New York: Viking, 1986).

46. Some biologists make a sharp distinction between natural selection and sexual selection: the former being defined as the selection of attributes that enhance relative "fitness" or reproductive success, whereas the latter concerns attributes that make individuals of one sex (usually males) more attractive to individuals of the opposite or "rate-limiting" sex (usually females). In practice, however, it is sometimes difficult to distinguish clearly between the two selective processes, which had already been noted as somewhat different by Darwin. Since both work on individuals, they have been treated as different elements of what philosophers would call individual "self-interest."

47. See especially Mancur Olson, Jr., *The Logic of Collective Action* (Cambridge, Mass.: Harvard University Press, 1965); Howard Margolis, *Selfishness, Altruism, and Rationality* (Cambridge: Cambridge University Press, 1982). Cf. Wright, *The Moral Animal.*

48. Garrett Hardin, "The Tragedy of the Commons," *Science* 162 (1968): 1243–48. For an illustration of the argument in game theoretical terms akin to those of a Prisoner's Dilemma, see Masters, *The Nature of Politics*, 169–179.

49. One of the ironies of the period of the Cold War was the vigorous ideological conflict between two groups, each believing that the ideal human circumstance is a highly complex society without any government at all. The dreams of both American laissez-faire and Soviet Communist ideologues coincided in their hopes that in the future, the state would "wither away" or be replaced.

50. See Robert Ellickson, "Property in Land," *Yale Law Journal* 102 (1993): 1314–1400. Ellickson's argument does not, however, spell out what seem to be cultural prerequisites for the availability of this strategy since, in many cultures, norms of reciprocity make it difficult to establish the institutionalized practices we associate with "fee simple" private property. See Robert D. Cooter, "Inventing Market Property: The Land Courts of Papua New Guinea," *Law and Society Review* 25 (1991): 759–795. These cultural factors should not, of course, be confused with the technical impossibility of privatizing indivisible resources (like the earth's atmosphere).

51. Technically, this has been described as "internalizing"—i.e., making "internal" to the costs of activity—what are otherwise "externalities" or costs which fall on future generations or helpless third parties.

52. Recent scientific research demonstrates that individuals with "psychopathic" (or "sociopathic") personalities do not follow established social norms in part because their brains process information differently from normal individuals. Whereas most humans quickly acquire conditioned avoidance responses to aversive or anxiety-producing stimuli, sociopaths do not do so. Moreover, sociopathic personality seems to be associated with abnormally low base-line levels of brain activity as well as unusually strong needs for stimulation and excitement. As a result, sociopaths fail to internalize routine social norms and do not show fear of punishment when engaging in risky behavior. Taken together, these traits suggest that a small proportion of every human population is biologically predisposed (but not genetically determined) to engage in highly selfish behavior. See Robert D. Hare and Daisy Schalling, eds., *Psychopathic Behavior: Approaches to Research* (New York: Wiley, 1978); Lee Ellis, "Relationships of Criminality and Psychopathy with Eight Other Apparent Behavioral Manifestations of Sub-Optimal Arousal," *Personal and Individual Differences* 8 (1987): 905–925; Sherrie Williamson, Timothy J. Harpur, and Robert D. Hare, "Abnormal Processing of Affective Words by Psychopaths," *Psychophysiology* 28 (1991): 260–273.

53. See Mancur Olson, Jr., *The Rise and Decline of Nations* (New Haven, Conn.: Yale University Press, 1982).

54. See Masters, *The Nature of Politics*, chs. 5–6.

55. The Italian reads "*verso il suo principio*"—literally, "towards its beginning." It is particularly important to note that this chapter concerns *religions* as well as states—and that its reference to states explicitly concerns "kingdoms" as well as "republics." Machiavelli is explicitly "concerned with composite bodies, such as are states and religious institutions, and in their regard I affirm that those changes make for their conservation which lead them back to their origins [*inverso i principii loro*]" (*Discourses*, III, 1, p. 385).

56. See Ridley, *The Red Queen*. For a comparable view of nature in the thought of Leonardo, see *Notebooks*, ed. J. P. Richter, 2.310–311, cited above, note 9.

57. For what follows, see Masters, *The Nature of Politics*, chs. 5–6.

58. Early or "pristine" state-forms based on irrigated agriculture have therefore exploited a wide variety of crops, including cotton rather than food (when, due to abundant resources of fish along a coast, fishing-nets enabled enormous increases in food output).

59. Compare Machiavelli's accounts of the incursions of the "barbarians" in the Western Roman Empire in *Florentine Histories*, I, 1–3; pp. 9–13. It is said that the Great Wall of China was built to keep out foreigners who sought to come, either peacefully or violently, to gain the benefits of the productive systems made possible under the Imperial system.

60. In contemporary physics and mathematics, the emergence of radical novelty from an unusual combination of circumstances is now often explained as a "singularity." For examples of this approach in a variety of fields, see Roger Penrose, *The Emperor's New Mind* (New York: Oxford University Press, 1989); James Gleick, *Chaos* (New York: Viking, 1987); and M. Mitchell Waldrop, *Complexity: The Emerging Science at the Edge of Order and Chaos* (New York: Simon & Schuster, 1992).

61. Between 1487 and 1490, Leonardo developed a futuristic proposal for a city built on two levels—perhaps at Vigerano—for Sforza; his draft text to accompany the drawings concludes: "Let such a city be built near the sea or a large river in order that the dirt of the city may be carried off by the water" (*Notebooks*, ed. J. P. Richter, 2.28).

62. *Notebooks*, ed. J. P. Richter, 2.300. This text has been dated around 1493 as part of a proposal for Duke Ludovico Sforza (Pedretti, *Literary Works*, 2.249–250). It should be no surprise that this project involved dikes and dams to control water.

63. See the discussion of Machiavelli's political career in chapters one and two above. Despite Machiavelli's close working relationship with Soderini, it is evident that he was frustrated by the Gonfalonier's indecision on many matters. Cf. Najemy, *Between Friends*, ch. 2 with *Discourses*, III, 9; p. 431.

Chapter 6

1. *Notebooks*, ed. J. P. Richter, 2.299.

2. The question of gender and dominance is a complex one. Because males are, among primates, generally more likely to initiate physical aggression than females, it was long thought that dominant roles were typically filled by males. This impression was reinforced by the emphasis on monkey societies—adult males are likely to show physical superiority over females based on large sexual differences in size. For an example of this view, see DeVore, *Primate Behavior*. For studies revealing a rather different type of dominance hierarchy in females than in males, even among monkeys, as well as important

differences between monkey and ape social structures: see especially Maryanski and Turner, *The Social Cage*. Moreover, other observations reveal leaders
engaging in dispute settlement and social management whose status did not
depend primarily on physical aggressiveness: see Frans de Waal, *Chimpanzee
Politics* and *Peacemaking among Primates*. This latter form of dominance
is often exercised by females, especially in primates with less size difference
between males and females and in human hunter-gatherer bands with little
need for intergroup conflict. See Sarah Blaffer Hrdy, *The Woman Who Never
Evolved* (Cambridge, Mass.: Harvard University Press, 1981); Goodall, *Chimpanzees of Gombe*; Glendon Schubert, "The Biopolitics of Sex: Gender,
Genetics, and Epigenetics," in *Biopolitics and Gender*, ed. Meredith Watts
(New York: Haworth Press, 1983), 97–128. For a review of recent literature on
primate social behavior, see Schubert and Masters, *Primate Politics,* paperback
edition (Lanham, Md.: University Press of America, 1994), Preface to paperback edition.

3. Along with increased differences in status and power among males, the
expansion of wealth and the emergence of the centralized state increased the
gender differences in status. In human societies, inequalities between males
and females have generally been greatly influenced by factors that also increase
differentiations of socioeconomic or political power. See Roger D. Masters,
"Explaining 'Male Chauvinism' and 'Feminism': Differences in Male and
Female Reproductive Strategies," *Women and Politics, Symposium Issue on
Biopolitics and Politics,* ed. Meredith W. Watts 3 (Summer/Fall): 165–210,
reprinted as *Biopolitics and Gender*, 165–210.

4. For a summary of the emergence of this negative view of Machiavelli's
teaching, which coincided with the increasing role of direct popular support
and corresponding decline of the hereditary aristocracy and the church as the
foundation of modern political authority, see Adams, "Rise, Proliferation, and
Degradation of Machiavellianism," in Adams edition of *The Prince*, 227–232.
The paradox of Machiavelli's increasingly negative reputation as his critique of
medieval politics became more widely adopted did not escape contemporaries.
Hence Christopher Marlowe introduces *The Jew of Malta* with a Prologue in
which "Machevill" begins as follows:

> Albeit the world think Machevill is dead,
> Yet was his soul but flown beyond the Alps,
> And now the Guise is dead, is come from France
> To view this land, and frolic with his friends.
> To some perhaps my name is odious;
> But such as love me guard me from their tongues,
> And let them know that I am Machevill,
> And weigh not men, and therefore not men's words.

Admired I am of those that hate me most:
Though some speak openly against my books,
Yet will they read me, and thereby attain
To Peter's chair; and when they cast me off,
Are poisoned by my climbing followers.
I count religion but a childish toy,
And hold there is no sin but ignorance.
Birds of the air will tell of murders past?
I am ashamed to hear such fooleries.
Many will talk of title to a crown.
What right had Caesar to the empery?
Might first made kings, and laws were then most sure
When like the Draco's they were writ in blood.
Hence comes it, that a strong built citadel
Commands much more than letters can import. . . .
(Marlowe, *The Jew of Malta*, ed. Craik, pp. 9–10)

Written around 1590, this play could be viewed as a continuation of Machiavelli's use of the theater (e.g., *Mandragola*) to spread his ideas. Note Marlowe's suggestion that at the end of the sixteenth century, Machiavelli's influence has been greater in France and England than in Italy (cf. below, chapter seven, note 97).

5. See also the discussion of forms of government in *Discourses*, I, 2, where Machiavelli explicitly describes "one and the same" society [*città*], like Sparta or Rome, in which "there was principality, aristocracy, and democracy" (pp. 109–111). One reason for the multiple meanings of the word "prince" is the uncertainty, at the time of political events, of the ultimate results of a leader's actions. As the comparison of Cesare Borgia (*Prince*, ch. 7) and Moses (*Prince*, ch. 6) suggests, how is one to know—at the moment a leader kills some members of his society—whether he will be a "founder" who creates lasting political institutions?

6. To be sure, Machiavelli does not use the word "tyrant" in *The Prince*, as perhaps befits his analysis of politics from the perspective of the leader himself; "of princes people speak with the utmost trepidation and the utmost reserve" (*Discourses*, I, 58; p. 257). As a comparison of the discussion of such leaders as Hiero, Agathocles, and Julius Caesar in *The Prince* and *Discourses* will reveal, however, Machiavelli makes a clear distinction between such leaders and those, like Moses, Lycurgus, Solon, Theseus, Romulus, or Cyrus, who founded lasting regimes based on law.

7. On the praise of France as one of "the well–ordered and governed kingdoms in our times," compare *The Prince*, ch. 19; pp. 74–75. That the rule of law

is responsible is implied by the criticism of the errors of Louis XII and "Rouen" (his minister, Cardinal Georges d'Amboise) in ch. 3; pp. 13–16.

8. This point is only reinforced by the fact that Eisenhower's success was probably due as much to choice and calculation as to impulses of "nature": see Fred I. Greenstein, *The Hidden Hand Presidency: Eisenhower as Leader* (New York: Basic Books, 1982).

9. On Hannibal as a "past master in warfare" whose crossing of the Alps was an exceptionally "difficult" action, cf. *Discourses*, III, 10 (pp. 436–437) with I, 23 (p. 172).

10. Machiavelli's phrase is *da uno comune consenso d'una universalità*—literally, "by a common consent of a *universality*" or *"community"*; in *The Prince*, Machiavelli uses the word *universalità* to refer to any collectivity that is the base of support of a leader (e.g., ch. 9; p. 41 and Mansfield's note 5). Hence France is "well-ordered" because its founder knew "the hatred of the generality of people [*universalità*] against the great, which is founded in its fear" and created legal institutions (a "third judge"—presumably the Parlement of Paris) to avoid the danger that the king would "make himself hated by the people" (*Prince*, ch. 19; p. 75).

11. See especially Darwin, *Expression of the Emotions in Man and Animals*; Konrad Lorenz, *Studies in Animal and Human Behavior*, vols. 1–2 (Cambridge, Mass.: Harvard University Press, 1970–1971); Frank, *Passions within Reason*.

12. For the technical analysis, see van Hooff, "Facial Displays of Catyrrhine Monkeys and Apes"; Ekman and Oster, "Facial Expressions of Emotion"; and Eibl-Eibesfeldt, *Human Ethology*, ch. 6.3. For a summary of the evidence reported below, see Masters, *The Nature of Politics*, ch. 2.

13. For the selection of these criteria, see Roger D. Masters, Denis G. Sullivan, John T. Lanzetta, Gregory J. McHugo, and Basil G. Englis, "The Facial Displays of Leaders: Toward an Ethology of Human Politics," *Journal of Social and Biological Structures* 9 (1986): 319–343. On the frequency of different types of display during a political campaign, see Roger D. Masters, Denis G. Sullivan, Alice Feola, and Gregory J. McHugo, "Television Coverage of Candidates' Display Behavior during the 1984 Democratic Primaries in the United States," *International Political Science Review* 8 (1987): 121–130.

14. For further evidence and an assessment of the significance of this characterization, see Masters, *Beyond Relativism*, ch. 5.

15. Alan J. Fridlund, G. E. Schwartz, and S. C. Fowler, "Pattern Recognition of Self-Reported Emotional State from Multiple-Site Facial EMG Activity during Affective Imagery," *Psychophysiology* 21 (1984): 622–637; Gregory J. McHugo, John T. Lanzetta, Denis G. Sullivan, Roger D. Masters, and Basil Englis, "Emotional Reactions to Expressive Displays of a Political Leader," *Journal of Personality and Social Psychology* 49 (1985): 1512–29.

16. Roger D. Masters and Denis G. Sullivan, "Facial Displays and Political Leadership in France," *Behavioral Processes* 19 (1989): 1–30, and "Nonverbal Displays and Political Leadership in France and the United States," *Political Behavior* 11 (1989): 121–153.

17. Siegfried Frey, Alfred Raveau, Guido Kempter, Catherine Darnaud, and Gabriel Argentin, "Mise en évidence du traitement cognitif et affectif du non-verbal," *MSH Informations* 70 (1993): 4–23.

18. A. Michael Warnecke, Roger D. Masters, and Guido Kempter, "The Roots of Nationalism: Nonverbal Behavior and Xenophobia," *Ethology and Sociobiology* 13 (1992): 267–282; A. Michael Warnecke, The Personalization of Power, Senior Fellowship Thesis, Dartmouth College, 1991. As these reports indicate, careful statistical analyses indicate that, controlling for perception and emotional response, cultural differences in nonverbal performance have an independent effect on viewer response.

19. Among nonhuman primates generally, threat displays directed toward inappropriate targets are a sign of low-status males, and can even be elicited by artificially lowering the neurotransmitter serotonin (which is higher in dominant than subordinate animals). See Roger D. Masters and Michael T. McGuire, eds., *The Neurotransmitter Revolution: Serotonin, Social Behavior and the Law* (Carbondale, Ill.: Southern Illinois University Press, 1994), esp. ch. 9; Michael T. McGuire, Lynn A. Fairbanks, Michael J. Raleigh, "Life History Strategies, Adaptive Variation, and Behavior Physiology Interactions: The Sociophysiology of Vervet Monkeys," in *Sociophysiology*, ed. Pat Barchas (New York: Oxford University Press, in press). As a result, among playschool groups of children, one social role has been described as the "dominated aggressive" individual (Hubert Montagner, *L'enfant et la communication* [Paris: Stock, 1978]). On the cultural difference in responses to appropriate anger/threat displays, see the references in notes 16–18.

20. John T. Lanzetta, Denis G. Sullivan, Roger D. Masters, Gregory J. McHugo, "Viewers' Emotional and Cognitive Responses to Televised Images of Political Leaders," in *Mass Media and Political Thought,* ed. Sidney Kraus and Richard Perloff (Beverly Hills, Calif.: Sage, 1985), 85–116. This effect is observed in both the physiological reactions of facial muscles and in verbal reports of emotion: Gregory J. McHugo, John T. Lanzetta, and Lauren Bush, "The Effect of Attitudes on Emotional Reactions to Expressive Displays of a Political Leader," *Journal of Nonverbal Behavior* 15 (1991): 19–41; Roger D. Masters and Denis G. Sullivan, "Nonverbal Behavior and Leadership: Emotion and Cognition in Political Attitudes," in *Explorations in Political Psychology*, ed. Shanto Iyengar and William McGuire (Durham, N.C.: Duke University Press, 1993), 150–182.

21. Denis G. Sullivan and Roger D. Masters, "Biopolitics, the Media, and Leadership: Nonverbal Cues, Emotions, and Trait Attributions in the

Evaluation of Political Leaders," in *Research in Biopolitics,* ed. Albert O. Somit and Steven Peterson (Greenwich, Conn.: JAI Press, 1994), 2.239–275.

22. Roger D. Masters and Stephen J. Carlotti, Jr., "Gender Differences in Responses to Political Leaders," in *Social Stratification and Socioeconomic Inequality,* ed. Lee Ellis (Boulder, Colo.: Praeger, 1994), 2.13–35; Roger D. Masters, "Gender and Political Cognition," *Politics and the Life Sciences* 8 (1989): 3–39. On the differences in emotional responses of males and females, see James W. Pennebaker and Tomi-Ann Roberts, "Toward a His and Hers Theory of Emotion: Gender Differences in Visceral Perception," *Journal of Social and Clinical Psychology* 11 (1992): 199–212.

23. Roger D. Masters, "Differences in Responses of Blacks and Whites to American Leaders," *Politics and the Life Sciences* 13 (1994): 183–194.

24. Roger D. Masters, "Individual and Cultural Differences in Response to Leaders: Nonverbal Displays," *Journal of Social Issues* 47 (1991): 151–165.

25. Denis G. Sullivan and Roger D. Masters, "'Happy Warriors': Leaders' Facial Displays, Viewers' Emotions, and Political Support," *American Journal of Political Science* 32 (1988): 345–368. Facial conformation also plays a role, as is evident from differences in perceptions and responses of subjects to neutral excerpts of unknown candidates. Indeed, it has long been popularly believed that personality can be "read" by decoding facial conformation: for a recent example, see Rose Rosetree, *Face Reading Secrets: See Others as They Really Are!* (Baltimore: Oppenheimer, 1994).

26. Lewicki, Hill, and Czyzewska, "Nonconscious Acquisition of Information." On the structure of the brain, see Gazzaniga, *The Social Brain*; Stephen M. Kosslyn and Olivier Koenig, *Wet Mind: The New Cognitive Neuroscience* (New York: Free Press, 1992); Francis H. C. Crick, *The Astonishing Hypothesis* (New York: Scribners, 1994).

27. Compare Larry Arnhart, *Aristotle on Political Reasoning* (DeKalb, Ill.: Northern Illinois University Press, 1981).

28. *III Henry VI*, 3.3.182–185, 191–193. This speech contains one of three explicit reference to Machiavelli in the Shakespearean corpus; for the others, see *Merry Wives of Windsor*, 3.1.101–102; *I Henry VI*, 5.4.74.

29. For this case, and the problem in the United States more broadly, see Kathleen Hall Jamieson, *Dirty Politics: Deception, Distraction, and Democracy* (New York: Oxford University Press, 1992).

30. Roger D. Masters, Siegfried Frey, and Gary Bente. "Dominance and Attention: Images of Leaders in German, French, and American TV News," *Polity* 25 (Spring 1991): 373–394.

31. Edmond T. Rolls, "The Processing of Face Information in the Primate Temporal Lobe," in *Processing Images of Faces,* ed. V. Bruce and M. Burton (London: Ablex, 1989). For a fuller discussion of the neuronal basis of face recognition and its implications for political philosophy, see Masters, *Beyond Relativism*, ch. 5.

32. Shanto Iyengar and Donald Kinder, *News that Matters* (Chicago: University of Chicago Press, 1989).

33. To be sure, writing had from its very beginnings a political role. Early kings used writing to record their victories on monuments or to register their edicts on parchment. But political dialogue and debate occurred by word of mouth: the widespread and inexpensive availability of the printing press—as distinct from writing—hence constitutes the essential innovation that transformed modern politics in the seventeenth and eighteenth centuries.

34. Compare Rousseau's analysis of the indirect effects of printing: *First Discourse*, in Masters and Kelly, *Collected Writings of Rousseau*, 2.20, note.

35. See V. I. Lenin, *What Is To Be Done?* (New York: International Publishers, 1929).

36. See Claude Lévi-Strauss, *Tristes Tropiques* (New York: Atheneum, 1974), esp. the remarkable chapter entitled "A Writing Lesson."

37. Sullivan and Masters, "Biopolitics, the Media, and Leadership."

38. Gary Bente, Siegfried Frey and Johannes Treeck, "Taktgeber der Informationsverarbeitung," *Medien Psychologie* 2 (1989): 137–160.

39. Masters, Frey, and Bente, "Dominance and Attention: Images of Leaders in German, French, and American TV News."

Chapter 7

1. *Notebooks,* ed. I. Richter, 9.

2. On Machiavelli's claim of novelty, see *Prince*, ch. 14, p. 61; *Florentine Histories*, p. 8; *Mandragola*, Prologue, p. 9; *Discourses*, Dedicatory Letter, pp. 94–95. When Machiavelli asserts that he seeks to "enter upon *a new way, as yet untrodden by anyone else*," (*Discourses*, I, Pref.; p. 97), he compares himself to explorers like Amerigo Vespucci and Columbus, acknowledging that such innovation carries great risks: "it has *always been no less dangerous to discover new ways and methods than to set off in search of new seas and unknown lands.*" Amerigo Vespucci's travels to the Canary Islands in 1503 were doubtless known to Machiavelli, not only through his assistant Agostino Vespucci (a kinsman), but because the explorer wrote widely known letters to Piero Soderini; Leonardo also apparently knew Amerigo Vespucci and refers explicitly to his account of cannibalism in the Canary Islands (*Notebooks,* ed. J. P. Richter, 2.130–131 and note).

3. See the works cited above, chapter two, note 2. It needs to be added that, for some social historians, the question itself implies an incorrect view of cultural and political change, attributing to individual human will or "agency" what are in actuality deeper historical processes. Even more widespread on the European continent than in the United States (as represented, for example, by the *Annales* school of history in France), this tradition was already clearly

articulated in Hegel's *Philosophy of History* and Tocqueville's *Democracy in America.* While my argument is focused on individual thinkers, it is not my intent to dismiss such accounts or to imply that human intentionality has the power often attributed to it by Anglo-Saxon social scientists. See below, note 13.

4. While individual "natural rights" are common to such modern theorists as Hobbes, Locke, and Rousseau as well as central to the American and French Revolutions, such a concept is denied or ignored in the philosophical traditions represented by de Maistre and Nietzsche as well as in such political systems as Nazi Germany or Maoist China. Popular sovereignty is not central to some modern philosophers (Hobbes or Marx) and regimes (Franco's Spain or the Ayatollah Khomeini's Iran). Conversely, secular science and politics existed in pagan antiquity—an epoch in which Sophists like Antiphon spoke of the natural equality of all men and regimes like the Athenian democracy had a measure of popular rule. It follows that modernity should probably be defined in terms of more general *principles* rather than by the presence or absence of specific theoretical or institutional features. On the problem of defining what is specifically "modern" in politics, see Robert Wokler's thoughtful essay, "Democracy's Mythical Ordeals: The Procrustean and Promethean Paths to Popular Self-rule," in *Democracy and Democratization,* ed. Geraint Parry and Michael Moran (London: Routledge, 1994), 21–46.

5. Rousseau, *The Social Contract,* 1.8–9; in Masters and Kelly, *Collected Writings of Rousseau,* 4.141–144.

6. On Bacon's role in the emergence of modernity, see Robert K. Faulkner, *Francis Bacon and the Project of Progress* (Lanham, Md.: Rowman and Littlefield, 1993), ch. 3 *et passim.* Faulkner's work is of major importance in challenging the current devaluation of Bacon's thought in Western intellectual and scientific history. The study is particularly invaluable in tracing the influence of Machiavelli on Bacon, although my interpretation of Machiavelli suggests he had intimations of many views that, for Faulkner, originated with Bacon.

7. To cite only one example, Aristotle—in this respect broadly representative of the attitudes of ancient Greece—distinguishes sharply between theoretical wisdom (*sophia*), practical wisdom or moral reason (*phronesis*), and technical reason or art (*techne*). For the articulation of these three modes, and their relationship to the hierarchy of nature, custom, and law, see James Bernard Murphy, *The Moral Economy of Labor: Aristotelian Themes in Political Economy* (New Haven, Conn.: Yale University Press, 1993), esp. 106: "Whenever practical wisdom (*phronesis*) is contrasted with theoretical wisdom (*sophia*), for example, *phronesis* is taken to include *techne*" (citing *Nichomachean Ethics* 1141a20–b22, 1142a11–30, 1143b14).

8. For a fuller elaboration of this point, see Masters, *Beyond Relativism.*

9. John Travis, "Cosmic Structures Fill Southern Sky," *Science* 263 (1994): 1684.

10. In most human cultures and societies, religious doctrine, ritual, nature, convention, and law are not discrete categories, but part of a seamless conceptual web of practices, beliefs, and activities. Hence, in languages as different as ancient Hebrew and Japanese, there were no distinct words for "religion," "nature," or "science." E.g., see Mircea Eliade, *Cosmos and History* (New York: Harper, 1963) and, for the Mesopotamian religions prior to the Hebrews, James B. Pritchard, ed., *The Ancient Near East* (Princeton, N.J.: Princeton University Press, 1958).

11. See Roger D. Masters, "Nature, Human Nature, and Political Thought," in *Human Nature and Politics*, ed. R. Pennock and J. Chapman (New York: New York University Press, 1977), 61–110, and "Classical Political Philosophy and Contemporary Biology."

12. Equally important, though beyond the scope of this essay, was the development of a new mathematics, overcoming the Aristotelian distinction between measure and number and making possible the differential calculus—i.e., a mathematics of continuous motion. On Aristotle and the difference between ancient and modern mathematics, see Michael J. White, *The Continuous and the Discrete* (Oxford: Clarendon Press, 1992) and, for a fuller discussion, Masters, *Beyond Relativism*, ch. 2. On the emergence of the modern view, see also the citations in note 41 below.

13. One reviewer of an earlier manuscript setting forth the interpretation in this book put the objection as follows: "much of what you find in Leonardo and Machiavelli can be found in a general way in the humanistic and artistic avant-garde of the late fifteenth and early sixteenth centuries. Leonardo and Machiavelli need to be treated as illustrative examples rather than as links in a chain." Just as biological evolution is the study of change that is the product of *both* the transmission of existing genetic structures (gene replication) *and* changes or innovations (genetic mutation), so cultural history must be a combination of the slow process of imitation by which learned behavior is transmitted from generation to generation with individual innovations; debates in historiography can therefore legitimately focus on the *extent* of the innovative change that can take place in the mind of a single individual. The account presented here could be said to answer the debates in historiography by documenting the disproportionate range and power of the innovative ideas and actions of both Leonardo and Machiavelli (cf. note 3 to this chapter).

14. *Notebooks*, ed. J. P. Richter, 1.356.

15. Ibid., 1.328.

16. Brizio, "The Painter," 24.

17. *Notebooks*, ed. I. Richter, 194–195. For the context of this passage and

its echo in Machiavelli's dedication to *The Prince*, see above, chapter two. In politics, the equivalent of Leonardo's description of the power of the painter would seem to be the creative power of Machiavelli's legislator or founder.

18. On the painter as *universale*, see *Notebooks*, ed. J. P. Richter, 1.250–251, 252–253.

19. *Notebooks*, ed. I. Richter, 195.

20. Ibid. Cf. Plato, *Republic*, VI.509d–511e; VII.514a–521b; X.601b–603b.

21. Leonardo's priorities are clearly indicated by his reaction to the denunciation of his practice of dissection when he was working under the patronage of Giuliano de' Medici in Rome. Having been commissioned to develop solar mirrors that could be used in the production of cloth, Leonardo was assigned a German specialist who failed to do his work; when Leonardo complained, the artisan denounced Leonardo for conducting illegal autopsies. The drafts of Leonardo's letters to his patron—and his decision to leave Rome for Milan—indicate clearly enough that Leonardo used his inventiveness with applied technologies to create the opportunity for his primary interests in pure scientific research. See *Notebooks*, ed. J. P. Richter, 2.407–410; Bramly, *Leonardo*, 383–389; Emilio Lavagnino, "Leonardo in Rome," in Istituto Geografico d'Agostino, *Leonardo*, 127–138.

22. *Notebooks*, ed. J. P. Richter, 2.107–108. This text has been dated around 1508 (though it is not clear whether when Leonardo was in Florence or after his return to Milan): Pedretti, *Literary Works*, 2.89.

23. See Zammattio, "Mechanics of Water and Stone," 190–207; *Notebooks*, ed. J. P. Richter, 2.180–204, 240.

24. See Costantino, *Leonardo*, 119–121. For Leonardo's texts on the deluge and other comparable catastrophes, see *Notebooks*, ed. J. P. Richter, 1.305–313, 608–609; 2.365–368.

25. Brugnoli, "Il Cavallo," 90–91.

26. André Chastel, "Treatise on Painting," in Reti, *Unknown Leonardo*, 230. For the text cited, see *Notebooks*, ed. J. P. Richter, 1.245; the passage is dated from 1504, when Leonardo was in Florence (Pedretti, *Literary Works*, 1.327).

27. Brizio, "The Painter," 45–46.

28. Ibid., 46. The absence of *written* evidence of Leonardo's influence on Machiavelli becomes trivial when one thinks that *visually* Machiavelli would have had many occasions to *see* Leonardo's painting. This would have been true, moreover, even without reference to the role that Machiavelli may have played in securing the commission for Leonardo or the Signoria's approval of supplementary payments to the artist in 1505. For one possible implication, see Appendix III.

29. "O painter, when you represent mountains, see that . . . the bases are always paler than the summits. . . and the loftier they are the more they should reveal their true shape and color." This passage is cited by Heyden-

reich ("Military Architect," 147), for it is a technique that played a role in the aerial perspective maps for Leonardo's canal projects and other military plans as well as one used in his paintings and drawings.

30. See Chastel, "Treatise on Painting," 216–239. Leonardo began writing the *Treatise* on 22 March 1508 while in Florence contesting the will of his uncle Francesco; at the time, he was staying at the house of Braccio Martelli, who was also well known to Machiavelli. Cf. *Notebooks*, ed. J. P. Richter, 1.12.

31. It is therefore worth noting that manuscripts containing some of Leonardo's theoretical observations are often interspersed with practical matters. For example,

In Codex Madrid II calculations and rough sketches dealing with the deviation of the Arno (from 1503 to the end of summer 1504) or the fortification of Piombino (autumn 1504) alternate with studies for the conversion of volumes and observations on gliding and musical instruments. We also find here and there remarks on totally different subjects, some of which have proved to be of capital importance—such as the note that gives the data of an accident that befell the cartoon for the mural of *The Battle of Anghiari* [recording a violent storm that broke at the moment Leonardo started to paint on 6 June 1505]. This little note serves as a reminder that the period of 1505 to which the manuscript belongs is also—and in a sense is especially—that of *The Battle of Anghiari*, commissioned in October 1503. Leonardo therefore had the notebook at hand during the two years when, in spite of his work as engineer, his mind was on this project of the governing council of Florence. One might have expected it to contain remarks concerning the elaboration of the work. In fact, however, the observations deal mainly with anatomy or how the eye sees—that is, with general problems. These may be connected with the council's complex project, but they only deal with it through Leonardo's customary problem-solving approach." (Chastel, "Treatise on Painting," 220)

32. On this project, see Brugnoli, "Il Cavallo," 86–109.

33. Ibid., 87. There is good evidence to suggest that a manuscript by Leonardo, explaining his methods for *Il Cavallo*, was purchased by Benvenuto Cellini and was the basis of the techniques described by Boffrand as having been used in the statue of Louis XIV. His monument, completed in 1699 (and destroyed in the French Revolution), was smaller than Leonardo's, with a combined height of the horse and rider of 6.82 meters (ibid., 92, 106).

34. Tarchiani, "Leonardo in Florence and Tuscany," 103–106; Bramly, *Leonardo*, 347–349.

35. See Chastel, "Treatise on Painting," 220, who quotes Vasari's statement that "His fame had grown so great that all lovers of art, indeed the whole city, wanted him to leave them something to remember him by, and

everywhere they spoke of nothing other than to have him carry out some great and wonderful work."

36. Perhaps the most valuable single study is Cassirer, *The Individual and the Cosmos in Renaissance Philosophy*. See also Duhem, "De l'accéleration produit par une force constante," 3.514ff and *Études sur Léonard de Vinci*; Valéry, *Introduction to the Method of Leonardo da Vinci*; Kouznetsov, "Rationalism of Leonardo da Vinci and the Dawn of Classical Science"; John Herman Randall, Jr., "The Place of Leonardo da Vinci in the Emergence of Modern Science"; Jacob Klein, *Lectures and Essays* (Annapolis: St. John's University Press, 1985); Alexandre Koyré, *Galileo Studies*, trans. John Mepham (Atlantic Highlands, N.J.: Humanities Press, 1978), esp. Part 2.

37. *Notebooks*, ed. J. P. Richter, 1. 11.

38. Ibid., 2.289.

39. *Notebooks*, ed. I. Richter, 5–6.

40. On these problems, see White, *The Continuous and the Discrete*.

41. *Notebooks*, ed. J. P. Richter, 1.28. Cf. 2.171–172: ". . . the point may be compared to an instant of time, and the line may be likened to the length of a certain quantity of time, and just as a line begins and terminates in a point, so such a space of time begins and terminates in an instant. And whereas a line is infinitely divisible, the divisibility of a space of time is of the same nature." See also the texts cited in Pedretti, *Literary Works*, 1.123–126.

42. *Notebooks*, ed. J. P. Richter, 2.308–309. This passage, which has been dated around 1503–1505 (i.e., during Leonardo's stay in Florence), is crossed out—though perhaps because Leonardo had copied it elsewhere: see Pedretti, *Literary Works*, 2.256.

43. *Notebooks*, ed. J. P. Richter, 2.137

44. Ibid., 1.11.

45. Ibid., 1.12.

46. On *The Last Supper*, see Bramly, *Leonardo*, 256; for a typical sketch, ibid., 276–281. There is a story that Leonardo's perfectionism cost him much conflict with the prior of Santa Maria delle Grazie, who was frustrated by the artist's failure to complete the face of Judas, the last of the apostles to be painted. Leonardo is said to have replied that he was still looking for the perfect face to illustrate Judas's treachery—and that, if not able to find it in the streets, he would paint the closest he had yet seen . . . the prior himself.

47. Bramly, *Leonardo*, 280. See also the bitter attack on human cannibalism as "a supreme wickedness, which does not happen among the animals of the earth" (*Notebooks*, ed. J. P. Richter, 2.130–131, cited above).

48. Ibid., 1.15–16. These texts seem to have been destined for the *Treatise on Painting*, and date from around 1490; the first phrase is part of a copy of the first chapter of Peckham's *Prospectiva Communis*. See Pedretti, *Literary Works*, 1.109–110.

49. *Notebooks*, ed. J. P. Richter, 2.111. By "great author" here, Leonardo seems to mean "nature" rather than the traditional Christian view of God. Such references are rare in the *Notebooks*, suggesting that this text is intended for public dissemination. Given the theological opposition to dissection, Leonardo's presentation of the results of his work with human cadavers obviously could have created difficulty. Perhaps more striking is the claim that Leonardo seeks to "demonstrate" not only "the nature of men" but the varieties of "their customs"— i.e., a total science of human life.

50. Ibid., 2.315–334.

51. Ibid., 2.329. Such collections of aphorisms were by no means unique in the Renaissance; what makes Leonardo's interest in their collection so interesting is that he also pioneered in comparative anatomy and physiology, with the aim of attaining a complete theory of human and animal behavior.

52. *Notebooks*, ed. J. P. Richter, 2.50–73; Pedretti, *Literary Works*, 2.60–70, 191–194. For analysis of Leonardo's military engineering and weapons, see Heydenrich, "Military Architect," 136–165; Birn Dibner, "Machines and Weaponry," in Reti, *Unknown Leonardo*, 166–189; Calvi, "Military Engineering and Arms," 275–306; Pedretti, *Royal Palace at Romorantin* and *Leonardo: Architect*.

53. *Notebooks*, ed. J. P. Richter, 2.51. See *Art of War*, Book VII (*Chief Works*, 2.70) where Fabrizio, the general presenting military strategy, says "Therefore, always deferring to a better judgment, I believe that . . . the wall should be made high and should have ditches inside and not outside." Is the "better judgment" that of Leonardo?

54. *Notebooks*, ed. J. P. Richter, 2.446. This text—dated from 1515 when Leonardo was in Rome (Pedretti, *Literary Works*, 2.371)—goes on to recount the honors given Archimedes when, on the conquest of Syracuse, the Romans found him dead: by implication, Leonardo seems to be contemplating the fame that would be due the genius who could harness the new military technologies and put them in the service of a well-organized regime. See also the riddle whose answer is "Of great guns, which come out of a pit and a mould" (i.e., bronze cannon): "Creatures will come from underground which with their terrific noise will stun all who are near; and with their breath will kill men and destroy cities and castles" (*Notebooks*, ed. J. P. Richter, 2.371), dated around 1505 (Pedretti, *Literary Works*, 2.282).

55. *Notebooks*, ed. J. P. Richter, 2.300 (cited as the epigraph to chapter five), written around 1493 as part of a plan to create ten satellite cities around Milan (Pedretti, *Literary Works*, 2.249–250). See also the following text also written when Leonardo was in Florence around 1505 (ibid., 251): "Aristotle and Alexander were teachers to each other. Alexander was rich in power, which gave him the means of seizing the world. Aristotle had a great intellect,

which gave him the means of seizing the rest of the knowledge contributed by all the other philosophers."

56. See the reproduction of the map in Heydenreich, "Military Architect," 144–145.

57. Pedretti, *Literary Works*, 2.249 (a text not transcribed in the Richter edition).

58. *Notebooks*, ed. J. P. Richter, 2.300 (cited above, p. 131).

59. Pedretti, *Literary Works*, 2.250–251.

60. Ibid., 250.

61. *Notebooks*, ed. J. P. Richter, 2.297; the fragment is dated from around 1493–1494 (Pedretti, *Literary Works*, 2.246).

62. See especially the document in Appendix I.3. On the controversy between Leonardo and Soderini, see Vasari's *Leonardo*, 400 and Tarchiani, "Leonardo in Florence and Tuscany," 104–106. The probable connection linking Machiavelli to Leonardo's work on *The Battle of Anghiari* is reinforced not only by the description of the battle, written in Leonardo's notebooks in the handwriting of Machiavelli's assistant Agostino Vespucci (*Notebooks*, ed. J. P. Richter, 2.348–349; Pedretti, *Literary Works*, 1.381–382), but by another entry in Vespucci's hand from 1504: "Stephano Chigi, Canonico . . . servant of the honorable Count Grimani at S. Apostoli" (*Notebooks*, 2.465; Pedretti, *Literary Works*, 2.384).

63. "For just as those who sketch landscapes place themselves down in the plain to consider the nature of mountains and high places and to consider the nature of low places place themselves high atop mountains" (*Prince*, Dedicatory Letter; p. 4).

64. "The painter is lord of all types of people and of all things. If he wants valleys, if he wants from high mountain tops to unfold a great plain extending down to the sea's horizon, he is lord to do so; and likewise if from low plains he wishes to see high mountains" (*Notebooks*, ed. I. Richter, 194–95).

65. See Masters, "Machiavelli and Hobbes: Theory and Practice at the Origins of Modernity," and above, chapters two and three.

66. See A. Richard Turner, *Inventing Leonardo* (New York: Knopf, Random House, 1993), 227–232.

67. On Leonardo's theories of hydraulics, "Leonardo has absolute priority both in the theoretical aspect and in practice, where he presents the most varied and brilliant inventions" (Frederico Sacco, "Da Vinci's Geology and Geography," in Istituto Geografico d'Agostino, *Leonardo da Vinci*, 463). On Leonardo's innovations in the practical applications of hydraulics, see also Carlo Zammattio, "Hydraulic and Nautical Engineering," in the same collection, 467–482.

68. *Notebooks*, ed. J. P. Richter, 2.297; Pedretti, *Literary Works*, 2.248. In the chapter of the *Discourses* entitled "Weak states will always be uncertain in

coming to a decision, and slow decisions are always injurious," Machiavelli ends with the example of the reaction of Florence to Louis XII's invasion, concluding: "I decided to avail myself of a fresh incident to repeat what I had said, since it seems to me to be a matter of which republics, especially those that resemble ours, should take careful note (II, 15; 316). While the explicit reference is to the Republic's delay in accepting the French king's terms of neutrality, could Machiavelli also have in mind the Signoria's hesitation in forming a citizen army and the abandonment of the scheme to divert the Arno?

69. Although Machiavelli rarely refers to the Bible explicitly (for an exception, see *Prince*, ch. 13; p. 56), his indirect references—like the attribution of the Mosaic miracles to Machiavelli's own times in Italy—are sometimes of the greatest importance (ch. 16, p. 103). For instance, today's readers, unfamiliar with the Bible, are often unaware of the way the account of Moses at Mount Sinai in Exodus provides historical evidence for the assertion that "Moses, Cyrus, Theseus, and Romulus would not have been able to make their peoples observe their constitutions for long if they had been unarmed" (ch. 6, p. 24).

70. One good indication of this point is the distinction between Agathocles the Sicilian in chapter eight of *The Prince* and Moses, Cyrus, Theseus, or Romulus in chapter six.

71. E.g., Rousseau, *Social Contract*, 3.6, ed. Masters, p. 88. Although thus far the argument of Pocock in *The Machiavellian Moment* is sound, it can be questioned whether—as Pocock claims—this reflects Machiavelli's acceptance of the specifically *Aristotelian* form of republicanism. See the thoughtful critique in Vickie B. Sullivan, "Machiavelli's Momentary 'Machiavellian Moment': A Reconsideration of Pocock's Treatment of the *Discourses*," *Political Theory* 20 (1992): 309–318.

72. There is an ambiguity in Machiavelli's discussion of fortune that is reinforced by this passage. In chapter twenty-five of *The Prince*, there are of course *two* allegories of fortune—to a river and to a woman. The latter suggests that the conquest of fortune requires violence and force: "because fortune is a woman . . . it is necessary, if one wants to hold her down, to beat her and strike her down" (p. 101). Even without reference to Leonardo's discussion of the need to "coax" a river, it should be obvious that Machiavelli's "dikes and dams" cannot be built entirely by force. Moreover, Machiavelli emphasizes that leaders have often been killed or overthrown in retaliation for rape (*Discourses*, I, 7, p. 127; III, 5, pp. 395–395; III, 6, pp. 400, 417; III, 26, pp. 477–478). The distinction between the ways of "the fox and the lion" (*Prince*, ch. 18; p. 69) is paralleled by the dual allegories of fortune in chapter twenty-five.

73. Indeed, the recovery of ancient history and thought was only made possible by the accident that the Christians used Latin: "it is true that Christianity did not succeed in wiping out altogether the record of what outstanding men

of the old religion had done; which was due to the retention of the Latin language, for this they had to retain so that they might use it in writing down their new laws." The very possibility of the Renaissance was itself the product of the error of "Saint Gregory and other heads of the Christian religion," who did not realize that if they used "a new tongue" to write their laws, there would "have been no record of the past left at all." (*Discourses*, II, 5; p. 289).

74. See chapter three, note 75.

75. On the need for such "purging" in nature, compare *Notebooks*, ed. J. P. Richter, 2.310–311 (cited above, note 9 to chapter five).

76. *Florentine Histories*, IV, 23; pp. 169–170. On Leonardo's drawing of a device to flood an enemy camp, marked "toward Lucca" (possibly as an illustration of Brunelleschi's project), see Pedretti, *Literary Works*, 2.58–59.

77. See again note 72 (especially Machiavelli's view of rape) and compare the discussion of fortresses below (esp. notes 83 and 84).

78. "Water is the driver of nature" (*Notebooks*, ed. I. Richter, 18 [cf. pp. 19–48]). Cf. Aristotle, *Physics* 198a–b (*The Complete Works of Aristotle*, ed. Jonathan Barnes [Princeton, N.J.: Princeton University Press, 1984], 1.338–339). On the mathematical implications of the difference between the motions of water and of objects falling through the air, see note 45 above.

79. Letter from Machiavelli to Guicciardini, 17 May 1521, in *The Prince*, ed. Adams, 133–135.

80. *Mandragola*, 7. This song was written at the request of Guicciardini in 1526.

81. See chapter two, note 4.

82. On the role of "*accidenti*"—events that cannot be foreseen, and hence cannot be included in general rules or predictions—in Machiavelli's political thought, see John P. McCormick, "Addressing the Political Exception: Machiavelli's 'Accidents' and the Mixed Regime," *American Political Science Review* 87 (1993): 888–900. It would seem that this traditional or Aristotelian view of the priority of practical wisdom over technical knowledge explains the classical view of "moral character" which underlies Machiavelli's persistent emphasis on *virtù*: see Cary J. Nederman, "Machiavelli and Moral Character: Principality, Republic, and the Psychology of Virtue," paper presented to the 1992 Annual Meeting of the American Political Science Association, Chicago, Illinois, September 1992. As Nederman concludes from his consideration of this dimension of moral psychology: "The body of literature debating the so-called 'modernity' or 'originality' of Machiavelli's political thought, especially in *The Prince*, has grown to truly staggering proportions . . . . The present inquiry provides a plausible explanation for the inability to resolve these issues of 'modernity' and 'originality,' namely, that Machiavelli was in a sense trapped between innovation and tradition, between *via antiqua* and *via moderna*, in a way that generated internal conceptual tensions within his thought as a whole and even within individual texts" (p. 23).

83. The possibility that "fortresses" are intended to represent all the technological applications of Leonardo's science of nature is reinforced by the extensive description of military fortifications that we find in his *Notebooks*—and by the fact that Leonardo designed fortresses for a number of cities, including of course the mission to Piombino in 1504 which seems to have been arranged by Machiavelli. In this case, as in the description of "fortune" as a flooding "river," it may well be that Machiavelli is using the poetic device of the synecdoche (in which the part stands for the whole—as "head" stand for "cattle"), rather than an allegory in the common sense.

84. *Discourses*, II, 24; pp. 352–353, 356. Because other advances in technology have reinforced this skepticism: "if there ever was a time when they [fortunes] were useless, it is now on account of artillery" (ibid., 353). The summary statement in *The Prince* should probably be read as irony: "So, having considered all these things, I shall praise whoever makes fortresses and whoever does not, and I shall blame anyone who, trusting in fortresses, thinks little of being hated by the people" *(Prince, ch. 20; p. 87).*

85. The superiority of prudence over theoretical wisdom or philosophy is made explicit in Machiavelli's endorsement of Cato as "prudent" and patriotic in *Florentine Histories* V, 1 (p. 183): "Whence it has been observed *by the prudent* that letters come after arms and that, in provinces and cities, captains arise before philosophers. For as good and ordered armies give birth to victories and victories to quiet, the strength of well-armed spirits cannot be corrupted by a more honorable leisure than that of letters, nor can leisure enter into well-instituted cities with a greater and more dangerous deceit than this one. *This was best understood by Cato when the philosophers Diogenes and Carneades, sent by Athens as spokesmen to the Senate, came to Rome.* When he saw how the Roman youth was beginning to follow them about with admiration, and since *he recognized the evil that could result to his fatherland* from the honorable leisure, he saw to it that no philosopher could be accepted in Rome." The philosophy or science of Leonardo is "honorable," but it must be judged in terms of the utility of the city; Machiavelli inverts the relationship between theoretical wisdom (*sophia*) and practical wisdom (*phronesis*) characteristic of ancient thought and epitomized by Aristotle. Cf. Murphy, *The Moral Economy of Labor*, ch. 3.

86. *Discourses*, III, 24; p. 466. In this chapter, however, Machiavelli focuses primarily on tricks and stratagems like the use of elephants or "soldiers with flames on their spears"; that is, he does not mention the type of technological devices which Leonardo designed.

87. Ibid., II, 27; p. 371; *Art of War*, Book IV; pp. 652–653. For Leonardo's design, see Costantino, *Leonardo*, 19, 97.

88. *Art of War*, Book VII; p. 711.

89. Ibid., Book II; p. 607. "It is true that much more harm is done by harquebuses and light artillery than by the heavy" (ibid., Book III; p. 638).

90. Ibid., Book VII; pp. 703–710.

91. Ibid., Book III, p. 639.

92. Ibid., Book I, p. 587.

93. As Paul Valéry said of Leonardo, "His philosophy is wholly *naturalistic*, markedly opposed to the purely *spiritual*, very much given to word-for-word physico-mechanical explanations" (*Introduction to the Method of Leonardo da Vinci*, 13). Note, as Valéry goes on to suggest, the paradox that "When the subject is the soul, observe how very close he is to the philosophy of the Church" because, in the doctrine of resurrection, "reason demands, and dogma imposes the restoration of the flesh" (ibid.). That this legacy of Christian doctrine is not equivalent to traditional faith will be obvious to any reader of Leonardo's *Notebooks*—or of Valéry's essay.

94. One could say that while Leonardo's art, science, and even architecture focus on "simple bodies" (a painting, an individual philosopher's knowledge of the world, a building), Machiavelli was primarily concerned with what he calls "mixed bodies" (cities, readers of books, audiences of plays). For Machiavelli's distinction between "simple" and "mixed bodies," see *Discourses*, II, 5, p. 290.

95. See Faulkner, *Francis Bacon and the Project of Progress*, for a more detailed exposition of this point. Of particular importance, I believe, is Bacon's insight that the scientific and technological components of the modern project need to be organized and institutionalized. Ultimately, I believe this shift reflects Bacon's awareness of the impact of printing in the diffusion of ideas, making it possible to replace the informal network of apprenticeship, face-to-face communication and written manuscripts with the fully modern means of transmitting ideas across space and time. We cannot forget that, for both Leonardo and Machiavelli, printing was as new as computers and the electronic media for the current generation.

96. See John T. Scott, "The Sovereignty of Construction and the Construction of Sovereignty in Galileo and Hobbes," paper presented at the 1994 Annual Meeting of the American Political Science Association, New York, N. Y., September 1–4, 1994. As Scott shows, Hobbes's meeting with Galileo in 1636 represents a major aspect of his thought which has unfortunately been ignored by most commentators; this gap is all the more deplorable because the facts of the meeting are not open to the questions that could be raised with regard to the meetings of Leonardo and Machiavelli. On the mathematical differences between the foundations of ancient and modern science, see Masters, *Beyond Relativism*, ch. 3 (and the references there cited). To have a fuller understanding of the role of Leonardo's innovations in mathematics and natural science in the emergence of modernity, it is necessary to analyze in detail the difference between Leonardo and Galileo (the focus of work in progress by John T. Scott).

97. On the importance of Machiavelli's influence on the young Thomas Hobbes, see Arlene Saxonhouse, "Hobbes's *Three Discourses*: Political Foun-

dations and the Beginnings of Modern Political Thought," paper presented at the 1994 Annual Meeting of the American Political Science Association, New York, N. Y., September 1–4, 1994. An additional historical circumstance, which perhaps provides the transition between Machiavelli and both Bacon and Hobbes, cannot be documented here but will be the focus of a future publication: the apparent role of Machiavelli's *Prince* in the transformation of the English monarchy by Henry VIII. Henry's decision to take control of the Church of England, ignoring papal authority in the "great matter" of annulling his marriage to Katherine of Aragon, led to the suppression of the monasteries (with the attending distribution of wealth to Henry's supporters) and hence to a secular control of religion, ending the "two swords" of medieval Christendom. Until 1529, Henry's policy was utterly dependent on a papal annulment, even though the pope himself had apparently once implied that Henry might try the case in England. It is therefore worth knowing that, according to Cardinal Reginald Pole, Thomas Cromwell showed him a manuscript of *The Prince* in 1529; for Cardinal Pole, Henry's change of policy was due to the influence of Machiavellian precepts (Adams, "The Rise, Proliferation, and Degradation of Machiavellianism," 227–228). In later years, "Pole attributed Henry's policy to Machiavelli's devilish how-to book and identified the book's author with the Antichrist" (Athanasios Moulakis, "Which Machiavelli?" *Perspectives on Political Science* 22 [1993]: 85). Careful consideration of the history of Henry VIII's behavior does suggest a sharp change in his policies after 1529, abandoning the courtly or chivalric style of his early years in favor of the secular and ultimately brutal tactics that make his later reign seem particularly "Machiavellian." The events at the time of this transition are described carefully in Alison Weir, *The Six Wives of Henry VIII* (New York: Ballantine, 1991), who comments that by 1530 Henry VIII "was, in truth, no longer the same man who had lodged a plea in Archbishop Warham's ecclesiastical court in 1527. The despot was emerging, determined to have his own way, and even if necessary to alter the process of law to get it" (p. 215); Weir attributes the change in policy to Cromwell (pp. 220–221). Thomas Cromwell could easily have known Machiavelli or his works, since he had been a soldier in Italy in the early years of the century, and was in Florence in 1527. There are many examples of Henry VIII's "Machiavellianism": Henry's treatment of rivals and disobedient subordinates, including Cardinal Wolsey, Archbishop Fisher, and Sir Thomas More, calls to mind Cesare's punishment of Remirro de Orco (*Prince*, ch. 7, pp. 29–30); his disposition of the wealth of the monasteries illustrates Machiavelli's advice that "of what is not yours or your subjects' one can be a bigger giver" (ibid., ch. 16; p. 64); his willingness to rely on the rising urban "people" against the nobility reflects Machiavelli's established hostility to rule by the feudal aristocracy. If the secularization and centralization of the English state made possible the adoption of a Hobbesian science of politics, the religious controversies between English Catholics and Protestants made it seem necessary.

98. Thomas Hobbes, *Leviathan*, ed. Herbert W. Schneider, Library of Liberal Arts (New York: Macmillan, 1958), 23.

99. The difference between the proto-modern formulations of the early sixteenth-century innovators and the fully modern premises of Hobbes can be seen by contrasting the endless desire of Hobbesian man with a prescient passage from Leonardo's *Notebooks:* "That man is of supreme folly who always wants for fear of wanting; and his life flies away while he is still hoping to enjoy the good things which he has with extreme labour acquired" (ed. J. P. Richter, 2.296).

100. "[T]here are three kinds of brains: one that understands by itself, another that discerns what others understand; the third that understands neither by itself nor through others; the first is most excellent, the second excellent, and the third useless" (*Prince*, ch. 22; p. 92).

101. "And as to the faculties of the mind, setting aside the arts grounded upon words, and especially that skill of proceeding upon general and infallible rules called science—which very few have and but in few things, as being not a native faculty born with us, nor attained, as prudence, while we look after somewhat else—I find yet a greater equality among men than that of strength. For prudence is but experience, which equal time equally bestows on all men in those things they equally apply themselves unto" (*Leviathan*, ch. 13: p. 105).

102. Cf. Rousseau, *Discourse on Sciences and Arts*, in Masters and Kelly, *Collected Writings of Rousseau*, 2.20.

103. The works that Machiavelli saw printed in his own lifetime, apart from the *First Decennale* (a poetic summary of Italian history from 1494 to 1504), were the *Art of War* and *Florentine Histories*. Even after Machiavelli's death, one of the principal means of spreading his ideas and his fame remained the theater, as is evident in the works of both Shakespeare and Marlowe.

104. Of particular value in analyzing this point is Tracy B. Strong, "How to Write Scripture: Words, Authority, and Politics in Thomas Hobbes," *Critical Inquiry* 20 (1993): 128–178. In addition to serving as one of the rare commentators to give adequate attention to the theological dimension, Strong has very usefully analyzed the frontispiece engraving of *Leviathan* to show the importance of the image as an epitome of Hobbesian teaching. On the role of such a symbolic presentation of thought, compare Sullivan, "Bruegel's Proverbs" and Robert S. Westman, "Nature, Art, and Psyche: Jung, Pauli, and the Kepler-Fludd Polemic," in *Occult and Scientific Mentalities in the Renaissance*, ed. Brian Vickers (Cambridge: Cambridge University Press, 1984), 177–229.

105. E.g., Francis C. Hood, *The Divine Politics of Thomas Hobbes* (Oxford: Clarendon Press, 1964).

106. Rousseau, *Social Contract*, 4.8 (ed. Masters, p. 127). Note that Henry VIII had achieved, in practice, what Hobbes recommends in theory: see note 97.

107. On the relation between Hobbes and behaviorist psychology, for example, see Henri Taijfel and R. S. Peters, "Hobbes and Hull: Metaphysicians of Behavior," in *Hobbes and Rousseau*, ed. R. S. Peters and M. Cranston (Garden City, N.Y.: Anchor, 1968).

108. See again the example from contemporary cosmology cited at note 9 to this chapter from Travis, "Cosmic Structures Fill Southern Sky," 1684.

109. "Suppose that Leonardo da Vinci were suddenly transported to the United States in 1994, says Dr. Arthur Caplan, an ethicist at the University of Minnesota. What would you show him that might surprise him? Dr. Caplan has an answer. 'I'd show him a reproductive clinic,' he said. 'I'd tell him, "We make babies in this dish and give them to other women to give birth."' And that, Dr. Caplan predicted, 'would be more surprising than seeing an airplane or even the space shuttle'" (Gina Kolata, "Reproductive Revolution Is Jolting Old Views," *New York Times*, January 11, 1994, p. 1). Although Bacon had spoken of the creation of "new Natures," few moderns based their political principles on the prospect that it would one day be possible for humans to make living beings in factories. Indeed, one might say that the failure to project this extension of the premises of a technological science points to the deepest internal flaws of the modern project. See Leon Kass, "The New Biology: What Price Relieving Man's Estate?" *Science* 174 (1971): 779–788

Conclusion

1. Letter, Leo Strauss to Alexander Kojève, 28 May 1957, in Strauss, *On Tyranny*, rev. ed., 279.

2. See William J. Connell, "The Republican Tradition, In and Out of Florence," in *Girolamo Savonarola: Piety, Prophecy and Politics in Renaissance Florence*, ed. Donald Weinstein and Valerie R. Hotchkiss (Dallas: Bridwell Library, 1994), 95–105.

3. Ibid., 97–100. In this as in other respects, Connell's essay is a balanced and highly valuable survey of the literature of the last generation.

4. *Tercets on Ambition*, 113, in *Chief Works*, 2.737

5. Recognition of this point is made more difficult by Machiavelli's presentation of scientific knowledge through images or symbols rather than "laws of nature" or abstract algorithms. For a catalog of the images in *The Prince* alone, see the Appendix to Russell Price's forthcoming edition of *Il Principe*.

6. Byrne and Whiten, *Machiavellian Intelligence;* Andrew Whiten and Richard W. Byrne, "Tactical Deception in Primates," *Behavioral and Brain Science* 11 (1988): 233–273; Ridley, *The Red Queen*, ch. 10. For the theoretical implications of deception and conscious intentionality in primates, along with

a review of observed examples of its existence, see Roger D. Masters, "Conclusion," in Schubert and Masters, *Primate Politics*, 235–239.

7. Robert D. Kaplan, "The Coming Anarchy," *Atlantic* 239 (February 1994): 44–76.

8. John Locke, *Second Treatise of Civil Government*, ch. 2, §4, in *Political Writings of John Locke*, ed. David Wooton (New York: Mentor, 1993), 263.

9. Ibid., §6, p. 264.

10. Ibid., ch. 5, §36, p. 279.

11. Janet Kramer, "A Chaos in the Head," *The New Yorker* (June 14, 1993), 52.

12. Both Machiavelli and Leonardo therefore planned to have their writings published—and though several of Machiavelli's works did appear in his lifetime, the most important publications of both were posthumous. Whereas Machiavelli and Leonardo were truly pioneers in adapting military strategy, tactics, and fortifications to the new world of firearms, they did not place as much emphasis on the more peaceful technology of printing: for Leonardo, because he was committed to painting and the arts; for Machiavelli because he relied on theater and poetry as a means of communicating with a broader public.

13. *Discourses*, II, 17–18 (*Chief Works*, 1.367–377)

14. Masters, *The Nature of Politics*.

15. Masters, *Beyond Relativism*.

16. Rousseau, *Social Contract*, 2.7; ed. Masters, p. 69.

17. Rousseau, *Discourse on the Sciences and Arts*, in Masters and Kelly, *Collected Writings of Rousseau*, 2.1–22.

18. In this case, however, the praise is at first puzzling, since we later discover that Scipio's own army "rebelled against him" due to "his excessive mercy," which led to the charge by Fabius Maximus that he was "the corruptor of the Roman Military" (*Prince*, ch. 17; p. 68). The puzzle is quickly resolved when Machiavelli adds that while this behavior would have been damaging "in the empire," it produced Scipio's "fame and glory . . . while he lived under the government of the Senate" (ibid.). In short, as the next footnote will confirm, Xenophon's *Cyropedia* is desirable as a way of teaching *republican* leaders.

19. In this chapter of the *Discourses*, Machiavelli begins his recommendation by remarking that "just as *all sciences demand practice* if we desire to attain perfection in them, so this [knowledge of terrains and of countries] is one that calls for a good deal of practice" (III, 36; p. 510). Later, he remarks, "A person who has had *practice*, for instance, will see at a glance *how far this plain extends, to what height that mountain rises, where this valley goes,* and everything else of this kind, for of it all he has already acquired a *sound knowledge*" (p. 511). Rather than Leonardo's theoretical "science" of painting, Machiavelli recommends the practical "sport" of hunting as the means to acquire "knowledge."

Appendix II

1. This translation is taken from the Mansfield edition of *The Prince* (pp. 107–11). Unless otherwise indicated, the footnotes are my own.

2. "Petrarch, *Triumph of Divinity, 13*" (Mansfield's note).

3. The reference is presumably to Filippo Cassavechia and Pagolo Vettori, Francesco's brother. As Machiavelli indicates later in this letter, he has shown his own manuscripts to Filippo: hence both should be "safe."

4. Vettori was the ambassador of Florence in Rome.

5. Compare the discussion of fortune in *The Prince*, ch. 25—and the passage at the end of this letter on Machiavelli's uncertainty whether or not to give his manuscript to Giuliano de' Medici.

6. "Giuliano" (Mansfield's note).

7. The Secretary to Giuliano de' Medici.

8. Presumably a reference to the labor of Sisyphus.

9. Compare the argument of *The Prince*, chs. 12, 17, and 18.

Appendix III

1. See chapter one above and the extracts from Machiavelli's dispatches in Appendix I as well as chapter two.

2. *Art of War*, Book 7 (*Chief Works*, 2.705). Machiavelli instead gives a different contemporary example: "Genoa, when she rebelled against King Louis of France, made some small forts on those hills that surround her; these, when they were lost (and they were lost quickly) caused the loss of the city" (ibid.). In this case, Machiavelli elsewhere explicitly describes the "fallacy" when "the Florentines built fortresses in order to hold" Pisa (*Discourses*, II, 24; p. 396)—but does not mention his role in the decisions involved.

3. *Art of War*, Book 7 (p. 713). Cf. *First Decennale*, 499–504; *Chief Works*, 3.1456.

4. In comparing these two chapters, it is noteworthy that the account in the *Discourses* refers explicitly to the fact that "in another of my works" he has "discoursed at length on the futility of mercenary and auxiliary troops and on the advantage of one's own"; in neither *The Prince* nor *The Art of War*, however, does Machiavelli give us explicit analysis of his own attempt to raise an army for Florence. More broadly, consider the discussions of actions in the war against Pisa and the role of the Committee of Ten, the body for which Machiavelli had the post of Secretary—e.g., *Discourses* I, 38, 39 (pp. 204–209); II, 24 (pp. 352–359).

5. Machiavelli's text in this chapter is notable for several reasons. First, he begins by describing precisely the problem that confronted him as an

administrator and indicating it is "too long and too deep" for him to discuss: "how dangerous it is to take the lead in a new enterprise in which many may be concerned, and how difficult it is to handle and direct it, and once directed on its way, to keep it going, would be too long and too deep a topic for us to discuss here. Reserving it, therefore, for a more convenient place . . ." (*Discourses*, III, 35; p. 500). Although some assume that Machiavelli never wrote the promised analysis (see Crick's note at this point), it is conceivable that the more "convenient place" is chapter six of *The Prince*. Second, the criterion governing the narrower problem of advising (as distinct from administrating) is governed by the same principle that Machiavelli argues is used to judge princes: "men judge of actions by the result" (ibid. Cf. *The Prince*, ch. 18). Finally, but most telling, Machiavelli equates the problem confronting "the advisors of a republic and the counselors of a prince," speaking no less than five times in the chapter of "the city or the prince" as posing identical problems. The only solution Machiavelli can offer for one who gives advice is "by putting the case with moderation instead of assuming responsibility for it, and by stating one's views dispassionately and defending them alike dispassionately and modestly" (III, 39; p. 501). Is it far-fetched to apply this procedure for advising to Machiavelli's published works too?

6. See the documents in Appendix I, esp. 2, A-B and 4.

7. See especially the letter to Guiccardini of 17 May 1521, cited in chapter three. On Christianity itself, rather than the Catholic Church, as the source of corruption and political weakness, see *Discourses*, II, 2; p. 277.

8. Niccolò Machiavelli to Antonio Tebalducci, 27 August 1505: "To the Magnificent Antonio Tebalducci, commissioner general in camp, his patron. In the field. *Magnificent Man.* Keep what I am writing you secret. The consultative meeting this morning decided upon conferring the [marshal's] baton to Messer Ercole, but they want to put off announcing it for a day or two in order to see what they have to do to placate Marco Antonio, fearing that they may raise the devil. It would be a good idea to do two things: first, for Signor Iacopo and Messer Annibale to send someone here to let people know that the glory for the rout is not all Ercole's because he sent word several days ago seeking to have his prowess proclaimed; two, for you to write to some authoritative friend here and point out that Marcantonio is not going to share the camp nor will he be followed by Signors Luca and Iacopo—as they assume— because such an assumption has delayed the decision in favor of Messer Ercole. In short, the honesty of Signor Iacopo and Messer Annibale has made this third man too insolent and has given him too much prestige. You can remedy the situation. Tear up this letter" (*Machiavelli's Correspondence*, #103). By way of contrast, compare Buonoccorsi's letter to Machiavelli a month earlier, expressing concern because he "did not know how secure the letters were" and reporting that "we have begun actively to make preparations of

such a nature as to make someone else think again about his own situation" (ibid., #102).

9. Najemy, *Between Friends*, 89–90.

10. See above, chapter one and Appendix I.3 as well as Bramly, *Leonardo*, 336–340. This point would, of course, be strengthened were it true—as some claim—that Leonardo's letter to "Messer Nicolo" was addressed to Machiavelli.

11. It is true that, in Florentine foreign policy, Machiavelli was a partisan of an alliance with France—a policy orientation not always shared by Vettori and others (see Najemy, *Between Friends*); in the *Discourses*, Machiavelli is critical of the excessive suspicion of the French by Florentine leaders (e.g., II, 22; pp. 344–346). For Machiavelli, however, reliance on a foreign ally was never a substitute for a state's independent strength.

12. See, for example, *The Account of a Visit Made to Fortify Florence: A Letter to the Ambassador of the Republic in Rome*, reporting on his activities as Overseer of the Walls and Secretary of the Commission in charge of them (*Chief Works*, 2.727–734). The text of this letter reports the views of "the General" (unnamed) rather than of Machiavelli himself.

13. There may be evidence for this hypothesis in a letter by Vettori to Machiavelli: "in the letter of 27 June [1513], he [Vettori] alluded to problems he had had or was having with an unnamed 'amico nostro,' in whom Machiavelli had warned not to place any trust" (Najemy, *Between Friends*, 141). Even if the "friend" was not Leonardo, moreover, Vettori's letter reminds us that Machiavelli was not the only Renaissance political figure to write with circumspection.

14. "The principalities are either hereditary . . . or they are new. The new ones are either altogether new, as was Milan to Francesco Sforza" (*Prince*, ch. 1; p. 3). Since Francesco claimed legitimacy through his marriage to the daughter of his predecessor, Duke Filippo Maria Visconti, Machiavelli silently dismisses Francesco's claim to legitimate succession. Cf. the implicit criticism of Ludovico, ch. 14; p. 58.

15. Costantino, *Leonardo*, 29.

16. *Florentine Histories*, V, 33 p. 227. The editor, Harvey C. Mansfield, Jr., adds the following note to this passage: "NM here departs from his source, Biondo, from whom it appears that at least 70 died in the battle of Anghiari." More telling, this account contradicts the description of the battle found in Leonardo's *Notebooks* (ed. J. P. Richter, 1.348–349). This entry is apparently written in the hand of Agostino Vespucci, one of Machiavelli's secretaries (Bramly, *Leonardo*, 337). It is plausible that Machiavelli would have arranged for a description of the Battle of Anghiari to be available to Leonardo when he was planning his painting (it was once even thought that this description was written by Machiavelli himself), but this only heightens the contrast between

Vespucci's text in the *Notebooks* (which describes "great carnage") and Machiavelli's history (Bramly, *Leonardo*, 337). There is, after all, no a priori reason to assume that, in case of contradiction, it is Machiavelli's *Florentine Histories* that must be exact.

17. The "discrepancy" between Machiavelli's "famous description in the *Istorie fiorentine* of this 'bloodless' battle" and "the carnage depicted by Leonardo" is "one of the great puzzles of Renaissance scholarship" (William Connell, personal communication).

18. Heydenreich, "Military Architect," 142–143. See, however, the documents in Appendix I.2.

19. For the discussion of Brunelleschi's plan, see chapter seven above; on the diversion of the Arno, see the analysis of the documentary evidence in chapter one. If I correctly interpret Machiavelli's correspondence with the camp at Pisa during September 1504 (Appendix I.4), Colombino, who directed the project in the field, preferred the plan of Giovan Berardi (two small channels rather than one) to that of Leonardo, did not dig them deeply enough, ignored Machiavelli's technical criticism, and generally confirmed the negative opinions some had felt about his ability. Technological innovation is difficult because it depends so heavily on the cooperation of skilled assistants. Leonardo, of course, repeatedly confronted the same problem. E.g., Bramly, *Leonardo*, 386–387; *Notebooks*, ed. J. P. Richter, 2.407–410.

20. Pedretti, *Literary Works*, 2.51.

21. *Prince*, ch. 20; pp. 83–87; *Discourses*, II, 24; pp. 354–359.

22. *Discourses*, III, 24 (*Chief Works*, 1.466).

23. *Notebooks*, ed. J. P. Richter, 1.11; Bramly, *Leonardo*, 341. The device was a submarine that could be used to sink ships and kill their crews.

24. *Florentine Histories*, V, 1; pp. 185–186; Rousseau, *Discourse on Sciences and Arts,* in Masters and Kelly, *Collected Writings of Rousseau*, 2.3–24.

25. *Prince*, Dedicatory Letter, p. 4.

26. Ancient writers often used the dialogue form, or present different points of view, as if the standpoint is that of a human judge in a controversy (rather than a divine observer capable of predicting the outcome). This perspective is as evident in the dialogues of Plato, Xenophon, or Cicero as in the more didactic writings of Aristotle. Exceptions, such as the poetic form of Lucretius's *De rerum natura*, retain the standpoint of a specific human observer without the more extreme pretense of objectivity of moderns as diverse as Hobbes and Hegel. As similar contrast could be found in the difference between ancient drama or epic and the omniscient narrator of the classic modern novel.

27. The failure to change the manuscript of *The Prince* seems intentional, since Machiavelli's former assistant Biagio Buonaccorsi copied the work for sale in its current form in 1520. See Fachard, *Biagio Buonaccorsi*, 160, 215. On

the hypotheses concerning Machiavelli's changes in the text of *The Prince* after 1513, see Najemy, *Between Friends*, ch. 5.

28. In 1515, for example, it appears that Giuliano de' Medici, Lorenzo de' Medici, Leonardo, and Machiavelli were all in Florence. The dating of the Windsor sheet containing the images of a deluge (1515) makes it possible that at this time both Machiavelli and Rucellai heard Leonardo describe the storm of 1456 at the Orti Oricellari, where Machiavelli himself read the manuscripts of the *Discourses on Titus Livy* and *The Art of War*. Cf. de Grazia, *Machiavelli in Hell*, 358; Pedretti, *Studi Vinciani*, 17, 34–35.

29. Is it possible that Prospero is actually modeled on Leonardo? The similarity in methods—using a knowledge of science and technology to control nature, create "miracles," and establish the perfect society—gives room to wonder if Leonardo's reputation might have spread from the court of Francis I to Shakespeare's England. One hint is consistent with this possibility. In *The Tempest*, Prospero is the legitimate Duke of Milan. The register of Leonardo's death at Amboise identifies him as "noble *Milanese* and sometimes director of painting of the Duke of Milan" (*Notebooks*, ed. J. P. Richter, 1.352). On the difference between Machiavelli and Bacon (which on this view would also be a difference between Machiavelli and Leonardo), see Faulkner, *Francis Bacon and the Project of Progress*, esp. ch. 3.

30. Machiavelli to Giovan Battista Soderini, 13–21 September 1506, *Machiavelli's Correspondence* #121. Leonardo had left Florence for Milan, at the urgent request of King Louis XII, in May 1506, ostensibly for only three months; once Leonardo was in Milan, the French king asked a prolongation of his stay at the cost of breaking a formal agreement with the Signoria. The timing of this letter thus coincides with the realization that Leonardo had left Florence more or less definitively, and thus would probably never finish *The Battle of Anghiari*. This decision greatly angered Piero Soderini (Giovan Battista's uncle and Machiavelli's patron), see Bramly, *Leonardo*, 353.

31. See Najemy, *Between Friends*, passim.

Index

accidents, 145, 191, 192, 338n82. *See also* fortune

Accioatoli, Robert, 25, 289n76

Adams, Robert M., 324n4, 342n97

adaptation, biological, 89–93, 128. *See also* natural selection

aerial perspective, 52, 171–72, 176, 298n12; use in maps, 14, 17, 52, 265, 275n19, 280n40, 333n29

Agathocles the Sicilian, 54, 73–74, 299n22, 325n6, 337n70

aggressiveness, 101, 102, 121, 140, 323n2

agonic modes of behavior, 101–5, 106. *See also* competition; fear; threat

Alexander VI (pope), 18, 277n28, 282n43, 305nn60, 62; and Cesare Borgia, 68–71, 72, 305n58

Alexander the Great, 291n9, 335n55

Alexander, Richard D., 117–18, 120, 319n25

allegory, use of, 46–47, 59. *See also* fortune

altruism, 114–15, 318n19; reciprocal, 117–18. *See also* cooperation

Amboise, Charles d', 21, 22, 184, 260, 261

Amboise, Georges d' (cardinal of Rouen), 14, 261–62, 275n22, 304n48, 305n62, 326n7

Anabasis (Xenophon), 24, 288n73, 318n17

analog signals, 102, 314n33

anatomy, Leonardo's studies of, 179, 182, 313n27, 335n51; empirical approach, 173–74, 309n4, 333n31

anger/threat: facial displays of, 140–43, 156. *See also* threat

Anghiari, Battle of: Machiavelli's account of, 262, 347nn16, 17. *See also Battle of Anghiari, The*

animal (social) behavior, 6, 124, 134, 210, 318n19; compared with human behavior, 85–107, 220, 313n23; cost-benefit approach to, 115–19, 319n30; intentionality in, 93, 311n14; Leonardo's contributions to field, 182–83, 335n51. *See also* animal nature; primates, nonhuman; *individual animals*

animal kingdom, Leonardo's divisions of, 309n4

animal nature, 315n3

Leonardo's view of, 269n3, 316n9

Machiavellian theory of, 6, 44, 65, 109, 209–10; compared with human nature, 86–92, 96, 98–99, 101–2, 103–5, 106–7

See also animal (social) behavior

anthropomorphism, 93, 97, 99

Antiphon the Sophist, 113–14, 310n9, 330n4

antiquity, 47, 207–8, 213, 217, 330n4; citizen armies in, 65, 303n44; compared with modernity, 161; importance for Machiavelli, 77–78, 191, 197n7, 302n41; politics, 221, 302n41; population increase results, 110–11. *See also* Greek philosophy; paganism

apes. *See* primates, nonhuman

Appiani, Jacopo, 16, 21, 25, 174, 263, 308n77

architecture, Leonardo's contribution to, 14, 183–84

Ardinghelli (secretary to Giuliano de' Medici), 37, 293n35

Ardrey, Robert, 99, 313n23

aristocracy, 152, 325n5

Aristotle, 29, 31, 196, 210, 293n28, 335n55, 348n26; analysis of comparative anatomy, 313n27; on human nature, 5, 217–18, 314n37; on inequality and education, 219–20; on justice, 114; Leonardo on, 291n9; mathematics, 180, 331n12; *Nicomachean Ethics*, 302n41,

Milan: Leonardo in, 14, 21–22, 194–95, 260,
286n59, 349n30; Leonardo's map of, 14,
171, 275n19
military forces, 74, 305n64; in river and
fortune analogy, 61, 189, 301n37. *See also*
citizen army
military strategy, 129–30, 278n35, 344n12;
Machiavelli on, 21, 23–24, 26, 192–94,
302n40. *See also* warfare
military technology, 51, 216–17
Leonardo's contribution to, 52, 58, 173,
182–83, 258, 336n54; for Cesare Borgia,
14, 15, 25, 276n23; early plans for, 13–14,
275n17; for the Florentine Republic,
16–17, 282n44; parallels in Machiavelli's
strategy, 21, 23–24
Machiavelli's attitude toward, 193–94, 263,
339nn84, 86
See also artillery; fortifications
Mill, John Stuart, 203, 315n38
mobility, in modern society, 165–66, 167
modernity, 7, 202–5, 228; and Hobbes,
200–201; and integration of theory and
practice, 163–69, 296n53; Leonardo's
contributions to, 7–8, 11, 169–86;
Machiavelli's contributions to, 7–9, 11,
27, 29, 50, 85, 195, 265, 338n82; origins,
159, 161–63, 207–10; and present status
of Western civilization, 212–18; transition
to, 218–28
Mona Lisa (Leonardo), 21, 52, 170, 186,
285n56, 298n12; perspective, 171–72
monarchies, 133, 152
Mondale, Walter, 144, 147
monkeys, 106, 124, 211, 313n21, 323n2; social
displays, 100, 140
morality, 1–2, 5, 318n19; classical view of, 31,
187, 199, 338n82; for Machiavelli, 31,
75–78, 80–82, 83, 290n3
moral reason (*phronesis;* practical wisdom),
192–93, 330n7, 338n82, 339n85
Mosaic Law, 73, 168
Moses, 75, 188, 306nn66, 70, 325n5,
337nn69, 70
as a founder, 50, 63, 68, 72–74, 87, 201,
301n37, 303n43; regime based on law,
325n6
Hobbes on, 201
motion, 178–79, 195–96, 334n41; in art, 171,
174–76
Murphy, James Bernard, 330n7

Nabis (Spartan prince), 54, 299n21
Najemy, John H., 268, 278n33, 306n69,
308nn2, 3
nationalism, 31, 131; and contemporary
violence, 155, 158–59, 204–5. *See also*
patriotism
nation-states, 211, 213. *See also* centralized
government
Native Americans, 121, 122, 164
natural law, for Hobbes, 197
natural selection, 91–94, 97, 101, 309n6,
310n8, 317n9; in analysis of social
behavior, 115, 319n27; and cooperation,
115–19, 319nn25, 27, 30; on individual
and group level, 123, 319n27, 320n32;
and sexual selection, 321n46
nature, state of, 107, 214–15, 220; for
Hobbes, 88–89, 197–98; for Rousseau,
120, 215, 220, 223
Nazi Germany, 139, 164, 330n4
Nederman, Cary J., 338n82
neo-Darwinian theory, 115, 309n6, 310n8
networks, social, 97, 105–6, 313n21
neuroscience, 102, 144, 210, 223, 311n13
newspapers, 7, 149, 151–55
Newton, Isaac, 178, 179, 265, 300n26
Nicomachean Ethics (Aristotle), 302n41,
318n17
Nietzsche, Friedrich, 81, 135, 162, 315n3,
330n4
nonverbal behavior, 101–4, 118, 135, 139–46,
314n33; among primates, 100–104,
138–40; on television, 148–49, 156
Notebooks (Leonardo), 3–4, 12; letter to
"Messer Nicolò", 21–22, 266, 285n57;
parallels with Machiavelli's writings, 23,
26–27, 191; publication, 186–87. *See also*
individual topics
novelty (innovation), 208, 331n13
in Leonardo's contributions: to the fine
arts, 170–78; to mathematics and
science, 178–81
in Machiavelli's writings, 161–63, 169,
187–88, 191, 329n2, 338n82; relationship
to deviousness, 44, 45–47, 296n53; type
found in *The Art of War,* 197n7
nuclear weapons, 217, 223, 303n44
Nuvarola, 15, 278n32

obedience, political, Hobbes on,
197–99

warfare (*cont.*)
    analogy, 60–61. *See also* military strategy;
    military technology
water: allegory of history and fortune, 59;
    Leonardo's fascination with, 174, 180–81,
    190. *See also* canals; floods; rivers
Weir, Alison, 341n97
whirlwind, descriptions of, 24, 26–27,
    288n74, 289n25, 349n28
wisdom, 187, 188–89. *See also* practical

wisdom; theoretical wisdom
wolves, nature of, 88–89, 91–92, 96, 100
woodchucks (marmots), 94–95, 97, 106
Xenophon, 45, 188, 219, 226, 318n17, 344n18;
    and scythed chariots, 24, 288n73; use of
    dialogue form, 348n26
Yeltsin, Boris, 139, 151, 152

Zhirinovsky, Vladimir, 148, 151